Scalable Planning

Concurrent Action From Elemental Thinking

David C. DiNucci

May 2012

First edition: April 2012

ISBN-13: 978-1475211160

ISBN-10: 1475211163

Typeset using LyX to LaTeX. Diagrams edited and rendered with elepar.com's L23 (for ScalPL diagrams), Blender (for 3D pebbles), and xfig and variants (for others).

Dedication

To Robbie Babb and Lane Browning.

Short Contents

Contents   vii

List of Figures   xiii

Author's Preface   xvii

Acknowledgments   xix

1 Introduction   1

2 Activities and Resources   21

3 Fundamental Activities: Actons   43

4 Predictability: Concurrent Observers, Buffers, & Broadcast   71

5 Making It Go: The Director   83

6 Encapsulation: Building More Complex Activities   107

7 Constants, Repositories, Activation, and Recursion   123

8 Revisiting Computation   137

9 Nondeterminism and Atomicity   157

10 Axiomatic Semantics   175

11 Sets   195

12 Objects   203

13 Arrays   229

14 Data Parallelism   255

15 Engineering Correct Plans   285

16 The Future: What If?   299

Index   305

Contents

Contents   vii

List of Figures   xiii

Author's Preface   xvii

Acknowledgments   xix

1 Introduction   1
   1.1   Computation, Traditionally   1
   1.2   Plans, Activities, Platforms   2
   1.3   Limitations of Traditional Sequential Computing   3
   1.4   Why Sequential Processors Run Hot   6
   1.5   Scalability & Speedup   7
   1.6   Complexity and Decomposition   10
   1.7   Some Traditional Approaches to Concurrency   11
         1.7.1 Programming Models   11
         1.7.2 Pitfalls of Traditional Concurrency   14
         1.7.3 Dealing with Latency   15
   1.8   Scope, Goals and Directions of This Book   16
   1.9   History of This Approach   18
   1.10 Disclaimer   20

2 Activities and Resources   21
   2.1   Introduction   21
         2.1.1 Plans and Activities   21
         2.1.2 Resources   22
         2.1.3 Permissions   23
   2.2   Resources   24
         2.2.1 Control State   25
         2.2.2 Using and Manipulating Control State   27
         2.2.3 Mutually Exclusive Access to Resources   28
         2.2.4 Waffles Example   29

2.3	Delineating Activities from Their Contexts	31
	2.3.1 Roles and Transitions	32
	2.3.2 Usages vs. Permissions	33
	2.3.3 Plan Interface	34
	2.3.4 Plan/Context Conformance	35
2.4	Strategies Are Plans	38
2.5	Representing Strategies as Text: SPLAT	38
2.6	Summary	40

3 Fundamental Activities: Actons   **43**

3.1	Activity Properties	43
	3.1.1 Determinism	46
	3.1.2 Serializability	48
	3.1.3 Safety, Liveness, and Fairness	52
3.2	Proposal for Actons and Tactics	56
	3.2.1 The Basics	56
	3.2.2 Liveness and Fairness	58
	3.2.3 Some Common Representations for Tactics	59
	3.2.4 Termination ($\perp$ Transitions)	61
	3.2.5 Beltedness	62
	3.2.6 Predictability (Concurrent Access to Resources)	62
	3.2.7 Summary of Acton/Tactic Definition	63
3.3	Examples	63
	3.3.1 Waffles	64
	3.3.2 Software Subroutines as Tactics	65
	3.3.3 Natural Events as Actons	67
	3.3.4 ACID Transactions	68
3.4	Summary	69

4 Predictability: Concurrent Observers, Buffers, & Broadcast   **71**

4.1	Common approaches to shared access	71
	4.1.1 Concurrent Observers	72
	4.1.2 Broadcast/Multicast	72
	4.1.3 Throttling and Buffering	73
4.2	Predictability	74
	4.2.1 Snapshots: An Implication of Predictability	74
	4.2.2 Predictability as "Wrinkle in Time"	76
	4.2.3 Optimizing Snapshots	77
4.3	Revisiting the Scenarios, in Light of Predictability	78
	4.3.1 Throttling and Buffering	78
	4.3.2 Multicast	80
	4.3.3 Concurrent Observers and/or Broadcast	80
	4.3.4 Potential Oversimplifications	81
4.4	Summary	82

5 Making It Go: The Director   **83**

5.1	Introduction	83
5.2	Duties of the Director	84

	5.2.1	Semantics	85
	5.2.2	Embedding/Mapping	91
	5.2.3	Scheduling	92
	5.2.4	Communication	94
5.3		Example of a Simple Director	98
	5.3.1	Embedding (Static)	98
	5.3.2	Content State Movement	100
	5.3.3	Finding Content State	102
5.4		Remaining Director Duties	103
5.5		Summary	104

6 Encapsulation: Building More Complex Activities   **107**

6.1		Issues with Interfacing Strategies	107
	6.1.1	Breaking Existing Plans Down into Smaller Plans	108
	6.1.2	Building Existing Plans Up into Bigger Plans	110
	6.1.3	Activity Lifetime	111
6.2		Forming Activateable Plans from Strategies	112
	6.2.1	Formal Resources: Roles for Strategies	112
	6.2.2	Strategy Interfaces: Resources as Finite State Machines (FSMs)	115
	6.2.3	Predictable Roles Revisited	117
6.3		Finite-lived Composite Activities	119
	6.3.1	Finishing an Activity	119
	6.3.2	"Cleaning Up" an Activity: Garbage Collection	120
6.4		Summary	121

7 Constants, Repositories, Activation, and Recursion   **123**

7.1		Constants	123
7.2		Repositories	124
	7.2.1	Introduction	124
	7.2.2	Constant Paths (Repositories as Constants)	125
	7.2.3	Resolution of Constants (Time and Source)	125
	7.2.4	Resolving in Parent Repositories	126
	7.2.5	Constant recursion	127
	7.2.6	Content Domains as Types	127
7.3		Activation: How Contexts Really Work	129
	7.3.1	$plan Role Binding	129
	7.3.2	Delaying/Sensing Plan Activations	131
	7.3.3	Recursion: Activating a Plan within the Same Plan	132
	7.3.4	The Root Plan and Root Context	133
7.4		Summary	134

8 Revisiting Computation   **137**

8.1		Introduction	137
8.2		Sequential Computation	138
	8.2.1	Plans and Computation	138
	8.2.2	Example of TDSP and its Computation: Binary Search	138
	8.2.3	Computations as Functions	140

8.2.4   Example of Function Corresponding to Computation . . . 143
8.2.5   Structured Planning 144
8.2.6   Summary: Sequential Algorithms and Computation   . . . 144
8.3   Concurrent Computation   145
8.3.1   Algorithms, Programs, Computation 145
8.3.2   Example of Concurrent Computation 147
8.3.3   Characterizing Input and Output for Strategies 149
8.3.4   Computations as Functions 150
8.3.5   Example of function corresponding to computation 151
8.3.6   Structured Planning 154
8.4   Summary 154

9   Nondeterminism and Atomicity   157
9.1   Nondeterminism 157
9.1.1   Definition 157
9.1.2   Syntactic (Strategy) Computation Determinism 158
9.1.3   Semantic (Tactic) Computation Determinism 160
9.1.4   Result Determinism (Specifically, Semideterminism)   . . . 161
9.1.5   Re-creating Computations 165
9.1.6   Other Kinds of Nondeterminism   166
9.2   Atomicity 167
9.2.1   Definition 167
9.2.2   Atomicity Using an Atomic "Start" Acton 169
9.2.3   Atomicity Using Activation Formal Resources 171
9.2.4   The Downside of Atomicity 172
9.3   Summary 172

10   Axiomatic Semantics   175
10.1   Intro 175
10.2   F-Net Syntax 177
10.3   F-Net Semantics 179
10.3.1   Initialization Axiom   180
10.3.2   Time Axiom   181
10.3.3   Atomicity Axiom 181
10.3.4   Safety Axiom 181
10.3.5   Liveness Axiom 181
10.3.6   Firing Axiom 181
10.4   Theorems 183
10.4.1   Nodes in Computation Are Partially Ordered 183
10.4.2   States for a Resource in Computation Are Totally Ordered 183
10.4.3   Computations as Functions 185
10.4.4   Tracing a Computation   186
10.4.5   Computations with Identical Resource Traces are Isomorphic 188
10.5   Summary 192

11   Sets   195
11.1   Motivation   195

11.2 Paths and Formal Resource Sets 197
11.3 Role Sets and Splice Bindings 198
11.4 Bundlings 199
11.5 Wildcards 199
11.6 Resource Sets 200
11.7 Summary 201

12 Objects   **203**
12.1 Intro to Object-Oriented Planning 203
    12.1.1 Outline of (Some) OO Principles 204
    12.1.2 Strategies as Classes and Instances (Objects) 206
12.2 Encapsulated State 207
12.3 Partial Binding 212
    12.3.1 Binding Constraints 213
    12.3.2 Methods 214
12.4 Delegation 215
12.5 Class Structure (Subtyping) 219
    12.5.1 Strategies as Content Domains 219
    12.5.2 Superclass Designation 220
    12.5.3 Abstract Classes 221
12.6 Example 222
12.7 Summary 227

13 Arrays   **229**
13.1 Resource Arrays 230
    13.1.1 Form and Terminology 230
    13.1.2 Default Binding, Bindall 232
    13.1.3 Bindany 232
13.2 Binding Modifiers 233
    13.2.1 Reduction 237
    13.2.2 Selection 238
    13.2.3 Translation 239
    13.2.4 Mapping 241
    13.2.5 Permutation 243
    13.2.6 Combining Binding Modifiers 245
    13.2.7 Alternate Representations for Binding Modifiers 247
13.3 Delimited and Undelimited Resource Arrays 247
    13.3.1 Establishing Array Size: Delimiters 249
    13.3.2 Sensing Array Size 249
13.4 Example: Bounded Buffer Object (Queue, FIFO) 250
    13.4.1 The Plan 251
    13.4.2 Analysis 252
13.5 Summary 253

14 Data Parallelism   **255**
14.1 Creating Contexts Dynamically 255
    14.1.1 Basic Function of Dup 256
    14.1.2 Number of Replicants 256

14.1.3 Behavior of Role Bindings 257
14.1.4 Combining Dups 258
14.2 Using dups with binding modifiers for data parallelism 260
14.3 Examples 263
14.3.1 Linked List Object 263
14.3.2 Matrix Multiply 268
14.3.3 Matrix Multiply Variations 271
14.3.4 Quicksort 276
14.4 Embedding/Scheduling Data Parallel Plans 282
14.5 Summary 283

15 Engineering Correct Plans   **285**
15.1 Introduction 285
15.1.1 Correctness of Tactics 285
15.1.2 Correctness of Strategies 286
15.1.3 Specifications for strategies 288
15.2 Refactoring 289
15.2.1 Refactoring Control State 290
15.2.2 Refactoring Tactics 292
15.3 Related Formal Models 292
15.3.1 UNITY/Guarded Commands 293
15.3.2 Petri Nets 293
15.3.3 Turing Machines 294
15.3.4 Chemical Abstract Machine (CHAM) 297
15.3.5 Other Models 297

16 The Future: What If?   **299**
16.1 Publishing More Existing Research 299
16.2 Making "Scalable Planning" Simply "Planning" 300
16.3 Creating a ScalPL-Friendly World 301
16.4 Rethinking Apps 302
16.5 Conclusion 303

Index   **305**

List of Figures

1.1   Speedup curves.   9

2.1   Four resources and 2 contexts. Plan A's context has 3 role bindings,
      with observe, update, and replace permissions.   23
2.2   Activity to dry a dish (in context).   25
2.3   Some common icons used to represent control states.   26
2.4   Dish drying example, with control states.   27
2.5   A strategy for making and eating waffles.   30
2.6   Junction dot shorthand.   31
2.7   Transition bindings within resource.   33
2.8   Potential interface for the **serve** plan, graphically.   35
2.9   Conformance of role usage to role binding permissions.   36
2.10 Conformance of role content domain to role binding (resource) con-
      tent domain.   37

3.1   Activities can be considered as pebbles in a bucket.   45
3.2   Mutual time dependence and circular time dependence.   49
3.3   Many common shapes are belted in some orientations (belt at plane). 50
3.4   Non-belted pebble, alone and with belted circular dependences. . . .   50
3.5   Gridlock on the roads, and deadlock in an activity cross-section. . .   54
3.6   Work-around for inter-resource dependences.   55
3.7   Simple liveness and fairness scenarios.   59
3.8   Possible **mix** tactic.   65

4.1   Predictability via snapshots (single, multiple, optimized).   75
4.2   Simple throttling/buffering in ScalPL.   79
4.3   Multicast.   80
4.4   Single updater/producer, multiple observers.   80

5.1   Reasons counts, evolving over time.   86
5.2   Example of rivalries.   89
5.3   CDS operation.   96
5.4   A resource and associated FSM. 101

6.1 Problems with encapsulating part of plan into a separate context. . . 109

6.2 **repaint** plan is (a) invented, (b) sketched, (c) visualized after integration, and (d) shown in final form. 111

6.3 How control state moves between actual and formal resource. 114

6.4 Four formal resources and associated FSMs and usages. 116

6.5 C (right) child of P (left), with binding X in P seemingly predictable. 118

7.1 Four equivalent ways to bind role "months" to constant 15. 125

7.2 Equivalent: Context label represents a constant on $plan role. . . . 130

7.3 Anonymous bindings to help alternate increment and add_to_total. 132

8.1 TDSP (C function) for simple-case binary search. 139

8.2 Computation of binary search for inputs 'r', "abefrsv", and 7. . . . 140

8.3 A simple ScalPL strategy, and its computation. 146

8.4 A ScalPL computation for waffles. 148

8.5 Functionalized concurrent computation for waffles. 152

9.1 Universe of plans, categorized by determinism. 158

9.2 Two deterministic plans. 159

9.3 Left may be deterministic or not depending upon tactic A. 160

9.4 Possible computation prefix for Figure 9.3 (right plan). 161

9.5 Simple strategy, two potential resulting computations, and the functionalized computation. 162

9.6 Plan Comm activates 3 times, each observing its **in** role and updating its **to** role. 164

9.7 Computation subgraph equivalence rule for Comm (#I & #J generic). 165

9.8 Top strategy (1) deterministic if A and B atomic, but not if decomposed (2) or strategies (3 & 4). 168

9.9 Strategy A from previous example modified to be atomic. 170

10.1 Sample F-Net with contention. 187

10.2 Possible traced computation for F-Net in previous figure. 189

10.3 Two isomorphic prefix computations for same F-Net. 191

11.1 "Do it in a circle" plan takes "it" and applies it in a circle. 196

11.2 Formal sets (x within y). 197

11.3 Splice binding to formal set x, one element of role set to u. 199

11.4 Using bundlings to bind role set m {x{j, k}, y, z{a,b}}. 200

11.5 Resource sets and set constants. 201

12.1 Resources with Instantiation Level 0, 1, 2, and 3. 208

12.2 Contexts with IL 0, 1, 2, and 3. 208

12.3 Left plan instantiates ClassA twice at IL 1, each twice at IL 0. . . . 209

12.4 Examples with IL 1 formal resources. 211

12.5 Method invocation example. 215

12.6 SpeakingCellPhone class, based on CellPhone. 217

12.7 Ported resource shorthand. 218

12.8 Digital Infinite Integer Class extends Infinite Integer Class. 224

12.9 `get_digit`, implementing method in `Digital_Inf_Int_Class`. . . . 226
12.10`clone` and `deep_init`, methods in `Digital_Inf_Int_Class`. 226

13.1 Resource arrays of dimensionality 0 (usually called "scalar"), 1, 2, and 3. 231
13.2 Bindall (default) and Bindany (with ? label prefix). 232
13.3 Binding modifer: The pieces, and as represented in tools. 233
13.4 Primary bindings can also be secondaries, but cycles not allowed. . . 234
13.5 In each pair, left diagram is legal syntax, and right diagram shows what it represents in terms of flow of data during indexing. Parens enclose a hypothetical index issued by activity, and hash marks on array resource act as "address lines" for each dimension, from top to bottom. 236
13.6 Sample reductions. 237
13.7 Selections restrict other bindings, including other selections. 239
13.8 Examples of early and late translation. 240
13.9 Mappings, simple and not-so-simple. 241
13.10Examples of permutation binding modifiers. 244
13.11Array delimiter for dimensions 1 and 3 of C. 249
13.12Formal resource size sensor (dimensions 1 and 3). 250
13.13Bounded Buffer strategy. 251
13.14Tactic inc_and_test, used in Bounded Buffer Strategy. 251

14.1 One-, two-, and three-parameter form, plus 2 dups on 1 context. . . 257
14.2 Assorted bindings in conjunction with dup. 258
14.3 Dup order may matter, such as when dupall and dupany are mixed. 259
14.4 Using dups in binding modifiers. 261
14.5 Allocating and accessing free element of `dyn_info`. 262
14.6 A Linked List strategy. 265
14.7 Tactics used in Linked List strategy. 266
14.8 fmatmult: Matrix multiply. 269
14.9 fdotprod: Dot product. 270
14.10ac_red: Associative Commutative reduction. 272
14.11ac_red, another implementation. 273
14.12Matrix multiply revisited. 275
14.13Recursive Quicksort in ScalPL. 279

15.1 Simple translation of binary search from Chapter 8. 290
15.2 Removing program counter resource from binary search. 291

Author's Preface

I set out to write a book that I would want to teach from, for a class in concurrency and scalability, focusing on principles rather than necessarily on existing practice. This first edition is necessarily a trade-off, between fully achieving that goal and not getting the book done at all. Still, I hope and trust that it possesses ample valuable, consistent, relevant, and often novel information and insight, enough to make your investments here (of time as well as money) pay off. It was created with the meagerest of resources – including, perhaps, my intelligence, patience and sanity – but I have tried to balance some of those lackings with ample investment of my own time and effort. Even so, I chose the places to focus that effort, and if the result may at times seem "unripe" in places, I ask you to at least consider where you might favor its further development, and perhaps to help make that happen. And even those who relish discovering omissions, errors, and inconsistencies may find some glee here, and in the best of worlds, future editions will benefit from their input as well.

For those offended by the slightly narrowed margins, my apologies in advance. The format can be viewed in a positive light if you try, such as the preservation of trees required for printing paper versions. And if you like to scribble in the margins, I have already found myself (while marking up earlier proofs) that the white space surrounding the multiplicity of diagrams and section headings provides adequate room for many notes. If you feel that more white space around the edges would ease your reading, I hope it won't be too much trouble to insert a larger blank sheet behind that page. The narrower margins were not the result of taking a stand of any kind, just as yet one more way to minimize time to press under the circumstances while preserving diagram readability and media flexibility.

Acknowledgments

This research, and then this book, have spanned many years, and together have benefited from the kindness and support (emotional, monetary, advisory) of many people. I can only hope to adequately recognize even a fraction of them here.

The spark of this work was originally set at Oregon Graduate Center, OGC, subsequently known as Oregon Graduate Institute (OGI). (OGI has since been absorbed into Oregon Health & Science University, OH&SU). For the productivity of my time there, I thank my then-wife Tamae Sawano, who initially helped to encourage my enrollment and studies; my graduate advisor, friend, and neighbor Robbie Babb, who planted many of the initial ideas and challenges in me that ultimately led to the approach explored in this book; and many other professors at OGC/OGI (including Michael Wolfe, Richard Kieburtz, David Maier, Dan Hammerstrom, and Richard Hamlet) who were instrumental in providing insight into the puzzle that this approach is meant to solve. My thanks also to Harry F. Jordan, from UC Boulder, who also served on my committee and provided valuable feedback.

Later, Doreen Cheng, Louis Lopez, Robert Hood, and Ian Stockdale were among many who provided feedback on my intentions to develop this work further at NASA. Upon returning to Portland many years later, I struck up a friendship with Robert "Buzz" Hill which resulted in many hours in coffee shops discussing deep subjects, occasionally including concurrency, and during subsequent attempts at commercialization of this work, he, Polly Jennings, Pat Cauduro, Bob Dietrich, and Miki Tokola were open with their opinions and ideas as to how we might progress.

For this book itself, the two primary people who turned my writing attitude from a whim into a plan were Horst Simon and Randi Cohen. Although circumstances left me unable to make the most of their expertise and services, that was primarily due to the unique nature of this work, my situation, and the times: Their reputations for drive, knowledge, and professionalism are certainly well-earned. Most of the direct material support for the writing came from a handful of people. For several years, extended family Carmela Smith and Jan Keller provided me with significant life support in exchange for my assistance in other ways, during which time I wrote the majority of the book. Two friends and colleagues were also especially instrumental: Jon Inouye provided some important computer resources that helped tremendously, and Steve Neighorn (SCN Research) provided a web presence and ISP services (and occasional odd jobs). Carla DiNucci (my sister and a professional graphic designer) did a great job with the cover. Eugene Miya has also been very supportive throughout, and Michelle Gaudreau offered editing guidance and services based on her years of experience, which I unfortunately could only barely sample for this edition.

Lane Browning's motivational and emotional support cannot be overstated during what were intended to be the final months of this work. And even in the months since, that earlier enouragement continued as a vital force to bring it through to completion. (Readers of Lane's own enjoyable and skillful prose will quickly recognize that she had no direct writing/editing role here, and is thereby innocent of abetting the relative assault on the English language taking place within these pages.)

Thanks to these and the many other people who have kept me on a straight and healthy path for this entire period. Virtually to a person, the book negatively impacted my relationships with these people in various ways, and they not only accepted those impacts, but further fueled my drive and offered help. Specifically, many of the members of two groups certainly filled that role: The Humanists of Greater Portland (HGP), and The Wanderers (as guided largely by Don Wardwell, and sponsored by the Linus Pauling House and ISEPP, the Institute for Science, Engineering, and Public Policy). Also, the owners, employees, and fellow patrons of Common Grounds Coffee in Portland made me feel quite comfortable in the many hours per day, days per week, and weeks per year that I spent silently huddled there with my laptop and cup of tasty joe.

Every one of these people have their fingerprints in this book, and I thank them all.

Chapter 1

Introduction[1]

> The electronic part of the calculator will be somewhat elaborate, and it will certainly not be feasible to consider the influence of every component on every other. We shall avoid the necessity of doing this if we can arrange that each component only has an appreciable influence on a comparatively small number of others. Ideally we would like to be able to consider the circuit as built up from a number of circuit elements, each of which has an output which depends only on its inputs, and not at all on the circuit into which it is working. Besides this we would probably like the output to depend only on certain special characteristics of the inputs. In addition we would often be glad for the output to appear simultaneously with the inputs. – *Alan Turing, "Proposed Electronic Calculator", 1946.*

1.1 Computation, Traditionally

Alan Turing is often known as the Father of Computer Science, because some seventy years ago (circa 1937), he addressed the issue of what it really meant to compute something. In the process of proposing an answer, he formalized his ideas into a widely accepted mathematical model now known as a Turing Machine, which we'll explore some much later in the book. His work (together with others like Alonzo Church) provided insights into the kind of operations that an automated computer might need to perform if it is to solve a wide variety of problems, and, in turn, has made it possible to show (to some great extent) the capabilities and limitations of computers built to carry out those operations. Simply put, you can calculate the same sorts of things whether you describe how to compute it mathematically as a function (including recursion), or you express it as a "recipe" of steps to be followed one after another (or repeatedly). This implied that if you could build a computer that followed "recipes" of steps, you had all the power you needed to do great things – including creating computations that were so complex that nobody could figure out

---

[1]Those seeking just classic book introductory material may wish to skip to section 1.8.

1

precisely what they would do by just looking at them. It was only after that that Turing proposed how to actually build an automated computer to carry out such computations, such as in the description leading this chapter. (As it turned out, his computer was not the first.)

One simplification which Turing adopted as a basis for his computational model was that it would perform only one operation at a time, or in other words, that it would perform operations sequentially. It is easy to understand why he might have adopted this approach. Prior to the existence of electronic computers, the term "computer" referred to a person who computed, by following a set of directions or formulae. Sequential computation is a simplification of how we reason, how we address problems, how we teach others, etc. We have but a single mind, which allows us to consider only one (or a few) things at a time, a single mouth to communicate them, etc. Even if deep down many concurrent actions are occurring in our brains to facilitate each step, any time actions need to each occur at the same single point in space (such as in our mouth or ears or fingertips), they must happen at different times, sequentially, at some level of granularity.

This simple single-step oriented approach also largely allows one to completely separate the computation from the person or machine used to carry it out: We can check the order of the steps, and determine whether they do or do not solve the problem at hand, with a logical or mathematical mindset, while ignoring the physical aspects of precisely how the steps will be carried out. Turing's objective was to develop a model that was as simple as possible that would do the trick, and his simple sequential model of computation is indeed very powerful, seemingly as powerful for expressing computations as any model could possibly be. And it would also seem to be among the simplest, certainly simpler than a concurrent model, where many things might happen at a time. After all, how could keeping track of concurrent actions be somehow simpler than just one action occurring at once?

1.2   Plans, Activities, Platforms

The word "computation" itself has implications which are limiting. To many, it suggests numbers, data, and mathematics, and indeed, computers were original devised for such purposes. However, today, although these things we call "computers" still deal in such terms at the lowest levels (and actually even more abstractly, with ones and zeros, trues and falses, bits of charge, AND gates and NOT gates), one might not currently describe their primary utility as "computing" in that sense. In fact, if one was to name computers based on how they are used today, we'd probably call them "communicators" or "assistants" or "information accessors" – and such terms are indeed used for marketing computers to different audiences. So maybe those are all just aspects of computation?

Throughout this book, we will wish to consider computation more broadly. Instead of just describing what happens in a mathematical formula, we will want to describe pretty much anything that happens. Any time there are entities that do something, that interact, that change and/or sense their environment, we will consider that as computing, but to avoid too much confusion or controversy, we will instead usually just say that they are carrying out an activity, a broader scope than is usually applied to computing alone. Later on, we will more formally define what we mean by the word computation, which (in brief) will be a description of precisely what goes on within an activity. (This is fairly consistent with the way computer scientists, including Turing himself, use and used the term.)

This brings up other terminology confusion. The instructions presented to a computer are generally called a program (or software). Yet, if we develop similar instructions for use by a person, such as for how to prepare some food, we might call it a recipe. And if we were to develop a set of instructions for how to build a house or to run a company, we might call it a plan. And yet another term, algorithm, is often used as a generalization of computer programs, but this term also has been implicitly endowed with certain properties over the years. Rather than bouncing among such terms for no apparent advantage, for the purposes of this book, we will use the term "plan" when we wish to encompass the most general meanings. So, we will consider a program just as a plan made to be understood by a (particular) computer, and an algorithm as a plan which is intended to be easy to turn into a program, and a recipe as a plan intended for a person to create food, etc.

So, an activity will result from following a plan. Traditionally, the thing that carries out the plan (especially, a plan in the form of a program) would be called a computer, but we believe it would be too much of a deviation from standard usage to refer to a company, or car, or homemaker, as a computer. Instead, we'll use the more general term "platform" as the site where a plan is carried out to result in an activity, so a computer, an office, a person, a network of computers, etc., are all examples of platforms. Even this may be considered a bastardization of common usage, but at least the term platform has largely escaped the sort of precise definitions often provided to terms like "computer" that could only serve to confuse the reader.

1.3 Limitations of Traditional Sequential Computing

We said that Alan Turing (and others) simplified the concept of computation by restricting it to be sequential. As with most any simplification, there are limits to its generality, which seem to become more obvious the further we push until the simplifications eventually become obstructive rather than helpful, reminding us of the differences between reality and the simpler fantasy we have created.

One way to see the limitations of this sequential approach is to consider using it for modeling or describing common behavior in the world around us. We live (and have evolved) in a concurrent world, among concurrent events, and we are therefore very good at dealing with them. Our cell phone rings while we're shopping, and we may stop to answer it even while the person behind the deli counter continues to slice our cheese for us. The people conversing in the next aisle don't bother us, because we don't expect to be affected by them or them by us. If, later, they're in the same aisle as we are, and we both reach for the same final bottle of capers, then we are affected by them, and may even need to work out some means of determining who gets the bottle, such as through a conversation. Sequential computation was never designed to model such actions, sponteneity, interactions, and jumbled ordering of events.

Second, regardless of our desire and attempts to reason about computation abstractly, as a logical and/or mathematical phenomenon, it is in fact a physical phenomenon. This is easy to forget precisely because a very central goal of manmade computational models has been to distill the abstract (computational, software) aspects away from the physical (platform, hardware) aspects so that the former could be dealt with in purely logical and mathematical terms, while the latter is constructed solely to support that abstraction. Although both software and hardware have undergone substantial evolution over the decades, the fact remains that computation only results when both the plan and the platform (e.g. the software and the hardware) are put back together. In their combination, we cannot violate basic physics principles such as lack of action at a distance. Computation is cause-and-effect, which in turn implies the movement of something from the causal to the affected entity, the requirement that such movement takes time (restricted by the speed of light), and that such movement (as well as other aspects of computation) consumes energy. Regardless of the logic involved in the computation, these other factors have their own real-world impacts, costs, and constraints, which must be considered, and sequential computation may not (and often is not) the best way to optimize them.

Third, the principle advantage of having any formal model of computation is in allowing the development of automated computers to perform that computation. And one of the main reasons for having such computers is to make that computation fast and efficient. And regardless of how fast one can make such a computer to carry out a single computation, it is easy to see that it can often go even faster if you put multiple computers together, and split up the computation so different parts are carried out on the different computers at the same time. However, even if each computer in a collection can carry out some part of the overall computation independently, separate from the other processors, at some point in time (and far more likely, at many, many points), some or all of these independent parts must interact (such as to move or trade information). We now have something which is not a typical sequential computation. How do we reason about this? Can we have the same kinds of independence of the plan (the abstract logic) from the platform that we do when dealing with just one sequential computation? It turns out that these are not at all a simple questions to answer.

These three limitations of sequential computing were clearly understood by Turing himself, as evidenced in the passage from his paper that began this chapter. Note that he did not turn to sequential computing to describe how that computer would work internally. Instead, he knew that it should be constructed of electronic components, and that in all likelihood, several components would need to work together, concurrently, at various points. He began by coming up with some basic ideas of what those components would look like and how they should each act independently in order to simplify the job of having them work together. As the remainder of this book will eventually show, his insights mentioned above into how to deal with the complexities of the concurrency in the interworkings of those parts were remarkably apt. One can only wonder now what might have happened if Alan Turing had held off on finalizing his model of sequential computation until carefully considering rules for putting such concurrent components together, and presenting that model as the general form of "computation".

In the early part of the second millennium, the impact of these three limitations of the sequential computing model came to a head. Prior to that time, computers worked (and were built) largely in the mold Turing and others had created, and the speed of any single computer was limited, to a great extent, primarily by physical manufacturing phenomena related to the speed and wavelength of light – i.e. how logic elements could be manufactured and how small and for what price and how closely they could be spaced to get electrical signals from one to the next quickly without leaking into places they shouldn't. Improvements in these technologies were made at a steady clip, so consumers were satisfied with the speed of the increases. There were only a few disciplines that demanded even faster computers than were on the market at any one time, and engineers in those disciplines (primarily in large industries and governments) did indeed tie several (up to thousands) of computers together to deliver the higher computational speeds they needed. The job of programming these so-called parallel computers was monumental in some cases, but the demand in the fields needing this extreme speed was high enough to afford the people and time necessary to surmount that challenge on a case-by-case basis.

But sometime after the year 2000, something extremely important happened: The ability to manufacture and pack more devices more tightly stopped being the limiting factor in making sequential computers faster. Instead, the amount of energy it took to drive and cool the tiny tightly-packed devices became the main obstacle. That is, increasing the number of logic devices (gates) that could be involved in a single computational sequence also increased the energy (and heat) involved in driving those devices, beyond the point of practicality. As a result, the industry largely stopped increasing the number of devices used to carry out each computational sequence, and thus let the speed of executing any one computational sequence level off. Still, the industry continued in its ability to make the devices smaller and tighter, which meant that even if the number of devices in any one computer's central processing unit (CPU or "core") was to be held roughly constant, the space required for the core still became smaller and smaller. The result: The industry could now put multiple cores on a single computer chip, each capable of executing one computational sequence, or "thread": First two cores per chip, then four, and upwards from there. So, in even the smallest computers, in desktops, in laptops, and even in handheld devices, there were now multiple cores, or processors. And in order to take advantage of the on-chip processing power, even the simplest programs had to be built to exploit concurrency, to run on multiple processors at once. Instead of just the big industrial or governmental users who had always fought to utilize multiple processors, the entire world of computer programming was being thrown into concurrency, with very few tools at our disposal.

And those big industrial or government users? They are largely using the same hardware and techniques they always have, but have also found even more processors to utilize, some which have long been there but until now ignored as probably useless for anything but very specialized tasks. Prime among these are GPUs, so-called Graphics Processor Units, processors originally designed (and only intended) for manipulating graphical information on its way to (and sometimes from) the computer screen. While the kinds of a GPU's operations (and specifically, the flexibility with which these operations can be performed) is very limited, they are indeed very fast when they work within those limits, and scientists have found that some of scientific computations are indeed limited enough to be performed far more efficiently there. This introduces the concept of not only concurrency, but heterogeneity – i.e. the idea that some sorts of computations are better equipped for some processors than others, and simply deciding when and how to move information from one processor type to the other becomes an additional (and unwelcome) level of complexity all on its own.

1.4   Why Sequential Processors Run Hot

For some insight into the trade-offs and complexities of carrying out concurrent plans versus sequential ones, consider a very small store, with just one register (with one line) for checkout. It has only a few customers per hour, so it easily handles them, and all is fine. This is akin to the functioning of an old-fashioned sequential computer. But the store grows more successful, and grows in both size and number of customers. The management decides that everyone can still be served with just the one check-out line (also called a queue), if they get someone who is very fast and efficient on the check-out register. And as it gets even bigger and more popular, they decide to still mainain just the one register and line, though they put more helpers on the one check-out line – one to find the price tags, another to ring up the sale on the register (which is the most optimized, state-of-the-art model), and another to help bag the purchase, so that they can all be kept busy. This is akin to a more recent model sequential processor, which may even allow customers to pass each other there at the register if it will help to speed things up (so-called OOO, or out-of-order, execution). Up to a point, this may remain feasible, even if not exactly sensible.

The obvious questions: Why make all the customers come from every part of the store to the one register? Why put so much effort into getting the one cash register working quickly? Why not just open up more lines, each with it's own cash register? Indeed, the way the problem has been stated, with each customer and product completely independent of the others, that's an obvious solution, and one that is used in the computer industry for very simple cases like this. So now we'll extend the analogy to be a little more computer-like. Assume that a large percentage of the customers in this store return or exchange products. And, in addition, this store has a rather extreme policy that if you come in for an advertised product which they don't have in stock, you'll get it for free (when it does come in, one per customer, with other purchase). But to try to limit the chance that the stock of any product will be totally depleted, and to help make up the cost of cases where they will give away products, they counter that policy with an even more bizarre (but well-publicized) policy: That the last 100 of any product in stock cost progressively more than the standard retail price, until the last item of any product in stock costs twice standard retail. (Returns and exchanges always receive the amount it was sold for.)

With these new rules, the outcome of any one cash-register transaction depends on what happened in previous transactions. With only one line, it is still possible, at least, to predict what price everyone in line will be charged for the products they are purchasing. With multiple lines, however, the amount charged to any one person is potentially influenced by transactions in another line. This can be problematic not only for each customer, who may not know what they will be charged until the cashier tells them, but also for the cash register attendants, who (for example) must determine with each transaction whether there have been other recent transactions for the same product at other cash registers, in order to determine the price to be charged. Note that even knowing what all the customers in each line want to do, one cannot predict the outcome for each customer (or the store overall) without knowing the relative rates at which each line will move – e.g. whether customer A will get to the cash register in line 1 before customer B gets to the cash register in line 2 to purchase the same product.

So, indeed, one way to avoid many such complications is to maintain just one line. At the same time, getting everyone in the entire store to funnel through that one line is an inconvenience, and at some point will very likely reduce the amount of business the store can do in a unit of time (and drive away customers). Getting that one cash register to function ever more efficiently, and routing customers between extreme points in the store and the line quickly and efficiently, becomes ever more problematic.

Another approach, however, is to determine the circumstances under which multiple lines will act the same as just one line – e.g. as long as there is sufficient stock of the items being purchased – and to advertise to the customers and store management the advantages of having multiple lines even in light of the lack of predictability they may cause. That is, concurrency involves trade-offs, especially regarding predictability, and it is not so rare to find that the predictability guaranteed by sequential approaches is not as valuable as it might have seemed, as long as one has the proper tools to understand and deal with the lack thereof.

1.5 Scalability & Speedup

At its most basic, scalability is the broad concept of the ability of an entity to benefit by growing larger. For example, in the physical world, the human form (or that of most other animals) does not scale well more than a certain percentage: An entity like King Kong cannot exist with flesh and bone like ours because the strength of the bones would not increase at the same rate as the weight of the body they would be required to support. (Bone strength, related to cross-section area, grows at scale squared, while weight, related to volume, grows at scale cubed.) This is why an elephant has such wide legs and feet. Likewise, a skyscraper is built with different design and materials than a two-story house.

In the computer world, it is often relatively easy to improve (scale up) factors like storage space or bandwidth (amount of information which can be carried between different places per unit time) by increasing size (e.g. number of disk drives or communication channels), but those may trade off against other factors such as the speed with which one can access any particular piece of information, or the number of amount of space it takes to describe the location of a piece of information (i.e. its address). It is not uncommon for such trade-offs to exist, and to result in a natural optimal size. In our case, the factor which we will focus on improving is primarily speed – e.g. reducing the time that it takes to complete a plan – and the size will refer to the size of the platform, or more specifically, the number of processors, or computing engines, in the platform, each capable of carrying out the steps of one sequential part of the plan at a certain rate. The performance is often reported in terms of speedup, or the ratio (expressed as a fraction) of the time to completion of a sequential activity (or concurrent activity using one processor) compared to a concurrent one (with multiple processors). Since the numerator is a constant, if the speedup is graphed (on the Y axis) against the number of processors (on the X), we would hope that the time would decrease, and therefore the speedup would increase, with the addition of each processor, resulting in a curve that would move up and to the right. In fact, if the speedup was to increase exactly at the same pace as the concurrency, then the speedup with n processors would be n, and the curve would be a line with slope 1. This is often called unitary speedup, and the plan may be referred to as being perfectly scalable. If the speedup increases regularly with each processor, but not exactly at full efficiency, then it the curve is still a line, and therefore called linear speedup. Generally speaking, unless the amount of work to be done by the plan is effectively infinite, there will be some point when additional processors do not increase speedup, so the line levels off, and adding more processors may at some point actually increase the time to completion ("too many cooks" problem). See Figure 1.1.

Unitary speedup is, at first glance, the best that one could do, and it is rarely achieved. There are, however, cases where even super-unitary speedup has been demonstrated, where using n processors goes more than n times faster than using 1 processor. This is because a single processor may operate at less than peak efficiency because it has insufficient resources like memory, and when the activity is split among multiple processors, each now has less to do, and so may operate more efficiently. One of the most basic reasons for the far more common case, sublinear speedup, is explained in (Gene) Amdahl's Law, which simply observes that if some part of a plan is not amenable to concurrency at all, and so must be executed on only one processor, it can have a drastic impact on speedup. For example, if 10% of an activity is "inherently sequential", and can only benefit from one processor, then even if the rest is perfectly scalable, the speedup with n processors will be $t/(.9t/n + .1t)$, so with 9 processors, the speedup is only 5 (i.e. $t/(.9t/9 + .1t)$), and with even a million processors, the speedup is less than 10 (i.e. $t/(.9t/1000000 + .1t)$. This observation was countered more recently with so-called (Jon) Gustafson's Law, which basically argues that for many problems, making the amount of

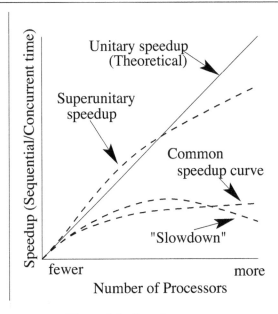

Figure 1.1: Speedup curves.

total work arbitrarily large can make any "inherently sequential" percentage arbitrarily small, so Amdahl's observation is not as troublesome as it might at first seem.

(Some definitions of terms like "linear speedup", "superlinear speedup", etc., require the property to be present even as the number of processors goes to infinity. We feel such cases are rare enough to make such definitions largely useless. More recently, terms like "soft scaling" are sometimes used to refer to how a problem scales to larger processors when the problem size – usually related to the amount of data to be processed – is increased commensurably at the same time.)

But even parts of a plan that would seem to lend themselves to concurrency typically suffer from sublinear speedup, for many real-world reasons. In fact, speedup often becomes "slowdown", with a plan taking longer with more processors. More processors means more more total distance between arbitrary processors, which means increased overall **latency** – the time that it takes to communicate even a small amount of information between two processors. And processors can't usually just be packed together: Processors, whether machines or people, consume energy and produce heat, so appropriate plumbing for those must also accommodated. Processors may fail/sicken/die and need to be replaced, and so physical access is important. At the same time, more processors also means more communication per processor (for each to communicate with each other), magnifying the latency problem. And just as it is cost-prohibitive and troublesome to have a private dedicated phone or data line from your house to each person or site you might communicate with, processors will usually communicate through a network or switch that is not only slower than a direct line from each to each, it can become swamped at times, leaving some processors with the analog of a "fast busy" signal on a telephone when they try to use it, slowing things down even more.

There are only so many ways to reduce latency using improvement of transmission processes or technology. In computers, even reducing latency to near the theoretical limits imposed by the speed of light may not be enough to keep it from having an impact on overall computation time, if too many (needless) communications between distant points are performed. In other words part of the solution to latency comes in the planning/programming step, using techniques like latency hiding (discussed shortly).

1.6 Complexity and Decomposition

We have tended to be wary of concurrency in part because having multiple things happening at once could seemingly not possibly be simpler than having just one, especially after noticing that concurrency uniquely introduces some properties (like nondeterminism) which we don't even need to deal with in a purely sequential mindset. Still, science is rife with examples of improving and simplifying our understanding by thinking "outside of the box", of simplfying our model of something by adding more dimensions or degrees of freedom. For example, although a Ptolemaic geocentric universe had a more familiar perspective than in a Copernican heliocentric system, describing planetary motion in the former was more complicated, and less elegant and generalizable, than in the latter. If we had continued to limit ourselves to seeing our world as being constructed of but a few elements (Earth, Water, Fire, and Air, for example), we certainly would not have the understanding or predictive ability over matter that we now have. This is often posed as a balance between Occam's Razor, which favors a simpler explanation, and what is sometimes called Einstein's Razor, which advises that theories should be as "simple as possible, but no simpler". Perhaps theories based on sequential models of computation have been too simple to work very naturally.

Another lesson can be gleaned from the element analogy. We have not only progressed past those four elements, but into a view of matter built of molecules, and molecules built of atoms, and those of subatomic particles, and those of quarks, etc. Yet a farmer isn't likely to look past genetics when trying to breed a sweeter or more hearty tomato, a surgeon might not be concerned below the organ or tissue layer when performing an operation, and even a chemist will not care about particles below atoms and electrons for most common reactions. Adding more detail or understanding is not necessarily useful for every purpose, only for when that extra level provides useful additional information.

When it comes to activities, which occur in time and space, the decision of where to stop delving deeper into structure seems even more complicated. Both time and space are generally considered as continuous quantities, capable of being divided into ever finer pieces without (practical) limit, rather than discrete quantities which have natural units (e.g. in size or mass) and boundaries. Is it possible, or advisable, to discuss "fundamental particles" of time or activity? Regardless of what we choose as a fundamental particle of action, couldn't we find other smaller activities from which the original could be constructed?

In this book, we will in fact attempt to decompose actions of any complexity into some which have some specific properties. We will figuratively consider such actions as fundamental action particles, which we will call actons (a play on the words atom and action). We use the term "elemental concurrency" to describe this approach of considering concurrency in terms of these fundamental particles. The idea is not that actons cannot be divided even more finely: Of course, they can. The idea is to get down to something which we can reason about more abstractly *if we like*, and to provide some guidelines for such reasoning. If we wish to go deeper and subdivide actons, that is possible, too.

1.7 Some Traditional Approaches to Concurrency

So what have people done up to now to address these issues? What have been their primary toolsets and techniques? We will cover some of the main ones here used in programming parallel computers, but hope first to comfort the reader by clarifying that these are the things we will try to protect them from in the remainder of the book. If this all begins to sound too cumbersome and complicated, it is, and that's why this book was written. So, it is here for the brave-hearted, to those who want to understand our motivations, and especially those who will later want to delve into Chapter 5, but for others, if this section should feel too burdensome, feel free to skip to the next without too much penalty.

1.7.1 Programming Models

The most obvious ways to achieve concurrency when starting with sequential processing is to provide some way for multiple sequential activities (programs, processes, threads) to interact. The two primary traditional approaches have been:

- "Shared Memory", where some subset of resources (generally memory or storage) are accessible by multiple activities running on different parts of a platform (or, if you like, different platforms). In the store example, this could be a shared store room or warehouse (or at least inventory list) used by all the cash registers. Because these resources are shared, alterations by one activity can be observed/sensed by another, resulting in communication. It is quite common for some of these shared resources, often called locks or semaphores, to be used for regulating access to other shared resources. Such a lock can be envisioned as a token of some kind assigned to (e.g. placed near) another shared resource, and before observing or changing that other shared resource, an activity is required to pick up the token first, replacing it when finished. This ensures that one activity won't be in the middle of doing something with the shared resource while another comes in and unexpectedly changes it around at the same time.

- "Message Passing" (or "Shared Nothing"), where one activity can send (provide) a message (generally a copy of some part of some local information available to it) to another activity. Typically, unless the receiving activity is already waiting for the message to arrive, that message sits in a hidden buffer (storage area) in the receiving activity, akin to a mailbox (or voicemail box), until that activity explicitly "receives" it. In the store example, a message-passing solution might represent cashiers trying to determine the current stock of an item by calling or texting one another to find out what they have at their register (e.g. recently returned). When using message passing, an activity can wait until a message shows up, and may also typically inquire as to what kinds of messages are waiting (e.g. in the mailbox) to be received, and perhaps how large they are. It is also common for the sender to specify a "tag" or "type" for the message, and the receiver to specify that it wants to receive the next available message with that tag or type, rather than the next overall. Even in cases where the activities can communicate very quickly, there is generally time and space overhead involved just with copying information, between activities and/or to and from mailboxes.

One reason these two approaches became popular is that they were relatively easy to implement, such as in computer hardware. If there are just a few processors, and they are close together, they can all be configured to access the same memory, facilitating the first model. If there are more than a few processors, and/or they are further apart, some sort of communication lines ("wires", "network", "switch") can be set up between them to allow data to be moved from one to the other, facilitating the second model. For this reason, the choice of which approach/model of concurrency was used was traditionally determined by the architecture (configuration) of the computer system. Not only was programming difficult, regardless of the model, it was not at all independent of the hardware, thereby trouncing a primary goal of computation since its inception. In fact, even within the two approaches above, the precise style of message passing and/or shared memory often depended upon the specific brand or features of the processors. These differences have been ameliorated significantly with the adoption of standards, such as MPI (Message Passing Interface) for Message Passing and OpenMP for Shared Memory.

One approach to minimizing the disparity between Shared Memory and Message Passing has been to create platforms which are capable of either, or more accurately, are somewhere in the middle. The most common approach was Virtual Shared Memory, or NUMA (Non-Uniform Memory Access). The idea is that, even if there were lots of processors and/or they were far apart (connected by wires), thereby looking externally like a message-passing computer, the programmer can still use a shared memory model as long as there is special hardware and/or software to automatically decide when information should be moved (sent) around from one processor to the next to make it available for access there. The NUMA name arose from the very different access times which result, depending on whether the data being accessed is already nearby or not, in contrast with more typical shared memory where the time to access memory is more uniform, always being a relatively fixed distance away. Though somewhat successful, NUMA is indeed another style of hardware, and programming it effectively requires the programmer to understand when it might try to move data, to minimize spurious or unimportant transfers through clever programming, just as one would do with message passing.

These were by far not the only models of concurrency which were attempted. For example, since much scientific computing often required processing large arrays (or matrices) of numbers, often combining them in standard ways with similar standard mathematical operations, special hardware was created to optimize such calculations, by allowing different processors (or different parts of the same processor) to work on different matrix elements at the same time, even while specifying the operations to be performed only once. This was called (originally by Michael Flynn) a SIMD (Single Instruction Multiple Data) approach, to distinguish it from the communicating processors approach, which was named MIMD (Multiple Instruction Multiple Data). Hardware to perform such MIMD operations was often organized to combine sequences (or vectors) of numbers in fixed ways, leading to terms like vector hardware. Special software was developed to look at any particular computation and determine whether it was vectorizable (i.e. able to execute efficiently on such hardware) and how to vectorize it (i.e. make it do so). Even without special hardware, programs constructed to operate on matrices can also often be prepared to execute on MIMD machines somewhat efficiently, using an approach called SPMD (Single Program, Multiple Data), where the data is split up between the processors, and movement/exchanges are often handled automatically by underlying software.

So couldn't the differences between shared memory and message passing be hidden using a higher-level abstraction? One approach: Just express the plan completely mathematically, as a function, and let other software and/or hardware find the most efficient way to compute that function using the available hardware. Since a function only specifies what needs to be done rather than how to do it, if the computation can exploit concurrency, perhaps an additional software step can determine the best way to do that, whatever the platform may be. This approach has had some level of success, but it is also somewhat lacking from a computation perspective, where one tries to understand (or specify) what to do (or what is beng done), not just the mathematical relationship between the initial conditions and the final state. Functional approaches focus on the "what", usually leaving the "how" as a completely separate step, often accomplished by a non-human counterpart (e.g. a compiler or run-time system) which may be limited in its abilities.

There are, of course, a multitude of other techniques, languages, models, etc., that have been proposed over the years. In fact, the approach to be presented in this book (ScalPL) can be considered yet one more option among many, and especially as a specific form of so-called Partitioned Global Address Space (PGAS). One difference is that it will be presented primarily as a tool to understanding the concepts inherent in any concurrency. It is entirely up to the reader as to whether they might also see it as a tool for harnessing those concepts and, specifically, for expressing plans.

1.7.2 Pitfalls of Traditional Concurrency

It may not be immediately obvious that the traditional approaches to concurrency mentioned above are so unsatisfactory. After all, why should such seemingly minor alterations to sequential practices – things like adding "send" and "receive" operations for message passing, or allowing multiple sequential processes to access shared memory – be so problematic?

We have already alluded to one of the main reasons: Unlike a traditional algorithm, a concurrent algorithm using shared memory or message passing must be developed with the target platform in mind. Not only must the developer be aware of which of those approaches will be supported by the platform, to do its work efficiently, he/she must also generally have some impression of the number of processors, how long it takes to communicate among processors, how memory is divided among the processors, etc. Without such information, it is difficult to make algorithms which are superior in almost any way (and especially performance-wise, the most commonly sought advantage) to sequential algorithms. So if one can choose to have algorithms which embody concurrency (and performance) only at the cost of dependence on the target platform, it begs the question of whether the term "concurrent algorithm" is after all an oxymoron. After all, the term algorithm itself implies platform independence. (The oxymoron aspect can be at least partially avoided by restricting oneself to terms like "message-passing algorithms" or "shared-memory algorithms", and parameterizing aspects which can affect performance.)

Another fundamental difference between sequential and concurrent computing is the introduction of nondeterminism. That is, assuming that each step in a sequential algorithm is well-defined and functional (produces a specific result for any specific starting point), the algorithm as a whole will also provide a well-defined and specific (deterministic) result, given a specific starting point and specific set of inputs. Although many concurrent algorithms also have this property, many do not, and they are called nondeterministic. Even if each step is perfectly well-defined and functional, and the inputs are fixed, different outputs may result. This is largely due to the fact that, like the check-out queue example, the exact time that the different parts will interact is not dictated by the algorithm, and results may differ when those interaction times change.

When using traditional approaches to concurrency like message passing or shared memory, it is rather difficult to prevent nondetermism from being introduced into an algorithm accidentally, even when it is not desired, or to understand or control the extent of that nondeterminism. This has led some to interpret "nondeterminism" as a dirty word, something to be avoided at all costs. It can be especially problematic in cases when the nondeterminism changes the behavior of the algorithm specifically under the "wrong" conditions, such as when parts of it are being intentionally slowed down for examination, such as during the debugging process. (Such problems are often called "Heisenbugs", because, like Heisenberg's Uncertainty Principle, the act of observation itself affects the phenomenon being observed.) However, in many cases, nondeterminism is not necessarily so bad, such as when the designer does not need to nail down the result of the algorithm for some given input to just one "right" answer in all cases. In return for allowing different results (or results in different orders), the designer may be able to speed up the production of one or all of the (correct) results by facilitating a "first-come first-served" approach among different parts of the algorithm. In fact, the inability to naturally express such nondeterminism in some languages (like those for expressing only functional relationships) can be, in some cases and by some people, considered a draw-back of those languages: They cannot, in any "pure" way, introduce nondeterminism without either doing it in a very unnatural way (e.g. introducing functions which are just so complex that they are for all intents and purposes non-functional) or changing the entire basis for the language. More recently, some of these languages have added constructs called monads, which have a vague similarity to constructs which arise in this book.

The nondeterminism issue can be considered as part of a larger issue – i.e. that keeping track of how information moves through a concurrent algorithm can be very hard. Over the years, techniques for controlling and keeping track of such things for sequential algorithms has been carefully developed and studied, under the topic of software engineering. Techniques such as information hiding, data types (including abstract data types), side effects, and more generally, restricting and controlling scope of influence have resulted in the ability to construct and reason about large complex algorithms, but similar techniques are difficult to adapt to situations where information is being passed around between different, potentially independently-developed, portions of an algorithm in a rather haphazard and uncontrolled manner. The resulting and lasting impression has been simply that developing correct parallel algorithms is hard.

1.7.3   Dealing with Latency

We have already described how latency is the time it takes a signal (or more usually, information) to get from one place to another, and how there's only so much one can do in the computer hardware to minimize it. After all, even if every possible bottleneck was removed, it would still take time to communicate, due to limits in the speed of light. So, various programming techniques have been adopted to help deal with its reality. For example:

- A primary way of dealing with latency is called **latency hiding**, which simply means finding something else productive to do while waiting for a communication. It is easy to understand that if someone sends us a letter in the mail, we usually aren't left twiddling our thumbs until it arrives, because there are other things to do locally. Perhaps the easiest way to hide latency, and one that's been used for decades when waiting for something to happen locally, is to work on some other (e.g. someone else's) completely unrelated plan while waiting. This will not help to speed up either one of the plans individually, but will speed up the collection of plans. More useful for a single plan, then, is to find other unrelated parts of the very same plan to work on. The problems, traditionally, have been (in part) identifying other work to do while waiting, and paying context switch overhead – the time it actually takes to record precisely where the (now delayed) plan (or part thereof) is, and then reestablishing the context of a plan (or part thereof) now being resumed after a delay.

- Latency hiding is also aided by getting information to where it's needed, even before it is needed there, and that means, in a plan, clearly expressing and (if possible) limiting which processors need to be informed when something changes. This means knowing both which parts of the plan will need the information, and where (physically) those parts of the plan will be dealing with it.

- When lots of processors do need to communicate at about the same time and in about the same way, it is often possible to optimize, an approach called collective communication. Sometimes, that optimzation relates to minimizing the distance. Sometimes it means minimizing the number of communications. Sometimes it means minimizing the time to complete a set of communications. These can all often be accomplished by having the processors work together in some way as a team, with advance knowledge of the overall goal.

- Vary granularity as necessary. That is, don't use more processors than will pay off. This starts by breaking the plan down into small enough pieces to use many processes when that works out well, but when it doesn't, providing a way to effectively glue some of those pieces together to form bigger pieces. That is, it is usually not sufficient to just make each communication smaller, since latency is suffered regardless of size, so it is important to actually minimize the number of communications if possible.

Attempts to optimize these are difficult, even in the context of so-called homogeneous platforms (where all of the parts such as processors are identical) and even with complete control and visibility over all of the plans being carried out on that platform at any given time. Not only are those sorts of restricted conditions oversimplified and unrealistic, but they carry their own costs. For example, a homogeneous platform can usually be constructed only by monolthic development and/or replacement of the entire platform at once, with rigid specs, while heterogeneity (the opposite of homogeneity) allows the piecemeal construction or augmentation of the platform with newer or older technology as finances allow.

That is one of the main goals (and hopefully accomplishments) of the Scalable Planning Language (ScalPL) introduced in this book: To facilitate the construction of plans in such a way that the above optimizations can be carried out independently of the plan, in an entity we will call the Director. It is an open question whether such techniques will be seen as productive even when used for plans that are not expected to require large-scale execution. In general, our approach here is to argue that they are, since tried and true principles of software engineering are being used, beneficial regardless of scale of the eventual platform.

1.8 Scope, Goals and Directions of This Book

The intent of this book is to provide some useful ways of thinking about concurrency. In the process, it will present some notation for capturing and combining concepts as they are explained. This notation, although graphical/visual in nature, is precise and complete enough to be considered a language (such as a computer language) in its own right, so we call it Scalable Planning Language, or ScalPL (pronounced "scalpel") for short. Some readers will notice similarities between ScalPL and more traditional notations such as flowcharts, entity-relation (ER) diagrams, UML, dataflow diagrams, Petri Nets, etc.

As a result, the book has at least three potential audiences:

1. Computer specialists and students who are familiar with sequential programming but have had little or no previous exposure to concurrency, and wish to learn of the inherent issues, concepts, and some solutions. As currently written, the book is not intended to be a historical treatise, or a survey of tools/languages that have been (or are being) used to address issues related to concurrency, so if such information is desired, the reader may wish to augment it with other texts.

2. Computer specialists and students who may have had previous exposure to concurrency and tools and languages to address the inherent issues, but now want to learn ScalPL as an alternate way of representing programs (and/or plans), and to learn when and how to use the constructs therein.

3. People who are not in the computer industry at all, but who wish to understand the impact and issues involved with concurrency, either purely to satisfy curiosity, or to make sense of wrinkles in the computer industry from a largely non-technical perspective, or to apply to non-computer related fields such as organizational planning, product design or systems maintenance.

Clearly, all aspects of the book won't be of interest to all three audiences, but all audiences may find value in Chapters 1 through 9, 11, 12, and 16.

Chapters 2 and 3 present (in a stepwise fashion) the basic constructs and principles used in the remainder of the book for developing concurrent plans, and Chapter 4 outlines some special cases which can be easily optimized. Chapter 5 describes how a Director might go about carrying out a plan (constructed according to guidelines in the other chapters). Chapter 6 adds a few new constructs and concepts to facilitate hierarchy and encapsulation, and in the process, to allow the planner to construct composite activities with almost any level of complexity, and with almost any desired external behavior. And Chapter 8 introduces a systematic way of thinking about algorithms and computations which applies to sequential computing but generalizes well to concurrent computing.

A few chapters relate primarily to managing how information is scalably stored and accessed by plans, rather than on concurrency per se. Chapter 7 discusses the way that names are associated with plans, and what a name means when used within a plan, and Chapter 11 introduces ways to manage visibility to sets (groups) of resources at one time

To finish out the more generally applicable chapters, Chapter 9 delves more deeply into the concepts of nondeterminism and atomicity, and some ways to find and/or control the level of these present in a plan. Chapter 12 introduces some Object Oriented concepts and constructs, and illustrates how they are integrated with ScalPL. (The subject of Object Oriented programming and design is far broader than the scope of this book, so the latter chapter can be seen as an introduction, or as a "terminology bridge" between this text and others where such matters are discussed in more depth.) The final chapter, 16, speculates on how a wide acceptance of approaches like the one described here could affect how we integrate expertise in the future.

The remainder of the chapters may be of more interest to advanced readers and concurrent programmers who wish to study the extent to which ScalPL can be used as a full-fledged formal language for developing computer software. These chapters can safely be skipped by other readers. Chapter 10, on axiomatic semantics, will examine the extremes of formality, equating the rules of ScalPL with mathematical axioms. Chapters 13 and 14 explain extensions within ScalPL for for operating on arrays and matrices in the same ways available in other concurrent computer languages, to exploit maximum concurrency when there is ample data to be operated upon. Chapter 15 applies some engineering principles and relationship to other formal models to building and analyzing plans, to help assure their correctness.

1.9 History of This Approach

This author's work on this subject began in about 1985, when he took a graduate lab course in software engineering from Dr. Robert G. "Robbie" Babb II, at Oregon Graduate Center (OGC) in Beaverton, Oregon (near Portland). Dr. Babb had been exploring an engineering technique, which he called Large Grain Data Flow (LGDF), for developing concurrent software. He had started with rather traditional dataflow diagrams used in software engineering, and after experimenting with a novel shared-memory parallel computer (the Denelcor HEP) which had a decidedly dataflow "feel", asked himself why these diagrams couldn't be used as the basis for a concurrent programming language for such machines.

Shortly thereafter, the author became Dr. Babb's graduate assistant, and together they considered implementations of LGDF on a few other shared memory computers, soon realizing (1) that there were some difficulties with implementing LGDF on other kinds of concurrent platforms, such as those based on message passing, and (2) there were some complexities/confusion with the notation Babb was using. The author went on to address and overcome these issues, resulting in a more limited (but also more precise and portable) notation called LGDF2. Eventually, the author went on to develop a formal mathematical model for that notation, called F-Nets (for Function Networks), as his 1991 PhD dissertation at Oregon Graduate Institute (OGC's new name). This formal model is essentially that presented in Chapter 10 of this book. In addition to Robert Babb, the dissertation committee consisted of Richard Kieburtz, Michael Wolfe, all of OGI, and Harry Jordan of the University of Colorado at Boulder, with Dr. Wolfe offering especially helpful reviews.

Upon completing the dissertation, the author began rebuilding LGDF2 (and F-Nets) into a form which would be useful for real programming and design tasks, by adding such things as arrays, encapsulation, and object-oriented constructs. The language containing these constructs (but based upon the F-Net formalism) became known by various names, most notably Software Cabling (SC). (At that time, the constructs had names such as chips, boards, wires, cables, sockets, memories, etc.) Eventually, with a change of terminology and focus, that language became the Scalable Planning Language (ScalPL) described in this book. Other attempts to extend LGDF2 (or its principles) were also attempted by others: ELGDF ("extended LGDF") was proposed by some researchers at Oregon State University around 1990, and Dr. Babb later proposed a product called LGDF3. Both of those developments (and any others, as far as this author is aware) were completely separate and markedly different from the SC/ScalPL approach presented in this book.

Determining a useful notation and semantics for SC was only part of the challenge, however. For such a thing to become widespread and successful, it must gain traction, or at least ample exposure. In late 1991, NASA Ames Research Center (NAS Division), where the author then worked, agreed to have the author develop a prototype of tools called NASPACT (NAS Parallel Algorithm Construction Toolset) to support the method, but the novelty of the approach made it a hard sell in that particular environment, and the project was essentially canceled before it began. NASA did, however, fund development of a subroutine package called CDS (Cooperative Data Sharing) which embodied the underlying architecture-independent communication model, explored here in Chapter 5. Later at NASA, the author headed the Distributed Architectures planning team of a joint "grid" (now considered "cloud") project between NASA and the NSF (called Information Power Grid), where he gained further insight into the demand for this sort of integrated approach, and eventually left NASA to form a startup, Elepar (a shortening of "elemental parallelism", a coined term to describe the approach used by ScalPL), which acquired the rights to CDS and intended to develop SC/ScalPL tools upon it. However, timing and location were poor, just as the "dot com bubble" was bursting, and the novel visual approach complicated matters. (In fact, some funding was reportedly denied specifically because the funding agencies separated all software engineering from concurrent software development, making superiority in both fields together more of a hindrance than a help to obtain that funding.)

In this book we take a wholly different perspective to presenting ScalPL than those earlier attempts. Rather than trying to "sell" ScalPL and presenting it in terms of tools or a development language, we shift the focus to the issues of concurrency that need to be addressed, regardless of development language or toolset, and use ScalPL to represent solutions to these issues in a form that allows those solutions to subsequently be conveyed and combined in a variety of ways. As such, we believe the book will be valuable, certainly to people who do not have tools to support ScalPL, but even to those who may not be interested in ScalPL for anything more than simply learning/teaching concurrency. At the same time, for those who are interested in the potential of ScalPL as a development technique, this book should also serve as a clear treatise on ScalPL's design principles.

1.10 Disclaimer

The purpose of this work (like most other books) is to broadcast ideas which may be of some use to readers, and nothing more. The techniques expressed in this work are not guaranteed to be correct or original, or to be correctly attributed when citations are present. We make no claim about the suitable application of these ideas for any particular purpose, even in cases where suggestions are made. We hope that you can enjoy and merit from the contents here, but cannot accept responsibility if you find them troublesome in any way, or suffer any sort of damages through their use.

Chapter 2

Activities and Resources

This chapter introduces the basic terminology, concepts, and notation to serve as a foundation for the rest of the book. This includes the definition and representation of plans, activities, resources, contexts, roles, bindings, permissions, etc. Abstract definitions will rapidly give way to concrete examples to illustrate how the constructs fit together.

2.1 Introduction

2.1.1 Plans and Activities

We will consider a **strategy** for computation very broadly and abstractly as describing a collection of **activities** and portions of the environment with which they interact. Each activity may affect some of the parts of the environment, and may be affected by some parts. When an activity affects its environment, it is likely (as a result) to also have an impact on other activities which are affected by the environment. In fact, this effect on other activities can be considered the only reason that an activity would modify the environment. Put another way, the environment can be considered as just a medium for allowing activities to impact other activities (or the same activity at a later time). We will not consider activities which have no effect at all on their environment, because there is (by definition) no way to determine whether such an activity has taken place.

The activities here will be considered to be intentional, and are therefore each the result of following some **plan**. The initiation of an activity from a plan will be called **activating** (or **executing**) the plan, and the entity deciding which plans to activate, and then activating them, will be called the **Director**. (The Director is not necessarily physically separate from the activities themselves, but it will be characterized as such here for simplicity.) Little more needs to be said about the Director, but for those who are interested in how it might work, a later chapter (Chapter 5) is dedicated to it.

While activities happen over a period of time, plans are just static things which guide activities. Plans are common in the real world in business and personal matters, with a recipe being the archetype of a plan for the activity of preparing food. In the computer world, algorithms and programs are examples of plans, and active processes or threads (resulting from running those programs or algorithms) are examples of activities. Although plans and activities are closely related, multiple activities may be activated from a single plan, and may even appear (externally) to behave very differently from one another.

Each activity in a strategy will take place within a **context**, represented graphically as a circle, signifying the relationship of the activity to its environment, as described shortly.

2.1.2 Resources

Since different activities will access (affect and be affected by) different parts of the environment, it is both unrealistic and unhelpful to regard the environment as one single monolithic entity, and instead more natural to consider it as being composed of independent pieces, which we will call **resources**. The specific way to effectively partition an overall environment into resources is largely subjective, but will be motivated in part to ensure that each activity can access the parts of the environment (resources) it needs without unduly interfering with activities accessing other parts (i.e. other resources) at the same time. In cases where different activities will indeed need to access exactly the same part of the environment (though perhaps at different times), decomposing that part further into smaller, more specific resources may serve little purpose, instead just requiring each activity to access more resources. The issues involved in considering the environment in terms of resources and activities are similar to those which we humans have collectively taken into consideration when deciding how to assign nouns to bits of our natural environment, and verbs to different discrete activities in our natural environment. In fact, there should be little confusion in using the term "verb" interchangeably with "plan" and "noun" interchangeably for "resource".

But this description of resources as simply being parts of the environment is slightly ambiguous and imprecise. If an activity creates something new within the environment, does that mean it is always creating a new resource? If that part of the environment changes, does the resource become a different resource, or does some part of it change while it maintains its identity?

Instead of being considered literally as part of the environment, a resource is more properly considered as a container or specifier for a conceptual part of the environment or for a particular kind of entity within the environment when present. That is, we will usually consider a resource as a placeholder or label in the environment, within which parts of the environment exist. In most cases, when some part of the environment is created (usually just constructed or moved from other resources), we will consider it as being created within such an already existing resource (container or label), and when it is destroyed, the (now empty) resource (container) remains. Those familiar with computer languages will recognize a resource as corresponding closely to the concept of a variable. The part of the environment associated with a resource, the part which affects or is affected by an activity, is called the resource's **contents** or **content**

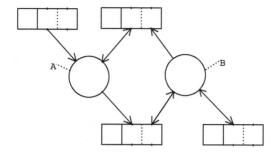

Figure 2.1: Four resources and 2 contexts. Plan A's context has 3 role bindings, with observe, update, and replace permissions.

state, and it corresponds closely to the value of a variable in a computer. To help characterize each resource, the resource itself has an associated **content domain** which is a specification of all of the different content states which that resource is capable of holding during its lifetime. That specification may be in any form which seems suitable for the task at hand. (It can be considered as a set which lists all the possible content states for that resource, or just a qualitative description of such a set – such as "an integer" or "a dog". For readers familiar with computer languages, a content domain is roughly equivalent to the data type of the resource.) A resource also has an **initial content state**, which is the content state of the resource before that resource is affected by any activities. Of course, the initial content state for a resource must be an element of its content domain.

There are cases when, instead of just creating new content for an existing resource, we will want to actually create new resources (i.e. with new names/labels), and/or to eliminate old ones, but those can wait. We will tackle those in Chapters 6 (encapsulation) and 13 (arrays).

We will represent resources graphically in our computational strategy as rectangles, as in Figure 2.1. Each may optionally be labeled with a meaningful name, and optionally a description of its content domain (in parentheses after the label, if any), and those (if any) can then optionally be followed by an equal sign and the initial contents in the form of a **constant**. (Much of Chapter 7 will be dedicated to describing different forms of constants.) Each context circle (housing an activity) will be connected to the resources it cares about in the environment (i.e. those it will affect or be affected by) by lines called **role bindings**. The justification for this notation and terminology will become clearer later, but simply put, each of these lines will designate the role that the corresponding resource will play within the activity. Generally, each context circle will be labeled with the name of the plan from which the activities in that context will result (i.e. when activated).

2.1.3 Permissions

Arrowheads called **permissions** on the role bindings (lines) indicate the ways that the activities and resources might interact. An arrowhead on the context (circle) end, called **observe** permission, indicates that the activity may observe the resource contents – i.e. that the outcome of the activity might depend upon that resource's content state. An arrowhead on the resource (rectangle) end, called **replace** permission, indicates that the *entire* content of the resource will be replaced by the activity. No arrowhead at all, called a **nodata** permission, will become useful only later, as it means that the activity will neither observe nor change the resource content state. And an arrowhead on both ends of the role binding is called an **update** permission, and it signifies every other possibility – i.e. that the activity might replace all or just part of the resource contents, along with potentially observing the contents.

It is important here to be clear on when to use the replace vs. update permission. Replace permission (the single arrow on rectangle end) is used *only* when the activity will *never* look at anything on the resource, and will *always completely* replace the entire resource content with new content. In other cases, where the activity would only sometimes replace the entire content, or replace only part of the content (sometimes or always), or do these things together with sometimes or always observing some of the resource contents, update permission (double arrow, signifying both observe and replace) must be used instead. This is because, in all of these other cases, even if the activity doesn't explicitly observe the contents of the resource, the content on the resource after the activity has accessed it might have something to do with the content of the resource before the activity accessed it (such as, the content might remain partially or completely unchanged from before the access), just as if the activity had first observed the resource, and then completely replaced the contents, some with what it had observed. That is, the permissions do not reflect what an activity actually does while accessing a resource's contents, just the sort of result that may be expected on the activity's resources when it has finished accessing them, relative to what was there when it began accessing them.

2.2 Resources

There are many potential ways to partition or organize the parts of an environment, needed by an activity, into resources. Say, for example, that we wish to have an activity representing the drying and stacking of a single dish. It seems logical to consider the dish being dried as a resource. Certain other parts of the environment, such as a towel or drying rack, and the water coming off the dish, aren't important to any other activities, so there is no apparent advantage in representing them as separate, explicit resources that outlive the activity and/or are visible outside of it. (We will later refer to such things as transient resources, there only for the use and duration of an activity.) As for the stack of dishes, we could consider each dish in the stack as a separate resource, but in that case there would be no discernable "stack" except as a collection of individual dishes, and since each resource has its own identity, we would need to plan and deal with the identities of each dish independently, for no apparent advantage. Future chapters will indeed discuss ways to organize collections of individual resources in an easy-to-manage way, each with their own identity, but for now, we'll consider the entire stack of dry dishes as a single separate

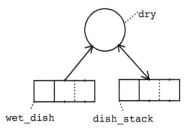

Figure 2.2: Activity to dry a dish (in context).

resource. So, in that view, our drying activity will take a wet dish, dry it, and add the now dry dish to (i.e. integrate it into) a stack of dishes, as in Figure 2.2..

2.2.1 Control State

Consider the permissions here. Although this activity is seemingly not taking or observing anything from the dish stack, it is important to use update permission for that stack because the resulting content of the stack will depend, in part, on the content before the new dish is added: All the dishes that were there before will remain there. But also, from what we know so far, the observe permission for the wet dish seems questionable, since we are doing more than observing it: We want to effectively take it away and put it (after drying) onto the dry stack, so we don't want another activity finding it (e.g. observing it) there on the "wet dish" resource later. It might seem more sensible to use update permission, so the activity could, say, erase the content of that resource and leave it empty, or even for us to invent and use a special new permission like "consume" for cases like this.

Such approaches are, in fact, common in other concurrency techniques, especially in so-called dataflow techniques. The idea there is that a resource (or whatever it is called in those techniques, often a variable or channel) has two primary qualities or conditions: full or empty, defined or undefined, present or absent. Furthermore, these other techniques use this condition to control access to the resource (or variable, or channel) by activities (or their equivalents): Whenever such a resource/channel is empty, it can be given new contents, but its current contents cannot be observed, and when it is full, the resource contents can be observed (at which time they are often removed) but not changed. While this can simplify operation and logic in some cases, it naturally leads to moving contents from one resource to another, quite often for no reason except to make a small change to the contents or to give it a new label (by putting it into a different resource, variable, or channel). For example, perhaps the dish went through a whole list of activities – e.g. was first clean, then had food on it, then became empty (but dirty), then was washed to become wet, and then our "dry" activity accessed it. In classic dataflow (and functional) approaches, the dish would move from one resource (variable/channel) to an-

25

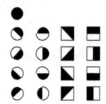

Figure 2.3: Some common icons used to represent control states.

other with each step, in order to keep track of which state it is currently in, and which activities should be able to access it next. In our case, as long as it is considered an individual dish throughout, we would like it to remain as one resource throughout.

So, we take a very different (and more general) approach here than traditional dataflow, instead treating control over which activity will/should access a resource next as completely independent of the resource's content. That is, in addition its content state, every resource will have a completely separate **control state**. Like content state, control state can change during the life of the resource, but unlike the content state, which an activity can observe and/or replace so that another activity can observe it later, the control state is not directly observable or usable by an activity: It's just used to control which activities (if any) can access the content state of the resource at any given time. And just as a resource's content domain represents all of the possible content states that the resource might adopt, the resource's **control domain** represents all of the possible control states which it can adopt. You can think of control state as a traffic signal for the activities which might access the resource, but unlike a traffic light, the number of "colors" (elements of the control domain) can be chosen uniquely for each resource, and the "traffic" (activities) allowed to progress (and access the resource) on any given control state can also be customized for each resource. Generally, one can think of control states like phases, each control state representing an adjective describing some externally-important property of the resource when it has that control state. So in our example, the phases that the dish might be in (dry, dirty, etc.) could be considered the dish's control domain, because these are adjectives that affect what we may want to do with the dish next.

Unlike content domains, which generally are not represented graphically in a strategy, a control domain (the set of possible control states for a resource) is generally small enough, simple enough, and important enough to the high-level understanding of a strategy's behavior that it *is* represented graphically. That is, for each resource, the planner decides the control domain it should have, in terms of names (meanings or adjectives) for each of the desired control states, and then assigns a unique icon and/or color to each control state. Common icons (which will be used in this text) are shown in Figure 2.3. It is sometimes helpful to include a legend of the control domain – the icons and/or colors being used for each name – at the left end of each resource's rectangle, as in Figure 2.4. The only restriction on the icons and/or colors to be used is: The **initial**

26

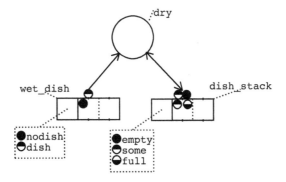

Figure 2.4: Dish drying example, with control states.

control state for each resource (i.e. the one which the resource will have when it first comes into existence) is always represented as a completely filled circle icon and/or the color green.

One might ask why we have suggested some flexibility in whether to use icons or colors to represent control states. It's purely for portability and convenience: The decision of which to use (or both) is often based on the medium being used to represent the strategy. If it is represented on a computer screen, colors are just as easy and inexpensive to represent as icons, and have the added benefit that changes are easy to effect and recognize. For example, as the control state of the resource changes over time, the color of the resource rectangle itself can be colored on the computer screen to reflect its current control state, and these changes can be easily perceived and quickly matched by the human eye – at least, for eyes that are not color blind. In a medium such as this book, icons may be preferable to colors because icons are typically much cheaper to represent in ink than colors, and since the diagrams in a printed medium are not dynamic, the ability to perform rapid recognition is not as important here. To show the current control state of a resource in a print medium, the icon representing that current control state is often highlighted (or shown alone) within the control domain legend at the left end of the resource rectangle. Both icons and colors (i.e. colored icons) are useful for cases where diagrams may be moving between printed and screen media, and/or when screen diagrams might be processed by users with color blindness.

2.2.2   Using and Manipulating Control State

To indicate the control states under which a particular activity is allowed to access a particular resource, the role binding line connecting the activity's context to the resource is shown as being attached to that resource with one or more **access dots** (i.e. between the line and the rectangle) consisting of the icons representing those control states, as in Figure 2.4. These dots are considered as part of the role binding. The associated activity can only access (i.e. observe, replace, or update, according to the arrowheads) the content of that resource

27

at any particular time if the resource then has a control state represented by one of the access dots. You can think of an access dot (or collection thereof) as a rudimentary switch which enables the transfer of contents to or from the resource, through the role binding, from or to the activity in the context, only when the resource has the same same control state as one of the access dots.

Once an activity is finished accessing a resource (perhaps just for the time being), it will assign that resource a new control state. The control states which that particular activity might assign to that resource are shown as another set of **new control state dots** inside of the resource rectangle, near the access dot(s) for the same role binding. To help keep track of which role binding these new control state dots are associated with, the resource rectangle is typically sectioned off into zones with vertical lines, so each zone will then have at most one role binding, a set of access dots, and a set of new control state dots. The left-most zone is just used to contain the control domain legend.

Figure2.4 shows the dish-drying example after incorporating control states. The control state of the `wet_dish` resource signifies whether a wet dish actually exists to be dried, with the initial control state (solid or green dot) representing the absence of a plate, and a different control state (a top-filled dot) representing its presence. (In a sense, the `wet_dish` resource represents the spot where the plate sits rather than the plate itself.) Likewise, the stack of dishes uses the initial control state (green or filled dot) to mean the stack is `empty`, a top-filled dot to mean that the stack is neither `empty` nor `full`, and a bottom-filled dot to mean that the stack is so `full` that no other dishes will fit. In this case, the `dry` activity can access a wet dish only when there is a dish there, and always changes that control state back to having no dish there. The activity can only put a dish into the `dish stack` when it is not full (either empty or partially full), and when it is done adding the new dish, leaves the stack as either partially full or completely full. (The example is intended to be part of a larger strategy: Otherwise, `wet_dish` has no way of getting from its initial `nodish` control state to `dish` control state, so dry cannot access a `wet_dish`.)

2.2.3 Mutually Exclusive Access to Resources

The access dots describe the control state which a resource must have before a particular activity can access it. The new control state dots represent the new control states which the activity might leave the resource with when that access is finished. But what control state does the resource have *while* being accessed by the activity? The answer to this question is especially important when two (or more) different contexts are bound to the same resource (via role bindings) with one or more access dots of one matching one or more of the other. That means that when that resource has certain control states (i.e. those shared among both sets of access dots), the activities in either context can access that resource. While this "either-or" approach may not be a problem, if both activities were to begin accessing the resource at the same time, or if one was to begin accessing it first, but the second was to access it before the first assigned it a new control state, then multiple activities could conceivable overlap in their access to the same resource at the same time.

There are some cases where that would not be a problem, such as where both activities were just going to observe the resource and not change it in any way. However, there are also plenty of other instances where it *could* cause problems, such as where one or both activities will change something about the resource, be it the control state or the data state, since the other might not be expecting the resource to be in a state of flux.

To prevent these undesired cases, we'll start by oversimplifying, by throwing the baby out with the bathwater. For now, we'll say that multiple activities cannot access a resource at the same time under any circumstances. We'll ensure this by forbidding multiple activities from initiating access to the resource at exactly the same time, and by removing the control state from the resource the instant that any activity begins to access it. (This may sound much like the description of shared memory locks/tokens in Section 1.7.1... and in fact, it is similar.) That answers the question of what control state the resource will have while it is being accessed by an activity: No control state at all. And since it has no control state at all, that control state cannot possibly match one of the access dots on any (other) role binding, and therefore the resource remains off limits until the activity that is accessing the resource (i.e. the one that stole the control state) assigns a new control state to it. Later on, we'll explore a tricky way to effectively allow multiple activities to access a resource at the same time under restricted circumstances, even while leaving this rule intact.

2.2.4 Waffles Example

For a more complete example of how the control states of several resources might interact with several activities, see the strategy for making, serving, and consuming waffles in Figure 2.5. The mix activity takes some flour, milk, and eggs, and if the batterbowl is empty (as indicated by the access dot), puts batter in the bowl and transitions its control state to nonempty (as indicated by the new control state dot). If the waffler is cold, the preheat activity heats it. The spoon activity takes some batter and puts it into a hot empty waffler, changing it to hot and full. The serve activity takes the waffle from the waffler (if the waffler is hot and full) and if the table has been set, moves the waffle to the table so that the table has food (whether it did before or not). The serve activity also adjusts the number of waffle requests, and sets the control state to either none (if it just satisfied the last request) or some (if it didn't). If the table has not been set, the set activity sets it. The ask activity senses the hunger from either eater (designated by hunger1 and hunger2) and relays it to the spoon and serve activities via the requests resource, while putting the hunger into a waiting state. Likewise, the eat activity decreases the hunger of the eater, and determines whether it is now happy or still hungry.

There are three new constructs in this strategy diagram. The first is the role binding (line) connecting the spoon activity to the requests resource. It has no arrowheads. We say that such a role binding has **nodata** permissions, meaning that it will neither observe nor replace the contents of the resource. Such a role binding is used to sense, and perhaps to alter, the control state of the resource,

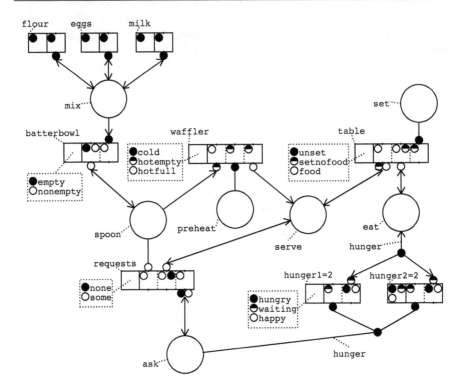

Figure 2.5: A strategy for making and eating waffles.

regardless of its content state. In this particular case, it's purpose is to sense whether there are requests for waffles before spooning (more) batter into the waffler. (This is also true for the **hunger** role binding on the **ask** activity.)

The second new construct is the so-called **junction dot** as shown both above and below the two hunger resources. (Unlike the other dots used so far, the color or shading of these dots is immaterial.) A junction dot effectively allows a single activity (such as the **eat** or **ask** activities here) to be bound to multiple resources (in this case, the two hunger resources) in an "or"-style relationship, so that the activity can access one or the other depending on which has a control state matching the associated access dot. In actuality, it is shorthand for replicating the activity to be bound in every combination specified by the dots, as in Figure 2.6. The overall effect, in many cases, is that the activity (**eat** and **ask** in this case) will deal with these two resources as though they were just one, and the one it accesses at any one time will be determined by which is ready to be accessed (according to its control state). If they are both ready to be accessed, the one to access will be unspecified – it could be either one, or in some cases, both individually. The precise effect will become clearer as we delve further into the behavior of activities (like **eat** and **ask**), in the next chapter.

The third new construct is the label (**hunger**) on one of the role bindings

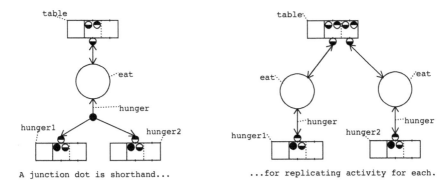

Figure 2.6: Junction dot shorthand.

for the `ask` activity and on one for the `eat` activity, and these will be explained more fully in the next section. In this particular case they are related to the junction dots: The `ask` and `eat` activities must have some way to refer to the two hunger resources collectively, and this is it.

Note that the strategy shows the conditions (in terms of control states) under which each activity can access each resource, and shows the conditions (control states) in which each activity might leave each resource after accessing it, and the type of access each activity will make to the resource contents (through the permissions) when/if access does occur. This diagram does *not* (necessarily) show the conditions under which each activity will commence or the circumstances under which it will try to access each resource. For example, it does not show whether the `mix` activity will start fetching the `flour`, `eggs`, and/or `milk` even before the `batterbowl` is `empty` and ready to accept the new batter. It doesn't show the conditions under which the `spoon` activity might try to access the `requests`, so it doesn't show when a lack of such `requests` (as represented by its control state) will interfere with that activity's progress. Some of these details and others can be filled in by the words describing the intent of each activity in the preceding paragraphs. This combination of graphical representation and words is very flexible and can be applied to describing a large number of complex activities, but there are times when more formality is required to avoid the potential misunderstandings or omissions which may result from using natural language. Much of the remainder of this text will focus on precisely that – i.e. to precisely describe activities in more formal terms, regardless of how complex or simple they may be, and to provide cognitive tools to help determine how those activities will behave in conjunction with other activities. Understanding the resources themselves and rules of access to them is only the first step.

2.3 Delineating Activities from Their Contexts

Just as the meaning of a verb is fairly independent of the specific objects to which it applies, we would like activities to be able to apply to more than a

31

specific set of resources. For example, even if we might consider the activity (verb) "throw" only in terms of something that a human with certain skills does to a ball of a certain weight and size, we would at least like it to generalize to different humans with those skills and different balls of that weight or size. How should an activity refer to its resources so that the activity will work in different contexts, bound to different resources?

2.3.1 Roles and Transitions

We have already described an activity as taking place within a context (represented by a circle), which is bound (with lines called role bindings) to the resources (rectangles) which that activity may access. By adding a name to giving each role binding, the inner workings of the activity can refer to those names instead of the resource names. We will call these names **roles**, as in, signifying the role that the associated resource plays within the activity – and this is why role bindings are named as they are, because they bind (associate) roles to resources. In that way, the same activity can function in a number of different contexts, without knowing the names of the resources, just by naming the role bindings of each to conform to those expected by the activity. Indeed, each role binding is considered to have a label, but perhaps not an explicit one: If it is not explicitly labeled, it borrows its name from the resource to which it is bound (so that resource must have a name). That explains why most role bindings in the waffle example were not labeled. When using a junction dot (as in the waffle example for the hunger resources), the role must always be labeled, since it is not generally possible to adopt names from multiple resources to a single role binding.

The situation is similar for control states. Since we now expect an activity (in a context) to be oblivious to the resource to which each of its roles is bound, it would naturally also be oblivious to the control domains of those resources, and oblivious to what other contexts might be bound to other control states of those resources, so the activity generally can't know which control state to assign to the resource in different situations (in the same context) or in different contexts to have the proper effects on other activities. So instead of having an activity deal explicitly with control states, when an activity finishes with a role, it will simply issue a name to that role, called a **transition**, specifying the general condition or circumstance in which it is leaving the role (or more specifically, the resource bound to that role). The set of all of the possible transitions (names) which an activity may issue to any specific role is called the **transition domain** for that role. Then, just as role bindings associate each role with a resource, **transition bindings** will associate each transition for a role with a control state for its corresponding resource. This association is expressed by labeling the new control state dots with the corresponding transition. That way, when the activity issues a transition to a role, the new control state for the corresponding resource is determined by just picking the new control state dot labeled for that transition. Just as it may or may not be useful to explicitly show control domain names in a graphical representation, it may or may not be useful to show transition bindings. Figure 2.7 shows an example each way,

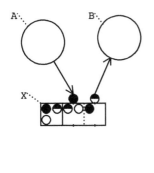
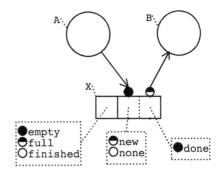

(a) Control domain and
transition names not shown

(b) Legends for control domain and
transition bindings shown

Figure 2.7: Transition bindings within resource.

and the waffle example showed that plenty can be gleaned without explicitly showing the transition bindings. If multiple transitions from the same activity are to result in the same control state, it may be represented as either a single new state dot with the multiple transition names, or as a separate, identical new state dot for each transition name associated with that control state.

Note that there's no need to provide any sort of naming or binding related to access dots as we have done with roles/resources and transitions/new control state dots. An activity has no direct visibility or control over its access dots: They are there for the benefit of the Director, to tell it when an activity can access a particular resource.

2.3.2 Usages vs. Permissions

Upon delineating an activity from the context it is within, the relationship of an activity to its context is rather analogous to a hand and glove, with the context being the glove, the role bindings being the glove's fingers, and the activity being the hand to fit into that glove, with the activity's roles being the hand's fingers. The glove's fingers (i.e. role bindings) serve to guide the hand's fingers (roles) to connect to the appropriate resources.

Earlier, we described the arrowheads on role bindings as permissions, describing what an activity in the context might do with the content state of the associated resource. Now that we can discuss an activity separate from the context it was in, we will leave the permissions with the role bindings, and say that each role of the activity has a **usage** which has similar names and properties. More specifically, a usage (either observe, replace, update, or nodata) describes what that activity may do to the content state of the resource to which that role is bound. A permission (on a role binding) will then come to describe the sort of usages which the role (within that role binding) may/must have. This will be described more fully shortly under conformance.

33

2.3.3 Plan Interface

We have now seen that activities are carried out within contexts (circles). Another name for a context is an **activity binding**, because it shows how the activity within the context relates to the resources around it via a set of role bindings. Summarizing from previous sections, each role binding of the context (i.e. activity binding) specifies:

- *a unique name*, either explicitly in the form of a label or implicitly adopted from the resource to which it is bound, denoting which of the activity's roles it is binding;

- *a resource*, denoted by the resource rectangle to which it is connected (with access dots), denoting the resource associated with that role;

- *access dot(s)*, denoting the control state(s) which the resource must possess for it to be accessible by the activity via that that role;

- *a permission*, represented by arrowheads, of observe (context end), replace (resource end), update (both ends), or nodata (neither end); and

- *a transition binding*, represented by a set of new control state dots and a label for each, denoting which new control state each of the activity's role's transitions represents.

The plan to activate within a context is denoted by labeling the context with the name of that plan. This implies that it must be possible to give names to plans, which will be covered in Chapter 7. It also implies that a plan must not only specify what happens within the resulting activity, but also how that activity will interact with the resources bound to the context (via role bindings), such as when the activity will (attempt to) observe the content of those resources, when it will (attempt to) replace the content of those resources, what the new content will be, and what control state transition to make to each of those resources and under what circumstances. These will be covered throughout the remainder of this book, but for now, we will address the question of when a particular plan can be (i.e. is allowed to be) activated within some particular context.

A plan is generally considered in two parts: Its **implementation** and its **interface** (or **signature**). The implementation is the (typically operational) part which we normally consider as the plan itself, the part that tells what an activity resulting from the plan will (or may) do when the plan is activated, and when (or under what circumstances) it will do them. This is stated as precisely as is desired by the planner for the matter at hand. The interface is just a declaration or list of the roles in the plan and their properties. Although the interface can sometimes be automatically derived from the implementation, it is often useful for the planner to specify the interface explicitly, as a double-check to ensure that the implementation is causing the sorts of external interactions that the planner intended.

Regardless of how the interface is created, it can be fairly rapidly compared with a context to determine whether that context is suitable for activating the

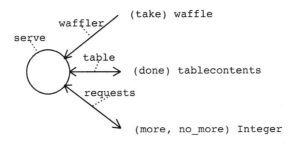

Figure 2.8: Potential interface for the `serve` plan, graphically.

plan. Extending the "hand in glove" analogy mentioned earlier, the implementation can be considered as the inner workings of the hand (plan), while the interface is like the shape and size (and number!) of the hand's fingers, which determine whether the hand will fit into a particular glove (context).

More specifically, the interface for a plan consists of (at least) a set of *roles*, each with (at least):

- A *name* (unique among the roles in the plan);

- A *transition domain*, listing the transitions which the activities resulting from the plan may issue to the role;

- *Usages*, describing how the activity will use the contents of the resource which is bound to the role (Observe, Replace, Update, or None);

- A *content domain* for the role, describing the sort of content which the activity expects to access (observe, replace, or update) on the resource bound to the role.

(More possible traits for each role will be identified later.) An interface is often depicted visually as in Figure 2.8, as sort of a disembodied context circle (palm of the hand), with attached labeled lines for the roles (fingers), each resembling a role binding except not bound to any resources. The arrowheads, which would represent permissions on a role binding, represent usages on the role lines. And the role lines are labeled explicitly with the transition domain (usually in parens at the end) and the content domain.

2.3.4 Plan/Context Conformance

A plan may be activated within a context, and is said to **conform** to that context (i.e. the hand fits in the glove), if and only if the role bindings of the context are named exactly (one-for-one) for the roles of the plan's interface (to be relaxed/softened later), and for each role in the plan's interface:

- The names in the transition domain of the role match exactly (one-for-one) the transition bindings on the role binding.

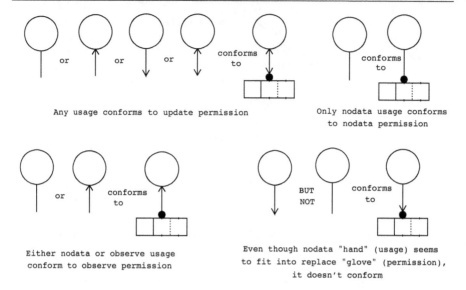

Figure 2.9: Conformance of role usage to role binding permissions.

- The usages of the role conform to the permissions on the role binding, as represented in Figure 2.9. In almost every case, this just means that the role ("hand finger") will fit into the role binding ("glove finger") only if there's room in the role binding for all/any of the arrowheads on the role. The one exception (in the lower right of Figure 2.9) is: If the role binding (glove finger) has a *replace* permission (arrowhead on the extreme end) but no *observe* permission (arrowhead on the context end), then that role binding will not accommodate a role with *nodata* usage (no arrowheads), even though there's "room in the glove". The reason for this exception is explained below.

- The content domain for the role conforms to the content domain of the resource to which it is bound, meaning that neither the activity nor the resource will be asked to handle (or store) content that it is not expecting. Specifically, as represented in Figure 2.10, if the role has *replace* usage, the role's content domain must be a subset of (perhaps equal to) that of the resource filling that role, and if the role has *observe* usage, the content domain of the resource filling that role must be a subset (perhaps equal to) the role's. Since *update* usage is effectively both *observe* and *replace*, an *update* role's content domain must be equal to the content domain of the resource filling that role – i.e. both the role's content domain and the resource's content domain must be subsets of one another.

Conformance between permissions and usages (including the exception to the "arrowhead room" rule described above) is defined to allow the planner to reason in terms of the very obvious permission arrowheads on role bindings in the diagram only, rather than (say) of the plan/activity within the context, so

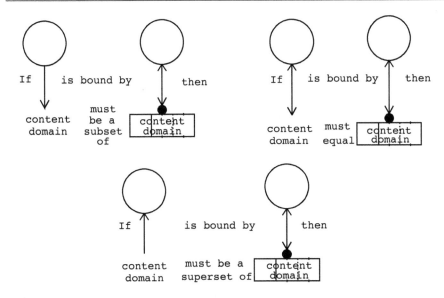

Figure 2.10: Conformance of role content domain to role binding (resource) content domain.

the conformance rules allow all (and only) those plans which preserve that reasoning, and won't ever cause unexpected things to happen when relying on that reasoning.

For readers interested in precisely why these rules are used to assure this: For example, if the permission on a role binding is *observe*, then an activity will not produce surprising results if the associated role has *nodata* usage, since that would be just as though the activity observed the resource but did nothing with what it observed. Likewise, if the permission is *update*, then an activity which only *observes* or does nothing (*none*) has the same outward behavior as one which *observes* the content and *replaces* it with the same content it just observed. The exception to the arrowhead room rule (disallowing *nodata* usage for a *replace* permission) is present because it violates this principle: *Replace* permission means that the activity is expected to replace the contents of the resource with something, and the lack of *observe* permission means that the new contents must be unrelated to what was there originally. An activity with *none* usage on its role, which leaves the resource contents alone, would therefore produce surprising results for such a role binding, because the results would be related (in fact, exactly the same as) the original content.

The result of trying to activate a plan in a context to which it does not conform can vary, but in the cases we've described so far, there's no sense in even trying: Since the context is statically labeled with the plan to be activated there, tools (or careful inspection) can and will warn the planner in advance if the plan does not conform to the context.

One of the first requirements given for conformance (above) was that the role bindings of the context be named exactly (one-for-one) for the roles of the plan's interface. This requirement will be loosened in two ways in subsequent sections and chapters, through constructs called anonymous role bindings and Binding Contraint Expressions, but the goal is always for the basic requirement to be followed rigidly by default, and only overridden with the planner's full knowledge and intent.

2.4 Strategies Are Plans

To this point, we have referred to a diagram containing resources and contexts as a strategy, and the things to be activated within the contexts as plans. But, in case it wasn't already obvious, a strategy is also a plan, in that it describes an activity, comprising many other activities, each from a plan, which may itself ultimately be a strategy.

This begs several questions. Does that mean that we can activate a strategy within a context of another strategy? If so, a strategy needs an interface, so how do we declare that, and how does the implementation of the strategy interact with the roles in its own interface? Is a strategy the only kind of plan? (Presumably not, or there'd never be an end to the nesting, with each context in a strategy containing another strategy with more contexts.)

Subsequent chapters will indeed address these very questions. Specifically, Chapter 3 will describe simpler kinds of plans, called tactics, and Chapter 6 will describe how to add an interface to a strategy, and ways to get activities within the strategy to interact via the roles (bound to resources in another strategy). For now, we have had our hands full just understanding the components of a strategy and how they interrelate.

2.5 Representing Strategies as Text: SPLAT

There are many good reasons for representing strategies graphically as we have been doing here so far (and will continue to do, primarily, throughout this book), and some of those reasons will be elucidated in Chapter 8, on computation. However, much present-day technology infrastructure (including computer software for processessing and editing files) has been optimized for dealing with textual forms. For this reason, we have developed a textual form for representing strategies, called **SPLAT** (for Scalable Planning Language As Text). We will primarily give just a flavor of it here.

The general form of a strategy in SPLAT is

```
plan interface strategy implementation
```

where italicized terms (*interface* and *implementation* here) represent so-called "non-terminals", which will be elucidated upon later, and non-italicized terms (like plan and strategy here) are literal terms which should appear in the SPLAT text just as they are shown. For now, since we haven't discussed the interface for a strategy, we'll leave *interface* blank. The *implementation* part in general is:

```
{ resources resource-list contexts context-list }
```

i.e. a declaration of all of the resources followed by all of the contexts (including role bindings). Each resource declaration consists of the name (if any) of the resource, the control domain (as a list of the control states, in parens, with the first being the initial control state), followed by the content domain, and optionally, an equal sign and initial content state. All this is terminated with a semicolon. If there is no control domain listed, it is assumed to be "init". So, the waffles example, to that point, might be:

```
plan strategy {
 resources
    flour () flour;
    eggs () eggs;
    milk () milk;
    batterbowl (empty nonempty) batter;
    waffler (cold hotempty hotfull) waffle;
    table (unset setnofood food) tablestuff;
    requests (none some) int;
    hunger1 (hungry waiting happy) int = 2;
    hunger2 (hungry waiting happy) int = 2;
```

Each context declaration then starts with the label (if any) followed by the role bindings in braces. Each role binding consists of the label on the role binding (if any), a symbol indicating its permissions (<- for observe, -> for replace, <-> for modify, and — for nodata), then the access dots (separated by "|" if more than one) and name of the resource filling the role, followed by the transition bindings of the form:

$$(transition > control\text{-}state, \ transition > control\text{-}state, ... \ )$$

If there's a junction dot, the access dot, resource name, and transition bindings for each branch are represented within braces. So, the remainder of the waffles example could be represented as:

```
activities
    mix { <-> flour ()
          <-> eggs ()
          <-> milk ()
          --> empty batterbowl (done > nonempty)}
    spoon {
        <-> nonempty batterbowl
                      (nomore > empty, more > nonempty)
        --> hotempty waffler(done > hotfull)
        --- some requests (done > some)}
    preheat { --- cold waffler (done > hotempty)}
    serve {
        <-- hotfull waffler (done > hotempty)
        <-> setnofood|food table (done > food)
```

```
                <-> some requests (zero > none, nonzero > some)}
        set { --- unset table (done > setnofood)}
        eat {
            <-> food table (more > food, nomore > setnofood)
            hunger <-> {
                waiting hunger1 (more > hungry, nomore > happy)
                waiting hunger2 (more > hungry, nomore > happy)}
            }
        ask {
            <-> some|none requests (done > some)
            hunger --- {
                hungry hunger1 (done > waiting)
                hungry hunger2 (done > waiting)}
            }
    }
```

The translation from a graphical to textual form isn't always smooth. For example, in the graphical form, not every resource (and as we will find out later, not even every context) must be assigned a name, and especially not a unique name, but unique names are required in SPLAT so that the proper associations can be made between contexts and resources.[1] This is usually addressed by appending non-unique names with a qualifier "#1", "#2", etc., to make them unique, or assigning nameless constructs full names "#1", "#2", etc. The convention is not to display these suffixes when converting to a graphical form.

And, speaking of converting to graphical form: Even tools which support a graphical form for strategies may store them in SPLAT when they are not on display, to allow intervention and/or editing using other text-based tools. Such tools may find it convenient to store information about the appearance of various constructs (such as the color or patterns of dots used for control states, or the position of resources or contexts on the screen) within the SPLAT file, but these specifications are not part of the SPLAT language itself. These are often stored as comments, and in a form which is not easily decipherable by humans, as so-called "structured comments". The important point is that SPLAT can be understood without the need to decipher this second-level information.

2.6 Summary

So far, we have said precious little about the overall behavior of plans in general, we have just presented one way of constructing a plan, called a strategy, from other plans, and of establishing the kinds of interactions those other plans can have with resources.

A strategy (which is one form of plan) consists of contexts, represented by circles, intended to embody activities ("verbs"), and resources, represented by rectangles, intended to hold content ("nouns"). Each context is labeled with

---

[1] In SPLAT, these associations are made by name matching, which is far less intuitive and obvious than the physical connections, using arcs, in graphical ScalPL.

the name of the plan which may be activated within that context to result in an activity, and is bound (connected) to resources by role bindings, each represented by a line/arc between the context circle and a resource rectangle. Each role binding is labeled for the name of a role in the plan/activity associated with the context, thereby designating the role in the activity being filled by the associated resource.

Each resource possesses two dynamic attributes: Its content state (or just content) and its control state. The resource's content domain represents all the possible content states which it might attain (usually in the form of a set, or data type), and its control domain represents all of the control states which it might attain. If a resource's content domain is represented at all in ScalPL, it is as a description of the domain (e.g. a set, or name or expression representing a set) described within parentheses immediately following the resource name (if any). While the form and purpose of content state (and therefore content domains) can vary from one resource and/or plan and/or discipline to another, control states are always exclusively for controlling which activities can gain access to a resource at any one time. Control states are represented by colors and/or shaded dots, and for any one resource, the control domain (set of unique control states) is often represented by dots within the left end of the resource's representing rectangle, each control state signifying a potential phase or characteristic which the resource (i.e. it's contents) might be in at any one time.

The control state of a resource affects, and is affected by, access to that resource by activities (within contexts). Every role binding from a context is connected to a resource with one or more access dots, each signifying a control state. The resource must have one of these control states before the activity in the associated context can gain access to the resource. When the activity does gain access to the resource, the resource is considered to effectively completely and instantaneously lose its control state, thereby preventing access to that resource by any other activity. Within the resource rectangle, near the role binding, there are also zero or more other labeled dots representing new control states and transition bindings. When an activity has finished accessing a resource, it issues a transition, represented by a name, to the assocated role, and the dot with that same name within the transition binding represents the new control state to be assigned to the resource, thereby making the resource again accessible by any activities (including, perhaps, the same activity) having access dots with that new control state.

Each role binding has a permission, represented by arrowheads on neither, either, or both ends of the role binding line, representing how the activity in the associated context will interact with the content state of the associated resource. Specifically these permissions represent whether the activity will effectively observe (arrowhead at the context end), replace (arrowhead at the resource end), or both (arrrowheads at both ends) the (entire) contents of the resource. Observe and replace together are also called update permission, since updating (replacing just part of) the contents can be considered the same as observing the entire contents and then replacing the entire contents, some with what was just observed. Replace permission alone is not sufficient if the activity will/may replace only some of the resource contents, or if it will replace

41

even the entire contents only sometimes: For these cases, replace permission is required.

The activity in each context results when the Director activates a plan. Each such plan consists of an implementation, which describes what it will/may do when activated, and its interface, which describes how the implementation will interact with the resources bound to the context in which it resides. The interface (or signature) of a plan consists of a set of roles, each with a name, a content domain, a usage, and a transition domain. The usages are very similar to the permissions associated with a role binding, and have identical names and meanings (observe, replace, update, and none). The transition domain is a set of names representing all of the transitions which might be issued to that role (by the implementation).

The interface for a plan is often represented graphically, as a circle (similar to a context) with lines emanating from it, one for each role – similar to role bindings, but not attached to resources. Each line is labeled with the role name and content domain, has arrowheads representing the usage, just as those on role bindings, and a set of names at the terminus representing the transition domain. This representation lends itself to a "hand in glove" metaphor for determining whether a particular plan conforms (i.e. would fit into) a particular context. That is, the roles on the activity must agree with the role bindings on the context in name, and for each, the usages on the role must be a subset of the permissions of the role binding ("room" for the role's arrowheads in the role binding). In one case, though, room in the glove is not a sufficient rule: A role with none usage does not conform to a binding with replace (only) permission, even though there is room. The transition domain of each role must correspond exactly to the labels of the transition binding on the role binding. If the role has *observe* usage, the content domain of the resource filling that role must be a subset (perhaps equal to) the role's, and if the role has *replace* usage, the role's content domain must be a subset of (perhaps equal to) that of the resource filling that role.

A particular role from a particular context can be effectively bound to multiple resources (one at a time) by utilizing a junction dot. The junction dot effectively splits the role binding into several to allow each branch to bind separately to a different resource. Any of those branches which becomes ready (by virtue of the resource's control state matching one of the associated access dots) may be accessed by the activity, at which time the control state is stolen only from that resource, and access continues only to that one until a transition is performed. In actuality, the junction dot is a shorthand for replicating the context, and providing each with one unique combination of the possible bindings. The precise behavior will depend on the plan in the context, to become clearer in subsequent chapters.

Chapter 3

Fundamental Activities: Actons

We now have a visual language for showing interactions between activities, but it is still less than satisfactory at describing the behavior of any one of those activities, or at providing much insight about how to construct any specific behavior. At best, it's similar to the situation of an ancient chemist, who may have a relatively good understanding of individual elements and ways to compose them, but who is unable to do more than guess about how those compositions will behave.

Is it possible to decompose activities into ever simpler activities and resources until we get down to activities that we can reason about in a more rigorous manner and which can be used to compose any other activity in pedictable ways? Such activities would serve as our fundamental particles of computation.

This chapter will devise guidelines for such "easy to deal with" activities, such "fundamental particles of computation". It is tempting to call these desired activities "atoms of computation", much as the fundamental particles of matter, but the term "atomic" has taken on its own meanings in the computing world. We will play on the words "atom" and "action" to call our simple activities **actons**. And we'll use the term **tactic** to refer to the plan for an acton.

The chapter will have three basic parts. In the first, we'll just survey the factors which can affect the interaction of activities, to provide a solid basis upon which to make decisions regarding our actons and tactics. Following that, we'll establish exactly what properties our actons and tactics will possess, and why, based on that initial survey. Then we'll consider some of the implications, and how actons might manifest themselves in the real world.

3.1 Activity Properties

As a fundamental activity, our primary goal is for an acton to be **independent**. That is, we want to make it so that everything important we can say about the behavior of an acton – i.e. a specification of the factors that make it unique among other actons – is true regardless of the presence or behavior of other activities in the environment. Among other things, this implies that, even if many actons occur concurrently, we should be able to explain the result in terms of the workings of each acton independently, and therefore as though only one acton was working at a time in isolation, one after the other. This property, that the result of a set of concurrent activities can always be regarded (i.e. produces the same results) as the same activities in some serial (sequential) schedule, is called **serializability**.

For an acton to be intentional (the result of a plan), we also need it to be **deterministic** – i.e. for the plan to be complete and unambiguous about its intended results, given the environment in which it operates. If we did not make such a restriction, and allowed an acton specification to allow any one of a number of outcomes given a fixed starting environment, then it would be very difficult to test since, being fundamental, we could ascertain no additional structure or information about how to get it to give one outcome over the others. Though it will be desirable at some level to allow non-determinism and/or to hide causality, it isn't useful in the most basic activity "particles". (Unlike Einstein, we have the power to dictate that God will not play dice there.)

Finally, we need to be able to give the circumstances under which an acton will take place. This includes both the conditions under which the acton may or may not commence, known generally as **safety**, but also some assurance that it will commence when it should and/or do something after it commences, known generally as **liveness**. Without both safety and liveness, even the most careful specification of an activity will be of limited utility, since activities could take place haphazardly or not at all.

These goals (especially determinism) require some clarification as to which aspects of an acton's behavior we consider "important" (e.g. must be reproducable/predictable). For example, in any real-world environment (or "platform", defined later), there is a limit to the number of actons (or activities of any kind) which can be carried out concurrently before additional activities start to affect the time that it takes others to complete (or perhaps to even commence). That means that it is not possible, in general, to make activities both independent and deterministic if we consider completion time (e.g. according to some clock) to be part of the behavior, so we will not consider measured time as behavior when defining determinism. (Others have, leading to concepts such as unbounded non-determinism, which we do not find productive for our analysis here.) There are other traits that will arise which we will also determine to be unimportant, and therefore not defined as "behavior" in these rules.

There is another important requirement for actons: That, by their combination, we be able to build any other desired activity from them (including, for example, activities that are non-deterministic or not independent). That is, actons must form a **basis** for all other activities. This chapter will focus on developing and describing actons so that they meet the other properties here, then subsequent chapters will further explore the behavior of their combination (i.e. within strategies like those described in the previous chapter) to demonstrate that they do indeed meet this requirement

The remainder of this section will focus, in turn, on those three main topics: Serializability (of activities), safety and liveness (ensuring that plans become activities at the appropriate times), and determinism (matching plans with ac-

Figure 3.1: Activities can be considered as pebbles in a bucket.

tivities), followed by a formulation for actons. To help illustrate (or at least help visualize in a mind's eye) the way that activities may interact, we'll consider them as though they are pebbles in a bucket, as in Figure 3.1. In this analogy, each pebble represents an activity, the vertical dimension of the bucket (from bottom to top) represents time, and the horizontal dimension represents (roughly) resources or space, so the height of any particular activity pebble represents the time period during which the activity existed, and the horizontal cross-section at any one point represents the resources it was using (or other space it was occupying) at that time. So, for example, a tall thin pebble would represent an activity which used a few resources for a long time, while a short wide pebble would represent one which used more resources but not very long. A pebble with an hourglass figure would represent one which accessed some resources, then stopped accessing some of them, then started accessing more again before ending. Notice that, in this analogy, we've simplified three-dimensional space as two horizontal dimensions in the bucket, and even then, the shape of each such pebble could get very complex and non-pebble-like if accesses to resources were modeled fairly accurately, with perhaps thin filaments leading to big globs (as the activity moved around or accessed remote resources), and lots of very rough edges (as the activity performed repeated small accesses of a particular resource), but in general, even very vague and simple shape considerations will help to illustrate the issues involved.

To make this analogy valid for our purposes, however, we must give the pebbles a few unnatural properties as we move them around. Since we don't want time translated to space and vice versa, each pebble must maintain its vertical orientation (i.e. the same point is always up) as we move it around, so that the same (vertical) axis always corresponds to time. In fact, we also don't want some resources changed to others, so we also can't allow them to shift around horizontally or spin around, either. In other words, the pebbles will primarily only be allowed to shift along their vertical axes, so we may lift them, or they may drop.

3.1.1 Determinism

Even before considering how the different pebbles in the bucket relate to one another, we can consider some properties of activities that can affect their shape (as pebbles), and how each activity (pebble) can affect others around it, and what affect they can have on it.

Recall that determinism applies to the relationship between a plan and the activity resulting from carrying out that plan. Specifically, if a plan is deterministic, then activating it in a given environment will always produce the same results – i.e. will always result in the same effects on the environment.

Since we have also set serializability as a goal for actons, it means that a plan for an acton must produce the same external behavior whether or not the acton is activated in the presence of other activities, which in turn means that its behavior cannot be affected by other concurrent activities. (Otherwise, it could act differently when serialized than when not.)

In the terminology and methodology of the previous chapter, this means that if an acton was to begin twice in a given context, and was to observe the same content state on the resources it accessed (i.e. the ones to which the context is bound), then the results (also on those resources) will be the same.

As stated earlier, time until completion (or time until the activity produces some other specific behavior) will not be considered behavior in itself in this discussion of non-determinism, so it is allowed to vary even if initial state doesn't vary. In terms of pebbles, that means that even for a particular plan and starting environment, the pebble representing that activity may be stretched or squeezed vertically without violating the rule on deterministic behavior.

Completion

One issue which will be faced repeatedly in the coming sections relates to completion. That is, if the behavior of a deterministic activity is dictated only by its plan and the state of the resources in the environment which it accesses, what if it can't finish carrying out that dictated behavior for any reason? For example, what if it gets partway through and then can't get the resources it needs to finish (because, say, some other activity has jumped in first to take them)? Or something catastrophic happens which terminates it unceremoniously? If this failure to complete depends on something other than the initial environment, then the supposedly deterministic plan has produced a different result than it might have under the same starting conditions elsewhere (i.e. only part of the complete result), and is therefore not acting deterministically.

It is common to use a different term for this sort of determinism: **atomicity**. That is, if an activity is **atomic**, it means that it will either complete, or will at least behave as though it never started. For the reasons mentioned, a serializable deterministic activity must be atomic by definition (because it must behave the same whether other concurrent activities are present or not), but activities can be made to be atomic even if they are not deterministic or serializable.

A common way to ensure activity is atomic is through **commit** and **rollback**. Specifically, an activity is made to have no permanent observable effect on its surrounding environment until it is completely done, at which time it commits, by (all in an instant) making all of its effects observable. In a sense, the atomicity of the entire activity is made dependent upon the atomicity of the commit alone, which takes much less time and is (theoretically and practically) therefore much easier to implement. If the activity is not able to commit (such as when it does not complete for reasons like those mentioned above, and therefore never makes it to commit time), it is rolled back, which means that all trace of the partially-completed, uncommitted activity is removed so that its detritus will not affect the progress of other activities. After a rollback, the activity may often be re-executed, but this will often depend on other factors (including liveness constraints, as discussed later).

As a special case, when a serializable deterministic activity is terminated abnormally for some reason, but it appears that situations have improved to the point where the original activity would now have been able to complete, and all of the original conditions which could affect its behavior are still available, it may be possible to re-execute without rollback. That is, since it is deterministic, it will be guaranteed to have the same results to the same original conditions, so by restarting the plan and feeding it the same initial conditions, it will exhibit the same behavior. By suppressing (or ignoring) any behavior which it got right the first time (and which is therefore duplicated during the re-execution), the remaining, uncompleted portion of the activity can be finished. We will call this **supplemental re-execution**.

Parts of an activity may be atomic without the entire activity being atomic: In fact, it's quite common. For example, it is common to ensure that access to a particular resource by an activity is atomic, by using locks or semaphores. By requiring that any activity wishing to access a resource first obtain a designated lock, and follow the access by releasing the lock, all intervening access will appear (to any other activity) as a single atomic action, no matter how complex. Generally speaking, though, locks are acquired one-by-one, so access to all locks will not occur as one atomic action. The relationship of locks to atomic activities will be further discussed in section 3.1.2.

Side-effect free and Stateless

Non-determinism can (sometimes or always, depending on your philosophy) be interpreted as merely deterministic behavior based on non-obvious inputs. That is, if some hidden resources (or resources with unknown state) are accessed by an activity, then its behavior might not be predictable even in light of its deterministic plan and knowledge of the state of all of the other more obvious resources accessed by the activity. Such hidden resources are sometimes called **side effects**.

Some of the most common sorts of side effects in computer software are due to resources (persistent state) hidden within the plan itself, in such a way that any activity resulting from the same plan will utilize that hidden resource (and the state that it carries). The result is that the outcome of such an activity, even if deterministic in some sense, depends on more than just the obvious external environment when the activity begins, it also depends (in that case) on the hidden internal "environment" affected by the history of plan, such as what other activities resulting from that plan did. In fact, an entire branch of software engineering, called object-oriented programming, is based on this approach, and "information hiding" is cited as a valuable concept of software engineering. So, like many other goals mentioned in this chapter, side effects are not altogether without merit for activities in general. For the purposes of establishing our basic "particles" of computation (actons), however, access to hidden resources must be avoided for the same reasons that any non-determinism must be. Hidden resources, as well as object-oriented techniques, will be added at a higher level of abstraction.

3.1.2   Serializability

Recall from above that serializability is the property that activities behave as though they are each acting in isolation, which also means that the result of a set of those activities could be explained just as well by the activities occurring one at a time, in some (but usually not just any) serial schedule. In terms of our bucket analogy, it can be stated in terms of a puzzle. The goal of this **pebble puzzle** is to take an arbitrary bucket full of pebbles and insert horizontal plates (consider strong panes of glass) into the bucket by lifting pebbles vertically, resulting in only one pebble between each pair of plates, such that each pebble is supported (against gravity) by (at least) the same pebbles as it was in the original bucket (i.e. those vertically below it there). That is, if any part of one pebble was vertically below another in the bucket (representing accessing a shared resource before it in the activity interpretation), it must remain below it with the plates inserted, but the plates will ensure that no two pebbles are alongside one another (concurrent in the activity interpretation). In other words, this corresponds to activities being **serialized**[1], obeying the constraint that if one activity (X) might depend on the results of another activity (Y) in the concurrent world, then the same activities can be considered one at a time as though X occurred after Y in a serial schedule, with the same result. As we will see, for some buckets of pebbles, it will not be possible to serialize them like this, so we would like to know why not, and how to make sure we can.

(A more natural, and in some ways more realistic, goal for the puzzle would be to stack the pebbles up vertically, one over the other, such as in a tube, rather than inserting plates into the bucket – but of course, that would violate the condition that we not shift the pebbles around vertically)

Activity (Pebble) Shape

One question that we can ask about the pebble puzzle is: Can we put conditions on the shape of the pebbles so that the puzzle always has at least one solution?

Clearly, some topmost pebble in the bucket (to the extent that there is one) must end up at the top of the solution, so consider picking up one of those topmost pebbles and sliding the first plate under it, then picking another topmost pebble (from those remaining) and sliding the second plate under it (pushing up and supporting the previous plate and pebble), and so on until

---

[1]This is not to be confused with the same term as it is sometimes used in object-oriented languages, which refers to converting the representation of an object to make it easier to transfer or store it on some other medium.

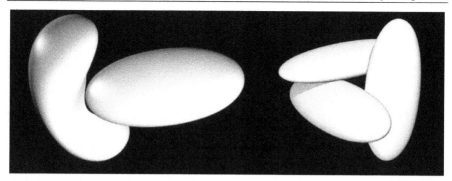

Figure 3.2: Mutual time dependence and circular time dependence.

all of the pebbles have been isolated between plates. Since each pebble picked from the bucket will be topmost when it is picked, any other pebble which was previously supported by it in the bucket must have already been picked and had a plate shoved under it, and so will now be (ultimately) supported by the new pebble. Goal achieved.

The problems with this approach come in when there is no topmost pebble because all of the visible pebbles are wedged in among other pebbles. For example, when a pebble is concave on the side (like an hourglass or c shape), another pebble can impinge on its side such that one cannot be pulled vertically without also pulling the other one, in a so-called **mutual time dependence**. (Note that it is not a problem for the top or bottom of the pebbles to be concave, such as a bowl-shaped pebble.) In fact, interlocking situations can occur even when no pebbles are concave on their sides, such as when three or more flat pebbles are arranged in **circular time dependence**, with each partially above and partially below the others in the spiral, such as in Figure 3.2. In these cases, the puzzle can't be solved, because these collections of interlocking pebbles may mutually support each others' weight: They can't be separated vertically and still support each others' weight.

So, to solve the puzzle (at least using this approach), pebbles must not interlock vertically in these ways. What pebble shapes are guaranteed to not interlock, such that there is always at least one topmost pebble? Spherical pebbles would do, as would cubic, cylindrical, or conic pebbles (or mixes thereof) if they are all oriented horizontally or vertically. In fact, all that's required is for every pebble to have a horizontal cross section, which we'll call a **belt**, such that as one progresses vertically up or down away from the belt, the pebble's horizontal cross section does not increase in any dimension – i.e. it effectively tapers off (or stays vertical) as one progresses upwards and downwards from the belt. Note that it is not sufficient just for the *size* of the horizontal cross section to shrink (or stay the same) while moving away from the belt: Each horizontal cross section must actually be completely coverable (without sliding/shifting) by any other such cross section which is closer to the belt. Some examples of belted shapes are shown in Figure 3.3. Two such pebbles can't interlock vertically, because the belt of one is either above, below, or at the same level as

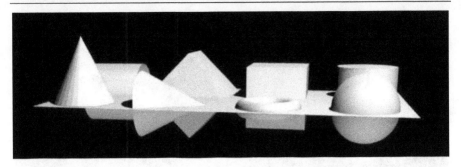

Figure 3.3: Many common shapes are belted in some orientations (belt at plane).

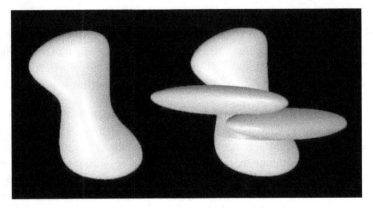

Figure 3.4: Non-belted pebble, alone and with belted circular dependences.

the other, and since they both taper away from their belts (without bending), there's nothing for the other to "grab onto". We will refer to pebbles or activities with a belt as being **belted**, and those with no horizontal cross-section qualifying as a belt as **non-belted**. Belted pebbles can always be serialized in the order of their belts (with pebbles with belts at the same time/level being serialized in either order), but alternate serializations are also often possible.

The introduction of even one non-belted pebble to the bucket can often allow such interlocks. By definition, for a non-belted pebble, progressing from bottom to top, there's a level where the cross section shrinks in at least one horizontal dimension followed by a level where the cross section grows in at least one horizontal dimension, such as in Figure 3.4. If it shrinks and grows in the same dimension, then another pebble (even a horizontally belted one) can fit into the concavity, resulting in interlock. If the non-belted pebble shrinks in a different dimension than it grows in (which could simply describe a wide flat pebble that is then tilted), then a few wide flat pebbles (which may be belted) can still form a spiral such that the lower pebble is supported by the ledge from the (lower) shrink, and upper pebble is beneath the ledge caused by the (upper) grow, again resulting in interlock. In general, the introduction of any non-belted pebbles permits interlocks and releases promises of serializability.

Artificial belts

Just as for pebbles, to guarantee serializability of any arbitrary collection of activities, each must each have an analogous belt – i.e. a point in time before which it may acquire (but not relinquish) resources, and after which it may relinquish resources (but not acquire any) – for the very same reasons that the pebbles must have one. Even when activities are not "naturally" belted, they can be made to be belted by holding onto resources longer than it takes for each individual access, to keep other activities from accessing them during that time, thereby effectively "filling in" the side concavity. This is generally called **locking** the resource. A common approach for creating a belt using locking is for an activity to lock any resource it needs just before the activity accesses it, then to not relinquish (unlock) any resources until the activity is complete, at which time all of the locks are released. In such cases, the top of the activity (after it holds all the locks) always qualifies as a belt, since the number of resources controlled by the activity never decreases (over time) before the belt. Such **top-belted** activities are roughly cone-shaped (small at bottom, and relatively wide and flat at the top). One reason that top-belted activities are common is that the belt also corresponds to commit time in a commit/rollback atomicity scheme (described earlier).

It is also possible to create artificial bottom belts for activities, by acquiring all of the resources that the activity will use as it begins, and then releasing them over time as they are no longer needed. These are inverse cone-shaped (large and flat at bottom, smaller at the top). The main difficulty with **bottom-belted** activities is in knowing which resources will be needed as the activity begins.

In the previous chapter, we described resources as having control states, which had the property that when an activity began to access a resource, the control state disappeared, during which time no other activity could access the resource, and then at some point, the activity could finish (temporarily or permanently) with the resource, at which time a new (possibly identical) control state would be assigned. This effectively locks the resource while the activity is using it, and thus can serve to construct an artificial belt, if used as described above.

The terms "belted", "top-belted", etc., are, as far as this author knows, coined here. The term **two-phase** was originally used to describe belted activities, in that they have a **growing phase** (below the belt) followed by a **shrinking phase** (above it).[2] Since then, the term two-phase has been largely abandoned and now is sometimes confused with another term, **strict two-phase**, which refers to what we are calling top-belted activities with atomicity.

---

[2]Kapali P. Eswaran, Jim Gray, Raymond A. Lorie, Irving L. Traiger: The Notions of Consistency and Predicate Locks in a Database System.

Non-blocking and Lock-Free

Although the way to guarantee that an arbitrary collection of pebbles will be serializable is to make them all belted, there are certainly some collections that can be serialized even if they are not all belted (or, for that matter, even if none of them are belted). For example, if the pebbles are all placed (vertically) into the bucket one at a time, then clearly they can be lifted out to solve the pebble puzzle (i.e. to insert the plates) one at a time in the reverse order, regardless of their shapes. This exact approach doesn't work in the activity world, because the vertical direction in bucket represents time, so placing them vertically downward into the bucket would be tantamount to transporting them backwards in time. That is, activities "grow" in the bucket as time progresses, from earlier (bottom) to later (top), with concurrent ones growing together.

However, even though pebbles can't be dropped down into the bucket, they can effectively be removed or "dissolved" (rolled back) from the bucket if they are found to obstruct serializability in some way, and "regrown" (re-executed) at a later time, thereby effectively moving them up in the bucket until they can "grow" to completion (to commit) in a spot where it is found that they are serializable. To determine if an activity like this is not serializable, without using locks, the general approach is for any higher-level overhang (access to a resource) to "look down" and see if there is any other pebble (activity) obstructing the line-of-sight, and if so, to rollback. (This is usually enforced by marking the resource with the activity name at each access, and noting whether the activity name on the resource has changed since last time.) Note that this is approach is not necessarily sufficient for all activity shapes: For example, the spiraled pebbles in Figure 3.2 don't have overhangs, but are not serializable. When locks are used, deadlock applies (see next section).

3.1.3 Safety, Liveness, and Fairness

Safety is the property that an activity will only produce a desired result, or only under appropriate circumstances. Liveness (or progress) is the property that it will eventually produce a desired result. Fairness is a property that, if multiple activities are trying to access some resource, especially repeatedly, perhaps under very specific circumstances, they will each succeed in achieving that access to within some margin of an equal number of times or equal probability.

The primary safety property which has permeated this chapter is that multiple activities will not access the same resource at the same time (indicated by the solid nature of pebbles in that analogy which keeps them from occupying the same space at the same time), primarily to assure the serializability and determinism properties. This is enforced in our activities by the construction in the last chapter, that an activity cannot access a resource until/unless the control state of the resource matches one of the access dots on the corresponding role binding, and that while an activity is accessing the resource, that resource will have no control state, thereby not allowing access by another activity. Control states were actually seen to be more general than simply a form of locking, to also help dictate the order in which different activities could access a particular resource, thereby enforcing other safety constraints, so that activities could only access a resource at all if it was in the proper control state (condition, or phase) to be accessed by that activity.

Liveness denotes the circumstances under which something must occur. Even that loose characterization of liveness demonstrates a major problem with the concept: Must occur when? We have already stated that we don't wish to make the time until completion a behavior governed by our determinism requirement, and putting a fixed time on the accomplishment of a task is contrary to that objective. Even if we omit all mention of time limits, and simply require that an activity eventually occur or complete, a definition of liveness is still elusive, in part because, even using very simple traditional sequential concepts of computation, it is theoretically impossible to determine, just by looking, whether certain plans (e.g. sequential computer programs) will ever complete or succeed in doing certain things.

There are only a few aspects of ScalPL which even lend themselves to liveness constraints – i.e. are observable/apparent from outside of an activity such that their occurrence can be established in a larger context. These few include when a plan is activated into an activity, or when an activity, once it has begun accessing a resource, finishes accessing it. These will be addressed in a subsequent section, when the entire computational model is put together.

Finally, fairness is a very complex subject, both to specifically define specifically and to enforce (whichever definition is adopted). That is, even in common everyday situations, while it may be convenient or desirable to wish for resources to be shared fairly, entire branches of government and other bureaucracies are often established for trying to define and impose that fairness, and even then, what seems fair to one is often deemed unnecessary red tape to another, and not fair enough by yet others. Generally speaking, with safety and liveness already guaranteed, fairness can always be included into a plan explicitly, such as by counting and limiting accesses to certain resources. In fact, implicitly making behavior dependent on past history (without making that history an explicit part of the environment) would violate our earlier determinism requirement. In other words, one can expect fairness to be only loosely adopted into ScalPL (at best).

Deadlock

A plan will, in one way or another, specify the resources to be accessed by an activity. If the resources are not available because they are being accessed by another activity, the activity can wait (or, in other words, continue to grow vertically in time) until the other activity relinquishes them, which will preferably happen soon. However, the resources will never become available if each activity in some collection of activities each needs a resource already held by another activity in the collection. This situation is called **deadlock**. If taking a cross-section of the bucket, deadlock is characterized not only by where the pebbles are, but the horizontal directions they want to grow in (representing resources they want) as they progress upwards (representing time). In the cross section, each pebble in the deadlocked set is blocked from growing in its desired direction by another pebble in the set which is already there, yielding an outline resembling cars gridlocked in a city block which cannot progress due to each

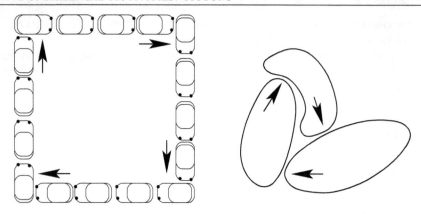

Figure 3.5: Gridlock on the roads, and deadlock in an activity cross-section.

other, as in Figure 3.5. Deadlock can be avoided if an activity (or pebble), while it is awaiting its own forward progress, can shrink (i.e. relinquish some resources) enough to allow enough forward progress by another to, in turn, shrink (relinquish resources) to allow enough forward progress for another, etc., to finally alleviate the deadlock. For belted pebbles, however, the fact that the pebble wants to grow in the first place means that it has not yet reached the belt (i.e. is below it), since shrinkage in any dimension is not allowed (until after the belt). Typically, shrinking and then reacquiring would make the activity non-belted. Generally, then, the way that deadlock is dealt with is (a) to have the Director watch over the other activities to detect when deadlock occurs, and if it does detect it, (b) to terminate and roll back at least one of the deadlocked activities, thereby removing it as an obstruction, and then likely (c) restarting that activity later on (especially if required by liveness constraints). If this termination and retry occurs to many activities in lockstep, these new activities may all deadlock again, resulting in another rollback, etc., ad infinitum. This synchronous retry and rollback cycle is called **livelock**, and can prevent liveness even in the absence of any persistent deadlock. A common approach to avoiding livelock is to have the Director wait a random amount of time, or have each delay exponentially longer periods (exponential backoff), before retrying any particular activity.

One approach to avoiding deadlock is to impose an order (or partial order) over the resources, and to constrain the activities to only acquire resources in that order. In terms of the bucket analogy, this can be interpreted as restricting pebbles to stretch only in a N or W direction as each progresses upwards in the bucket. Wherever a horizontal cross-section is taken, there must be some pebble (the most northerly and/or westerly one) which is not obstructed from growing by another pebble, and it can therefore get all the resources it needs, allowing it to finish and another pebble to become the new most northerly or westerly one, etc. If the activities need to acquire their resources in a particular order (as will be discussed in 3.1.3 below), or if plans must be portable among a variety of environments where the resources may be ordered differently, this may not be a suitable solution.

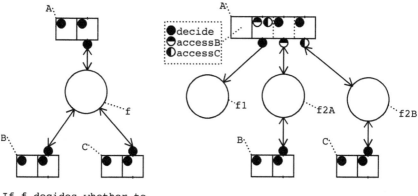

If f decides whether to access B or C based on A's contents, then it's not bottom-belted...

...but can be broken down into bottom-belted activities by adding control states.

Figure 3.6: Work-around for inter-resource dependences.

Inter-resource Dependences

For a deterministic activity, the resources accessed by the activity must be the same each time, or access to some resources must be decided by the plan as a result of observing the contents of one or more other resources. We'll use the term **inter-resource dependences** to describe this latter case. An activity with inter-resource dependences might behave no differently than one without, since one cannot tell from observation (especially from any one activation) how an activity is deciding on the next resource to access.

However, because an activity with inter-resource dependences must acquire its resources in a specific order, and in fact must do some amount of work (computation, decision-making) after acquiring one resource before acquiring others, such an activity cannot be truly bottom-belted. In addition, it may not be possible for a collection of activities which include some with inter-resource dependences to avoid deadlock (as described in the previous subsection) by acquiring resources in a specific order, because activities with inter-resource dependences may not be free to acquire their resources in that order.

Using the concepts and tools described in the previous chapter, there are ways to achieve the results of inter-resource dependences even when using only bottom-belted activities, by splitting the resource acquisition among different activities. For example, suppose that plan f is to access resource A first, and based on the content it finds there, it is then to also access either resource B or resource C, as represented by the question marks in the left diagram in Figure 3.6. That would be an inter-resource dependence, but plan f could be broken down as on the right, into plans f1, f2A, and f2B, where f1 accesses only A, f2A accesses only A and B, and f2B accesses only A and C, all without inter-resource dependences. By arranging the control states to allow f1 to activate first and set A's control state to allow the appropriate one of f2A or f2B to activate, the same result can be achieved, and the inter-resource dependence would effectively be moved to be between plans rather than within them.

Concurrent Observations

To this point, all accesses to resources have been treated equally – i.e. as exclusive, in the pebble analogy – regardless of whether those accesses have been observations or modifications of the resources. However, an activity which is only observing some of its resources can still be independent and deterministic even if those observations are concurrent with other activities which are also observing the same resources, and allowing such concurrency can (of course) reduce time to completion. In the pebble analogy, this would seem to correspond to overlapping pebbles, and to complicate the serializability analyses already mentioned.

Many concurrency models will make special rules specifically for this case, creating such things as "reader locks" as opposed to "writer locks", with the property that multiple activities can obtain a reader lock on the same resource at the same time, but a writer lock cannot be obtained on a resource if either a reader lock or a writer lock is being held (i.e. is active) for the resource. In the pebble analogy, this would correspond to certain parts of certain pebbles being allowed to "pass through" each other in a ghostly way, but others not, making the whole analogy a little feeble and non-intuitive.

A simpler (and in some ways more elegant) approach to solving this issue, while preserving the rather simple pebble analogy, can be to consider observations of a resource as acting like very short (i.e vertically thin) accesses. In this way, an observer cannot block another observer for more than a very short time, but an activity which may modify the resource (and therefore has a thicker access) can block out both observers and other modifiers. This approach also has difficulties – e.g. what if an activity wants to observe the resource for more than an instant, and therefore wants to block out modifiers? We will delve much further into these issues in the next chapter.

3.2   Proposal for Actons and Tactics

We now have sufficient information to devise a useful form of fundamental activities, which we are calling actons, and their plans, which we are calling tactics.

3.2.1   The Basics

First, for reasons outlined in the previous section, we will require that actons be deterministic (relative to their tactics). In part, this means that they won't have side-effects, and will therefore not access any hidden resources. We also, for those reasons stated previously, require that actons will be serializable. Putting these together, that means we will also require that they be atomic.

Second, and perhaps foremost, we will require that all tactics be represented in a manner that makes it easy to activate them as bottom-belted activities (actons) – i.e. represented such that all of the resources which the resulting acton will access are apparent even before the tactic is activated into that acton. In part, this means ruling out inter-resource dependences. The reasons for this requirement are manifold:

1. Bottom-belted activities completely bypass the issues of deadlock, except potentially while the plan is being activated/initiated, to form the belt. (More information on how a plan is activated into an activity will be addressed more fully in Chapter 5 on the Director.) Once the belt is formed, and the acton is underway, that acton can only relinquish resources, and therefore cannot be stuck waiting for a resource being used (e.g. locked) by another activity. This makes it much easier to ensure liveness, in the sense of carrying out whatever the plan (tactic) dictates without obstruction.

2. Activities without inter-resource dependences are simpler to specify formally and mathematically. In mathematics, a mapping (such as a function) is defined as a relationship between two sets (a domain and range, or co-domain). These sets, in the case of activities, are the content domains and control domains of the resources which it accesses. Specifying such mappings without even knowing whether some of resources will be accessed or not requires the use of special techniques, called lazy (or non-strict) mappings, which try to work around potentially non-existent information. If there are no inter-resource dependences, so the set of resources accessed is constant, this is not necessary. In fact, since we have already required that actons be deterministic, the mappings mentioned here are indeed strict functions. This will be addressed in greater detail later.

3. Bottom-belted activities make it much easier to implement the simplified approach to concurrent observers discussed earlier – that is, by treating observations as very brief accesses. Note that, if activities are to be belted at all, any such quick access must take place right at the belt. Therefore, any part of the activity which takes place before the belt would be unable to take advantage of such resources. By putting the belt at the beginning of the activity, the entire activity can make use of such resource observations.

Together with the constructs in the previous chapter, this alone provides a fairly complete description of how actons will work. As with any plan, a tactic (the plan for an acton) will have an interface consisting of a set of named roles, and for each, a usage (observe, replace, update, or nodata), a content domain, and a transition domain. And, as with any plan, those roles must conform to the role bindings for the associated context. Combining the safety requirements of the previous chapter (regarding control states for access to resources) with the lack of hidden state (side effects) and lack of inter-resource dependences mentioned here, we can conclude that an acton will not exhibit any effect unless/until all of the role bindings associated with its context are ready – i.e. are bound to resources with control states which match associated access dots.

Because actons are atomic, if and when one does exhibit any effect, it must exhibit its entire effect – i.e. for each role, it must produce whatever transition and content state is dictated by its tactic after observing the contents of its observable resources. In fact, since tactics are deterministic, they must behave as mathematical functions, producing the same result whenever the inputs (arguments) are the same.

Summing up, then, a tactic's implementation is basically the representation of a function which

- takes in (as arguments) the content states of its observable roles (i.e. the content state of the resources bound to the roles having observe and/or update usages), and

- produces (as results)

    - the content states of its replaceable roles (i.e. the content states of the resources bound to roles having replace or update usages), and

    - a transition for all of its roles.

An acton, then, is the evaluation of this function, with a specific set of arguments – i.e. the resource content states, designated by role bindings on its context. This is not quite as cut-and-dried as it might at first sound, because the tactic may not even produce transitions for some of its roles. We'll deal with those loopholes shortly.

3.2.2   Liveness and Fairness

This details when a tactic can activate into an acton (safety), and what the acton will do if it does anything at all (since it is atomic and deterministic), but doesn't address any conditions under which a tactic will (or must) activate. That is, with no further liveness requirements, a tactic would conform to these rules even if it did abslutely nothing, even if all of the conditions for it to activate were met. This suggests that, in addition to the safety constraints, we need a **liveness** constraint for this approach to be very useful.

Consider the strategy snippets in Figure 3.7. Assume that all of the contexts shown there contain tactics. In the case on the left, the tactic in the single context is ready to activate and nothing can possibly change that until it activates, so this is one case where we would clearly like to assume/require that the tactic will indeed eventually activate, and if/when it finishes and returns the same control state to the resource, that it will then eventually activate again, etc. Now consider the case on the right, where there are two contexts, only one of which can activate at a time. Again, we would clearly like to require that at least one of these eventually activate. In this case, however, if/when that one finishes and returns the same control state to the resource, is it OK for the same one to activate again? And again? Perhaps every time, with the other one never activating? Put another way, should **fairness** constraints be added to prevent one from "unfairly winning" every time?

We have already discussed some issues that can arise when adding fairness constraints. In some cases, the planner might want the two contexts to take

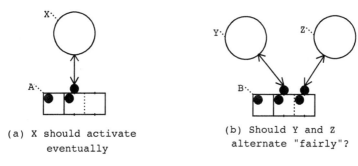

(a) X should activate
eventually

(b) Should Y and Z
alternate "fairly"?

Figure 3.7: Simple liveness and fairness scenarios.

turns evenly, and in others, the planner might think it's OK for one to activate a few times before the other one, but not too many. In some cases, the planner might not care if they are forced to take turns or not, and in yet others, the planner may specifically not want to limit them to taking turns – especially in the more realistic cases where one or both contexts have other role bindings which might alter their readiness in other ways. Moreover, if there is some sort of limit to the number of times that one should activate before the other one, information about the number of times that the one has activated must be stored in some hidden place. That is, contrary to our earlier-state goals, the behavior of one or both tactics would become history dependent, instead of just being dependent upon the control and content state of the resource.

So, we choose to avoid adding any fairness constraints, preferring to leave it to the planner to add those explicitly if they wish (e.g. with extra role bindings and resources). This allows us to keep the liveness constraint very simple: If a tactic is continuously ready to activate, then it will eventually activate. In the competing contexts example, when one tactic activates, it is defined as making the other unready, at least momentarily, thereby breaking the continuity of its readiness and "restarting the clock" on liveness.

3.2.3   Some Common Representations for Tactics

So, a tactic is the representation of a function that takes the content states of observable roles as arguments and produces transitions for all roles, and content states for replaceable roles, as results. What sorts of forms might such a function take? As it turns out, a very workable form is as a (more traditional) deterministic sequential plan, such as a program in a traditional computer language (like C, Java, or even Fortran).

We intentionally haven't discussed such sequential plans much, to avoid confusing matters. A deterministic sequential plan consists of specific steps to be followed one by one, sequentially (by default). Most of the steps act upon (i.e. use or modify) the contents ("values") of so-called variables (similar to resources) according to very specific rules, such as by using mathematical operations to specify the new content of some based on the existing content of others. Some steps result in changing the order in which the steps will be executed (out of direct sequence), such as jumping to a specific step or declaring that some series of steps should be repeated, sometimes based on the content of some of the variables. Regardless of what the step does, its outcome is completely determined by the state of the plan when it executes, which is affected only by previous steps, and typically consists only of the values of the variables. The sequential plan is considered to be finished when the last step is finished, or when some specific "stop" step is reached. Because each step is has a very specific result based on the variable contents when it begins, and the order of the steps is also very specific, the overall result is deterministic. That is to say, if the variables start out with a given set of contents, that will completely determine the order in which the steps will be followed, and the result of each step, and ultimately, whether the plan will ever finish, and if it does, what the final contents of the variables will be.

So, a sequential plan which terminates can be considered as expressing a function from the initial contents of its variables to the final contents of its variables. If all of the variables always start with some fixed content except for some subset of them, the plan can be considered as a expressing function from the initial contents of that (non-fixed) subset of variables to the final content of all the variables, or for that matter, to the final content of any subset of variables (even the same subset). Therefore, consider associating a subset of the variables of a sequential plan with the roles of a tactic, and when the tactic is to be activated, the content of the variables corresponding to the observable roles are initiated with the contents of the associated resource content (with all other variables initiated to some predetermined fixed content). Then the sequential plan is initiated, and if it completes, the contents of the variables corresponding to replaceable roles is considered as the new content state for the resources associated with those roles. Such a sequential plan is then just the sort of function, from content states of observable roles to content states of replaceable roles, we demand for a tactic.

This is part of what a tactic is supposed to do. The rest is to also express a functional mapping from that same starting point (i.e. content state of each of its observable roles) to a transition for each of the roles. For that, consider creating a new kind of step of the form "Issue transition X for role Y" to the language expressing our sequential plans. The result of such a step is determined by the following rule:

- If any step of the form "Issue transition Z for role Y" has already been performed by the plan (i.e. specifying the same role, Y in this case, but same or different transition, X or Z in this case), the step has the same effect as "stop".

- Otherwise, (if an "Issue" step has not already been performed for the same role), the step has the effect of declaring that the transition for role Y will be X. Also, if role Y has replace usage, then it also has the effect of declaring the new content state of the resource associated with Y as the content of the variable associated with Y – i.e. just like before, but now, right at the time of the "Issue" step, rather than waiting until the sequential plan is finished.

With this addition, then, a sequential deterministic plan which terminates can indeed be considered as a valid implementation for a tactic. (As will be seen shortly, even if such a plan doesn't terminate, it will still qualify.) Note that the function denoted by the sequential plan is independent of the order in which it issues its transitions, or the length of time it takes to issue them: The only salient attribute of the implementation is the function it represents – i.e. which final content states and transitions result from a given initial content of the observable roles.

There are indeed other possible representations for tactics than the one proposed. For example, the development of functional computer languages has provided ways to express ever more elaborate functions, so could be used for this purpose as well. Perhaps most importantly, the precise representation doesn't matter, and the representation style for two different tactics (even used within the same strategy) can be different, as long as the rules for interpreting that representation are clear. Regardless of whether a functional computer program or a sequential plan or more traditional function is used to represent a tactic, the important thing from the standpoint of the ScalPL methodology is that it is a function, not that it is any specific function. That is, it may not even be clear, upon looking at a particular functional or sequential program which function it expresses, and ensuring that it expresses the function that the planner wants it to express is a separate issue, beyond the scope here, but it is usually possible (within bounds) to at least ensure that it is indeed a function. Among other things, this means that if a sequential plan, such as a computer program, is going to "blow up" (terminate abnormally and finally), it should always do so under the same local circumstances, which are themselves only dependent upon the starting conditions – i.e. deterministic.

3.2.4 Termination ($\perp$ Transitions)

We have glossed over the case where the function (however it is expressed) does not terminate. The standard mathematical way of dealing with the situation is as we will do here: Rather than treating such a case in an entirely alternate way, we will simply give a name to a fictitious value which represents the lack of a value – i.e. the value "produced" when the function doesn't terminate. That value is called "bottom" and is represented as $\perp$. (This use of the term "bottom" has virtually nothing to do with other uses of the term here, such as in "bottom-belted": It is just a coincidence.) Specifically, we will say that if a tactic function never produces a transition for a particular role, then that is equivalent to saying that it produces the $\perp$ **(bottom) transition** for that role. We will also require that the transition binding for all roles implicitly binds the $\perp$ transition to the $\perp$ **(bottom) control state** of the associated resource, which corresponds to that resource having no control state at all. We will also define the content state of a resource as being $\perp$ if and only if the control state of the resource is $\perp$. Put together, this is just another way of saying that if an acton never issues a transition for a given role, then the control state for the associated will remain with no control state, and the content state will also be unavailable.

3.2.5 Beltedness

Considering non-issued transitions as being equivalent to a $\perp$ transition is especially useful for implementing and reasoning about bottom-belted actons, with tactics represented by sequential deterministic plans. For example, to enforce bottom belts, consider activating a tactic in a context only if all of the associated roles are ready, and upon activation, first stealing the control state from all resources bound to its roles (as one atomic action), and then initiating the sequential plan as described earlier (after initializing some variables with the observable content states). As soon as any "Issue" step is performed within that plan, for any role, the new control state (and potentially content state, if replaceable) is assigned to the corresponding resource, and other tactics may be activated immediately as a result. If "Issue" steps are never performed for some roles, then those are effectively the same as issuing $\perp$ transitions, and the associated resources remain without control state. This is exactly the approach we will focus on for the remainder of this book. It may be unknown and unknowable how much longer a plan might need to execute to change some of those $\perp$ transitions to real live (issued) transitions, but that's beside the point: As long as there is a clear rule on how long (usually forever) the steps in such a plan will be followed, the plan is deterministic, in that it either will or will not eventually issue a transition for each of its roles, so the roles which will be considered as $\perp$ will be well-defined.

Note that just because the rules here are made to facilitate bottom-belted actons, they do not absolutely require that actons be bottom-belted. For example, it would be possible and legal to implement actons as top-belted – i.e. to acquire resources only as they are required by the plan, and to wait until the the plan terminates to commit and make its effects (transitions and new content states) atomically felt. This would also require deadlock detection and remediation (e.g. rollback and re-execution) in order to satisfy liveness constraints. Perhaps most troublesome, if the plan truly had to terminate before such an activity could commit, then non-terminating plans would never commit (so the idea of $\perp$ transitions would not be useful). Another option would be to always carry out some maximum fixed number of steps for the plan, and if that happened (without the plan terminating first), the transitions not executed would be considered $\perp$, and the activity would still commit. This would still be deterministic (i.e. always the same result for the same initial state) if and only if the rule for whether a plan would be bottom-belted, top-belted (requiring termination), or top-belted (with fixed number of execution steps) was fixed, since this latter decision would effectively determine the specific function (from initial content states to final transitions and content states) that the sequential plan represents.

3.2.6 Predictability (Concurrent Access to Resources)

The introduction of $\perp$ transitions also makes it easy to express the special case regarding concurrent observations. Recall that, in an earlier section, we said that one way to think about concurrent observations is simply to require them to be relatively short. That way, an observer cannot block another observer for more than a short time, but an activity which may modify the resource (and therefore has a longer access to the resource) can block out other activities which either observe or modify as long as necessary, maybe forever. For this reason, we will consider any role binding (a) which has no replace usage, and (b) which binds all of its transitions to the same control state, as a special case, since this is the kind of one we would like to be "short". We will call such roles **predictable**, because (except for that pesky possibility of a $\perp$ transition, where a transition is never issued) we can predict what the new control and content state of the resource bound to such a role will be as soon as the access begins – i.e. the same content state as when it starts, and the control state to which all the transitions are bound. And since we want to get rid of "that pesky possibility of a $\perp$ transition" for these roles, the special case rule will just be: Predictable roles (i.e. those as just defined) will never issue a $\perp$ transition. In other words, they will always result in some non-$\perp$ transition, and therefore in the predictable control state, eventually. Chapter 4 will be devoted entirely to justifying and explaining the implications of this special case, so we won't go into this any more deeply now.

3.2.7 Summary of Acton/Tactic Definition

Summing up, we have defined a tactic as a plan which is deterministic, and has no inter-role (inter-resource) dependences: In other words, all of the resources which it will access are known before it is activated. Because it is a plan, it has an interface and an implementation, and it is activated within a context, so the role bindings for the context identify the resources which will be accessed.

Safety properties dictate that the resulting acton will exhibit effects (i.e. be activated) only if all of the roles of its context are ready (bound to resources with the same control state as an access dot of the binding), and liveness properties dictate that it will be activated within a finite time of those roles becoming and remaining continuously ready.

Once activated, liveness and atomicity properties also dictate that all of the effects specified by the plan will eventually be felt. Serialization and determinism properties mean that those effects will be decided completely by the content state of the observable roles and the plan itself, and that the effects will be only the transitions issue to all of the roles and the new content state for the replaceable roles.

Finally, any role binding which does not have replace permission, and for which all transitions are bound to a single control state, is called a predictable role binding, and is guaranteed to (eventually) issue one of those transitions to that role (not $\perp$). This means that the eventual control state and content state of the associated resource are known as soon as it is known that the tactic has indeed activated into an acton.

3.3 Examples

That is all we'll say for now about what a tactic and acton are, from an official or abstract point of view. This section will deal with the ramifications of such a definition.

3.3.1 Waffles

When the example strategy for making, serving, and consuming waffles was presented in the previous chapter, actons had not yet been discussed. At the time, we said:

> This diagram does *not* show the conditions under which each activity will commence or the circumstances under which it will try to access each resource. For example, it does not show whether the mix activity will start fetching the flour, eggs, and/or milk even before the batter bowl is empty and ready to accept the new batter. It doesn't show the conditions under which the spoon activity might try to access the requests, so it doesn't show when a lack of requests (as represented by its control state) will interfere with that activity's progress.

Now, however, if we reveal that all of the activities there within the contexts are actons – i.e. that their plans (mix, spoon, etc.) are tactics – the reader can get much greater insight into the workings of the plan.

For example, that being the case, mix will occur iff (short for "if and only if") the batterbowl is empty (the ingredients are effectively bottomless in this plan); Spoon will move batter from the batterbowl to the waffler iff the waffler is hot and empty (changed from cold by the preheat activity) and there are requests for waffles. The serve activity will only occur (moving waffle from the waffler to the table and decrementing requests) if the waffler has waffles in it and the table is set (i.e. anything other than unset); An eater (the two designated by hunger1 and hunger2) will ask for (i.e. register a request for) a waffle iff it is hungry, at which time it will change to waiting, and will eat a waffle iff it is waiting and there is a waffle on the table.

Recall that earlier, we described a text form called SPLAT for expressing strategies, with a basic top-level syntax of

> plan *interface* strategy *implementation*

We will now use the SPLAT for expressing tactics, but replacing the word strategy with tactic, i.e.

> plan *interface* tactic *implementation*

The interface is enclosed in braces "{", "}"), and the whole thing is usually preceded by the name of the tactic (plan) and a colon. (The reasons for that will become clearer in Chapter 7.) The implementation will appear in braces decorated with vertical bars (i.e. "{|", "|}"). Each role in the interface will begin with 3 characters symbolizing the usage, then the name of the role, then the transitions in parentheses, and then the content domain (type). If there is just one transition called done, it may be omitted (i.e. empty parentheses). The usage of a role is designated by mimicking the arrowheads on the role, as

```
mix: plan  { <-> flour(done) flour
             <-> eggs(done) eggs
             <-> milk(done) milk
             --> batterbowl(done) batter }
tactic
{|
Transfer 1 egg from eggs to batterbowl.
Issue done to eggs.
Transfer 1 cup of milk from milk to batterbowl.
Issue done to milk.
Transfer 1 cup of flour from flour to batterbowl.
Issue done to flour.
Mix contents of batterbowl until well combined.
Issue done to batterbowl.
|}
```

Figure 3.8: Possible mix tactic.

"-->" for replace, "<--" for observe, "<->" for update, and "---" for nodata. So, for example, the mix tactic might look as in Figure 3.8.

3.3.2 Software Subroutines as Tactics

Computer programmers might want a few more specifics about what a sequential plan might look like to be considered as a tactic. This section is for them, and can be safely skipped by those not so interested.

The earlier description of using a deterministic sequential program as a tactic mentioned essentially copying information between the content state of resources and the content of variables within the program representing those resources. Computer programmers know that such copying is often undesirable, and can often be avoided with the use of pointers (or formal variables, "proxies" for actuals). That is, when the subroutine is called (invoked) by another program (the caller), it is (generally) passed a fixed set of parameters or arguments from the caller, and when it is finished, a result value may also be returned to the caller. In addition to the return value, it is common for languages to provide some means for the subroutine to directly access and modify data structures held by the caller, typically by using the arguments as proxies or pointers to those structures. This is effectively another way to effectively pass information between the caller and the subroutine, even without copying the information itself back and/or forth. To ensure that the subroutine and caller understand the rules of engagement, the subroutine typically has a header (or prototype) which specifies precisely the sorts of access that it intends for each of the arguments, such as whether it will just read its contents (in), provide completely new contents (out), read and provide new contents (inout), etc. These intents can be used to optimize the calling process as well as to ensure that nonsensical code is easily identified, such as the caller providing a constant as an argument and the subroutine attempting to modify it.

Tactics can be made very similar in structure to these subroutines. A tactic accesses a fixed number of roles, which can be handled very much like arguments. Each of these roles will have observe, replace, or modify permission, very much like the access intents specified for subroutine arguments. Instead of pointing to data structures in a caller, however, they can be made to point to the content states of the resources to which the roles are bound, and rather than returning a value at the end, simply accessing and modifying these content states is satisfactory as the only form of communication. More specifics about what and how such subroutines are called and what happens when an "Issue" statement is executed are covered in Chapter 5 (The Director). Generally speaking, the specialized header (interface) of a tactic, and the Issue statements, are generally converted in a preprocessing step to specialized subroutine headers and service calls, so that the tactic becomes a fully legal subroutine in the host language which interfaces correctly with the Director. Some of this will become clearer in Chapter 5.

The primary differences between a tactic and a sequential subroutine are

1. a tactic does not "return" values to a "caller" when done, but instead relinquishes its arguments independently, one by one, via "Issue" statements;

2. before (or as) it relinquishes each argument, a tactic must declare a transition for it; and

3. the arguments must be the only means of interacting with its environment (i.e. resources).

Although there is no specific requirement for a "return" construct for tactics (as there is for subroutines) since the end of the tactic is implied when all of the resources have been relinquished (i.e. have had transitions issued to them), a similar construct can still prove useful for easily wrapping up execution of the tactic, including relinquishing any as-yet unreliquished resources with some default transition (which will be assumed to be the first one listed in the interface).

The most troublesome of these differences is the third. Sequential languages support a myriad of mechanisms other than the arguments for a subroutine to interact with resources like archives, computer devices, the main program, other invocations of the same subroutine, other routines ("methods") within the same object or class, etc. These include:

- System services which return information such as "time of day", non-deterministic pseudo-random numbers, or information about the current state of the computer or other environment.

- Input/output statements and related system facilities

- "common", "global", or "external" declarations which make data structures visible across several subroutines or subroutine invocations

- "save" declarations to maintain data between subroutine invocations

- Dynamic memory allocation ("malloc", "free", "new")

- Read access to data structures (such as file buffers, heap data, or stack frames) which may have random data left over from other work.

To the extent that a collection of subroutines is used to implement a single tactic, some of these constructs can be used in a restricted fashion to communicate between those subroutines. For example, dynamic memory can be allocated, used, and deallocated within a single acton, and global, common, or external variables can be used to communicate between portions of a single tactic as long as care is taken to ensure any left-over persistent state will not be used in subsequent executions, and that the results are perfectly repeatable/deterministic.

Although language processors can often detect and protect against a subroutine assigning values to (or otherwise modifying) a read-only argument, which corresponds to an observable resource for a tactic, tactics must also not be able to observe an "old" value which may be in a replaceable resource. In general, this sort of requirement is not enforced by many existing language processors (or language semantics), but it could be included, and is in some more modern parallel languages. In fact, a tactic can be allowed to read such a resource as long as it is only reading what it (itself) has previously written into the resource during the same acton, so it is theoretically possible for dataflow analysis within the tactic's implementation to allow this as well. In the interim, a much simpler solution is to initialize replaceable resources (as opposed to readable or updateable ones) with constants each time an acton is initiated, and then to allow the tactic to either read or write to the associated argument without restriction. Efficient approaches are described in the next two chapters.

Resources are powerful enough to substitute for virtually all of the restricted language mechanisms mentioned above, as will be more fully explained in subsequent chapters.

3.3.3 Natural Events as Actons

Many events that occur in a common day satisfy the requirements for actons, but that may depend on the perspective from which we consider them. For example, two people teaming up to carry out some activity can be considered in terms of the individual activities carried out by each person during the interaction (such as hearing a sentence or accepting an object, followed by a verbal response or providing an object), in which case the interaction must necessarily be regarded as several actons, but the same interaction can be interpreted in terms of the team, in which case the overall activity can be regarded in terms of the resources or inputs required by the team followed by the results or declarations produced by the team. In some cases, this overall activity may meet the definition of an acton, in others it may not. Later chapters will show how to capture both of these levels of granularity in a single plan using hierarchical composition.

3.3.4 ACID Transactions

A **transaction** typically refers to an activity which accesses resources at least some of which belong to a database. Simply put, a database can be considered as a very large set of resources which has a relatively long lifespan, which has some explicit and implicit logical constraints which hold (e.g. regarding the way that information in one resource relates to that in another), and which is usually optimized to make it easy to locate specific content in one or many such resources. Transactions must assure that the logical constraints continue to hold. Generally speaking, a database for which these constraints hold is said to be **consistent**.

Transactions with certain properties, called **ACID**, are common. ACID stands for Atomicity, Consistency, Isolation (or Independence), and Durability.

- Atomicity is essentially the same as what we have described here – either the transaction (activity) occurs completely, or it doesn't occur at all.

- Consistency means that the results of the transaction do not violate the consistency constraints.

- Isolation/Independence means that the transactions can be explained independently from one another, which is the same meaning we have assigned to serializability, for reasons explained earlier. However, many implementations of ACID do not take this as strictly as we do here.

- Durability means that once a transaction has completed, its effect is permanent. In most cases, this goes without saying, but since databases often have data cached/replicated in several places at once, some in long-term (e.g. disk-based) storage and others in short-term (e.g. RAM-based) storage, this is a reminder that the effects of the transaction must be felt permanently, in long-term storage.

Essentially, then, Atomicity and Isolation go together to form what we have called independence or serializability, and Consistency is roughly similar to what we have called safety, though the conditions are different. (We will discuss consistency of resources more in Chapter 15.) One significant difference between an ACID transaction and an acton is the requirement in the latter (but not necessarily the former) to be deterministic.

Although liveness is not stated as a required property of ACID transactions, it is certainly desirable that a transaction succeed in some finite amount of time after it is initiated. The character of liveness is different than in our situation, where activities follow one another in something of a chain reaction. In part, because of this looser requirement, ACID transactions are quite often implemented as top-belted, with commit/rollback/re-execute logic and deadlock detection, with no aversion to inter-resource dependences. (In fact, database transactions are usually rife with such dependences, consulting some resources to help find others.)

3.4 Summary

Our goal was to create a "fundamental particle" of computation or activity. We decided to call such an activity an acton (a play on the words atom and activity), and the plan for such an activity a tactic (to represent that it is intended to be part of a strategy, as described in the previous chapter). We set as requirements that tactics and their associated actons be independent, so that they could each be considered in isolation from other activities, deterministic, so that they could be understood entirely in terms of their input an output behavior, and have liveness (progress) and safety properties to make them suitable as a basis for building whatever kind of activity we might ultimately desire.

We discussed some ways of accomplishing our serializability goals, the most direct being to require that actons be belted, where the acton acquires access to (but does not relinquish access to) resources up to some point in time (the belt), after which time it can relinquish access to (but not acquire access to) resources. (These are also known in the literature as two-phase activities, being divided into the growing phase and shrinking phase, respectively.) We also discussed different trade-offs between different kinds of belted activities, such as top-belted activities (where all resources and effects are withheld until the activity finished, at which time those effects were made felt atomically in an action known as commit), and bottom-belted activities (where all of the resources required by the activity are obtained atomically at the beginning, and then relinquished one by one). Since only bottom-belted activities completely avoided deadlock, thereby complying directly with liveness and/or determinism requirements, we decided to facilitate those, even while leaving it free for a platform to implement them otherwise. To facilitate bottom-belted actons, we forbade inter-resource dependences (where it would be necessary to access one resource before knowing which others to access). The deterministic behavior of actons also helps to facilitate their construction as bottom-belted while preserving liveness conditions, since if an acton is unable to complete, it can be re-executed with the same results as long as the initial resource states are still available (which would be necessary even to facilitate roll-back for top-belted activities).

The result of these decisions, as well as the earlier characterization of plans having an interface defined by roles, each with permissions, transition domains, and content domains, was that an acton's behavior can be completely defined in terms of a function, from the content states accessible on its observable (including updateable) roles to the new content states for its replaceable (including updateable) roles and the transitions for all of its roles. Such a function (i.e. tactic) can be represented in many ways, but perhaps the most practical is as a traditional sequential deterministic plan (algorithm or program).

The only minor complication with that simple functional characterization is whether $\perp$ is an acceptable transition and/or content state result, where $\perp$ represents the lack of a result – i.e. a plan which can't figure out what result to produce, or which decides not to produce a result, for one or more of its roles. A practical middle-ground was adopted, where $\perp$ was always a possible if the role either (a) had replace (including update) permission, or (b) had transition bindings to more than one control state. If neither of those are true, then by excluding the possibility of a $\perp$ result, it is possible to determine (predict) the new content and control state of the associated resource even before the acton has completed, and that is a very useful result, so such a binding is called predictable, and a $\perp$ result is considered impossible (i.e. illegal, disallowed).

Chapter 4

Predictability: Concurrent Observers, Buffers, & Broadcast

A potentially problematic aspect of ScalPL, as we have described it so far, has been the limitation allowing only one activity to access a resource at one time, as enforced by control state, and specifically the properties that (1) the control state of a resource must match an/the access dot on a role binding in order to be accessed by the associated activity, (2) only one activity can begin accessing a resource at one time, and (3) the resource will remain without any control state during the period in which it is being accessed by an activity. Then, near the end of Chapter 3, we added a proviso about predictable roles, which we defined as those with no replace (or update) permission, and for which all of the transitions were bound to a single control state. We said that these predictable roles would not issue a bottom transition, or in other words, that they would always issue some transition in some finite time. It was hinted that this would somehow help to alleviate the problems (if any) associated the aforementioned limitations.

In this chapter, we will first look at approaches that have historically been used to efficiently share effective access to resource content among different activities at the same time. We then take a closer look at predictability (i.e. predictable resources) and the way that a Director can make the most of it to provide efficient overlapped access. Finally, we review the historic approaches as they might be expressed in ScalPL, in light of the predictability optimizations.

4.1   Common approaches to shared access

Before getting into how the rule on predictable roles will help to provide the flexibility and efficiency we need, we first review some common techniques and scenarios for delivering that efficiency through shared access to resources.

71

4.1.1 Concurrent Observers

As anybody who has ever visited an art museum or classroom knows, it's often very advantageous (and very little problem) to have many entities concurrently observing a single resource. In fact, if that's all they'll be doing, there's no reason not to have as many concurrent observers as can be accommodated by the platform. In cases where so much concurrency cannot be accommodated, it really changes little but the time to completion if some of them must wait their turn (for the "next show"). The potential problems come in when one or more of the activities might decide to follow the observation of a shared resource with modification, in our case either to the content of the resource, or to the control state (i.e. the ability of others to access/observe the resource).

4.1.2 Broadcast/Multicast

Closely related to concurrent observation is the concept of broadcast or multi-cast. Generally speaking, **broadcast** is the act of making information available (often for a very limited period of time) for multiple entities to observe or not, at their discression, typically with no feedback as to whether it was observed by zero, one, or millions of entities. The information is often produced as a **stream** – i.e. as a constant signal, or individual data, or **frames**, produced in rapid succession. **Multicast** is essentially a broadcast that is limited in scope to a fixed set of potential recipients. For multicast, since the list of intended recipients is sometimes known, it may make sense in that case to try to ensure that all intended recipients indeed can observe the information, and to provide feedback to the producer if and when that occurs, but that feedback may or may not be part of any particular implementaton.

The reason for even having a special name or category for broadcast is that it's sometimes very easy to implement efficiently in the real world. An example is a movie theater: The movie projector is effectively broadcasting the light, and the loudspeakers are broadcasting the sound, and this process can be the same whether there is an audience of one or one hundred. Any sound or light not picked up by audience members effectively disappears harmlessly. Broadcast is common in cases where signals naturally propogate outward and then disappear, so light, sound, radio (and TV), etc., can work well on a broadcast model.

Multicast may be implemented as broadcast with some special protection (e.g. authorization or encoding) that allows only the prescribed receivers to observe the broadcast, but there are many other options. For example, consider passing some object down an aisle during a presentation, for close analysis by audience members independently. The advance knowledge that everyone on the aisle (or room) is intended to see the resource allows an optimization of moving it from one to the next, instead of (say) having each get up to look at it, or passing it back to the producer each time to then be passed to another person who had not seen it. Note that in this particular case, even those who don't really want to observe the resource may be called upon to perform some action, such as passing it along to the next potential observer.

4.1.3 Throttling and Buffering

Concurrent observation usually applies to information which changes relatively rarely, so that multiple observers may happen upon the information while it is not being modified. Broadcast and multicast often apply to cases where information is produced regularly or even continuously, but still where observers are able to process the information at least as fast as they encounter it. A third case is where the information is (at least sometimes) produced at a rate higher than that at which observers are able to process it.

If overall speed is not of the essence, it is sometimes possible to slow the producer down (also known as **throttling**) to a rate where the observers can always consume each item as it is being produced. If it is not necessary for the observers to observe every piece of information, another alternative is for the producer to create it at full speed, but to have observers simply observe what they can and let the rest go, unobserved. (This is the usual broadcast model: You snooze – or take a bathroom break – you lose.)

However, another common case is where it is important for the observers to observe all of the information, and where the rate of the producer is faster than that of the observations only spurts, but where the overall rate of observation, over time, averages out to at least as fast as the information is produced over time. In such a case, a technique of **buffering** (also known as **double buffering** or **multi buffering**) is often used, where the producer is allowed to produce more than can be immediately processed by the observers for limited amounts of time, and this information is stored (or buffered) at the receiver until it can be observed. It is often important for the information to still be observed in the same order that it is created, so it is rather common to use a FIFO (first-in, first-out) storage area, also known as a queue, for any information waiting to be observed. Consider checkers at a grocery store waiting to observe groceries to tally up the price. At especially busy times, the queues (lines) of people waiting for checkers may get longer, but over time, the lines abate during the slower periods. (This is also a common role now played by digital video recorders, DVRs, which continue to buffer a video broadcast while the human viewer pauses the display, but can perhaps still catch up with the broadcast later by skipping through commercials.)

As long as the queue can hold enough information, and information can be added (at one end) at a different rate as it is removed (at the other end), and the overall rate of removal is greater than or equal to the rate that it is added, then no information will be lost, even if the producer continues without stopping.

Part of this classical solution is usually to allow the producer to continue producing as long as there is "room" in the queue, even if some of that information will never be eventually observed. (For example, people might be allowed to shop and get into the grocery store queue even if the store has a strict closing time, at which point those who have not yet checked out would just be kicked out without their groceries.) In these cases, adding a queue to a plan can actually change the behavior of the entities involved, not just the efficiency (or level of concurrency), in that it may (for example) lead some entities to waste effort/output that they wouldn't have if the queue had not been present. This can be avoided if the consumer (from the queue) somehow keeps the producer (to the queue) informed, using some more direct/immediate means than just emptying out the queue, on how much more information it is ultimately prepared to consume/observe, so that the producer can be sure not to produce more than that. In the grocery store example, this might mean an announcement of when one must be finished shopping, or the precise cutoff point in the queue, which would allow one to be serviced before closing.

4.2   Predictability

Although each of the scenarios described above can be (and often is) treated as a separate case, they can also (surprisingly) be treated as just many specific cases of a more general circumstance – i.e. the result of one or more activities knowing in advance the kinds of access that other activities will be performing to the communication medium (which we will consider as a resource). Another way to say this is that, when one or more activities can declare in advance what the entire state of a resource will be when they are done accessing it, other activities can (and in ScalPL, due to predictabiity and liveness constraints, sometimes must) move forward based on that advance knowledge, even before the previous activity is (activities are) finished. This is exactly the function and result of the predictability rule. The next section (4.3) will show how the previous techniques and scenarios can be interpreted this way, but first we must more abstractly understand the effects of the predictability rule.

Note that if an activity has finished accessing all of its non-predictable roles, it can't do anything else which will have any outward effect. The control and content state of all of its other (predictable) roles are already defined by the rule, so the activity is for all intents and purposes (and we will say, actually) done. A corollary of this is that if an activity has only predictable roles, then the moment it starts, it is done.

4.2.1   Snapshots: An Implication of Predictability

Consider the very simple snippet of a strategy in Figure 4.1 (a), having two contexts bound to a resource, one (updater) which modifies the content state and transitions the control state to allow the other (observer) to activate, which then observes the resource and transitions the control state back. Both of these are assumed to also access some other resources, not shown. Note that observer is bound with a predictable role binding, but not updater (because it has replace permission, as part of its modify permission). How does the predictability rule affect the behavior of this setup?

After updater provides new content state for the resource and transitions the control state, suppose that observer becomes ready to access the resource (by virtue of its unshown resources achieving the proper control states). observer can then go ahead and access the resource, stealing the control state as usual, until it is finished with its observations, at which time it performs the transition, reassigning the new control state to the resource allowing updater to access it again. This is perfectly acceptable behavior.

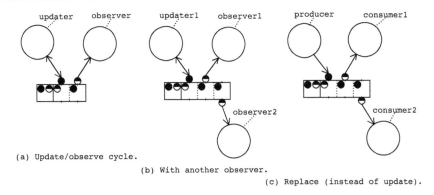

(a) Update/observe cycle.

(b) With another observer.

(c) Replace (instead of update).

Figure 4.1: Predictability via snapshots (single, multiple, optimized).

But what if **observer** takes a very long time to issue that transition? What if it might take forever? If it did take forever, it would violate the predictability rule, which says that it must eventually at least *act* as though it issues a transition, in effect sending access to the resource back to **updater**. Even determining whether **observer** will *ever* eventually perform the transition is not as simple as just looking at its plan, because it's not generally possible to tell by just looking (as Alan Turing helped us to understand). In that case, if the Director is going to enforce the rules (semantics) which we have set up, part of its job will be to ensure that **observer** at least looks as though it has performed its transition in finite time.

So the next question is how it might do that. It's not as simple as the Director just forcing a "fake" transition for **observer** while that activity continues to observe the content, because that transition could allow **updater** to start accessing and modifying the resource's content state at the same time, leading to the problems outlined earlier. Nor is it as easy as the Director just forcing a fake transition for **observer** and then blocking **observer** from observing the content any longer, since **observer** might have progressed (e.g. with its other resources) if the Director had but not interfered in that way.

No, the rules of predictability require that if **observer** looks like it might take forever (whatever that might mean) before issuing a transition to that predictable resource, the Director must facilitate both the transition and the continued progress of **observer**. The Director can accomplish this by (1) giving **observer** its own **snapshot** (i.e. copy) of the content state, then (2) issuing a "fake" transition to the resource on behalf of the **observer** activity, and then (3) suppressing any "real" transition for that resource which **observer** might finally get around to issuing itself. And although we prefaced this with "if **observer** looks like it might take forever", it is perfectly fine if the Director does all of this without waiting at all, such as just as soon as **observer** activates. We will go into more suggestions for optimizing these snapshots in a bit.

4.2.2 Predictability as "Wrinkle in Time"

Up to this point, we've considered a resource as a part of the environment, a named representing a content state (e.g. an entity like a sheet of paper or a car) and somehow marked with the control state denoting what activity can access it next. And while that's still sort of true, this introduction of snapshots and "fake" transitions now also introduces the notion that different entities might see the same resource as having different content and control states at the same time.

To see this more clearly, consider the center plan (b) in Figure 4.1. Just as in the previous example, when the `updater1` activity transitions the control state of the resource, one of the observer activities (say `observer1`) can perhaps activate, and with the aid of the Director, get a snapshot and predictively transition the control state back to allow `updater1` to access it again. But in this case, if `updater1` works quickly, updating the content state and transitioning the control state again, perhaps even while `observer1` is still busy accessing the first version (snapshot) of the content state, `observer2` could activate to access the new, second version of the resource content state, and again the Director could intervene to get a snapshot for it, and predictively transition the control state so that `updater1` could begin work on creating a third version of the content state. With enough predictable observer contexts on the right, this could continue to almost any level, with many versions of the content state all extant at once, each being accessed concurrently by a different observer activity.

Although it may seem as though the introduction of predictability and these "games" by the Director has just made dealing with resources more complex, it really hasn't for the activities concerned. Indeed, a more accurate way to consider it is that time has become more flexible. That is, in the example, `updater1`, `observer1`, and `observer2` can each be considered to have their own clock, and according to their own clock, all accesses to the resource are happening in a sequential fashion. But because there is no comparison between their clocks, they aren't made aware that `updater1` has moved ahead in time relative to `observer1` to activate a second time, and moved ahead in time relative to `observer2` to activate yet again. Predictable roles are a means of imposing a "wrinkle in time", allowing different activities to be working concurrently (physically) with that resource as it exists in different (logical) time frames.

Having different versions of a resource's state floating around might seem quite confusing, but recall that they are logically all rigidly ordered in time, and all but one are "old", dispensable versions which have already been logically superceded by newer ones. The planner never needs to consider that there are multiple versions outstanding, since it is the Director's job to ensure that all works the same way as it would if only one was accessing the resource (and its single content state) at a time. Put another way, it is not apparent to an entity outside of the Director whether the Director helped by making copies and issuing predictive transitions, or whether the Director did nothing and the activities themselves just progressed according to the stated rules. Logically speaking, all can be reasoned about just as it was before we started this discussion of predictability. The only subtle difference is between the implementation of a tactic and its outward behavior (as an acton), since the latter is now being helped along a little in some cases by the Director, to ensure that predictability rules are enforced (i.e. that a transition will ultimately be issued).

4.2.3 Optimizing Snapshots

Making a snapshot (or copy) may not be free, in either the time it takes to make it or the space it takes to store it. It is worth considering, then, whether there are ways to make them unnecessary or more efficient.

First, we've already mentioned that if an activity performs a transition to the predictable role "soon enough", just naturally in the its normal course of operation, then there may be no reason at all for the Director to make a snapshot. The two issues are:

1. How soon is "soon enough"? Some activities may observe the role for just an instant before they will perform a transition, others for relatively long periods, and some perhaps never explicitly performing one. And even multiple activities emanating from the same plan might take different amounts of time, so it's impossible for a Director to know for sure how long to wait before giving up and providing the "fake" transition and snapshot for a predictable role. Still, it *is* rather common for multiple (e.g. successive) activities from the same plan to access a given role for about the same period of time, so if the Director can keep records on how long that plan's activities took in previous incarnations, it may be easier to guess how long to wait on subsequent ones before giving up and issuing one itself.

2. The advantages of delaying a snapshot, to minimize the time and/or space of creating the snapshot, are counterbalanced by the advantages of hurrying the snaphshot, to perhaps let other activities (e.g. the updaters in our example) continue sooner. The updater in our example may be held up only until the transition is performed by an observer, so it may very well get more work done more quickly if the Director performs the snapshot and fake transition quickly, allowing both the observer and updater to work concurrently. On the other hand, the updater may also not be ready again soon, or ever for that matter, regardless of how quickly the transition from the observer is performed, since its other (unshown) resources may not be ready, in which case, there's no reason for the Director to expedite the transition (and expend the space and time for a snapshot).

And even when the Director does issue a fake transition, it is not always necessary for it to create a snapshot. In general, even ignoring predictability, if the next activity to access a resource does not have observe (or update) permission to that resource, there is no reason for the Director to provide it with the previous content state of the resource. Specifically, if that next activity has replace permission (and not observe) to that resource, then the Director may just as well give the activity a new "blank slate" for the content state. (In fact, this is a common and efficient way of assuring that the activity truly obeys the "replace but don't observe" permission on the role binding, by giving it no previous content state to observe.) In such a case, the Director might just as well allow a previous observing predictable activity to continue accessing the (old) content state even after issuing a fake transition, without making a snapshot.

To see this in more detail, consider Figure 4.1 (c), which is the same as (b) except that the activity on the left (`producer`) has replace rather than update permission to the common resource. In this case, each time a `consumer` on the right gets access to the content state, the Director can immediately "fake" a transition to allow `producer` to activate again (if its other roles are ready) to start creating the next content state, without performing a copy, even while the `consumer` continues to access the content state created previously, *as long as its new content state is created in a different location than* (rather than writing over the top of) *the previous one.* In such a case, the time overhead of creating a snapshot is gone, but the space overhead remains, so if space is tight and the content state might be very large compared to available space on the platform, it may still be beneficial for the Director to wait for some period to see if the `consumer` will explicitly finish access and issue the transition, thereby allowing the `producer` to reuse the space for that content state (by over-writing or de-allocating/re-allocating it).

In some cases, the time and/or space overhead of snapshots may also be obviated by the fact that the activity with predictable roles (those on the right in the examples) and the activities producing the content (on the left in the examples) might already be using/accessing different copies of the content state due to communication methods used between them. For example, if content state is being created in one building or computer processor, and observed in a different (perhaps distant) one, simply communicating the content state from the source to the destination using technology like traditional fax, email, or computerized message passing will often automatically create a copy as part of the communication process. In broadcast media like radio, television, or projection, not only is a copy often made at the source (e.g. light bouncing off the subject and into a camera, or a laser beam reading a DVD into a stream of bits on a wire), once the signal is broadcast, each recipient effectively gets its own copy, now separated from the source and from each other.

4.3   Revisiting the Scenarios, in Light of Predictability

Now that we have considered some of the optimizations and implications of predictability, we now revisit the cases from the beginning of this chapter, to see how they might be represented within ScalPL.

4.3.1   Throttling and Buffering

Consider Figure 4.2 (a), which is a simplification of the previous example, with one consumer (observer) instead of two. When `consumer` activates, the Director can instantly (predictively) transition the control state of the resource back to be accessible by `producer`, which upon reactivation can begin creating the next content state in a different area, to be considered by the Director as the

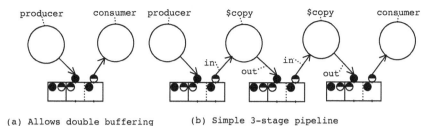

(a) Allows double buffering   (b) Simple 3-stage pipeline

Figure 4.2: Simple throttling/buffering in ScalPL.

subsequent content state (i.e. next version) for the resource. In computing, this technique is sometimes called **double buffering** – the use of two content areas so that one activity can create new content while the old content is still being utilized.

Suppose that we wish to disengage the producer and consumer even further, to allow further buffering (a queue) between them, while still suffering minimal copying overhead. One simple way to achieve this is as in Figure 4.2(b), which is similar to the previous example, but additional resources have been explicitly inserted to serve as additional stages of buffers, in a pipelined fashion. As might be expected, each $copy activity (effectively) simply copies the content state from its in role to its out role without modification, and then issues the associated transition, so the overall effect is to move the content state along all of the stages from producer to consumer. This may not appear to have low overhead at all, seemingly requiring two explicit copies of the content to get it from the producer to the consumer regardless of whether there is a build-up of content between the producer and consumer or not. But the **dollar-sign prefix** on $copy indicates (as it will throughout this book) that this copy construct is known (i.e. intrinsic) to ScalPL, so it is supplied as "standard equipment", and ScalPL knows how it works. In the case of $copy, that means that ScalPL will allow the one $copy tactic to be used generically for copying any kind of content, as long as the content domain for in is the same as that for out.[1] Moreover, the Director can thereby also be in on $copy's specification, and can optimize the plan accordingly if it wants. For example, the Director knows that it can get the same result by effectively "short circuiting" the stages if they are all empty (i.e. all in their initial state) when producer issues its transition, by just automatically treating the content state of the first resource as though it is the content state of the third one in that case, feeding it directly to consumer with no actual copying. More generally, whenever $copy is copying from a resource which is only replaced by other tactics, it (or the Director) can usually achieve its goal without copying by simply treating (renaming) the content state of the resource playing the in role as the content state of the resource playing the to role.

Such optimizations by the Director can generally be assumed by the planner, as long as they don't assume *too* much cleverness on its part, but in Chapter 13,

---

[1]In technical computerese, it would be said that $copy is polymorphic.

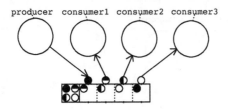

Figure 4.3: Multicast.

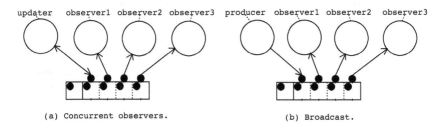

(a) Concurrent observers.   (b) Broadcast.

Figure 4.4: Single updater/producer, multiple observers.

after introducing arrays, we will show another approach to efficient buffering where the planner explicitly shortens or lengthens the buffer depending on how full it is, instead of relying on optimization of $copy.

4.3.2   Multicast

Now consider Figure 4.3. Here, producer creates new content state in the shared resource, and then transitions the control state to allow consumer1 to activate. As soon as it does, the Director can predictively transition the control state so that consumer2 can activate, and when it does, the same will allow consumer3 to activate, and when it does, the same will allow producer to activate again. In other words, as soon as producer issues its transition to the resource, all three consumer activities can concurrently observe the content state, even while producer may be creating the next version of the content state, with no snapshots required. Note that, in this case, every consumer activity is guaranteed to gain access to each version of the content state produced by producer (assuming that other roles don't keep one or more of them from activating at all). This is effectively a multicast from producer to the consumers.

4.3.3   Concurrent Observers and/or Broadcast

The plans in Figure 4.4 are similar to the previous example, except there is only one control state in the control domain of the resource, so all activities compete (in some sense) for the resource. Recall that the objective of concurrent observers was to prevent an observer from blocking another observer, even while an update should block new observers from coming in during the update. In

Figure 4.4(a), role binding permissions show that `updater` may update the content of the resource, and the three `observer`s only observe the content. The Director may use the predictability rule to allow multiple concurrent observers (without snapshots), but not to allow observers to access content state being updated by `updater`. This is, then, exactly the behavior normally associated with concurrent observers, with the additional flexibility that the Director here may also allow `updater` to activate on a separate, logically subsequent snapshot of the content state even while observers continue to access the previous one, providing even more concurrency than is usually afforded using other tools or representations.

Figure 4.4(b) is identical, except that the activity on the left (`producer`) has replace permission rather than update permission for its role binding. Since this means the producer does not need a snapshot, the Director will have little reason for ever allowing the observers to interfere with `producer`, especially if they are far apart and therefore do not physically access the same copy of the content state. The result, then, is that `producer` is free to produce new versions of the content state as rapidly as it likes, and the observers are free to absorb (observe) it as quickly as they care to, perhaps even catching every new version of content state multiple times or perhaps missing some versions. This is essentially identical to broadcast – perhaps surprising since it is so similar to the previous example.

4.3.4 Potential Oversimplifications

The broadcast and multicast examples here can be criticized for not capturing some of the "essence" of broadcast. For example, broadcast is usually defined as being independent of the number of receivers (observers), and here, each receiver must be explicitly shown in the plan. This is a shortcoming of the expressibility of our notation so far, and can be relaxed in future chapters as other constructs are introduced to allow dynamic modification and/or separate specification of parts of a strategy.

There are also generally some stated assumptions in broadcast paradigms about the relative speeds of the producer and observers and their access to the resource (i.e. the communication medium), to ensure a high likelihood that little (if any) content will be missed or re-observed by the observers. (In fact, the content is usually visualized as one continuous signal stream, or signal, rather than as independent frames of information.) These are real-time constraints, addressed separately in ScalPL, but unfortunately beyond the scope of this book.

Finally, in the real world, the producer and receivers of a broadcast are usually assumed to have some physical distance between them, meaning that the content generally takes time to propogate from the former to the latter, creating an implied buffering (e.g. a queue) of content between them (within the communication medium), and the length of that queue may be of different effective lengths for different receivers (at different distances from the producer). The simple example which was presented here is sufficient for modeling that, simply because it doesn't specify which version of the content each receiver will observe. However, if there is further interaction (via other unshown resources) between the producer and some consumers other than what is shown here, and those interactions might have different delay properties than the broadcast medium, a fully accurate representation might require the explicit introduction of buffering/queuing between the producer and receivers for the broadcast resource, such as that shown previously in Figure 4.2.

4.4 Summary

While proposing the form and function of tactics and actons in the previous chapter, we introduced the notion of a predictable role, meaning one that did not have replace (or modify) permission, and for which all of the transition bindings were to the same control state. We observed that, except for a case in which such an acton would produce no transition at all, the content state and control state of the resource bound to the role could be fully predicted as soon as the access began. We used that as justification for actually requiring that an acton issue (or at least seem to have issued) a transition to all of its predictable roles in some finite time. We didn't go into detail, but said it could help to overcome the limitation that only one acton could access a resource at one time.

This chapter has delved into the repercussions of the predictability rule, especially in terms of what the Director must and can do to enforce it, and the sorts of optimizations the the rule facilitates. Specifically, since access to a resource via a predictable role can delay other accesses to the resource for at most a finite amount of time, and time within ScalPL is not explicitly modeled, any such access can also be modeled as occurring in as brief an instant as one (e.g. the Director) deems to make it. In any event, the Director is held responsible for assuring that actons will (behave as though they) issue a transition to all of their predictable roles, even while also ensuring that subsequent accesses will not be allowed to interfere with content state in a way which would violate basic ScalPL rules.

The implications of that are manifold. Multiple activities accessing the same resource with predictable roles (which implies none having update permission) must not be allowed to interfere with each other for more than a finite time, and therefore each can just as well be allowed to not interfere with each other at all. Likewise, an activity with predictable access to a resource cannot be allowed to interfere for more than a finite length of time even with one which *does* modify the content, so in some cases, the predictable access *must* be given its own copy of content state (either retrieving it itself or being helped along by the Director), thereby implying buffering or queueing of content state, at least logically. And all of this can (and in some cases must) be accomplished while never violating the basic premise that, in terms of the ScalPL rules, only one access at a time is logically taking place.

Chapter 5

Making It Go: The Director

Chapter 3 described a strategy as consisting of contexts and resources, with each context assigned a tactic (i.e. a special form of plan) which, when ready, may be activated to become an acton (a special form of activity). The precise mechanism by which it would be activated was glossed over, and simply described as the job of an entity called a Director. Chapter 4 went even further, saying that the Director was also responsible for enforcing the special rule for predictable roles. Technically, the planner does not need to know how the Director carries out this work, so this chapter (which will describe such things) is not mandatory reading in order to understand ScalPL. However, any planner may want to get an idea of how different constructs might work on different platforms, to understand efficiency/portability tradeoffs, etc., and this chapter will help them to do so. It may also provide confidence (to potential skeptics) that ScalPL can indeed be efficiently implemented on a number of platforms.

5.1   Introduction

A plan, in itself, is static. To become an activity, there must be a real-world **platform** that is willing and able to carry out the plan. The platforms we will consider here will generally be one or more computers and/or people, usually with some set of temporary or **transient resources** at their disposal. These transient resources are not to be confused with the resources discussed so far: They are managed by the platform itself, in the cause of carrying out the plan, such as scratch paper, extra memory, or tools.

In our discussion here, whether a particular person or computer should be considered a platform in itself, or part of a larger platform (such as an organization, or a computer "grid" or "cloud") is entirely subjective. In other words, platforms are often hierarchical, consisting of other platforms, so we may refer to subplatforms (parts of larger platforms which may in themselves be considered platforms in their own right) and superplatforms. This chapter will begin to address the question of how a platform (whether independently or as part of a larger platform) goes about carrying out a srategy (which has been activated).

Discussion of platforms and the techiques they may use to carry out a plan is a double-edged sword. Since ScalPL has been specifically designed to be platform independent, the planner has very little direct influence over the platform or how it does its work, and doesn't technically need to know these things in order to develop a plan that works. For that reason, the reader can understand and benefit from the rest of this book while skipping this chapter. However, the planning approach (ScalPL) itself is specifically designed with knowledge of how these platforms work and their drawbacks and contingencies, so if the designer wants insight into why ScalPL looks the way it does, or when it might be beneficial to use one construct over another to make the plan work better on more platforms, this is a good place to start.

We will call the entity that takes care of activating a plan on a platform a **Director**. For now, we'll pretend that there is only one Director, but later we will discuss the prospect of there being perhaps many, working together, perhaps each with an expertise with a special style of platform, or perhaps even a special kind of plan.

5.2 Duties of the Director

The jobs of a Director are many, and varied. In many treatises on such things, the Director is not described as any one entity, but a collection of them, with some duties performed by an operating system, some by so-called middle-ware, and (in some cases) some manually by the application itself. But our goal here is not to describe any particular existing system, or to recommend how these should be organized on any future one, just to list the sorts of responsibilities which must be tended to, and some ways to tend to them. Those are responsibilities such as:

- Semantics: Ensuring that the rules of ScalPL are followed, such as ensuring that plans are activated when (and only when) the proper conditions are met, and that permissions, etc., are obeyed.

- Embedding/Mapping: Deciding where (i.e. on which platform(s), or parts thereof) any particular activity will take place.

- Scheduling: Deciding when a particular activity will take place, such as relative to other activities on the same platform or part of platform.

- Communication: Ensuring that information (such as the control and content state of resources) gets to where it needs to go in an efficient manner.

- Allocation and Garbage Collection: Using transient resources wisely, which includes allocating the necessary resources for newly created constructs (activities and resources) and deallocating those no which are no longer in use.

- Fault tolerance: Ensuring that damage is minimized when unforeseen and/or undesirable circumstances arise, and (when possible) continuing to make progress in spite of those circumstances (or when they subside).

- Security: Ensuring that external forces cannot intentionally adversely affect the behavior.

- Privacy: Ensuring that external entities cannot gain access to information on the platform, unless intended by the holder of the information.

- Real-time urgency: Ensuring that important deadlines are met by certain plans or parts thereof.

The following sections will address parts of the first four of these, each in turn. Some of the remaining bullets will be addressed in later chapters.

5.2.1 Semantics

The main job of the Director is simply to do its job at all – i.e. to ensure that the plan is carried out according to its specification and to the rules of ScalPL. This job can can be separated roughly into:

- Safety: Ensuring that a tactic can activate into an acton only when the conditions (i.e. control states) are right

- Liveness: Ensuring that a tactic will eventually activate, and when it does, will make progress toward its deterministic result.

- Determinism: Ensuring that each tactic indeed acts like a tactic – i.e. that the content results to resources filling replaceable roles (i.e. roles with replace or update usage), and transition results to all of the roles, are completely determined by only the tactic and the original contents of resources filling observable roles (with observe or update usage).

Safety

The only factor (discussed so far) that controls whether a tactic can be activated into an acton is the collective control states of the resources filling its roles – i.e. whether each has a control state matching one of the access dots on the associated role binding. One fairly straightforward way for a Director to keep track of this for all the contexts is to simply keep a **reasons count** (or **RC**) for each context, recording the number of that context's roles that are *not* yet ready. In other words, when a strategy begins, when all of the resources have their initial (solid/green) control state, each context holding a tactic is assigned a reasons count equal to its total number of role bindings (i.e. the number that could potentially be not ready) minus the number of those bindings which have an initial access dot (i.e. the number which are actually ready). If the reasons count for any context is zero, which in this initial case means that all of its roles have an initial access dot, that means there are no more reasons that the tactic within that context should not activate – so the Director is able (and sometimes obliged) to activate it.

Figure 5.1 shows a simple 3-context strategy at 3 points in time, from top to bottom. Assume that X, Y, and Z are tactics, and the left zone in each resource is labeled with the current control state of the resource (rather than the control

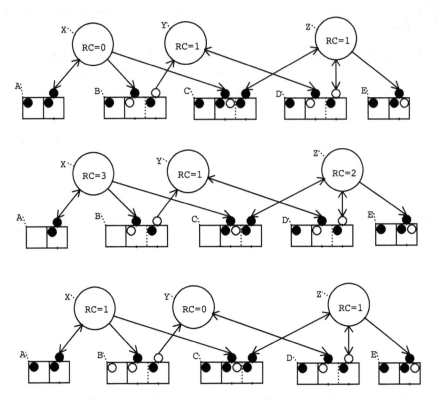

Figure 5.1: Reasons counts, evolving over time.

domain), shown empty when the resource has no control state. We show the reasons count of each context within its circle. In the top illustration, each resource has the initial control state, and only the left context has a reasons count of 0, so it is ready to activate. (For the center context, resource B has the wrong control state, and for the right context, D has the wrong control state.)

When the Director does activate a tactic (due to its reasons count reaching zero), it's first job is to effectively "steal" the control state away from all of the resources bound to its roles. This is accomplished, for each of its roles, by incrementing the reasons count of every context bound to the same resource with the same access dot, to record that there is now one more reason that that context cannot activate. Since the context which is activating is one of the contexts being incremented in each case, the reasons count of any activating context ends up being equal to its total number of roles (i.e. its reasons count was zero when it activated, and then is incremented once for each of its roles during the stealing process), reflecting that all of its own resource now have no control state. In the second illustration of Figure 5.1, X has activated in the left context, so the Director has incremented the RC of all of the contexts bound to A with a black access dot (only X), all those bound to the B with a black access dot (only X), and all those bound to C with a black access dot (X and Z).

86

When an acton within a context posts a transition to a role, the role binding and transition binding is consulted to understand which new control state is to be assigned to which resource. Then, the reasons count is decremented for each of the contexts bound to that resource with an access dot reflecting that new control state, signifying that all of them are one step closer to activating now that the resource has that control state. If any of those reasons counts reaches zero, then the tactic for that context becomes a candidate for activation. In the third illustration in the example, tactic X has issued transitions to all three roles. In issuing the one to A, changing it to black, the Director has decremented the RC for X; in issuing one to B and changing it to white, the Director has decremented the RC for Y; and in issuing the one to C and changing it to black, the Director has decremented the RC for both X and Z. As soon as the RC for Y had been decremented to zero, the Director was free to activate it.

That's pretty much the entire process for determining which contexts can activate their tactics. Note that, using this approach, there is no need to ever explicitly record the control state for the resources, since the reasons counts of the contexts, together with the (static) strategy itself, encode all the information required to decide when contexts can be activated or not. However, it is often still useful for debugging purposes, as well as other reasons to be introduced in subsequent chapters, to keep the control state of each resource in a form that can be understood and consulted by outside entities.

Also note that the entire process is event driven, which means that the Director doesn't need to be busy and/or aware at all times while the tactics are busy with other work: It can sleep (or be otherwise occupied) until a tactic performs a transition. In fact, instead of employing a separate entity as the Director, the issue statement itself can often serve in lieu of the Director for this function, often performing all reasons counts adjustments itself, and perhaps only calling on more complex logic of a full Director when a count reaches zero to help activate the associated tactic.

This approach can work even when there are multiple Directors (or concurrently active issue statements), but care must be taken to ensure that the activation of a tactic is always treated as one atomic action (so that tactics cannot be activated simultaneously in two different contexts bound to the same resource), and that operations to reasons counts are not fouled by concurrent access. The atomicity constraint requires that the RC for at most one context bound to any given control state of any given resource be decremented at any given time, or at least, if multiple such RCs are decremented concurrently and result in a zero RC, that only one of them result in an activation (thereby re-incrementing them).

The most efficient way to enforce these constraints with multiple Directors will depend on the platform, but generally speaking, the decisions revolve around how to partition/group access to the RCs. The two most obvious choices are to either treat each RC separately, meaning that the Director must acquire and/or release each of them independently, or to treat them all as part of one entity, allowing the Director to acquire and release them all at once, or something in the middle.

- Treating all RCs as part of one entity makes it easy and efficient, as the result of an issue statement, to acquire them all, perform the necessary decrements, and if any result in a zero RC, to effectively steal the control states from all of the associated resources by incrementing all of the RCs associated with that context's resources (i.e. the old control state), all as one atomic action. The major drawback to this approach is that it creates contention even between completely independent contexts. For example, in Figure 5.1, activity X could not issue a transition to A while Z issued a transition to D because the RCs for both X and Y would be accessed as a unit, even though those actions would have no logical bearing on one another.

- Accessing each RC independently makes less contention, but increases the overhead to acquire and release all of them independently. On performing an issue statement, each associated RC can be acquired independently by a Director to be decremented, but if any become zero, all of the RCs for that context's control states still need to be acquired at one time for its atomic activation – i.e. to increment them all to model the stealing of the control states. Even this is easier said than done, because if different Directors try to acquire some or all of the same RCs, they could easily deadlock with one another. This deadlock potential could be avoided by having each Director acquire the RCs in some fixed order, but it would mean (in general) first releasing the RCs already acquired (for the decrement operation), meaning that the RC could change between the time they are released and reacquired, making the reacquisition for naught.

A middle ground can be achieved by observing that the contention issues arise only when multiple contexts are bound to the same resource with identical access dots. We will say that contexts A and B are **rivals** for a resource (or in a symmetric **rivals relation**) if they are bound to that resource with identical access dots. What we wish is for a Director to acquire the reasons counts for all rivals at once. To this end, we will define a **rivalry** as the transitive closure of the rivals relation, meaning that if one context is in a rivalry, and it rivals another, then the other is also in the same rivalry, and so are *its* rivalries, etc. (independent of the resource involved). If all of the access dots on a context's role bindings are unique for their resource, that context is therefore alone in its rivalry. As a result, all of the contexts are partitioned among rivalries. In Figure 5.1, the two rivalries are {X, Z} and {Y}, since X and Z are both bound to resource C with black access dots. In Figure 5.2, the rivalries are {V,X,Y} and {W,Z}. As a result, if (for example) plan W in the latter figure was to perform a transition to resource B, it would acquire all of the reasons counts for rivalry {V,X,Y}, decrement the RC for X, and if it became zero, it would already be able to increment the RCs for V and Y without reacquiring any other RCs.

Liveness

So now that we can keep track of which contexts are allowed to activate (due to their RCs reaching zero), the question is which ones should (or must) be activated to preserve our rules, and how quickly, and how to do so with a limited platform.

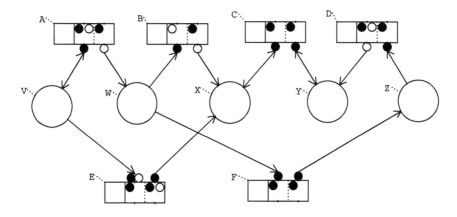

Figure 5.2: Example of rivalries.

In the best of all worlds, whenever a tactic became ready to activate, it would activate, and the resulting activity would proceed non-stop until it was finished. Well, almost: Even in the best of worlds, not all ready tactics can typically activate, since only one of those bound to the same control state (i.e. identical access dots) of a single resource can activate at once (and the others become unready). But even ignoring this contingency, the real world is much more troublesome: There are not generally enough transient resources available to activate all ready tactics and then to let them all proceed unencumbered. So to deal with contention for limited transient resources, how long can the Director delay the activation of a tactic?

The ScalPL rules state that if a particular tactic is continuously ready, then it will eventually activate, and (after activating) will eventually exhibit its deterministic behavior with regard to its resources. The implication is that those tactics which are not continuously ready are not required (by the semantic rules) to activate. A tactic in a context which shares no control states (i.e. for which every role is the only role bound to its resource with that color of access dot) will always remain continuously ready once it becomes ready, but for tactics which *do* share one or more control states with other contexts (so that multiple roles are bound to a resource with the same color of access dot), there may be no way to tell in advance whether it will continue to remain continuously ready or not. In such a case, one reasonable approach, lacking further guidance or information, is to always activate the one which has waited the longest (i.e. has been given the longest period to become unready) when appropriate transient resources become available (or known to soon become available). In a small, localized platform, this can be implemented by maintaining a single "run queue", and adding tactics to the end as they become ready, and removing tactics from the front to activate. If a tactic in the queue becomes unready, it is removed from the queue, and if it becomes ready again, is added back to the end. In a larger more distributed platform, maintaining a single run queue may be problematic, and it is not at all necessary. For example, a large platform consisting of smaller platforms could have a separate run queue for each smaller platform (though this in itself is also not always optimal).

Determinism

Once a tactic is activated, it must act deterministically, or else the platform is not truly supporting ScalPL. That is, the results (the new content state of resources filling replaceable roles, and the transitions to all of the roles) from an activity must be completely determined by only the content of the resources filling observable roles and the tactic which was activated. Note that this doesn't necessarily imply that the relationship between the initial contents and the results must be simple, obvious, or intuitive, even after observing the tactic, though that would obviously be desirable. The tactic is considered to act deterministically just as long as it always produces the same results for the same inputs (i.e. observable content state).

Since most computers and computer languages are deterministic in nature, they provide a very good basis upon which to build deterministic tactics. However, as mentioned in 3.3.2, they may also allow constructs that subvert determinism. Specifically, they may allow the activity to detect state (which may change from one activation to the next) other than that on its observable resources. For example, a platform may allow an activity to:

1. Communicate with devices which are not being modeled as resources, such as computer files or devices. (If access to such devices are required, they should be modeled explicitly as resources.)

2. Invoke "system functions" which provide access to other information, such as the time of day, or the amount of time that operations have used up, or how busy the computer is. (Again, such information can be modeled as being present on a resource, and accessed explicitly there.)

3. Communicate directly with another activity, or to find other information about another activity. (All communication with other activities should go through resources.)

4. Intentionally retain state internally between different activations of the same tactic, using constructs with names like "common" or "saved" or "static" storage/variables. (Resources make fine places to store state between tactic activations, and although it is not internal to the tactic, it is easy to ensure that only a single tactic is bound to it.)

5. Access left-over "garbage" state, such as on uninitialized variables or memory (or other transient resources), which are relatively unpredictable. The ability to access such state serves very little productive use, but can save a Director time by not requiring the extra step of initialization, which is often not technically required. (In non-compute environments, consider finding left-over numbers on a pad of scratch paper, and intentionally or accidentally using them in new calculations or decisions.)

6. Observe state on resources bound to roles with replace (but not observe) usage.

So, to ensure that tactics behave deterministically, these must be avoided. Some may be avoided syntactically, for example, just by ensuring that there is no use of "common" or "saved" variables in #4, or use of I/O statements or calls to system functions in #1 and #2. It may not be too difficult for a planner to intentionally circumvent such simple checking (such as by calling subroutines written in a more cryptic language to perform them), but often the goal is to avoid accidental inclusion of such elements, rather than to avoid subversive intentional inclusion.

Regarding #5 and #6, the answer is relatively simple: Initialize all variables, and all resources having replace (but not observe/update) usage, with some established fixed state when the activity begins. Some computers are able to dynamically sense when a program tries to access uninitialized storage, so might only need to initialize the storage at that time, thereby avoiding common situations where time is spent to initialize storage, even when the first thing the program will do is to store different state there.

5.2.2 Embedding/Mapping

In a platform consisting of subplatforms, the Director must also decide (or find out) which subplatform(s) to use for any particular activity. The decision can depend on a number of factors, including (for example) which subplatforms have (or are likely to have) available transient resources, which are most suitable for a particular activity, and which will be closest to (or will otherwise facilitate the simplest and/or quickest communication to) other subplatforms which will host other activities which will need to (sometimes) access the same content state (on common resources) with this one. Some or all of this information may be difficult to ascertain, but can sometimes be approximated or forced. For example, it may not be known precisely which transition might be issued to a particular role by a particular activity, and therefore what the new control state will be for the resource bound to that role, and therefore which activity will have access to it next, but the transition can often be guessed (predicted) based on previous frequency statistics.

The two extreme approaches to embedding are purely static and purely dynamic. In purely static embedding, no run-time information (such as the current location of resource contents) is used to determine where tactics should activate. Instead, each context in a strategy is assigned a subplatform where the tactics which activate within it should reside. In purely dynamic embedding, various run-time information, such as the availability of transient resources, the current location of resource contents, and the location of other activities may all be taken into account when deciding where a tactic should be activated. Generally, there is some middle ground, where static formulae may take some easily accessible dynamic metrics into account when computing where a tactic should be activated.

Another aspect of embedding is **mobility** – i.e. whether a single activity can move from one subplatform to another (after it has become an activity). ScalPL was designed with the assumption that actons will generally not be mobile, so will stick to a particular subplatform for their entire existence, but this is primarily for practical (rather than semantic or theoretical) reasons. Mobility can often consume extra time and trouble by requiring that transient resources are properly carried along or copied to the new location in the midst of their use. If actons are sufficiently short-lived, their mobility may be unnecessary, and mobility between actons is handled naturally by the normal movement of resource content states.

5.2.3 Scheduling

So, supposing that a tactic is activated (using the rules and techniques outlined under Semantics and Liveness, above), what then? Must it immediately start progressing, and using transient resources? And should it (or must it) continue to use those transient resources on its subplatform unabated until it is done, even if it doesn't seem to be getting much accomplished and other tactics can clearly use them? And what does "done" even mean?

If, as recommended earlier, actons are bottom-belted, the Director must know that all of the roles are ready for it to be activated, and that means having information about the control states of the resources bound to the tactic's context, which may just be in the form of Reasons Counts. But even if the Director knows these control states, that does not imply that the content state of the observable resources will necessarily be immediately available to the new activity. In fact, it is often wise to leave content state where it is created until it is determined where it will (or might) be needed next as the result of subsequent activations. So when a tactic is activated (i.e. the control state is stolen from its associated resources), there may be a time lag before all of the necessary content states can be moved to the subplatform where that tactic's body will commence execution, and until that time, there's little reason to assign any transient resources to the activity.

Once the content of observable resources are moved (or otherwise made available) to the appropriate subplatform, the general strategy is to assign any transient resources it may need and then to allow the activity to follow through to completion, unabated, when possible. In other words, the Director's sequence of operations is to first activate the tactic into an acton by forming a belt (i.e. atomically stealing the control state from its associated resources), then to efficiently move all of the observable content states of the associated resources to one (sub)platform, and only when they have all arrived, to then allocate transient resources and initiate the associated tactic to act upon the resource contents, and (as dictated by the tactic) issue transitions which may then make other contexts ready.

In the best of worlds, the sequential plan associated with the tactic would complete in some known and limited timeframe, thus making it easy to thereafter free the transient resources the activity was using (including processor time) to other actons. However, in general, complexity theory (Turing computability) shows that it is not possible to predict how many more steps will be needed to complete a sequential plan, or even to tell whether such a plan will ever terminate, assuming unlimited transient resources (represented in a Turing Machine by an infinite tape). Although all platforms are limited, between the extensive memory available on today's modern computers and the other resources reachable through a network, it is indeed effectively infinite. Even so, it is indeed possible to predict that an acton will terminate in a given time by artificially restricting the execution of an acton to some fixed number of steps or computer cycles, but (a) to be deterministic, the number of steps must indeed be exactly the same whenever the tactic is reexecuted, (b) it is becoming difficult in modern computer architectures with out-of-order (ooo) execution to deterministically limit execution to the "first n" instructions, and (c) it can be impractically difficult to come up with a viable fixed limit for each tactic, much less for each acton created from that tactic, which allows the tactic to produce useful results the vast majority of the time while restricting it from "running away" in others, as anyone who has had experience with older batch schedulers which required such estimates can attest.

Regardless of whether actons can be limited in their execution time, in many cases it may be advantageous to have at least a few actons sharing a single (sub)platform when multitasking is efficient. For example, modern computer processors are often optimized to look for alternate instructions to execute when a fetch to cache and/or local memory (where resource contents are assumed to reside) results in a stall, so having multiple actons in a runnable state at once can provide more options for such a processor to avoid stalls overall.

Taking all this into account, a practical way of proceeding, at least when the platform consists of one or more computers, is to initially assign some estimate to each acton for how long it will take to largely complete. If/when an acton runs over that estimate and other work is waiting, the acton would be stalled/frozen, and the platform would make its transient resources available to other waiting actons for some amount of time. Such a transition from one activity to another is called a **context switch**. When there are no other actons, or other actons have had similar opportunities to execute, transient resources are reallocated to the stalled/frozen acton for another chance, as many times as necessary. As time progresses, less time or less frequent opportunities could be given to the acton, to ensure it doesn't monopolize transient resources which could be used by other actons which may actually accomplish something. If the acton does ever complete, the amount of time it actually held transient resources could be recorded as a new estimate, for future activations, for when the first context switch should take place (if it is not completed by then). This approach of using context switches is similar to traditional timesharing, except that rather than using very small fixed quanta (execution times) between each switch, the quanta are potentially variable, and hopefully so large that execution of any acton could complete within one quantum (or a few quanta), thereby greatly minimizing the overhead of context switching. This is practical here because, unlike traditional timesharing which is often introduced to allow fair sharing between different users, the goal here is to maximize compute efficiency to complete multiple actons often devoted to accomplishing a single task (e.g. strategy). If mobility is required, this stalled/frozen state, between quanta, is likely the best time to effect it.

5.2.4 Communication

The introductory chapter covered some traditional communication models, most notably shared memory and message passing. Briefly, again:

- Message passing is akin to sending a letter or email: The entity with the information (the sender) has some idea of the entity that will need the information (the receiver), even if the sender may not necessarily know their precise location of the receiver, so the sender packages up (a copy of) the information, adds enough information to uniquely identify the intended receiver, and then leaves it to a transport service (e.g. US Postal Service or internet protocols) to find the recipient and deliver the message. When communication is slow relative to the distance between the communicating entities, and relatively large amounts are sent at once, message passing shines, because the message can be on its way (or already delivered) even before the recipient realizes it needs the information, making it excellent for hiding latency. On the other hand, in cases when the next entity needing information is not known, it is not so natural, and when the amount being communicated is small, overhead of packaging up the information can swamp the advantages.

- Shared memory is akin to a group of entities working closely together on a common document or white board. They are assumed to all have direct access to the shared area, and so communicating is simply a matter of putting something into the shared area where it can be observed and potentially changed by others. Advantages are mostly realized when the entities are close together and amounts communicated are relatively small, in which case overhead is small. When entities are far apart, and especially when next entity to access the information is known in advance, shared memory does not have the same advantages as passing messages.

The resources in ScalPL have been designed to support either or both of these approaches adeptly, depending upon the circumstances. That is, plans are blind to which activity will need the information next, or how far away it might be. Those factors are decided by the control states, role bindings, and the Director's embedding decisions of where the plans will be activated.

A Portable Communication Substrate: Cooperative Data Sharing (CDS)

To facilitate this sort of flexible communication, ScalPL is typically built upon a communication style which is between message passing and shared memory, called **Cooperative Data Sharing**, or **CDS**. CDS is then implemented to use message passing or shared memory (or whatever other tools might be available) depending on what is apt for the situation and platform. The result is that the entities using CDS to do the communication (which in the case of ScalPL would be the Director and the "issue...transition" steps, for example) do not need to worry about how the platform is laid out in order to get communication to happen efficiently.

CDS is built upon the following constructs:

- The platform is roughly partitioned into **CDS virtual processors**, each with a unique id, and each capable of hosting one or more activities. The only constraint on a virtual processor is that all of the activities hosted by a single virtual processor should be considered few enough and close enough to share communication space (described shortly as a whiteboard). So, in a computer network, one virtual processor might embody one computer processor, or a collection of them which share memory, but not multiple computers that are far from each other (e.g. experience a high latency between them). Virtual processors are spawned, either by some human or by another virtual processor, and each then initializes itself.

- Logically, each virtual processor has its own **CDS whiteboard**, which is an area in which **CDS regions** may be allocated, deleted, copied, etc. One can consider CDS regions as areas on the whiteboard (e.g. enclosed within boxes or circles) holding information. CDS regions may be different sizes, may grow or shrink, etc.

- A **CDS ticket** is a small document which identifies a particular CDS region in the CDS whiteboard. It effectively just points to the region. Any activity which needs to access a CDS region needs to possess a CDS ticket to the region, and if the activity wants to modify the region (the size or the information therein), the CDS ticket needs to possess modify permission.

- Each virtual processor has any number of **CDS queues**, each uniquely identified (in that virtual processor) with an integer, and each capable of holding a number of CDS tickets in a first-in first-out fashion. These queues can be considered as in/out boxes (mailboxes), in which tickets are kept in order. By default, CDS queues are accessible by other activities, but they can be restricted, to which virtual processors can add tickets to, and take tickets from, each CDS queue.

Based on those constructs, the following operations are available (as vaguely illustrated in Figure 5.3):

- spawnvp(*locations*): Spawn one or more virtual processors on the platform, as specified by *locations*. Each new virtual processor is responsible for invoking initvp (below). (The form of *locations* is intentionally vague here.)

- initvp(*wbsize, loqueue, hiqueue, queuesize*): Initialize this as a CDS virtual processor, with a whiteboard of size *wbsize*, and queues numbered *loqueue* to *hiqueue*, holding a total of at least *queuesize* tickets. (If this is somehow invoked before a corresponding spawnvp, it will not complete until such a spawnvp is invoked.)

- *vp*=myvp(): Return my virtual processor id.

- *pvp*=parentvp(): Return my parent's virtual processor id (i.e. that of the virtual processor which spawned me).

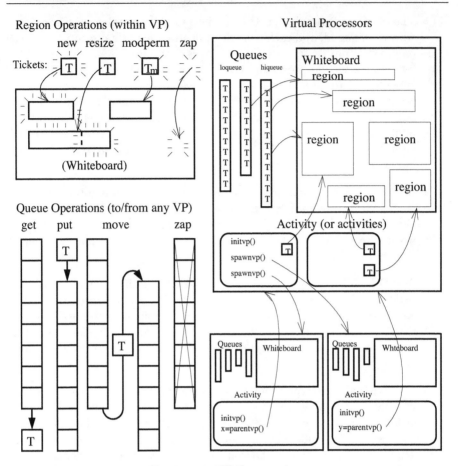

Figure 5.3: CDS operation.

- *ticket*=newticket(*size*): Create a new region of a given size on this virtual processor's whiteboard and return a ticket (with modify permission).

- modperm(*ticket*): Grant modify permission to *ticket*. (No effect if ticket already has modify permission.)

- resize(*ticket*,*newsize*): Change the size of *ticket*'s region to *newsize*. The ticket will also be granted modify permission, if it doesn't already have it.

- zapticket(*ticket*): Render a ticket unusable. Region will (eventually) be automatically destroyed if no other tickets to it exist.

- zapqueue(*vp*,*ticketqueue*): Remove and zap all the tickets from a queue *ticketqueue* in virtual processor *vp*.

- putticket(*ticket*,*vp*,*ticketqueue*,*zapq*,*zapt*): If *zapq* is TRUE, first zapqueue(*vp*,*ticketqueue*). Then, in the same atomic action, add a copy of ticket *ticket* to the end of ticket queue *ticketqueue* in virtual processor *vp*, and if *zapt* is TRUE, zapticket(*ticket*). Even if ticket is not zapped, it loses modify permission (if it had it).

- *ticket*=getticket(*vp*,*ticketqueue*,*remove*): Obtain a copy of the ticket from the head of ticket queue, and if *remove* is TRUE, remove it from the head of the queue. Ticket will not have modify permission.

- moveticket(*vpfrom*,*ticketqfrom*,*remove*,*vpto*,*ticketqto*,*zapqto*): Equivalent to putticket(getticket(*vpfrom*,*ticketqfrom*,*remove*), *vpto*,*ticketqto*,*zapqto*,TRUE). In other words, it takes a ticket (or copy thereof) from the head of one queue and adds it to another, optionally after zapping the latter and optionally remaining it from the former.

- With a valid (unzapped) ticket, you can access the contents of the region which the ticket points to, but you may only modify those contents if the ticket has modify permission. Upon finishing with a ticket you should zap it (using zapticket or putticket). If everyone follows these rules, CDS will ensure that others will not modify any region to which you hold a ticket.

These constructs and operations have been designed in this way to work well (and consistently) regardless of whether the virtual processors are far apart or close together, and to allow CDS to worry about the best way and best time to get information from one virtual processor to another. Internally, if multiple virtual processors are actually so close that they can share information among each other without message passing, CDS will just secretly merge their whiteboards, so communication among them simply becomes passing tickets around through the CDS queues. However, if a ticket is put into a far away CDS queue, CDS will automatically pass the contents of the associated region in a message to the other virtual processor, and place those contents into the destination's CDS whiteboard as a new region before adding its ticket to the queue there. In addition, CDS internally keeps a count of how many tickets there are for each region, and if that count goes to zero, CDS automatically deallocates the region. If a request is made for modify permission (using modperm) for a ticket, CDS checks to ensure that it is the only ticket for the region, and if not, CDS either waits to see if the other tickets are eventually zapped (thereby making it the only ticket), or (eventually) makes another copy of the region and modifies the ticket to point to the new copy. This is how CDS ensures that others will not modify any region to which you hold a ticket.

(The full CDS definition contains lots of other options as well, such as whether to wait for a ticket if the queue is empty on a getticket or to just fail, whether to wait awhile or copy immediately to facilitate modperm, ways to move and convert information within regions, operations on multiple queues at once, and actions (handlers) to initiate when queues become too empty or full, but those aren't central to the gist here.)

ScalPL Atop CDS

While CDS can be used on its own, independent of ScalPL, the goal here is to explain how the Director might use CDS to implement ScalPL.

The content state of a resource in ScalPL conforms closely to the content of a region in CDS. Obtaining observe permission to a ScalPL resource therefore corresponds closely with obtaining a ticket to the region, and obtaining update permission to a resource corresponds to obtaining modify permission to the ticket. If a ScalPL activity has replace permission (only) to a resource, without observe permission, that would be represented in CDS by creating a new region (with `newticket`).

At first glance, the control state of a resource in ScalPL seems to conform loosely with a queue in CDS. That is, like a control state, a CDS queue makes the contents available to other entities, can be used to denote the entities to which it is available, and sometimes, where those entities are. So one might consider a one-to-one correspondence between each control state of each resource in a ScalPL plan and one queue (in some virtual processor), and whenever an acton issues a transition to a particular role, to determine the control state to which that transition is bound, and to put the ticket for the associated region into that queue. That turns out to be a bad idea. Not only does it potentially result in moving regions around needlessly (e.g. when control states are transitioned by nodata roles, even with no intervening access to the resource contents), each resource has at most one control state at a time, and most of the effects of control state are already handled by the Director anyway (as explained earlier in this chapter).

So, more sensible is to treat queues for what they are – ways of efficiently getting information between virtual processors. The two main kinds of information we need to move are (1) the control state of resources and/or transitions to them, to the virtual processors hosting the parts of the Director that are keeping track of the contexts bound to those control states, and (2) the content states of resources, to the virtual processors hosting the actons accessing those resources.

5.3   Example of a Simple Director

This is an example of how a simple Director might work, to demonstrate how some of the issues in previous sections might be integrated into a solution. Implementing a full Director is beyond our scope, but it is our intent to demonstrate the feasibility of implementing one.

5.3.1   Embedding (Static)

Consider that an embedding step (described earlier) performs the following two steps:

- Statically assigns each context to a virtual processor (VP), perhaps multiple contexts per VP. When we say "context c is assigned to VP v", we mean that any tactic to be activated in context c will take place on VP

v. In addition, if actons are bottom-belted (as they will be here), the actual initiation (as in, allocation of transient resources) can (and will) be delayed until after all of the observable resource contents are local to VP v.

- Statically assigns each rivalry to a VP, perhaps multiple rivalries per. By "rivalry r assigned to VP v", we mean that the decision of which tactics will be activated in rivalry r (i.e. in a context within that rivalry) and when they will be activated will be made on VP v.

It is generally advantageous to always assign a rivalry to the same virtual processor as at least one of the contexts in that rivalry. For example, if a rivalry contains only one context, it can minimize communication overhead to have the same VP always handle both. There may be exceptions, such as when particular parts of the platform are specially equipped to handle only scheduling within rivalries, rather than any "real work" that takes place within contexts.

Note that neither contexts nor rivalries need to be statically assigned, such as during an embedding step: We have just made that choice in this case for the purpose of our example. Instead, for each rivalry, all of the reasons counts could (for example) be held on a single CDS region, which could then be accessed (remotely if necessary) by any context performing a transition, thereby effectively moving the rivalry from place to place. Likewise, the place to activate a tactic could be determined by a rivalry dynamically at the time the decision to activate is made, perhaps based upon where the resource contents that will need to be observed by that context currently reside (i.e. to minimize travel time before the actual activation), and/or upon which VPs have the lightest computational load at the time of activation.

In addition to information where each context and rivalry is embedded, before a context can initiate a tactic (as bottom belted), it will need to know that the specific content states it is to observe (or update), including the tactic to activate (discussed in later chapters as $plan), are local to the context's VP. It is not good enough to just know that some content state for each of the appropriate resources is currently present on the VP, since some may be out of date: There may be other copies of the content state for the same resource elsewhere which have since been modified (i.e. are more up-to-date versions/snapshots). So the context must also check to ensure that the correct *version* of each content state is present. To achieve this, we will append onto each content state of each resource a version number, hidden from the view of activities accessing that content state. That version number will start at zero, and then will be incremented each time that state may be changed – i.e. each time the resource is accessed by an activity with replace (or update) usage. Then, a context can consult the version number of any content state (for a particular resource) on its VP to see if it's the one it really needs.

It is the rivalry's job to tell each context which versions of the content states it needs before initiation. That is, when the rivalry decides (based on control states and/or reasons counts) which context within that rivalry should activate next, and informs that context (which may be on the same or a different VP) thereof, it also informs it which versions it needs for each of its observable (and updateable) resources. This means that the rivalry itself must have this version number at its disposal, which in turn means that it must be informed of this when it is informed of a transition (or new control state) by a context. So, each rivalry keeps track of not only the reasons counts for the contexts within its rivalry, but also the version number of the content state of each resource which may be observed by those contexts.

5.3.2 Content State Movement

That provides a big picture view of how information about control states and version numbers gets from place to place and when (from context to rivalry during transition, and from rivalry to new context during activation), but when does the content state actually move from one place to another, from the last context which replaced (or updated) it to the next one that needs to observe (or update) it, and which entity initiates the movement?

For the first of these (i.e. when to move the content), there are several options, based on balancing four factors:

1. the benefits of hiding latency (i.e. initiating movement of the content state as early as possible);

2. the penalty for using communication bandwidth and/or storage space needlessly (i.e. for moving and/or storing content state that isn't eventually used at its destination);

3. the ability to hide latency (i.e. knowing where the content state may be needed next sufficiently long before it is needed there); and

4. the likelihood the content will be needed on any particular VP.

The first two of these depend on the platform and the last two depend primarily on the plan (i.e. strategy) and embedding. For example, if the strategy calls for a tactic to produce some content state very early, and specifies that there is a 100% chance (perhaps as a result of predictability) that it will next be observed in a particular context much later (i.e. after many other activities), then these parameters (i.e. values for factors 3 and 4 in the list) might make it possible to initiate movement of the content from the producer to the observer long before it is needed there, regardless of how the platform behaves regarding factors 1 and 2. This is essentially a message-passing ("push") style of communicattion. If, however, there was only a 10% probability that the content would be observed in that future context (i.e. that a tactic would be activated there), then the decision of when to move the content (if at all) could depend on factors like 1 and 2. For example, if the platform had very slow communication (1), but plenty of available bandwidth (2), then it might be sensible to begin moving the information to the potential observer right after it is created, just in case it *is* needed there. But, if the platform has fast communication (1) but low bandwidth or restricted storage on the destination VP (2), it might make more sense to put off the communication until the certainty it is needed increases, such as until after the context on that VP actually activates a tactic to observe

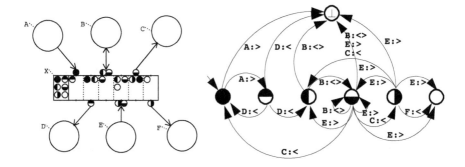

Figure 5.4: A resource and associated FSM.

the content state, thereby insuring 100% that the content will be needed there. This latter case would resemble more of a shared-memory ("pull", "on-demand") style of communication.

To come up with information to help determine the fourth factor, one must understand the possible patterns of access of the content state for the resource. That is, from any given starting control state (i.e. after a particular tactic has finished accessing the resource and issued a transition), will (or might) the content state be observed again? Before it is replaced? In every case, or only sometimes? To answer these sorts of questions, it helps to model the resource's control states as a so-called Finite State Machine (FSM), also known as Finite State Automata (FSA) or State Transition Diagram. Once this representation has been developed, any number of approaches from established theory can be used to analyze the patterns and/or probabilities.

An FSM, as depicted on the right of Figure 5.4, is simply a set of states, represented as circles, and a set of transitions, represented as directed arcs (arrows) from one state to another. A lone arrow with no initial state is used to identify (point to) one of the states as the initial state, and one or more states may be identified as final states by showing them as two nested circles. Simply put, an FSM is a very general way of representing sequences of states and/or transitions that lead from the initial state to other states: Such a sequence is considered to be represented by the FSM if and only if one can obtain that sequence of states and/or transitions by starting at the initial state and following the transition arrows one at a time, recording the states and/or transitions along the way. Such a sequence always ends when an end state is reached. In our case, each state in the FSM will represent a control state from the resource being modeled, and the transitions in the FSM will represent possible transition bindings of the resource – i.e. the activation of a tactic, and the issuance of that transition by the resulting acton.

Figure 5.4 shows a particularly (ridiculously) complex example of a resource and a corresponding FSM. To construct an FSM from a resource, simply create one state in the FSM (represented by a circle) for each control state in the resource's control domain, and if the resource is a formal resource, one final state (sometimes represented by a circle within a circle) for each element of the transition domain of the resource (from within the transition box). For a very precise/complete drawing, add another state circle representing the bottom ($\perp$) control state, the stateless condition that a resource ends up in when a transition is not issued by a particular acton. Then draw an arc (arrow) from state A to state B whenever the resource has a role binding with an access dot corresponding to A, and a transition binding corresponding to B. For any role binding that is not predictable (i.e. has replace or update permission, or transitions to multiple control states), add another FSM transition from the state corresponding to the access dot to the bottom control state. Label each arc to identify the context, the role name (if not obvious), the transition name (if important and not obvious), and the permissions on the role binding. (In the example, we use the label notation $C:p$ for context C and permission p, where p is < for observe, > for replace, and <> for update.) Mark the FSM state corresponding to the initial control state as the start state, by adding an arc pointing from nowhere to it.

Such an FSM, then, can be used to illustrate if (and how) it is possible to get from any control state to any other control state for a resource (or to any resource transition, for formal resources) – i.e. which tactics must activate, and the access permissions on the role bindings used by those activities. In the example, since the only arcs from the initial state are for A with replace permission, we know that the initial content state will never be observed. Then, from the next control state (represented with the dark top light bottom), all three outgoing arcs/transitions are labeled $D:<$, so we know that if a tactic activates in D, it may observe the content state created by A. (Note that even though D's role binding has observe permission, tactic D could theoretically have nodata usage on that role, still obviating the need to move the content state to D.) Two different control states (the initial again, or the left-dark right-white) are potentially reachable via D, and for the latter, all transitions originating there are labeled $B:<>$, so B may also need the content state created by A, meaning that from A, a Director might want to immediately communicate the content state to both D's and B's VP to hide latency. Further analysis is possible.

Again, this control state analysis is primarily to determine the parameters of factor 4, above. Taken together, the four factors can be used to (statically) determine when content state should be moved from one place to another, and therefore, what should initiate the movement: If the movement is to occur immediately when the transition occurs, the context can initiate it, but if it is to sit where it is until a rivalry determines that a particular tactic will be activated, that same rivalry can initiate movement of the content state.

5.3.3   Finding Content State

As discussed, there are cases where the current location, or desired next location, of content state may not be known (or knowable) statically. This is especially true when multiple contexts (assigned to different VPs) update or replace the content, and then any one of many contexts (assigned to different VPs) may subsequently observe that content depending on which transitions are issued by intervening contexts. There are also other less extreme cases, such as when there are multiple updating contexts, and only one potential subsequent observing context, but because that potential observer activates only rarely, and perhaps especially because platform bandwidth is limited and/or latency is low, it is desireable not to move the content state to the observer's context until it is needed there, meaning that the content may sit (in the interim) on any number of different VPs where it was last updated.

On the other extreme, if bandwidth is plentiful and latency is high, it may be advantageous to immediately move any replaced or updated content state to multiple VPs where it might potentially be observed (to hide latency), just in case it is. And between those extremes, it may make sense to move the content close to any potential observers (or to just the most likely observer), and then allow the last leg of the trip to be made (for some observers) only when the observer activates.

In these cases, it is important to keep track of where the content state may be, so that when a context with observe or update permission activates a tactic, the content state can be rapidly moved to the new location. In most cases, this tracking can follow the tracking of control state. That is, assuming an activity knows the location of the content state (such as because it has just replaced or updated it, or at least observed it, so it is on the same VP as the activity), when the activity issues a control state transition and passes the new control state info to the new rivalry, it can also pass the location of the content state to that rivalry. If the rivalry decides to activate a tactic in a context which does not already have that content state locally, but which needs it, the rivalry can also initiate movement of that content state to the context's VP.

The main issues arise when, between activations which access the content state of a resource, there are one or more activations in contexts which do not access the content state because they are bound to the resource with nodata permission. In these cases, the content state does not technically need to be passed to these intervening contexts. However, even here, the location of the content state can be passed to the contexts of those intervening activities, which can then still pass that location on to subsequent rivalries upon control state transitions, etc., so that when a tactic activates in a context which *does* need the content state, it will know where it is. Another option is for a context or rivalry to immediately disseminate the location of the content state directly to other rivalries which might need to make use of it, without it passing through intermediate contexts. (The assumption here is that the location of the content state is easier to pass than the content state itself, because it is likely to consume less bandwidth. If that's not the case, then passing the content state itself would be preferred, as mentioned earlier.)

5.4 Remaining Director Duties

The above sections have just touched on the issues to be addressed by a Director, and some ways to go about them. It would seem beyond the scope of this book to actually include a full implementation of a Director, but the above discussion provides significant insight into the data structures and communication protocols which a Director can use to carry our ScalPL plans efficiently on a number of different plaftorms.

Several of the duties described earlier have not been covered here, specifically:

- Allocation and Garbage Collection

- Fault Tolerance

- Security

- Privacy

- Enforcing Real-Time urgency/Constraints

Some of these will be addressed in subsequent chapters, or at least, cannot be well addressed until information in subsequent chapters has been introduced. In the simplest cases presented so far, many of these are straightforward or not especially applicable.

5.5 Summary

A plan describes the conditions under which activations are to take place, and what is to happen when activations occur, but generally speaking, more work is required to ensure that the plan follows the appropriate rules, and makes effective use of a platform (the entity carrying out the plan) and the transient resources at its disposal. Here, we describe the entity performing this work as the Director. (Other treatises will use different terminology, and many will not describe it as a single entity, but a collection thereof.) General functions performed by the Director include:

- Semantics: Ensuring that the rules of ScalPL are followed, such as ensuring that plans are activated when (and only when) the proper conditions are met, and that permissions, etc., are obeyed.

- Embedding/Mapping: Deciding where (i.e. on which platform(s), or parts thereof) any particular activity will take place.

- Scheduling: Deciding when a particular activity will take place, such as relative to other activities on the same platform or part of platform.

- Communication: Ensuring that information (such as the control and content state of resources) gets to where it needs to go in an efficient manner.

- Allocation and Garbage Collection: Using transient resources wisely, which includes allocating the necessary resources for newly created constructs (activities and resources) and deallocating those no which are no longer in use.

- Fault tolerance: Ensuring that damage is minimized when unforeseen and/or undesirable circumstances arise, and (when possible) continuing to make progress in spite of those circumstances (or when they subside).

- Security: Ensuring that external forces cannot intentionally adversely affect the behavior.

- Privacy: Ensuring that external entities cannot gain access to information on the platform, unless intended by the holder of the information.

- Real-time urgency: Ensuring that important deadlines are met by certain plans or parts thereof.

Tbe chapter described a diverse collection of techniques and approaches that a Director can use to achieve many of these goals.

Chapter 6

Encapsulation: Building More Complex Activities

So far, we have described only one way of building actons into more complex activities; the strategies described in Chapter 2, consisting of contexts bound to resources with role bindings. These constructs are indeed powerful ways to combine tactics, but strategies (so far) do not have interfaces, allowing only two levels of planning for now: The strategy at the top, with tactics within each of its contexts. Our stated intention in deriving tactics and actons has been to build more complex plans and activities out of them, and that can be accomplished by endowing strategies with interfaces, thereby allowing strategies as well as tactics to be activated within contexts. Since strategies can be build to exhibit far more complex behavior that a tactic, and to possess properties which we have forbidden from actons, this is at least a step toward that goal. This chapter will first highlight the issues and complications of encapsulating a strategy so as to be activateable within the context of another plan, and will then propose a form for addressing those issues.

6.1 Issues with Interfacing Strategies

This goal of creating encapsulated strategies (with interfaces) can be considered from two perspectives. The top down perspective is to start with a large strategy built from the constructs described so far (resources, contexts, etc.) and then to ask how we might identify and encapsulate some part of it, a "subplan", so that we could replace that encapsulated part with a single context within which that subplan could be activated. The bottom up perspective would be to start with a strategy that needs to interact with some larger environment, whether that environment is another strategy, an operating system, or a grid infrastructure, and consider what kinds of new constructs we need to make that happen. Both of these perspectives can be regarded as addressing the same issue. The bottom line is that we need a way to specify an interface for a strategy (subplan), indicating how activities in the subplan are to access (if necessary) the resources bound to that context in the other strategy. This means that the activity must have a way of observing and/or replacing the contents of those resources and of issuing transitions to those resources.

First, some terminology. When an activity (say A) is activated within a context C of another activity (say B), we will refer to activity A as a **child** of activity B, and to activity B as the **parent** of activity A, and to C as being A's context (in activity B). We may also (rather sloppily) refer to A's plan as the child of B's plan, and B's plan as the parent of A's plan, even though there is no specific relationship between these plans in the general case, one just happens to reference the other, as any number of other plans might: It is just easier to refer to plan X as being the parent (or child) of plan Y, when the activities involved are understood, than to refer to plan X as being the plan of an activity which is the parent (or child) of another activity having plan Y.

6.1.1 Breaking Existing Plans Down into Smaller Plans

To understand some of the issues involved, consider circumscribing (i.e. drawing a continuous ring-like barrier around) some set of contexts and resources within a plan (say, plan P, for parent) with the intent of making the circumscribed portion into a separate plan (say, plan C, for child). That is, we hope to replace the circumscribed portion in P with a single context ("C's context") in which we can activate that separate plan (C) with exactly the same results as before the transformation. See Figure 6.1 for complications that may arise if that is done haphazardly.

First, the barrier cannot be drawn just anywhere: It must be drawn to slice through role bindings only, such that each sliced role binding connects a context on the inside of the barrier (i.e. within C) to a resource on the outside (i.e. within P). Otherwise, as shown in Figure 6.1(a), the resulting context won't properly connect to resources (i.e. role binding g goes between contexts C and Z rather than between a context and a resource).

Second, the encapsulation could result in two contexts from within C connected to the same resource outside of C, as in Figure 6.1(b). Since they could have different names and transition bindings, both role bindings would need to be represented coming from C's context to the same resource in P. If the logic of C requires them to both be bound to the same resource, then there should be a way for C to enforce that, rather than trusting the parent (P) to reliably bind them to the same resource when necessary.

Third, even if we don't allow multiple contexts from within C to bind to the same resource outside of C, there's still an issue with role names. That is, if the names of the role bindings are always carried unchanged as they pass through the newly-drawn boundary, there's no assurance that the names for the role bindings on C's context in P will be unique, since they may have originated from different contexts within C. See Figure 6.1(c). So C should have some control over what its roles will be named within P, regardless of what the equivalent roles were named within C.

Fourth, and strongly related to the third, even if the role binding names that pass through the barrier are unique for C, those names (or the names of the transitions) may become less meaningful as they pass through the barrier.

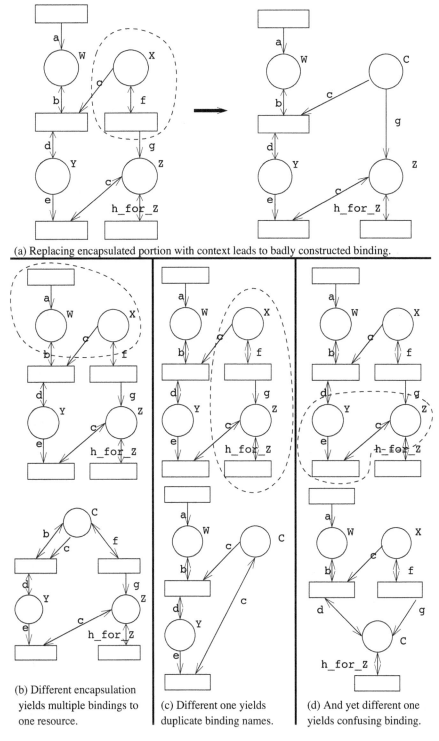

(a) Replacing encapsulated portion with context leads to badly constructed binding.

(b) Different encapsulation yields multiple bindings to one resource.

(c) Different one yields duplicate binding names.

(d) And yet different one yields confusing binding.

Figure 6.1: Problems with encapsulating part of plan into a separate context.

Within C, the role bindings are describing part of the behavior of one of the components of C, but within P (as a role binding on C's context), they are describing part of the behavior of C as a whole, from the perspective of P. Those may not be the same. See Figure 6.1(d).

And finally, in all of the examples from Figure 6.1, the role bindings in C which are snipped by the new barrier are now but dangling lines in C. That means that information about the corresponding roles which would could have been gleaned from the binding with the resource may not be apparent within C, information such as the transition domain (which can be gleaned from the transition bindings), the content domain (which is restricted by the resource's content domain), and perhaps even the role name itself (if borrowed from the resource name). This decreases the amount of correctness checking we can do for C, separate from P. To regain this abiity, we will want some way of bringing this information about these roles back inside of C, even if the actual role bindings to resources (in P) are accomplished external to C.

6.1.2 Building Existing Plans Up into Bigger Plans

Now we'll consider the same issue from the other direction. Instead of considering how to break an existing big plan down into smaller pieces, consider building a bigger plan up from existing pieces. Say that we're developing a plan for reconditioning furniture for resale, called `upgrade_furniture`. In addition to assessing the condition of the furniture, cleaning it, and labeling it, the plan will, under certain circumstances, require that a particular piece of furniture be repainted. However, the planner knows nothing about repainting furniture, so wishes to delegate that portion of the plan out to another planner. He puts a context into the `upgrade_furniture` plan as a place holder for a new plan called `repaint` to be developed separately. That context has two roles, one representing the piece of furniture, `furniture`, with update permission, and one describing the color of paint to use, `color`, with observe permission. Each has a single `done` transition signifying that the `repaint` activity is finished with it. See Figure 6.2(a).

Now another planner is to provide the `repaint` plan. She already has a plan called `strip` for stripping off the old finish (paint) from a piece of furniture (and dumping it into the `trash`), and another called `paint` for painting a piece of furniture, as roughly indicated in Figure 6.2(b) – which is not a legal ScalPL diagram. All she needs to do is to put these together, sequentially, into the `repaint` plan. The role names used by these plans are slightly different (`piece` instead of `furniture`, and `paint_color` instead of `color`). Even more troublesome, to make these smaller plans access the piece of furniture in the proper order (first `strip`, then `paint`), she would like to add another control state to `furniture` so that the end result (effectively if not literally) looks like Figure 6.2(c). But the planner of `upgrade_furniture` could not have guessed the internal workings or names used in `repaint` to make the roles and transitions work out right. After all, that's the whole idea of delegating that planning in the first place, to not *have* to know its internal workings.

So, what we would like is if the planner for `repaint` not only had control

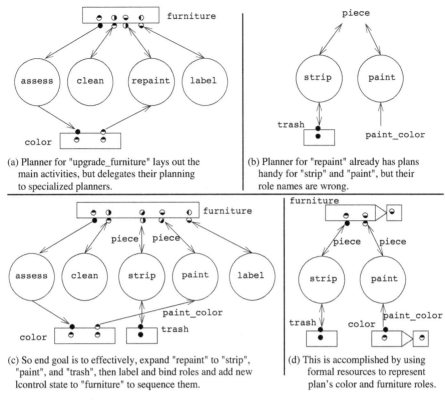

(a) Planner for "upgrade_furniture" lays out the main activities, but delegates their planning to specialized planners.

(b) Planner for "repaint" already has plans handy for "strip" and "paint", but their role names are wrong.

(c) So end goal is to effectively, expand "repaint" to "strip", "paint", and "trash", then label and bind roles and add new lcontrol state to "furniture" to sequence them.

(d) This is accomplished by using formal resources to represent plan's color and furniture roles.

Figure 6.2: **repaint** plan is (a) invented, (b) sketched, (c) visualized after integration, and (d) shown in final form.

over the role and transition names for each of the roles of that plan, but if she could also effectively introduce new internal control states for some of the resources it would access in its parent (**upgrade_furniture**) such that those control states would only affect, and be visible to, **repaint**. Figure 6.2(d) shows how we will eventually represent this, presented in the next section, in official, legal ScalPL form, so that it it can fit into the **repaint** context in (a).

6.1.3   Activity Lifetime

Getting the control state interactions right between the child strategy and the parent strategy is only part of the issue. Recall that our goal is to facilitate the construction of plans (strategies) which result in activities which behave any way we like, which can be anything from an acton to a nondeterministic, non-belted, non-atomic, non-serializable activity with internal state, resource dependences, and side effects.

So, at one end of that spectrum, if we want to be able to build strategies with activities which behave like an acton, it should be possible to make them deterministic, atomic, belted, and with no persistent internal state or other side effects. And some of these requirements, like atomicity and beltedness, have a more basic requirement – that the activity have a limited lifetime, at least logically. That is, while there may be cases where we want a context to simply serve as a convenient shorthand for the permanent inclusion of a substrategy (the way we have described `repaint`, above), in general, a plan associated with a context can be activated (e.g. only under certain circumstances), and may terminate and perhaps be activated anew again later, like an acton. Limited lifetimes can also aid in avoiding persistent internal state, when that is desired, since each time a strategy is activated, its resources therein could be made to start out with fresh versions of their initial control and data state.

Consider some alternatives for how we might make an activity (resulting from a strategy) finish. For example, there might be some event, such as activating some special "stop!" plan, or issuing some special transition or accessing some special resource, which might instruct the Director to bring the activity holding that context or resource to an immediate halt. While this might work in some cases, in most, it is contrary to many of our goals, which are to facilitate concurrency, and to make actions in one part of a strategy independent of those in another part. It would not even be clear what it would mean to bring an activity to "an immediate halt" from that perspective. (We would certainly at least want atomic activities, like actons, within the terminating activity which have effects visible from outside of the terminating activity, to complete or back out – i.e. to retain their atomicity.)

If we wish to create acton-like activities from strategies, we would like to facilitate the creation of a belt, or at least a "forward belt" – i.e. a point in time after which no further external resources can be acquired/accessed, even though external resources can be relinquished. If we can accomplish that, termination follows very naturally: If all of the resources external are relinquished after the creation of the forward belt, then the activity is, by definition, terminated, because it can no longer have any effect on its environment (i.e. the resources therein).

6.2   Forming Activateable Plans from Strategies

In this section, constructs to address the issues just raised will be presented.

6.2.1   Formal Resources: Roles for Strategies

To facilitate roles for strategies, we introduce a new form of resource called a **formal resource** which resides in the child strategy. A formal resource is visually distinguishable from a standard (non-formal) resource only by its **transition box**, an extra square attached to the right end with an isosceles triangle: See the resources named `furniture` and `color` in Figure 6.2(d). Each formal resource in a strategy represents one role in the child strategy's interface, that role having the same name as the resource. When the strategy is activated (as a child activity) within the context of another (parent) activity, and that role is bound there (with a role binding), the resource in the parent activity to which a role is bound is called its **actual resource**, so each role binding associates an actual resource in the parent activity with a formal resource in the child activity. (The actual resource in the parent may, in fact, be another formal resource, in which case it will also be associated with an actual resource in its parent, etc.)

Other than for its transition box, a formal resource looks and acts much like other resources, as far as the strategy it is in is concerned: As usual, the formal resource (effectively) has control states and content states, the control domain is commonly represented by dots in the left end of the resource's rectangle, and roles from contexts are bound to that rectangle with access dots, and the transitions for those roles may be bound to its control states.

The "magic" of a formal resource lies in its transition box. That box contains a set of dots, called **final dots**, which resemble control states, unique in color/pattern relative to each other and relative to the dots in the control domain. But instead of representing control states of the formal resource, these final dots actually represent the transition domain of the role which the formal resource represents, each dot being labeled with the name of one of the transitions in the role's transition domain. So, when a role binding in the parent effectively associates this formal resource with an actual resource, the transition bindings for that role binding will correspond to the *names* (*not* necessarily the colors/patterns) of these final dots in this transition box.

Although a formal resource behaves basically as though it has its own content and control state, it actually borrows both from its actual resource. The content state can just be considered as shared between both. The control state operates according to very specific rules, as shown in the furniture refinishing example in Figure 6.3:

1. Instead of starting out with an initial (green/solid) control state, the formal resource (e.g. `furniture` in the example) actually effectively starts with no control state at all. It automatically acquires an initial control state whenever the associated role binding in the parent is ready – i.e. whenever the control state of the actual resource in the parent matches an access dot on the role binding corresponding to the formal resource. So, if that role in the parent is ready, not only is the actual resource in the parent accessible by other contexts in the parent (if any) bound to that same control state (none in the example), but the formal resource in the child (`strip` in the example) is also accessible by any contexts in the child bound to its initial control state.

2. If such an activity (say an acton) in the child actually does access the formal resource (`strip` in the example), then (as usual) it steals the control state from the formal resource. However, in this case (when the formal is in its initial control state), the control state is also effectively stolen from the actual resource in the parent. And when (if ever) the activity in the child issues a transition to the formal resource, to some other control state (represented in the formal resource's control domain), this is visible only to the child: The formal resource in the parent is effectively left without a control state, for now.

113

Whenever a resource becomes ready for the context containing a child strategy (i.e. the control state of the actual resource matches the access dot of the role binding, the formal resource in the child for that role gets its initial control state.

When control state of formal resource in child matches a final dot, a transition of the same name as that dot is issued to the role, thereby transfering the control state back to the actual resource in the parent.

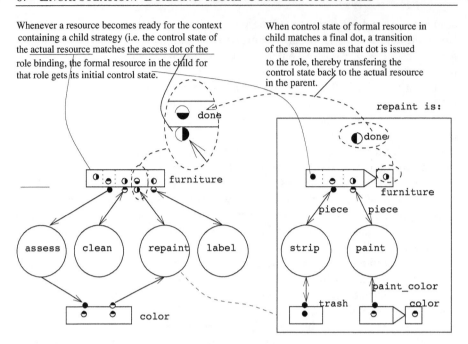

Figure 6.3: How control state moves between actual and formal resource.

3. However, if an activity in the child (**paint** in the example) issues a transition to the formal resource which corresponds to one of the final dots (in the transition box) rather than one in the control domain, then that designates that a transition of the same *name* (**done** in the example) is to be issued to the role in the parent, thus returning the control state to the actual resource there according to the binding for that transition (**done** in this case). Note that the color/design of the final dot in the child is unrelated to anything in the parent: It is used only in the child to find the name of the transition which should be issued to the parent.

The effect, then, is that if any activity in the child begins to access the formal resource (only possible when the associated role binding to the actual resource in the parent is ready), the child steals the control state of the actual resource for awhile, it rattles around in the formal resource of the child for awhile (while the state of the formal resource remains within its control domain), and then (perhaps eventually) that control state (and thereby the ability to access the content state) returns back to the actual resource in the parent when there is a transition matching a final dot. We will say that a formal resource is **active** if the control state has been thus stolen from the parent by its plan (the child) and not yet returned to the parent. From the perspective of the parent, there's no telling whether just one activity in the child accessed the resource in the interim, or one hundred activities. Note that even if the activity accessing the formal resource in the child is not an acton, but is instead yet another more complex activity resulting from another strategy, the logic is the same: Somewhere down the line, the thing actually accessing the formal resource *will* be an acton, and when it steals the control state, it will be stolen from the actual resource in its parent, and if that is a formal resource, it will be stolen from its actual resource in its parent, etc., all the way up until it is stolen from an actual resource that is *not* also a formal resource.

A few special rules pertain to formal resources to avoid any ambiguity.

1. No role bound to the formal resource can have a transition binding back to the initial control state (green/solid) of the formal resource. Why? If it *was* allowed, and the effect was to also return the control state to the actual resource corresponding to the access dot, it could be very counter-intuitive within the parent, since the role binding to the actual resource might not even have a transition binding to the control state of its access dot. And if the effect was to *not* return the control state to the actual resource, then the "new" initial control state of the formal resource would somehow be different than the "original" initial control state, in that it now wouldn't correspond to a control state on the actual. Both of these potential behaviors are confusing, and unnecessary.

2. No role bound to the formal resource can have an access dot corresponding to a final dot (from the formal resource's transition box). Why? If it *was* allowed, it would suggest that upon transitioning the formal resource to such a state, the result might be either to issue a transition back to the parent (as described earlier), or to allow another activity in the child to access the formal (or maybe both?). We wish the result to be unambiguous and final.

The use of formal resources which act in these ways avoids the issues and complications outlined in the previous section. For example, they:

- allow multiple activities within the child plan to access a single (actual) resource in the parent without requiring the parent to manage multiple role bindings to that resource;

- allow child to effectively add control states to a parent's (actual) resource which are only visible (and usable) in the child;

- allow a planner to specify the names of the roles presented to the parent for binding, which can be the same or different than the names of the roles used within the child; and

- allow a planner to specify the transition domain for each of the plan's roles (via the final dots), which can be the same or different than the transition domains of roles within the child.

6.2.2 Strategy Interfaces: Resources as Finite State Machines (FSMs)

As stated above, each formal resource in a strategy represents one role of that strategy, and the names of the dots in the transition box for each of those

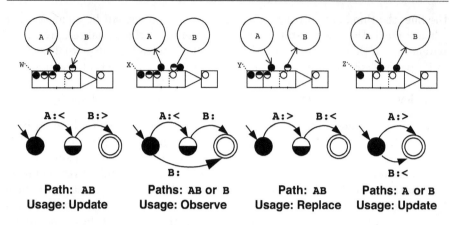

Figure 6.4: Four formal resources and associated FSMs and usages.

formal resources represent the transition domain for that role. The content domain of the formal resource also clearly represents the content domain for the role. So, just by inspecting the implementation for a strategy, key portions of the strategy's interface can be inferred. In fact, the final aspect – usages for the roles – can also be inferred, but it takes a bit more analysis.

By ignoring the content state and focusing only on the control state, any resource corresponds closely to a more traditional construct called a Finite State Machine (FSM), so all of the literature pertaining to FSMs can be used in analyzing patterns of access to resources. We will use it here to determine the usage of a role in a strategy, and later to determine other properties. (For those who have read section 5.3.2, the next paragraph is largely review.)

To construct an FSM from a resource, simply create one state in the FSM (represented by a circle) for each control state in the resource's control domain, and if the resource is a formal resource, one final state (sometimes represented by a circle within a circle) for each final dot (all of which represent the transition domain of the role corresponding to that formal resource). Then draw an arc (arrow) from state A to state B in the FSM whenever the resource has a role binding with an access dot corresponding to A, and a transition binding corresponding to B. Label that arc to identify the context, the role name (if not obvious), the transition name, and the permissions on the role binding. Mark the FSM state corresponding to the initial control state as the start state, by adding an arc pointing from nowhere to it. Such an FSM, then, shows if (and how) it is possible to get from any resource control state to any other resource control state or final dot (for formal resources). Figure 6.4 shows four examples of formal resources with some bound contexts (each assumed to have other role bindings to other resources not shown here), and under each example, the corresponding FSM, with states of the FSM patterned the same way as the control states of the resource. The arcs of each FSMs are labeled only with the context name and the permission of the role bindings (with < here meaning observe and > meaning replace): The roles and transitions are not shown (and

116

fairly obvious).

The usage of a strategy's role is determined by considering all paths in the FSM corresponding to its formal resource, starting at the start state, regardless of whether or not they reach a final state:

- If no paths traverse an arc having either observe or replace permission, then the usage of the role is nodata.

- If some or all paths traverse an arc with observe permission, but never one with replace (or update) permission, then the usage of the role is observe.

- If all paths traverse an arc with replace permission, and do so before traversing an arc (if any) with observe (or update) permission, then the usage of the role is replace.

- Otherwise, the usage is update.

In Figure 6.4, the possible paths from the start state are listed under each FSM, and under those paths, the corresponding usage dictated by the rules above. The first is a classic update usage, since A observes and then B replaces the content. The second shows two paths to the final state, one which has only nodata permission, yet the usage is observe because one path does have observe. In the third, even though B observes the content, the overall usage of the formal is deemed replace, because the original content is never observed, only always replaced in the first access (by A). Finally, the fourth allows either A or B to access the content, A with replace and B with observe. By the last rule above, it has update usage, precisely because the final content of the resource may be related to (and in fact, exactly the same as) the initial content, if B activates, but it may also be changed, if A activates.

6.2.3 Predictable Roles Revisited

The introduction of strategies also introduces a slight complexity regarding predictable roles. That is, based on the technique just outlined, some of the formal resources for a strategy may be deemed to have either observe (only) or nodata usage. So when the associated role is bound in the parent and if all of the transitions are bound to the same control state, we must decide: Should that role binding be considered predictable? If so, the activity (resulting from the strategy) must effectively issue a transition in some finite time, whether or not it explicitly issues one (by transitioning to a final dot of the corresponding formal). There are difficulties with either a "yes" or "no" answer.

If "no, it should not be considered predictable", then the parent can't really judge whether a role binding for a context is predictable without knowing something about the plan that is activated there (i.e. whether it is a tactic or a strategy, and if a strategy, whether it obviously ultimately issues a transition to the role). That seems counterintuitive, or maybe just illogical, especially seeing as how all of the original justifications for considering it predictable still exist – i.e. except for the possibility of no (or equivalently, bottom) transition, the future control and content state of the associated resource can be determined in advance, so it is useful for the parent to be able to act on that information.

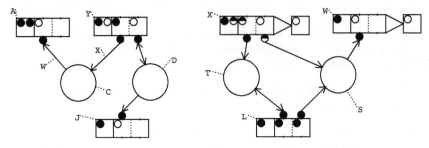

Parent strategy, D is tactic.   Child strategy C, T and S are tactics.

Figure 6.5: C (right) child of P (left), with binding X in P seemingly predictable.

But if the answer is "yes, it should be predictable", that can cause problems, too. For example, consider Figure 6.5 where role X for strategy C (the child) is predictable, and suppose that T activates in C, transitioning the formal resource X to its half-dot control state, effectively stealing the control state from the actual resource, Y, in the parent. But since role X is predictable, Y in the parent can predictably assume it will regain its control state, even before S in the child activates... seemingly meaning (according to the rules we've used so far) that the formal resource X within the child will re-attain its initial control state, but it will still possess the half-dot control state from earlier. Does the formal resource get two control states, contrary to all we've said up to now? Or does one get priority over the other?

We will define the results to be the most sensible and easy to manage. Yes, it will be considered predictable, but if a formal resource (like X, here) is already active, it will not follow the normal rule of adopting the initial control state if/when the role on the actual resource becomes ready. Only if the formal is inactive, such as if/when a transition is issued for the role here, will it be possible for the formal resource to re-attain an initial control state.

The reader might then wonder if this raises other complications with the liveness rules. That is, if the actual resource in the parent has re-attained the control state associated with the access dot, can't the parent expect the child to eventually access that resource, which it might never do only because the associated formal resource within it is still active? The simple answer is no: In the general case, the parent has no expectation that the child will access a role/actual in any specific time frame, because in the general case, the parent has no way of knowing what conditions are necessary within the child for the role to be accessed. Only if the child is a tactic and all of the other roles are ready does the liveness rule kick in.

Note that this means that if/when Y in the parent predictively re-obtains its initial control state, even before S in the child (C) has activated, D in the parent can activate and update the content state of Y. The Director must manage this correctly, ensuring that such an update does not affect the contents of Y being accessed (on role X) by S in the child (C). This is just an extension of the Director's job as already discussed in the chapter on predictability, Chapter 4.

6.3 Finite-lived Composite Activities

This description of formal resources explains how a child strategy can work with a parent strategy, effectively becoming a logical part of that strategy. In fact, the parent and child are almost too integrated: If the child strategy can be considered to represent a separate activity at all, it must be one with a very long lifetime, seemingly as long as the parent. This section will delve into ways of creating child activities with shorter lifetimes.

6.3.1 Finishing an Activity

To terminate the activity associated with a strategy, we will use an approach suggested in Section 6.1.3 relating to defining/declaring a "forward belt" for the activity.

One solution first requires that any strategy that wants its activities to potentially terminate include a formal resource named $plan, with one transition in its transition box, named done.[1] As with $copy, the $ prefix is used here for a reserved names – i.e. names which are meaningful to ScalPL itself, so would be confusing for planners to use for other (different) purposes.

An activity is said to **finish** (or to be finished) when the $plan formal resource is transitioned to done – i.e. when it (effectively) issues the done transition to that $plan role – i.e. when an activity bound to that formal resource issues a transition which corresponds to the resource's done dot. What "finished" means here is that all of the formal resources in the same activity (including $plan itself) lose their ability to possess an initial control state ever again. Specifically, (1) if any of the formal resources possess an initial control state when the activity is finished, they will lose their control state, and (2) if the role associated with the formal resource later becomes ready (i.e. the actual resource attains a control state matching an access dot for that role), the formal will *not* be given an initial control state, as it ordinarily would.

Note that, if one or more of the formal resources in the child are active when the activity is finished, the finishing will have no immediate effect on those resources: The formal resource has already transitioned out of the initial control state, so it has already been stolen from the actual resource, and activities within the child can continue to access that formal resource as usual, and perhaps eventually transition it to correspond to one of the formal resource's final dots, at which time a transition will be issued back to the parent. Once that has happened, however, regardless of what happens in the parent, the formal resource will never attain its initial control state again, as a result of finishing.

This is exactly the sort of behavior we would hope for when an activity reaches (or initiates) a belt. From the perspective of the parent, when the belt has been initiated, the activity has effectively terminated in the sense that the activity will have no further effect on resources in the parent, except possibly

---

[1]The presence of this formal resource will appear to contradict our earlier rules, because formal resources are always associated with roles, and there must normally be a role binding for every role when the plan is activated in a context, but no role binding named $plan will usually be apparent/required when activating a strategy containing a $plan formal resource. The reason that this is not really a contradiction will be addressed in the next chapter.

issuing transitions to complete work that has already been started – and the parent has no way of acting on the fact that those effects are not complete (transitions have not been issued), because there is no way for it to initiate any action on the absence of control state (in the actual resource).

When an activity in a context finishes, it allows a plan (likely the same one) to be (re)activated in the same context, according to the usual rules, creating a new (independent) activity, with the control and content states of resources initialized as usual. Note that this can happen, then, even while the previous activity finishes its work, because the activations will still be logically sequential: The new activity cannot access any resources until the previous activity finishes with them, because they will not have any control state, so the new one cannot have any effects which precede those of the old one.

Although finishing an activity my be considered as creating a belt for the activity, it might not technically be a belt at all. Specifically, if the activity has already accessed, relinquished (i.e. issued transitions for), and accessed more (or re-accessed) some of its formal resources even before finishing, then the activity will not satisfy the requirements for a belted activity – i.e. that resources are only accessed and *not* relinquished before the belt. So it is still the responsibility of the planner, if they want a belted activity, to ensure that resources are not relinquished before finishing the activity, just as they are responsible for ensuring that any formal resources that need to continue to be accessed by the activity after it is finished are indeed first accessed before it is finished.

6.3.2   "Cleaning Up" an Activity: Garbage Collection

We just stated that an activity may still do work, and may even continue to issue transitions to its parent, after it has finished. So if an activity does not go away when it finishes, when does it go away?

For the very reasons stated earlier, it is not the plan's responsibility to tell when it should "go away". Instead, the Director recognizes when resources (transient or "regular) are no longer being used effectively, in which case it frees them up to be used for more practical purposes. The general term used for recognizing and discarding unproductive resources in this way is **garbage collection**.

One case in which a Director will collect up and "discard" (i.e. make available for reuse) the resources used by an activity is when the activity has finished and none of its formal resources are active, either because they were not active when the activity finished, or they were subsequently transitioned to a final dot (thereby issuing a transition to the parent). In such a case, the Director will recognize that the formal resources will never regain an initial control state, or therefore any other control state, and will therefore not be accessible, and since the activity can only communicate with the environment (i.e. parent) via its formal resources, the activity can do nothing productive from here on out, and can be collected. This is the usual, and desired, behavior.

There may be other cases where a finished activity may want to effectively declare itself collectable even without issuing transitions to all of its active formal resources. An expedient way to do that is for the activity to transition those formal resources to a control state which is "dead" – i.e. which has no role bindings having that access dot. Just as with the inactive formal resources, the Director can recognize that this makes the formal resource unusable, which renders the activity unable to affect its environment (parent), leading the Director to collect the now-dead activity.

Even in cases where the formal resources do not enter dead and/or inactive states, there are often other cases where the Director can determine that some resources, and perhaps an entire activity with all of its resources, can be collected. For example, if any resource enters a dead state, then all tactics with atomic plans (e.g. tactics) bound to it will never activate again and can be collected, perhaps thereby leading other control states to be considered dead, etc.

6.4 Summary

One objective when devising tactics and actons was to allow them to be used as building blocks to build more complex activities having whatever behavior we might like, using constructs like resources, contexts, etc. We already discussed, in Chapter 2, how to put such constructs together into a form of plan called a strategy, but did not discuss there how to endow such a strategy with an interface (roles, etc.) so that it could be activated within a context. We also did not discuss there how to effectively terminate such an activity. Those issues are addressed in this chapter. In addition to building asmaller plans (strategies and tactics) into larger ones, the same approach can be used to help decompose large strategies into smaller ones.

The primary construct introduced here for strategies to facilitate these objectives is the formal resource, represented like a standard labeled resource (i.e. a rectangle) but with an additional box, called a transition box, attached to the right side of the resource rectangle with a triangle. The transition box contains one or more final dots, each with a unique label and color/pattern. The formal resource corresponds to a role for the strategy which contains that resource. That is, the name of the formal resource is the name of the role, the content domain is the content domain of the role, and the names of the final dots (inside of the transition box) represents the transition domain of the role. The usage of the role is determined by analyzing the control state transitions which can occur to formal resource, to determine whether or not the activities bound to the formal resource will observe the contents, replace them, neither, or both, and in what order. No transitions are allowed to go back to the initial (green/solid) control state of a formal resource.

When a strategy (a "child") with formal resources is activated within a context in another strategy (the "parent"), the formal resources in the child are interpreted as roles in its interface, and therefore the context must bind each of those roles to a resource in the parent, called the actual resource corresponding to the formal resource in the child. As a result of the binding, the formal resource and actual resource will effectively share content state (i.e. the formal borrowing it from the actual when necessary), and the initial control state of the formal will effectively be treated the same as the control state of the actual corresponding to the access dot(s) in the parent. That is, whenever the actual in the parent attains a control state matching an access dot, and not before, the formal will attain the initial control state, allowing any contexts in the child bound to the initial control state of the formal to access that formal, according to the usual rules. If such an access takes place, not only is the control state stolen from the formal (according to the usual rules), but also from the actual.

If/when a context bound to the formal (in the child) transitions to a final dot (in the transition box of the formal), a transition of the same name as that dot is effectively issued to the role in the parent corresponding to that role.

For all intents and purposes, a strategy usually activates within its context at the "beginning of time" and remains active there forever. However, the lifetime of a strategy may be shortened, thereby allowing it (or as will be seen in future chapters, other strategies) to be activated there again, with fresh content and control states for its resources, etc. The way to do this is to include in the strategy a formal resource named $plan, with one final dot in its transition box, named done. When a transition is made to that formal resource, to match that final dot, the strategy effectively finishes, meaning that none of the formal resources in the strategy will ever attain its initial control state again, or if some already have their initial control state, they will lose that control state. The overall result of this is that formal resources which have already been transitioned to some other control state, but have not been subsequently transitioned to match a final dot (in its transition box), will remain accessible by the strategy until/unless they do subsequently transition their control state to match a final dot. All other formal resources will be inaccessible from then on. The parent, then, will never see the child activity steal any more control states from the actual resources there, only (potentially) return some. Another activity is also allowed to activate within the same context, assuming that it meets the necessary other requirements.

Chapter 7

Constants, Repositories, Activation, and Recursion

We have described the relationship between a plan and an activity as being forged by a context: The context is labeled with the name of a plan, and that plan is then activated to form an activity. We have also covered the circumstances under which a particular plan conforms to a particular context, making that context eligible to be labeled with that plan. This still leaves lots of questions. How does a name get associated with a plan? Can the same name be assigned to different plans, an if so, how are ambiguities resolved? When is the plan activated? Is it possible to delay the activation? And is it possible to use the same context to (potentially or actually) activate different plans? More generally, how do we manage large collections of information associated with complex plans so that they can be accessed scalably?

7.1 Constants

The first few of the questions above have little to do with plans at all, but with constants. A constant is any piece of data or information which (in itself) does not change throughout the life of the activity in which it is used. A plan is one example of a constant: Although an activity created from a plan effectively changes over time as it executes, the plan from which that activity was created generally does not change.

Constants may take many different forms, depending upon what is being represented. For example, 5 and "abc" are examples of constants, and each would generally be expressed just that way whenever they are needed. But when a constant has a larger and/or more complex representation, and especially if the constant might be used in multiple places, it is often convenient to associate a name with it and to use the name to later represent that constant. Plans are a good example of constants to name for just these reasons.

A constant name can also be used as a placeholder for a constant when the actual value of the constant is not known yet, or when it may even occasionally change over time. This idea of a constant that changes over time may seem

123

contradictory, but recall that here we refer to a constant as something which does not change *throughout the life of the activity in which it is used*. For example, we might start with a rough guess for a plan and assign it a name, say, `planA`, and refine the plan over time while continuing to call it `planA` (revision control notwithstanding). Even though the constant associated with the name changes over relatively large time spans, `planA` is still considered a constant because it will not change within the lifetime of an activity in which it is used – i.e. that which uses `planA` as a label for one or more contexts – in that whatever `planA` stands for at the beginning of that activity, it continues to represent throughout the activity. If we need the value associated with a name to change *during* an activity, we have already addressed another better way to handle it, by naming a resource and using its content state as its value, to be changed during the course of activities. Following sections will address precisely how to assign a name to a constant, and how to deal with name ambiguities, and the precise form for many constants.

There are two places in a plan where a constant may appear, and we will eventually see (in Section 7.3) that one is just a convenient shorthand for the other. They are:

1. to indicate the initial content state for a resource; and

2. to label a context. The label is interpreted as the name of a plan constant.

In the first case, the name (if any) of the resource being initialized is followed by an equal sign and the constant representing the initial content state. If the construct `<name>` (i.e. some name, enclosed in angle brackets) appears somewhere in that constant (except within quotes), that construct will be treated as being equivalent to the constant named *name* (i.e. the name within the angle brackets), without the angle brackets, so if we have assigned the name `xxy` to the constant 17, then if the construct `<xxy>` occurs within an initial content state (including, perhaps, as the entire initial content state), it will be considered the same as the constant 17.

It is relatively common to use a resource just to make a constant value available to one or more contexts, by initializing the content state of the resource with the constant (as described above), and then binding only observe roles from context(s) to it. In such cases, the control state of the resource often goes unused – all of the control transitions go back to the initial control state (solid and/or green). Since this practice is so common, a shorthand is introduced: It is not necessary to actually draw the rectangle representing the resource at all, just the name of the resource (if any) followed by the initializer, with role bindings made directly to that text, often with no apparent access dots. See Figure 7.1.

7.2 Repositories

7.2.1 Introduction

A name may be declared for a constant (i.e. made available for later reference) through the use of a **repository**. A repository can be considered as a set of

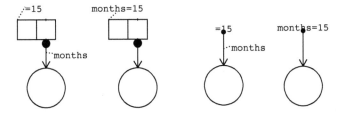

Figure 7.1: Four equivalent ways to bind role "months" to constant 15.

constant declarations, each consisting of the constant's name (unique within the repository) and its definition or value – i.e. the constant associated with that name. There are also other ways to think about it, like a storage area for constants indexed by their names (like a directory or folder or data base), or as a functional mapping from a set of names to a set of constants. The process of looking up the definition of a constant name and interpreting it as (or transforming it into) the value associated with that name is called **resolution** (or **resolving** the constant).

7.2.2 Constant Paths (Repositories as Constants)

A repository may itself be considered as a constant – for example, as a list of *(name, constant)* pairs. Since any of those constants may, in turn, be another repository, this allows repositories to be nested to any level. A constant within a repository can be referenced by following the repository name with a slash and the constant name. So, for example, `<this/that>` in an initializer would reference the repository `this` and then the constant `that` from within `this`, and the label `foo/bar/baz` on a context would first reference constant (repository) `foo`, then constant (repository) `bar` within that, and then constant `baz` (which should be a plan) within that. A complete constant name, together with all of the slashes and leading repository names, is called a **constant path**.

7.2.3 Resolution of Constants (Time and Source)

Constants (such as plans) can reference other constants in the ways mentioned previously (in initializers or context labels). It would be troublesome to resolve all referenced constants at the very time the referencing constant itself is declared (or "stored") within a repository, since the referenced constants may not be properly declared until later. On the other hand, delaying the resolution of all referenced constants until the plan holding the reference (i.e name) is actually activated can distract from other important work at that time. In the end, the available tools will specify a time or time range over which constants might be resolved (often called **link time**), sometime between the time the name is declared and the time it must be resolved, and it will be important to ensure that referenced constants have their desired definitions intact over that period.

Before any constant names are resolved, a **root repository** must be declared by the planner (using the available tools). This root repository serves as

125

the initial **home repository**, which is the term for the repository being used at any specific stage for resolving constant names. The first constant name to be resolved is usually specified at the same time as the root repository is, and is typically the main plan to be activated, as described below in Section 7.3.4. Although the search starts with a home repository, as a result of constant paths or other special path prefixes to be described shortly, the constant may actually eventually be located in a different repository. That (potentially different) repository will serve as the new home repository for any constant names subsequently referenced from within that constant. In other words, by default, all of the constants referenced by a constant will be sought in the same repository as the constant referencing them.

This facilitates a common technique for managing the definition of complex constants, like (perhaps) strategies, which often reference many other subconstants (e.g. the plans for each of the contexts in the strategy) which may themselves be complex. One particular constant name, BASE, has special status, in that if a reference is made to a repository itself (as the last name in a constant path, without referencing any particular constant within the repository), the reference is interpreted as being to the constant BASE within that repository, as if /BASE was appended to the end of the reference. And, as just described, if BASE is defined as a complex constant (such as a strategy), the same repository becomes the home repository for the constants referenced within it, which may in turn be other repositories, perhaps each containing their own BASE constants. In other words, each BASE can be considered as the root of a subtree, with the other constants in the same repository being the nodes branching from it. This effect can be suppressed by terminating the constant path with either a slash (/), in which case the last name in the path must be a repository, or a backslash (\), in which case the last name in the path can be either a repository or not. (Parts of this are simiar to web protocols, with BASE taking the place of index.html.)

A home repository can also be represented with a single dot (.), usually specified alone (since adding to the head of a path serves no purpose). Because of the rule described in the previous paragraph, this may refer to the constant BASE in the home repository, if one exists.

7.2.4 Resolving in Parent Repositories

Any constant path can be prefixed with a slash (/), in which case the root repository (rather than the home repository) is used to resolve it. This makes the root repository a convenient place to declare constant names which are widely referenced by other constants. However, this raises the potential of name conflicts: If there are several complex constants, perhaps developed completely independent of one other, they may each be organized to find a constant of a certain name in the root repository, but expecting it to represent completely unrelated concepts or values. In other words, the two levels of reference – either in the home or root repository – are not sufficient to allow each constant in each repository to reference the constants which are most pertinent to it alone. It's important to be able to move up some levels of a complex constant tree without necessarily going all the way to the root at the top.

To reference a constant which is up some levels, but perhaps not in the root, the prefix ../ on a path, perhaps multiple times, says to move up that number of repositories (to the home repository's parent, then it's parent, etc.) before finding the first name in the path.[1] Thus, <../../foo> would look for foo not in the home repository, or in the parent of the home repository, but in the parent of the parent of the home repository. Attempts to go beyond the root repository using ../ will always fail.

A single question mark (?) prefix on a path, called **searchback**, is like ../ except that it will go up any number of levels (including zero), all the way up to the root repository, to find the constant named after it, so <?global/nflags> would first look in the home repository for global, and if it was not there or was not a repository containing nflags, it would look in its parent for the path, then if not there, in its parent, etc. Searchback also works before one or more ../ to ensure that certain parent repositories are skipped over, so <?../global> would not find global in the home repository, because the ../ would first move up to its parent. If constants defined in a repository are interpreted as being potentially pertinent to (referenced by) all other constants in that repository (unless they are redefined at a deeper level between this definition and the referencer), searchback is a convenient way to reference the most pertinent definition of a particular constant name relative to where it is referenced.

7.2.5 Constant recursion

Constant references cannot be recursive, immediately or eventually. That is, a constant (say foo) which contains a reference to itself (e.g. <foo>), or which contains a reference to another constant which references back to itself (e.g. foo contains a reference <bar>, and bar contains a reference <foo>), etc., can never be fully resolved, and so should be completely avoided. It would be possible to make special rules to allow such constants to be fully resolved (e.g. by adding mechanisms to manually or automatically stop resolution after some number of cycles), or to allow them to be used even without being fully resolved (so-called lazy evaluation), but those don't suit our purposes. Some techniques described shortly will show how to obtain the same results as recursion in some cases, such as to allow a plan to activate itself. That will be sufficient for our needs.

7.2.6 Content Domains as Types

As described earlier, each resource has a content domain, describing all of the possible contents which the resource might contain over its lifetime. In computer terminology, this would usually be called the **type** of the resource, and instead of being expressed as a set, it is usually expressed as a name (like integer or name or person) describing a representative element of the set.

---

[1]This notation, and the aforementioned dot for home directory, was chosen (over some other perhaps more intuitive notation) because it is similar in function to similar notation used in various operating systems and web protocols to negotiate directories.

Complicating any statement regarding such content domains is that ScalPL itself is concerned with very few them: They are primarily for the benefit of tactics to pass information among themselves via resource content. Since ScalPL has little to say about how those tactics are represented (e.g. the language in which tactics are expressed, called the **tactic language**), it will mostly just be assumed that the planners developing tactics will agree on the content domains to be used for the resources. If all the tactics are developed in the same tactic language, those content domains will likely just be borrowed from the type system for that language.

However, there are a few content domains, and therefore forms of constants, which are important to ScalPL itself. The main two are integers (to be used in Chapters 13 and 14 for indices within binding modifiers) and plans. Within each, subsets of these domains can be specified. For integers, these are usually in the form of acceptable ranges (e.g. long or short integers, representing the number of bits or digits, or only positive or possibly negative, etc.) For plans, a signature can be specified, restricting which plans conform. (Most of this book is devoted to representations for plan constants.)

In addition to single (or **scalar**) constants like integers and plans, ScalPL is aware of three **collective** types of constants: Sequences, structures, and arrays. These are constructed from other constants, which may themselves be sequences, structures, or arrays.

- A **sequence constant** is an ordered collection of constants. A sequence is usually denoted as enclosed in braces {}, with its elements separated by either commas or white space. A homogeneous sequence is one where all the elements are considered as being members of a single content domain.

- A **structure constant** is a collection of elements, each having a name which uniquely identifies it within the elements of the structure. A repository is one example of a structure constant. If the order of the elements in a structure constant is specified, it may also be regarded as a sequence (by ignoring the names). A structure constant is generally specified like a sequence with each of its elements preceded by its name and a colon.

- An **array constant** is a homogeneous sequence, plus a sequence of integer ranges (usually represented in square brackets before the homogeneous sequence, with each range of the form $low:high$) representing a rectangular region. It represents an infinite array suitable for initializing a ScalPL array (to be introduced in Chapter 13) having the same dimensionality as the number of integer ranges in the sequence. The number of elements in the homogeneous sequence must match the product of the length of all of the ranges (i.e. $(high1 - low1 + 1) \times (high2 - low2 + 1)$, etc.). The elements of the homogeneous sequence are considered to initialize that region of the infinite array, consecutively with the first index varying most rapidly, next index next most rapidly, etc.

Similar to collective constants, upcoming chapters will also describe how to declare and work with collective resources, which are collections of resources which are themselves organized into structures and arrays. The collective constants mentioned here can be used to declare the initial content states of those collective resources, thereby effectively initializing the content state of several resources at one time.

Alternatively, most computer languages are also capable of declaring variables with array and structure types, much like ScalPL's arrays and structures, but of course without the concept of control state. When using such a tactic language, a single (scalar) resource in ScalPL may have a content domain capable of holding an entire array or structure from the tactic language. Even in this case, if ScalPL is appropriately informed of the form of records and arrays in the tactic language type system, it may be possible to specify initial content states for these tactic language collective variables within a ScalPL scalar resource with ScalPL collective constants.

The rules for initializing collective resources or a single resource with a collective type from a tactic language are as follows. A sequence (or a structure with ordered elements) can be initialized with a constant sequence of the same length, and where the type of each element of the constant conforms to the type of the corresponding sequence element which it is initializing. A structure can be partially or completely initialized with a structure constant (e.g. a repository), with correspondences made by name. Structure initializations are of four possible forms, indicated by asterisks optionally surrounding the equal sign:

=   (equal sign alone) Means the structure on the left and the structure constant on the right must have all of the same elements with all the same names

*=   (asterisk equals) Means that the structure (on the left) may have elements not mentioned in the constant initializer (on the right), and therefore left uninitialized.

=*   (equals asterisk) Means that the structure constant (on the right) may have elements not mentioned in the structure (on the left), and therefore some of the elements of the constant may go unused in the initialization.

=   (asterisk equals asterisk) Means that both the structure and the structure constant may have elements unmatched in the other.

7.3 Activation: How Contexts Really Work

7.3.1 $plan Role Binding

We mentioned in section 7.1 that the two uses of constant names – i.e. in angle brackets in an initializer for a resource, and as a label on a context – are actually two ways of expressing a single concept. This is because the label on a context is really just a shorthand for an initializer of a resource. That is, the label on a context is internally transformed into a reference to the constant of that name, which is treated as the initial content for a new resource, with a new observe

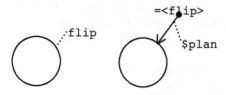

Figure 7.2: Equivalent: Context label represents a constant on $plan role.

role binding named $plan connecting that resource to the context, as shown in Figure 7.2.

This $plan role is quite special in that (in most cases) it is primarily for the use of the context itself, rather than for the activity (or plan activated to become the activity) within that context. That is, what a context *really* does is wait for the $plan role (and a few others, to be described shortly) to become ready, then the context itself observes the plan on its $plan role, and only then (subject to the usual rules of readiness) will the context activate that plan. Note that the context itself is not considered to "activate" just to observe $plan role, so there is no control state transition to the $plan role simply as a result of the context observing it, though the done transition on that role will be issued after the activity created by the context (and plan) finishes.

When the $plan role is bound to a constant resource as described above (e.g. as the result of just using the shorthand of labeling the context with the plan name), there is never a risk of the role not being ready, because the resource always maintains its initial control state. However, the same options are available for binding the $plan role as for binding any other role: One can explicitly specify a $plan role binding on any context in lieu of labeling the context, allowing any resource to supply the plan to be activated there. This not only means that the access dots on the binding together with the control state of that resource can be used to delay the activation of a plan within a context, it also means that the content state of the resource can be altered over time to change the plan to be activated within that context.

The $plan moniker will be familiar from section 6.3.1 where a $plan formal resource in a strategy was used to finish an activity. That $plan formal resource is considered to exist for every strategy, whether it is shown explicitly or not, and the $plan role corresponds to that formal, as would be expected by the usual rules. This will have repercussions described later, such as regarding recursion.

The potential of having plans as resource contents immediately raises some questions. Other than simply using a plan constant as an initial value (as happens when a context is labeled), how else can a plan get onto a resource in the first place? Is it possible to write plans that observe and/or replace other plans? These will be answered later, but for right now: There will be little if any need to consider the general case of plans which observe or replace other plans (on resources). We have already discussed one way to move plans from one resource to another: $copy. And we will introduce ways to move plans between resources, sometimes with minor modifications, but by far, the most common way for a plan to end up on a resource is as its initial value (e.g. implicitly by labeling a context).

7.3.2 Delaying/Sensing Plan Activations

Generally speaking, if the plan on the $plan role is a tactic, the plan will not activate until all of the roles on the context are ready (as described earlier). If the plan on the $plan role is a strategy, it can (and will) usually activate (e.g. bind its roles to resources) as soon as the $plan role is ready, regardless of whether any other roles are ready. However, there are times (especially for reasons outlined later) when a planner may wish to delay even the activation of a plan (strategy) until certain of its roles are ready. One way to accomplish this is to prefix the labels on one or more of the strategy's role bindings with an at sign (@), in which case it becomes an **activation role binding**, in which case the plan in the context (whether a strategy or a tactic) will not activate until that binding is ready, but once it is ready, the binding will behave as any other (without the @ prefix).

Any number of so-called **anonymous role bindings** can also be added to any context. These role bindings are characterized by the fact that they belong to the context itself, and don't actually correspond to (or bind) any roles from the activity in the context, even though they are similar to "normal" role bindings in other ways. They have three primary purposes: (1) to prevent a plan from activating in a context (until they are ready), just like activation role bindings; (2) to provide an external indication (via a control state transition to a resource) when a plan activates in the context; and (3) as described in Chapters 13 and 14, to supply information for array indexing and context duplication.

An anonymous role binding is distinguished from others by having a name starting with (and perhaps consisting only of) an underscore (_). One can consider this underscore as hiding the name (if any), leading to the "anonymous" moniker, and making it unnecessary (impossible) for any role of the activity within the context to correspond to it. A plan/activity in a context has no way of sensing whether there are any anonymous role bindings present on the context. An anonymous role binding never has update permission (but may have observe, for reasons to become clear in later chapters), and always has a transition domain consisting only of the done transition. So, an anonymous binding is always predictable, thereby (effectively) issuing its done transition as soon as the plan in the context activates. And again, since anonymous role bindings behave as activation role bindings, no plan will activate within the context until all of the anonymous bindings are ready.

A sample (simplistic) use of anonymous role bindings is illustrated in Figure 7.3, in which increment just increments the value it finds on its count role, and add_to_total adds the value from its contrib role to that on its total role. Both are bound here to another resource, latch, with anonymous role bindings which serve to ensure that the two activities alternate, effectively allowing count to keep the number of contributions added to total, and thereby (perhaps) allowing a later activity to calculate an average of the contribs by dividing

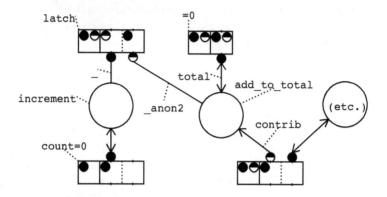

Figure 7.3: Anonymous bindings to help alternate increment and add_to_total.

total by count (say). Neither increment nor add_to_total is (or can be) aware that their context is also bound to latch.

Other uses of anonymous role bindings by the context will be described later (such as in Chapter 13 on arrays), where they will continue to affect only the way the context activates the plan within it, rather than being accessible by the resulting activity.

7.3.3   Recursion: Activating a Plan within the Same Plan

There are times when the most effective way for a plan to do its work is to "divide and conquer" – i.e. to break the work it needs to do down into smaller pieces and to then apply the same plan to each of the pieces. This approach is especially common in fields such as sorting, searching, and rendering (drawing), as well as in fields such as fractals. That is, for example, to sort a large list, one strategy is to simply pick some element (maybe at random) and break the list down into all of the elements larger than and smaller than that item, and then to sort those two lists the same way, until the lists get so small (e.g. fewer than 3 items) that the problem effectively vanishes. This sorting approach, called a quicksort (or quiksort), will be addressed in more detail later, but the important point is that the most natural way to express such a plan is just as it is stated – i.e. each quicksort activity will potentially activate the quicksort plan again twice (on its high list and low list).

Unfortunately, there's a minor inconvenience, described in preceding subsections of this chapter: One cannot just label a context in plan quicksort with quicksort, because labeling a context with a plan name is just a shorthand for setting the initial content state of a resource to that constant, so we'd be using a constant in the definition of itself – and that has already been ruled out.

The $plan role, and the $plan formal resource introduced in the previous chapter, provide a way around that inconvenience. Now that we know that these are related, it follows that the content state of the $plan formal resource is borrowed from the actual to which the $plan role is bound in the parent, as with any formal resource. That is, the content state of the $plan formal

132

resource is always the plan currently being activated, so binding a $plan role to that formal resource instructs the associated context to activate the same plan as the one that context resides within.

Due care must be exercised to avoid a similar trap as we just avoided with recursive constant definitions. That is, if there is nothing stopping a newly activated plan from immediately activating itself as a child, regardless of whether that activity will actually be used, then the same will be true with that child, etc., resulting in infinite recursion. So, when recursive activation is used, some means should ensure that the child will only activate under restricted conditions – i.e. when it will be actually needed. This can sometimes be accomplished using activation and/or anonymous role bindings, as just described, or with the control state of the $plan formal resource to restrict when it is ready. Another construct that can help (very much), called an activation formal, will be introduced in Chapter 9 on Atomicity.

7.3.4 The Root Plan and Root Context

This book describes a notation (ScalPL) for building plans. It is up to the planner to decide how much of their universe they wish to describe in this notation. In most cases, the plan described in ScalPL does not embody the entire universe in which the plan is to operate, and that plan must therefore interface with some amount of the outside "real world" environment which is not modeled within ScalPL, perhaps because that part of the world is already working (and understood) just fine. For example, the repositories mentioned in this chapter are typically maintained in the outside world (often as directories and files on a computer's file system), and thus any plan defined within a repository is also maintained in the outside world. Since many ScalPL plans are programs – i.e. they describe activities intended to be carried out automatically, by computers – the resulting activities (i.e. processes on the computer) often are intended to access information stored on a computer disk, maintained and accessed by other computer processes outside of those activities, and not described by ScalPL plans.

The question of how to integrate these external "real world" entities into a ScalPL plan is an important one. For example, one approach would be to add special language constructs within ScalPL to allow one to deal with entities that don't necessarily look or act exactly like ScalPL resources or contexts or plans. Instead, we take the view here that all the world looks enough like a ScalPL construct that it can be made to look *exactly* like one through a sufficient "glue" layer. For example, a computer file can be made to look like one or more resources or objects (described later), a device can be made to look like a formal resource, etc.

Although plans constructed with ScalPL may be composed of many component plans, we will consider that there is always one top level plan, known as the **root plan**, which is the one which (eventually) references all the others, and therefore (to prevent recursion) is not referenced by any of the others. It is around this plan where the the glue layer belongs. Put another way, the context in which this root plan will activate, called the **root context**, will be embedded in the real world, rather than in another plan. Since the role bindings on this root context are not to ScalPL resources, the notation for describing these bindings should not be expected to look (exactly) like ScalPL notation: The role bindings will be to real-world constructs, rather than to ScalPL resources, and analogies to control state, transition bindings, etc., need to be made between the real world (where they may not usually exist) and the role bindings.

Generally, then, any ScalPL runtime environment should support:

1. The specification of a root context to facilitate or specify role bindings to commonly accessed constructs in that environment (e.g. files);

2. The specification of a root repository; and

3. A root plan, which is usually the name of a constant within the root repository. If not specified, the name usually defaults to be simply a slash (/), meaning that the root plan is the constant named BASE in the root repository.

7.4 Summary

A context serves to activate a plan, and defines how the resulting activity fits into its environment by binding its roles to resources in that environment. In addition to the role bindings corresponding to roles within the plan to be bound, a context always has one additional role binding, named $plan, and potentially any number of other so-called anonymous role bindings. Anonymous role bindings are differentiated by having names beginning with (or consisting entirely of) underscore (_), and they never have replace permission and always one transition (named done), so they are always predictable. The context waits until the $plan and anonymous role bindings and activation role bindings (those prefixed by an at sign, @) are ready, then observes the plan present on the $plan role binding and activates that plan.

For most activities, the environment in which a context resides is another activity, resulting from another plan (i.e. strategy), and the roles from the context are bound to resources in that activity/strategy (its parent). However, at some level, as one moves up from parent to parent to parent, there becomes a point where it no longer becomes practical or realistic to consider the environment in terms of a strategy/plan, but instead in some other paradigm related to a real-world environment or (often) computer. This top-level context which is not considered to exist within a strategy is called the root context. For this root context, then, role bindings are non-standard. Also, instead of binding a $plan role, a root repository is specified, and one constant within that repository is specified (named) as the plan to be activated there.

Constants are defined (assigned names) within repositories. A repository is a form of constant itself (called a structure constant), which is a collection of name-constant associations, or identically, a functional mapping from names to constants. Since repositories are constants, this means that a repository may also be defined (assigned a name) within another repository, facilitating a hierarchical structure. When looking up (resolving) a constant name, the name is located (if present) within a particular repository called the home repository. If that constant is another repository, it is also possible to specify a constant within that repository by following that first name (that of the repository) with a slash (/) and then the name of the constant to be found there. Since that constant can also be a repository, this can be repeated to any number of levels. It is also possible to move up to the home repository's parent (i.e. the repository where it is defined) before attempting to resolve a name by prefixing the name with "../", and this can also be repeated any number of times. A sequence of constant names or .. concatenated in this way with slashes is called a constant path. In addition, starting such a path with a question mark (?) indicates that if the remainder of the path is not found in the home repository, resolution should be attempted in its parent, and then its parent, etc. One of the parents of the home repository is always specified as the root repository, and constants will never be resolved above the root repository, regardless of any use of ../ or ?.

By default, if the last name in a path specifies a repository, then it instead is taken to refer to a constant named BASE within that repository, as though /BASE was appended to the end of the path. If that is not desired, and the constant specified by the path is to be used instead, then the path should end with a lone slash (/) or backslash (\), depending on whether the path is known to be a repository (slash) or may also refer to a non-repository constant (backslash).

A plan is one form of constant, and can be (and usually is) thereby defined (assigned a name) within a repository. Like many other so-called complex constants, a plan may contain references to other constants. The repository in which such a complex constant is defined is taken to be the home repository for other constant references from within it. This is the motivation for the BASE construction: If BASE names a complex constant, then all of the constants referenced within it will be resolved (by default) from within the same repository as that BASE, as the home, and the complex constant together with all the constants referenced within it can be effectively addressed by the name of the repository which holds them.

Within a strategy, as described previously in other chapters, it is possible to specify the initial content state of a resource as a constant, following the name of the resource (if any) and an equal sign (=). Within that specification, other constants can be referenced by enclosing the referenced constant name in angle brackets (<>). If the resource being so initialized is being declared not for its control state, or to hold any other content state (other than its initial), then the normal notation for the resource to hold that constant (with rectangle, access dots, transition bindings, etc.) can be simplified by presenting only the (optional) resource label and initial content state, with role bindings directly to that text (with no rectangle apparent). And, if the $plan role for a context is bound to such a constant (i.e. the path of a plan in the home repository, enclosed in angle brackets), that whole construct can be simplified to simply labeling the context with the name of the plan – the more standard notation described earlier, before the $plan role binding was explained.

The $plan role corresponds (in the usual way) to the $plan formal resource within the plan, described in the previous chapter. In part, this means that it is always possible to observe the current plan on the `$plan` resource within that plan, and thus the plan can be activated recursively by binding the `$plan` role from another context to the `$plan` formal resource.

A repository is effectively just a structure constant – i.e. a functional mapping from names to constants. Two other forms of constants understood by ScalPL are sequence constants and array constants. A sequence is an ordered collection of constants, usually represented within braces (`{}`) and separated by spaces or commas. If all elements are considered to be from a single content domain, it is called a homogeneous sequence. An array is a sequence of integer ranges (the length of that sequence being the dimensionality of the array constant) followed by a homogeneous sequence containing items equalling (in number) the product of all the ranges. Future chapters will describe how to declare array resources within ScalPL, and (effectively) structure resources, and these constants can be used to initialize those. They may also be used to initialize regular (scalar) resources having content domains which appear to be arrays and/or structures in the tactic language.

Chapter 8

Revisiting Computation

We generalized all algorithms, programs, recipes, etc., into plans, and have preferred to speak of activities rather than computation. Still, we'd like to have a better characterization of what goes on inside of activities, in part to help us reason about them more formally, so we will now return to referring to that thing that "goes on" as computation. More specifically, a computation will be a record of what goes on within an activity, of obeying a plan and doing what it says. We attempt here to leverage much experience and practical knowledge garnered in our decades with traditional sequential algorithms toward our use and understanding of concurrency.

8.1 Introduction

We have now discussed two kinds of plans at some length, which we have called strategies and tactics. Tactics generally involve computation as it has been considered for decades, where steps (often expressed in a deterministic sequential language) are followed one-by-one, sometimes repeatedly or optionally, to produce outputs (or results). Strategies are very different structurally, being expressed in terms of resources and activities, which are potentially unsynchronized and concurrent unless there are specific reasons for them not to be, being restricted by control states and transitions rather than sequential steps. But can what happens within strategies and tactics be viewed as similar at some level?

To these ends, this chapter will first start by looking at traditional sequential computing, but from a somewhat fresh perspective. Then, we'll see if we can look at concurrency in a similar light. As a result, many readers will find the first part of this chapter, about sequential computation, more as a setup (by highlighting definitions and concepts) for the second part, about concurrent computation, than in conveying any particularly novel information on its own.

137

8.2 Sequential Computation

In this section, we take a brief vacation from concurrency to take a close look at **traditional deterministic sequential plans** and computation. The idea is to establish a deeper sense for terms like computation, and why sequential plans have evolved into their current form (e.g. structured programming). To avoid always using the rather cumbersome term "(traditional) deterministic sequential plan", we will often use the acronym **TDSP**. One particularly common and specific form of a TDSP is a sequential computer program, as expressed in a computer language like Java or C, and the reader is welcome to consider a TDSP as such, though the conclusions can be applied more broadly, such as to plans or algorithms which are not in program form (e.g. not in a specific computer language), but still expressed as a series of (potentially-repeating or optional) steps, with each step being explicit about what it does.

8.2.1 Plans and Computation

Here, we will consider a computation as a description of how a particular solution is reached, as a description of obeying a TDSP and doing exactly what it says. The term computation is often interpreted (elsewhere) as something that *happens*, rather than something that *is* (i.e. a description), because quite often a planner or user is not interested in the computation itself (as an object describing what happened), but in the solution/result produced by the computation. As far as most users of a plan are concerned, the computation (as a description) is unimportant enough to dispose of as soon as it exists, to the extent it ever does actually exist. Even so, this use of the term, as a description, is often used when formulating abstract computational models (like Turing Machines) .

If a plan is already a complete description of how *to* solve a problem, how does it help to have a specific description of how that plan *did* solve a problem, after the fact? Even starting with a particular TDSP, certain parts of the problem statement may remain open, to be specified at runtime via input values and/or initial state, and the precise solution may differ quite a lot depending upon these factors. The computation allows us to study how the solution resulted, how the TDSP led from a particular set of inputs and/or initial conditions (i.e. problem instance) to a specific solution instance, and this path can be especially useful when the solution leads to unexpected conclusions. Analysis of a computation is often called "tracing the execution" when debugging (i.e. finding out what went wrong with) a TDSP. (Henceforth, we will consider the term "input" to include all initial conditions, and "output" to include all final conditions.)

8.2.2 Example of TDSP and its Computation: Binary Search

We will use for our TDSP example a **binary search**. A binary search is an algorithm for finding something in an ordered (sorted) list, such as (say) a name in a phone book. The approach is to first look at the midpoint of the list, and if that's what you're seeking, you're done. If not, you at least know which half

```
function binsearch (char to_find, char list[], int n_elems)
{
    int to_check = n_elems / 2;       //First, check halfway.
    int jump_dist = n_elems / 4 + 1;  //Jump dist is half that.
    while (jump_dist != 0 &&          //While more to search
           tofind != list[to_check]) // & item not @ to_check,
    {                                 //(follow these steps)
       if (list[to_check] > to_find){ // If that one too big,
          to_check -= jump_dist;      //  decrease by jump_dist
       } else {                       // else, if too small,
          to_check += jump_dist;      //  increase by jump_dist
       }                              // (end of if).
       jump_dist = jump_dist / 2;     // Halve jump distance.
    }                                 //(end of while).
    return(to_check)                  //To_find is at to_check
                                      //(if in the list at all).

}
```

Figure 8.1: TDSP (C function) for simple-case binary search.

of the list it must be in, so you no longer consider the wrong entry you just checked or any of the entries in the wrong half of the list. Instead, you take the entries still in contention, and just repeat the process with those, finding the midpoint of those entries, checking the entry at that midpoint, etc. (It will take at most $1 + \log_2(n)$ tries to find, or rule out finding, the desired entry, where n is the number of entries in the list, and $\log_2(n)$ is the number of bits to represent n as a binary number.)

Figure 8.1 shows a simple binary search TDSP to find a particular letter in an ordered list of letters, though it only works correctly in very limited situations (where the list length is an integer power of two minus one, like 1, 3, 7, 15, 31, etc.). This TDSP could be expressed in the form of a tactic, by adding an appropriate header and some "issue" statements, but for now, we'll express it as it usually is in a sequential computer language such as Java or C, since we are trying to learn from them. (Even readers unfamiliar with computer languages like Java or C can hopefully get the gist, as anything after // is a plain English comment describing the C code to its left.) The function (subroutine) here is fed three values (arguments), represented internally by variables called to_find, which is the letter (character, or char) to find, list, which is a list of letters to search, and n_elems, which is the length of list. The result (location of to_find in list, if it is in the list at all) ends up in to_check, and jump_dist is just an extra variable used throughout to represent how far to move for the next test, if necessary. (Brief C lesson: a=b means the variable a gets the value in variable b, a+=b means to add the value of b to a, and the connectives "&&", "==", "!=", mean "and", "is equal to", and "is not equal to", respectively. Statements are separated from other statements with semicolon (;), with statements grouped together when necessary by curly

```
int to_check = n_elems / 2;              (i.e. 3)
int jump_dist = n_elems / 4 + 1;         (i.e. 2)
while (jump_dist != 0 && tofind != list[to_check]) {
  if (list[to_check] > tofind) {
  } else {
    to_check += jump_dist;               (i.e. 5)
  }
  jump_dist = jump_dist / 2;             (i.e. 1)
}
while (jump_dist != 0 && tofind != list[to_check]) {
  if (list[to_check] > tofind) {
    to_check -= jump_dist                (i.e. 4)
  } else {
  }
  jump_dist = jump_dist / 2;             (i.e. 0)
}
while (jump_dist != 0 && tofind != list[to_check]) {
}
return to_check;                         (i.e. 4)
```

Figure 8.2: Computation of binary search for inputs 'r', "abefrsv", and 7.

braces {}. Remainders after division are ignored for integers, so $15/4 = 3$, for example.)

Suppose we use this TDSP to find the 'r' (as to_find) in the 7-character string "abefrsv" (as list, n_elems as 7). It would first check 'f', then 's', and finally 'r', producing the computation in Figure 8.2 – i.e. a trace of the statements carried out to get to the result. (End of statement comments have been removed, and italicized annotations added to show newly computed values of important variables.) Note that although the TDSP and the computation resemble one another at a rudimentary level, the elements of the TDSP represent statements (steps) that may be executed in some order and/or under some conditions, while each of the elements of the computation represent the execution of one of those statements in response to some specific input, in the precise order that they were executed. So, although the form of the plan (TDSP) and of the computation are similar, to properly interpret what we are looking at, we must know which we're looking at.

8.2.3 Computations as Functions

A TDSP can be (and often is) considered as a function from its inputs (often its arguments) to its outputs, meaning that for any set of inputs, it will produce the same outputs (which is what the D in TDSP stands for). This is why computer languages like C use the term "function" to identify TDSPs. Here, we will use the symbol $TDSP_O$ (i.e. subscripted with the letter O for Outputs) to represent a TDSP as a function which produces outputs from inputs – i.e.

$$TDSP_O(Inputs) \rightarrow Outputs$$

But, we have just considered that, in the process of obtaining those outputs, the TDSP effectively also creates a computation (always the same for the same set of inputs), which could be considered as another result. We'll represent a TDSP which produces its computation as well as its regular outputs by subscripting with both an O and a C:

$$TDSP_{O,C}(Inputs) \rightarrow Outputs + Computation$$

(The + here does not represent mathematical addition, but a so-called disjoint union of sets, indicating that the function produces something from each set, both output(s) and a computation.) Since each of the steps in that computation is deterministic, and transforms the values of some variables (when the statement starts) into (possibly) new values (when it finishes), the whole computation (i.e. sequence of executed statements) together shows how all of the initial variable values (including the inputs) were transformed into all of the final variable values (including the outputs). That is, the computation, in turn, can also be regarded as expressing a function from inputs to outputs:

$$Computation(Inputs) \rightarrow Outputs$$

And clearly, the computation (as a function) produces the same outputs as $TDSP_O$ for the inputs which created it. Seeing the similarity between the first and third expressions (or signatures) above might even lead one to the incorrect conclusion that the computation produced by a TDSP can now be used in place of the TDSP (i.e. $TDSP_O$) to find the outputs for any inputs. The flaw in that reasoning is that the computation is not general: It will produce the same outputs as the TDSP for the same inputs that created the computation from the TDSP in the first place, but not necessarily any other inputs. (We might avoid such misdirection by subscripting Computation as well, with the TDSP and the inputs used to create it.) We can, however, safely consider another form of the TDSP, which is just like $TDSP_{O,C}$ but which ignores (throws away) the output and just produces a computation, which we'll call $TDSP_C$:

$$TDSP_C(Inputs) \rightarrow Computation$$

So, for example, Figure 8.2 can be considered the result of the binary search "subscript C" when evaluated on the inputs specified in the Figure caption, and the next subsection will show how it can be interpreted as a function.

By applying $TDSP_C$ to the inputs once to get a computation, and then applying the resulting computation to the same inputs again to get the outputs, we can get the same results we could have gotten from $TDSP_O$:

$$(TDSP_C(Inputs))(Inputs) \rightarrow Outputs$$

What is gained by this approach? If the outputs are created by a TDSP in order to create the computation anyway, why discard them and then recreate

141

them by evaluating the computation with the same inputs? We're not really proposing doing that, just separating computing the result from deciding which steps should be followed to compute the result.

One reason it could be beneficial is that, in general, a computation like this is a simpler function to compute than a TDSP. In traditional computing lingo, a TDSP is equivalent to a **partial recursive function**, the most complex and powerful form of function around, and that's basically a result of including constructs like the `while` statement in our example, which are very powerful but can also make it very difficult to figure out precisely what's going to happen when the function is evaluated. By the time the computation is produced, however, all of the effects of these so-called control statements (like `while` and `if` and their kin) has been felt, the computation has been "unrolled" from the TDSP, so that computation can now be regarded as just a sequence of non-repeating, non-optional steps, as "straight line code" or "a basic block", as a programmer might say. It is much easier to deal with such a function mathematically, without resorting to (say) recursive functions, and thereby to more easily see how the outputs resulted from the inputs.

Inside a modern computer, when evaluating a TDSP, the computer indeed tries very hard to produce as much of the computation as it can as early as it can, so that it can get a clearer idea of what is coming up in the future. That can help it to schedule the movement of information around the computer (such as fetching information from memory) so that it can be where it needs to be in a timely manner. The computer is restricted in how far ahead it can determine the computation trace, before some of the variables have been computed, but great efforts are made to do what can be done, such as to compute the variables needed to determine the computation first. In fact, this "straight line" sort of function, as represented by our sequential computation, is exactly the sort of function which today's graphics processor units (GPUs) are so efficient at computing, precisely because there are no surprizes about the operations to be performed next.

Considering it from the other direction, the act of planning (e.g. programming) can be considered as determining what computation should be produced, and then how to produce it, for any input of interest. One can then work backwards to consider a TDSP as a convenient, compact representation of all of the potential computations one might need to solve a particular kind of problem for any input, each like a strand of string, all of them folded/wound up until they look somewhat like each other. (In fact, when a particular sequence of statements must be repeated, computer programmers refer to it as a "loop", just as if one of those compuation strings had been looped onto itself in the TDSP.) Each decision point in the TDSP (in a control statement like `while` or `if`, for example) then represents the different ways in which to unwind a computation back off of the plan, depending on the values of various variables within the plan at that point.

8.2.4 Example of Function Corresponding to Computation

To reveal the mathematical function to which the binary search computation in Figure 8.2 corresponds – i.e. the **functionalized computation** – first omit all of the steps that have only to do with controlling the execution (i.e. all of the `while` and `if` statements, which have no effects other than changing the sequence of statements), since they have already done their job. This leaves only the intervening statements (which could in general each be statement sequences):

```
int to_check = n_elems / 2; (i.e. 3)
int jump_dist = n_elems / 4 + 1; (i.e. 2)
    to_check += jump_dist; (i.e. 5)
  jump_dist /= 2; (i.e. 1)
    to_check -= jump_dist (i.e. 4)
  jump_dist /= 2; (i.e. 1)
return to_check; (i.e. 4)
```

To consider this as a function, we will first switch to slightly more mathematical notation by abbreviating each of the variables above to its first letter, and will then name the different values assigned to that variable over time as the variable name augmented with an appropriate number of primes to indicate its instance – so, for example, the first value assigned to `to_check` will be called t, the second will be called t', etc. We use the equivalence symbol ($\equiv$) rather than equality ($=$) to represent that each of these names is actually just another name for the value, rather than just a temporary container of it as a variable might be. Translating each of the above statements one by one, we get:

$t \equiv \frac{n}{2}$
$j \equiv \frac{n}{4}+1$
$t' \equiv t + j$
$j' \equiv \frac{j}{2}$
$t'' \equiv t' - j'$
$j'' \equiv \frac{j'}{2}$

and the final return statement indicates that the value returned by the function is the final value assigned to `to_check` – i.e. t'', which reduces to:

$t'' = t' - j' = t + j - \frac{j}{2} = \frac{n}{2} + \frac{n}{4} + 1 - \frac{\frac{n}{4}+1}{2}$

We will use the Greek symbol Ξ to represent the functional form of a computation, subscripted by the program and arguments from which it resulted, so the computation resulting from the evaluation of binsearch('r', "abefrsv", 7) is:

$\Xi_{binsearch('r','abefrsv',7)}(t, l, n) = \frac{n}{2} + \frac{n}{4} + 1 - \frac{\frac{n}{4}+1}{2}$

It is apparent that, in this particular case, the t and l arguments (`to_find` and `list`) don't even appear in the expression on the right, since their contribution was solely in helping to construct the computation function, rather than factoring into the result mathematically: They were in a sense "used up" by the TDSP while constructing the computation. When applied to the same arguments as were supplied to the TDSP to produce it in the first place, this functionalized computation does indeed show precisely how (and which of) the original arguments were combined together to produce the answer:

143

$$\Xi_{binsearch('r','abefrsv',7)}('r','abefrsv',7) = \frac{7}{2} + \frac{7}{4} + 1 - \frac{\frac{7}{4}+1}{2}$$

$$= 3 + 1 + 1 - \frac{1+1}{2} = 4$$

8.2.5 Structured Planning

The binary search plan was expressed in a so-called structured style, in which indentation is used as punctuation to highlight so-called control statements, which separate and punctuate the otherwise "straight-line" statement subsequences (sometimes known as basic blocks) from which the computation will be built. When comparing the plan to the computation (in the form of an execution trace), the intuitive value of this indentation becomes clear: It helps to form associations between statements which are physically far apart, but which are in some sense logically close together. More specifically, any two statements which are adjacent in the computation will also be either immediately adjacent in the plan, or adjacent at the same level of indentation in the plan. [1]

We can make this more formal by defining two statements as being **logically adjacent** in the plan whenever they are either immediately adjacent there or adjacent at the same level of indentation. We can then say that two statements will be adjacent in the computation only when they are logically adjacent in the plan. In general, for any form of plan, if we can find some definition of logical adjacence for which this is true, and which makes each statement (or action) logically adjacent to only a small number of other statements (or actions), then we will say that plan is **structured** with respect to that definition. The power of having such a definition, then, is to be able to tell, just by looking at the plan, which few statements might be adjacent to any other statement in the computation – i.e. which statement might come next.

8.2.6 Summary: Sequential Algorithms and Computation

So, within the sequential world, a TDSP (e.g. an algorithm or program) describes how to solve a problem by somehow depicting all of the potential appropriate sequential computations, each a sequence of operations. Because the precise sequence making up that computation may depend upon the inputs (or other initial conditions), the TDSP (algorithm or program) isn't a computation (i.e. sequence) itself, but represents a number of different potential computations, with the precise one for the problem at hand being determined by the input. To facilitate this representation, the TDSP typically looks a lot like a computation, but with various parts (i.e. subsequences of operations) optionally included and/or repeated as necessary, based on some part of the state (such as the content of variables) as the sequence is being followed. The effect is that the TDSP can be regarded as taking all of the computations that it must potentially represent, and folding or winding them up into a common form.

---

[1] Slight liberties in this definition may be required to accommodate so-called "case" or "switch" statements, but the concept remains intact.

Conversely, a computation can be considered as an unwinding or unfolding of a TDSP.

Moreover, as programming matured, to make the correspondence between the TDSP and the computation more intuitive, structured programming approaches have been developed which help to illustrate which operations in the TDSP might end up being adjacent in any resulting computation, thereby simplifying analysis of the TDSP.

8.3 Concurrent Computation

In this section, we go back to concurrent plans (strategies) to see if we can exploit some of the insight gained in the previous section (regarding traditional deterministic sequential plans, TDSPs) but in the context of concurrency.

8.3.1 Algorithms, Programs, Computation

If we take a strategy to be a concurrent analog to a TDSP (as seems perfectly rational), we might assume that the computation associated with a strategy might resemble an unwinding or unfolding of the strategy, recording what actually happened during an activation of that strategy. Just as each execution of a statement in a TDSP was recorded as a unit in the sequential computation above, it makes sense that the activation of a tactic – i.e. an acton – in a strategy would be recorded as a unit in our concurrent computation. The atomicity and determinism properties of actons make them especially appropriate to act as the analogs of statement executions.

As the sequence of statements unwound from the TDSP, each was operating on and transforming an environment, which in that case could be regarded as the storage (e.g. variable values) and execution state (e.g. indication of the next statement to execute). All of the information needed (or at least available) about how each statement was affecting that storage and state was present in the sequencing of the statements and the text of the statement itself. In our concurrent computation, we know that each acton can only be affected by, and can only affect, the content and control state of the resources to which it is bound by its context. To preserve this information in the computation, perhaps in hopes of using it when interpreting the computation as a function, we would like to carry it into the concurrent computation.

This suggests the general form of our concurrent computation. First, realize that any ScalPL strategy, such as that shown on the left side of Figure 8.3 has the same meaning (also known as semantics) regardless of how the parts are laid out on the page as long as the parts and names and connections remain the same, so for the purposes of creating a computation, consider first reoganizing any such strategy in a linear, horizontal way, such as we have done at the top right of Figure 8.3. That is, all of the resources are laid out horizontally, and all of the contexts are situated just below them, but with all of the same names and bindings, etc. Assuming that a and b are tactics, the computation in this figure is almost completely determined in advance: First a will activate, and

145

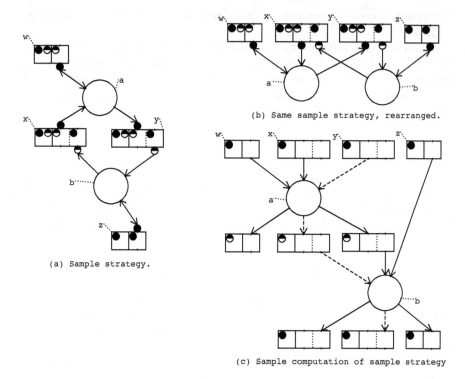

(a) Sample strategy.

(b) Same sample strategy, rearranged.

(c) Sample computation of sample strategy

Figure 8.3: A simple ScalPL strategy, and its computation.

change the control state of all three resources (and the content state of two of them), and then b will activate, and then nothing else.

We'll now effectively record this plan as it executes, to form a computation, as shown in the bottom right of Figure 8.3. We start that computation at the top with one **resource state rectangle** (or resource state node) for each of the resources from the strategy, each representing the initial control and content state of that resource. Then, each time a tactic activates, we will represent that activation with a new **activation circle** (or activation node) in the computation, labeled the same as the associated context holding that tactic, and we add new state rectangles below it to represent the new control and content states that it assigns to each of its resources (i.e. only those filling its roles, to which it is bound). Each activation circle is connected to the resource states above it (the "pre" states) and below it (the "post" states) for each of its resources, with arrows (similarly called "pre" and "post"). These arrows are similar to role bindings, but not quite:

1. These pre and post arrows always point down, and have no signal bindings, nor access dots connecting them to the resource states.

2. They are dashed (rather than solid) if they represent no information trans- fer. Specifically, a pre arrow will be dashed if and only if the associated role binding does not have observe permission, and a post arrow will be

dashed if and only if the associated role binding does not have replace permission. In other words, solid arrows represent potential flow of information between the resources and/or resource states and the tactic activations, while dashed arrows do not. (In later diagrams, these are represented as arrowless solid lines.)

The result is a graph, which starts at the top and proceeds toward the bottom. In general, any connected graph that consists of nodes (like our state rectangles and activation circles) and arrows where it is impossible to follow an arrow from any node back to that node is called a **Directed Acyclic Graph**, or **DAG** for short, so our computation is indeed a DAG. And any graph that contains two kinds of nodes, and for which each connecting line ("edge", or arrow in a directed graph) always connects one kind of node to the other (rather than to two of the same kind), is called a **Bipartite Graph**, so our computation is also one of those. Altogether, then, the computation for a strategy is a bipartite DAG.

In the case of TDSPs, we envisioned the computation as unwinding from the TDSP, and conversely, could envision the TDSP as being created from winding up all the computations that might be produced by it into a compact form. This new concurrent computation can also be envisioned that way, especially if we replace the dashed arrows in the computation with undirected lines (i.e. with no arrowhead), as we will subsequently. In that case, you can see how the computation can be folded up onto the algorithm, as long as the lines can stretch, and (if necessary) the circles and rectangles can fold. For example, consider the computation in the lower right of Figure 8.3 printed on a transparent plastic, dashed arrows replaced with solid undirected arcs, and then folding the plastic horizontally through the center of each the two activation circles and the center row of resource state rectangles. The resulting diagram would essentially fit exactly onto the strategy above it, modulo some access and control state dots. Just as in the sequential case, the plan (strategy) can once again be considered a folded up form of computations which might result from it.

8.3.2 Example of Concurrent Computation

So let's try to capture a computation for a more familiar concurrent algorithm – i.e. the waffle-making plan from Chapter 2, with the stipulation (from Chapter 3) that all of the activities therein are actons. See Figure 8.4.

Consider the mix, preheat, set, and ask activation circles on the first row. Notice that none of these shares any resources. They all act entirely independently. The vertical axis is not meant to represent (absolute) time, so the computation (in general) doesn't show the order in which they activated, relative to one another, or whether they all activated at the same time (concurrently). However, the lines/arrows do show that the mix, preheat and ask activations all occur before the first spoon activation. That is, the first mix, preheat, set, and ask activations in this computation are not ordered (relative to each other), but they are all ordered relative to the first spoon activation. A more formal way of saying that some things in a set are ordered and some are not is that the set is **partially ordered**, or that the set together with some ordering relation

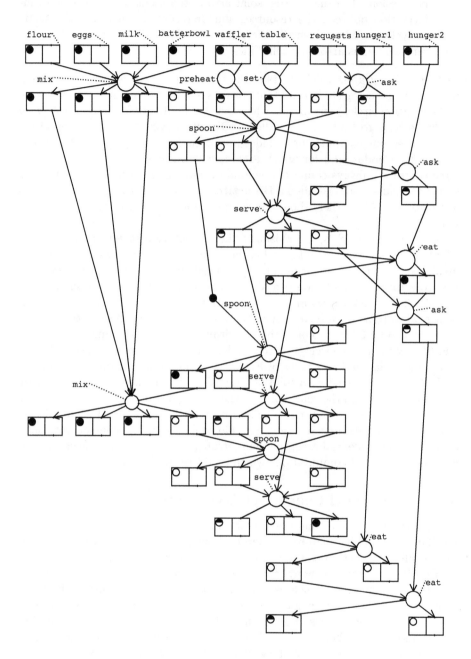

Figure 8.4: A ScalPL computation for waffles.

(indicated by our arrows) is a **partial order** (or **P.O.**). DAGs are one way of representing partial orders, in general. So, concurrent computations are partial orders of activations. They are also partial orders of resource states. All of the resource states for any one resource are totally oredered (i.e. a sequence), and so are all of the activations within any one context

In general, whenever two contexts holding tactics are bound to at least one common resource in a ScalPL strategy, the activations of those tactics within those contexts will be ordered in the computation, because only one can activate at a time, and that will create a new resource state which the other will use. If contexts are not bound to a common resource, the resulting tactic activations may or may not be ordered. For example, in this computation, the second `mix` activation is ordered relative to the `preheat` activation, because you can follow arrows from the `preheat` operation to that second `mix` activation. They don't have any common resources, but (for example) the second `mix` would not be activated until the `batterbowl` (filled by the first `mix` activation) was emptied by `spoon` activations, which could only occur after the `waffler` was preheated.

This computation may seem surprising or unfair in some ways. For example, we are modeling two eaters (with resources `hunger1` and `hunger2`), and they are both asking for waffles (one at a time for each), but there is no guarantee that they will get their waffles in the order in which they requested them, and in this case, they surely do not: Eater one asks, then eater two asks, eater two receives and eats the first waffle and asks again, and only after a new bowl of batter is made does eater one finally receive his first waffle. If this same strategy were to activate again, the resulting computation could come out to be very different: Maybe eater one would request and eat a waffle before eater two even requested one. The strategy in this case has not specified the specific order in which eaters one and two must request and/or eat their waffles: These are not determined by the strategy, meaning that the strategy is nondeterministic. The strategy does determine, however, that an eater will only eat after requesting a waffle, and will finish eating one waffle before requesting another.

8.3.3 Characterizing Input and Output for Strategies

Before continuing, we need to define what we mean by inputs and outputs, as they relate to a strategy. It seems logical to somehow relate input and output of the strategy to its corresponding formal resources, since those are the mechanisms by which such information would be fed to and from a strategy, and we have already used roles in describing inputs and outputs for one form of plan (i.e. tactics), not to mention that roles are the rough analogs of arguments and results as used in a TDSP function earlier in this chapter.

But strategies can exhibit far more complex input-output behavior on their roles than tactics can: In fact, that's been a primary motivation for our developing strategies in the first place. Instead of acting like an acton, atomically observing content associated with one set of roles and producing content on some (possibly overlapping) set of roles and issuing a single control state transition to all, a strategy may, in general, take or produce (or both) sequences of content and control states on some roles in various orders while taking or producing just single content states on others, etc. In some cases, it would be nearly hopeless to characterize, as input and output, all of the possible patterns of content and/or control state that a strategy might react to or modify/create on each of the formal resources, during its lifetime, relative to one another. (Many formal techniques, such as temporal logic, have been developed for characterizing patterns and interrelationships like this, but it is not clear that they offer us much advantage here.)

Fortunately, we don't need to describe such complex patterns, because, simply put, for any extremely complex input-output behavior one strategy might exhibit or require on its formal resources, another strategy will be capable of producing such behavior on the actual resources to which those formals correspond. To think otherwise, that a child strategy could exhibit or require behavior so complex that it could not be handled or created by another (parent) strategy, would not only nullify the whole reason for developing the child strategy in the first place, it would also lead to an odd reasoning that a child strategy was somehow more powerful (to be able to require or recognize certain complex behavior on its roles) than a parent strategy was (to be able to present such behavior to it on the actuals) – even though they are built with exactly the same constructs!

So, we can assume there is some parent strategy which has no formal resources which exhibits the proper behavior in its actual resources to satisfy the child strategy's needs for its associated formal resources. In a sense, this parent can be considered *as* the input/output specification for the child. If we consider the child and parent together, as one integrated strategy, we can then simply take the initial content states of some or all the resources (e.g. in the parent) as the input and the final control and content states of some or all the resources (e.g. in the parent) as the output.

8.3.4 Computations as Functions

In the sequential case earlier in this chapter, we spoke of considering a TDSP as either a function from inputs to outputs, calling it $TDSP_O$, or as a function from inputs to a computation, which we called $TDSP_C$. In the concurrent case, however, a plan (i.e. strategy) may be nondeterministic, and produce any of a number of different results for the same input (i.e. initial content states of its resources), so if we refer to the relation from inputs (initial resource content states) to outputs (final content states) as $Strategy_O$, and the relation from inputs to a computation as $Strategy_C$, then neither

$$Strategy_O(Inputs) \rightarrow Outputs$$

nor

$$Strategy_C(Inputs) \rightarrow Computation$$

is necessarily a function. However, perhaps suprisingly (as we will explain shortly), even for nondeterministic strategies, the computation produced by a strategy,

$$Computation(Inputs) \rightarrow Outputs$$

can be considered a function. So although the composition

$$(Strategy_C(Inputs))(Inputs) \rightarrow Outputs$$

still makes sense, the first evaluation (of $Strategy_C$) is not necessarily a function, but the second evaluation (of the resulting computation) will be.

To see the functional nature of the computation, simply recognize that each activation circle represents an acton which, by definition, expresses a function from the content states of its "pre" resource states (and actually just the observable ones) to the content states of its "post" resource states. (The content state of some of those "post" resource states – i.e. the ones without replace/update usage – are not changed from the corresponding "pre" content, but that's still a function, the identity function.) So, the content of the initial resource states is dictated by the initial inputs, and the content of each other resource state is dictated as the result of an activation node (i.e. the evaluation of a function on the "pre" resource states), which means the content of any resource state in the computation (including any that are considered part of the output) is the result of applying zero or more functions to some or all of the original inputs in an order dictated by the computation. In other words, a computation can just be considered a non-standard representation of functional composition.

This demonstrates not only that a computation always represents a function from some inputs to outputs, even for nondeterministic strategies, but that the content and control state of every one of resource states within the computation is completely determined by the inputs that created the computation from the plan/program, which is a rather stronger assertion.

8.3.5 Example of function corresponding to computation

Recall that in the sequential case, after the computation unwound from the algorithm, it contained some left-over remnants that were now useless, such as control statements originally used to help decide the next statement to execute – decisions which had already been made in creating the computation. When we deleted those useless statements, it was easier to understand the remaining structure as a function. That process and the result, which we called a functionalized computation, are very similar in the concurrent situation.

The extra remnants, in the concurrent case, are anything dealing with the control state portion of the resource states, since the entire purpose of control state is to control how the computation can unfold from the algorithm. We will create a functionalized computation by deleting all hints of control states, not only from the resource states, but also removing all dashed arrows (which are a cause and/or result only of control states, rather than of information flow).

Figure 8.5 contains the functionalized computation graph corresponding to the waffle computation in Figure 8.4. After removing the dashed arrows arrows, we have simplified what's left. For example, some of the resource states may still have one arrow in and one out, while others may have no arrows in, or no arrows out, or no arrows at all. First, unless they are the last representing their resources, delete the resource states with no arrows at all, since they are not unique in either contributing to or resulting from other activities. Then,

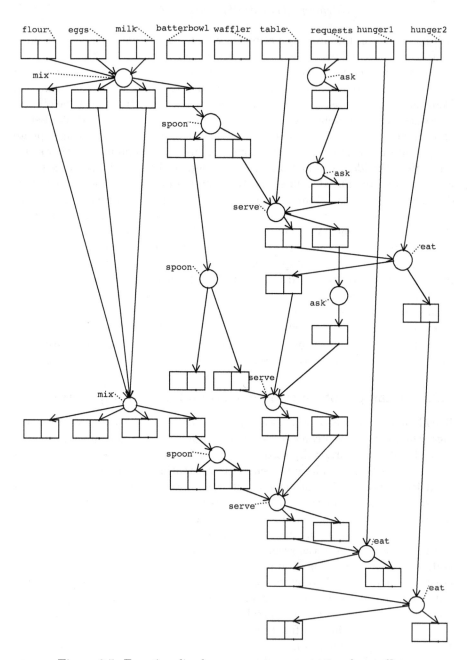

Figure 8.5: Functionalized concurrent computation for waffles.

if any resource states have only arrows out (and not in), merge them with the previous (above) one for the same resource: Since there were no intervening arrows in, those two resource states must represent the same content state for that resource. This may result in some resource states with multiple arrows out: That's OK for a functionalized computation graph.

Starting at any resource state, arrows can be traced back to find all of the potential contributors to its content. Note that some of the resource states are **content dead**, in the sense that their content state doesn't contribute to any future content states. In this graph, for example, the initial resource state for both `batterbowl` and `waffler` goes completely unused (both starting empty), and the 4th `batterbowl` resource state (of 6) is also content dead, because the content of that bowl is discarded when the new batter is mixed. (It didn't have to be that way, but that is how the plan was specified.)

This graph may not appear as a function at first glance, but that is almost entirely because it (and many or all of the intermediate acton activations) has multiple results. Traditional textual functional composition is based on the principle that functions return only a single value. To get a better grasp of a concurrent computation graph as a traditional mathematical function, one can consider each acton as a set of functions, one for each content state result (i.e. role with replace/update usage). So, for example, `mix` can be considered as four traditional functions, which we denote here by subscripting the function name with the result it produces:

$$mix_{flour}(flour, eggs, milk)$$

$$mix_{eggs}(flour, eggs, milk)$$

$$mix_{milk}(flour, eggs, milk)$$

and

$$mix_{batter}(flour, eggs, milk)$$

Now, the content of the four resource state rectangles below the first `mix` activation circle in the computation can be represented by these four functions evaluated on the inputs (initial content states) for `flour`, `eggs`, and `milk`. By using this same approach throughout, the content of the final resource state for `batterbowl`, for example, can be considered as

$$spoon_{batterbowl}(mix_{batterbowl}(mix_{flour}(flour, eggs, milk),$$
$$mix_{eggs}(flour, eggs, milk),$$
$$mix_{milk}(flour, eggs, milk)))$$

where $flour$, $eggs$, and $milk$ represent the original input values (content states) of those resources, and all function applications are traditional single-valued functions.

8.3.6   Structured Planning

For TDSPs, we presented a general characterization of structured planning. We said that a plan can be called structured if one can define a property of logical adjacency for elements of a plan, such that (a) an entity is logically adjacent to no more than a small number of other elements, and (b) elements that are physically adjacent in the computation are logically adjacent in the plan.

In the case of a strategy (i.e. a concurrent plan), the logical adjacency property is pretty simple: Two elements are logically adjacent in the plan if they are connected by a line (role binding). This qualifies as relating only a relatively small number of elements as being logically adjacent to any other element. And based on this, any elements that are physically adjacent in the computation (i.e. connected with pre or post arrows) are also logically adjacent in the plan. We therefore argue that ScalPL plans are structured with respect to this definition of computations and logical adjacency. The reason that strategies can be considered structured (in this way) is precisely because the computation can be considered (so directly) as unfolding from the plan, just as in the sequential case.

This structured aspect of ScalPL is relatively rare among concurrent planning techniques. In many traditional approaches to concurrency, the plan is represented as a completely disjoint set of TDSPs which interact in rather subtle and sometimes unpredictable ways, making it possible for parts of the plan which are far apart to interact closely in the computation, with very little indication of such in the plan.

8.4   Summary

A computation is a trace of what happens within a plan when it is carried out (in a specific instance). For traditional deterministic sequential plans (TDSPs) like sequential programs and algorithms, this trace will be the same whenever the inputs to the plan are the same, but it is not necessarily so for a concurrent plan (strategy), which may be nondeterministic: In that case, the computation may be different each time the plan is carried out, even with the same inputs. Still, regardless of whether a plan is deterministic or not, the computation tells exactly what happened, so if the computation *is* the same, the results are necessarily the same. In other words, the computation can be considered as a function from inputs to results, regardless of whether that computation was the result of a deterministic or nondeterministic plan.

In this view, the computation is what the planner wants to have happen (for a particular input), and the plan is the way to get there. In the sequential world, the effect of this goal has been to make plans look very much like the computations that result. They can even look exactly the same, if the desired computation is very simple – i.e. a sequence. But in general, there are parts of the computation that must differ from one input to the next, such as only including some operational subsequences on certain inputs, or to insert some subsequences repeatedly. Sequential plans have taken a form, called structured planning (or programming) which makes the correspondence between the plan and the resulting computations apparent. The computation can be considered as unwinding (in rather obvious ways) from the plan, or conversely, a plan can be considered as being constructed of the common aspects of the computations which it is to produce, glued together with conditional constructs (such as "if" and "while" shown here) that allow the parts to be included, excluded, or repeated as necessay into the computation. Structured planning makes it easier to understand which parts of the original plan might appear together in the computation.

While the computation for a TDSP is a sequence of operations, the computation for a strategy can be constructed as a partial ordering (P.O.), or directed acyclic graph (DAG), showing how actons carry some resource states to other resource states. Such a computation (or computation graph) can also be interpreted as an unfolding of its plan (the strategy), so strategies can also be considered as structured plans, being similar to the folding up of computations which could potentially result from it. These concurrent computation graphs can also be regarded as functions. In other words, seqential plans and concurrent plans can have a great deal in common, in spite of their obvious differences (which include nondeterminism in concurrent plans).

Chapter 9

Nondeterminism and Atomicity

Tactics are deterministic, by definition, and their resulting actons are atomic, by definition. In general, plans and their resulting activities, respectively, can be neither, either, or both deterministic and/or atomic. How can we recognize and/or ensure that a strategy is deterministic? That its activities are atomic? What do these terms really mean and are there different varieties? We will also introduce constructs to simplify atomicity enforcement. What are the benefits and drawbacks of enforcing each of these properties? How can we go about debugging a nondeterministic strategy?

9.1   Nondeterminism

9.1.1   Definition

> Nondeterminism: A property of computation which may have more than one result.
> – Free Online Dictionary of Computing (FOLDOC)

Nondeterminism is the property that something is not fully determined. As indicated by this definition, in our context here, that thing which is not fully determined is usually taken to be the result that will be delivered by a plan for any particular input. Now that we are familiar with the concept of *a* computation (rather than computation in general, as in that definition) as an intermediate entity between a plan and the result, we can break this property down a little more, to consider whether the computation itself is aso fully determined or not. From Chapter 8, we know that the same computation will always produce the same result for the same inputs, so if the plan always produces the same computation when given the same inputs, we can safely call the plan **fully deterministic**, regardless of whether referring to results or computation. (Since computations are graphs, the term "the same computation" should really read "an isomorphic computations" – i.e. one where there is a one-to-one correspondence between the activity instances in the two graphs and between the resource instances in the two graphs such that the edges and labels between

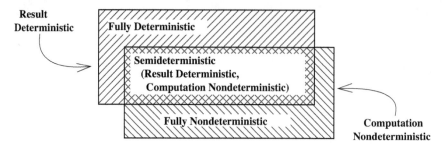

Figure 9.1: Universe of plans, categorized by determinism.

corresponding nodes correspond.) Conversely, if the same plan can return different results when given the same inputs, then these results must also result from different computations, so the plan can safely be called **fully nondeterministic**, regardless of whether refering to results or computation. But there is a third case, because a plan may yield different computations for a set of inputs while continuing to yield identical results in every case. We will call this last case **semideterministic** (to the best of our knowledge, a term coined here). Collectively, fully deterministic and semideterministic can be referred to as result deterministic, since they always return the same result for any input, and semideterministic and fully nondeterministic can be referred to as computation nondeterministic, since the computation may vary even with the same input. See Figure 9.1 to see how these different categories relate, with external labels referring to the large rectangles, and internal labels referring only to the same enclosed area (with same shading). In turn, fully deterministic is also sometimes called computation deterministic, and fully nondeterministic as result nondeterministic.

9.1.2 Syntactic (Strategy) Computation Determinism

Certain strategies can be determined to be computation deterministic (and therefore fully deterministic) by inspection, regardless of the definitions of their individual child plans, as long as it is known that those children are atomic and deterministic (e.g. like tactics). For example, if all contexts within a strategy hold tactics, and no two roles (from different tactics) are bound to the same resource with the same color of access dot, then the strategy must be deterministic. That is because, for any one resource, the lack of sharing of control states means that the resource's control state uniquely determines at most one context able to access that resource next. If the tactic in that context is indeed ready to activate (because the control states of all of its other resources also designate it as next), then it will remain forever ready to activate (until it does), because (by our initial assumption) there is no other context which could steal or alter the control state of any of its resources (by issuing a control state transition). And, since the ready context will always be ready, the liveness rules say that it must eventually activate, and when it does, it must deterministically assign (or not assign) a new control state to each of its

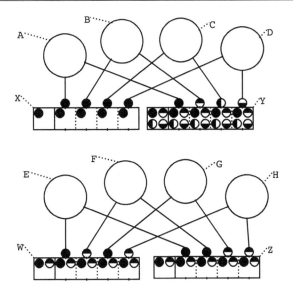

Figure 9.2: Two deterministic plans.

resources, which in turn can allow at most one other context to access each of those resources next. Since the initial state of all resources is determined by the input the entire computation is deterministic.

The same argument holds even if some control states are shared (i.e. have multiple matching access dots), as long as no more than one of the actons sharing that control state can access it at any one time, such as in Figure 9.2. In the top example, all of the actons share the initial control state of resource X, but they are each uniquely bound to one of the four control states of resource Y, meaning that Y alone dictates which can activate next. In the bottom example, both control states of both resources are shared by more than one context, but their combination still only permits one context to be ready at a time: The control states of W and Z together effectively encode the same four control states as the top plan, but in binary: Y's all black, top black, left black, and right black, respectively, are encoded by W/Z's black/black, half/black, black/half, and half/half. In general, if there is some set of contexts with atomic plans, and some set of resources, such that all of the contexts are bound to (at least) all of the resources, and the combined control states of all of those resources allow at most one context to be ready at any one time, then the order in which the plans in those contexts will access those resources is deterministic.

Perhaps it should go without saying that one way to verify syntactically that two or more contexts will not be ready at the same time is for all (or all but one) of them to provably *never* be ready at all. That is, if some contexts containing tactics are bound to a dead (unreachable) control state of some resource, they will never be able to activate, and therefore will not contribute to nondeterminism, even if they share control states with other contexts. Since dead states can be found syntactically, analyses above and elsewhere will assume

159

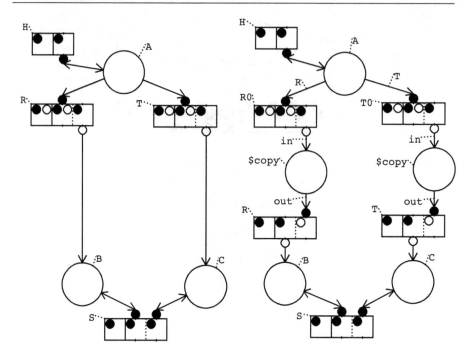

Figure 9.3: Left may be deterministic or not depending upon tactic A.

that such never-ready contexts have been excluded from consideration.

9.1.3 Semantic (Tactic) Computation Determinism

Some strategies cannot be judged to be computation deterministic (i.e. fully deterministic) without delving into the behavior of some of the tactics. Tactics are always deterministic (by definition), but their behavior can still determine whether a strategy containing them will be deterministic. For example, consider the simple strategy on the left in Figure 9.3. If we know that acton A will never give resource R the white control state in the same activation that it gives resource T the white control state, then we will also know that actons B and C cannot both be ready at the same time, so the strategy is deterministic. Conversely, if we do not know that about A, then we have no way of knowing whether B and C might be ready at the same time, in which case we must assume that the strategy might be computation nondeterministic.

Note that, in general, due to the potential arbitrary complexity of A (being partial recursive), it may not be possible to statically (syntactically) determine how it will act even after examining it. Practically speaking, however, with some small effort A's planner can often make it obvious (by observation) that it would issue the transition bound to the white control state to at most one of R and T.

The strategy on the right of Figure 9.3 is very similar to that on the left.

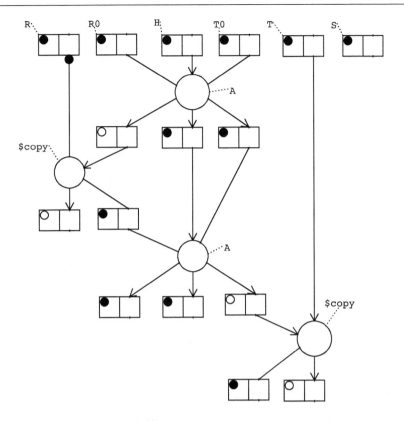

Figure 9.4: Possible computation prefix for Figure 9.3 (right plan).

The only difference is that the content and control state are transfered from R0 to R, and from T0 to T, by $copy actons (as introduced in Chapter 4). From this, one might suspect that the strategy on the right will also be computation deterministic under the same conditions on A as the strategy on the left. That suspicion would be *wrong*. The plan on the right is always computation nondeterministic. For example, consider any computation starting as in Figure 9.4 where A activates transitioning R0, the left $copy activates, A activates again transitioning T0, and the right $copy activates. As can be seen from the bottom state nodes in this computation prefix, either B or C could activate at this point, and since both access S, this would lead to different computations and potentially different results. This is the very nature of so-called **race conditions**: Effects are not necessarily felt, at some distant point or after some steps, in the same order in which they initially occurred, because the effect of one may overtake another.

9.1.4 Result Determinism (Specifically, Semideterminism)

As described earlier, all plans which are computation deterministic are also result deterministic. But some plans may be compute nondeterministic but still

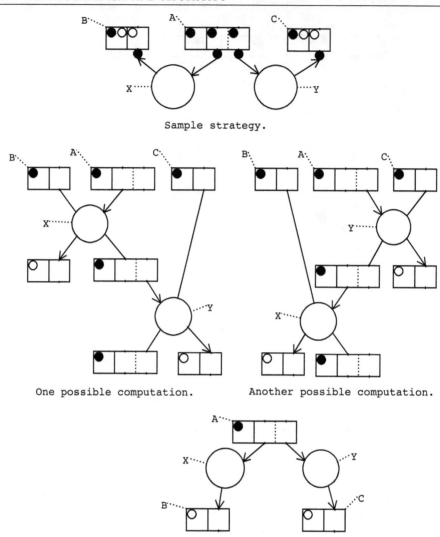

Sample strategy.

One possible computation.   Another possible computation.

Figure 9.5: Simple strategy, two potential resulting computations, and the functionalized computation.

result deterministic, which we referred to earlier as being semideterministic. Generally speaking, a semideterministic plan may provide a Director more opportunities for efficient scheduling on a platform than a fully deterministic one, because not only are there different scheduling options within a given computation (as with even a deterministic plan), but different computations.

One situation where an intuitively deterministic ScalPL plan may be only semideterministic is when many contexts share a single control state of a resource but all of them just observe the content state and don't change the control state, as in the strategy at the top of Figure 9.5 for resource A. That is, this occurs when some of the role bindings which share a control state are not only predictable, but also all leave the control state unchanged, making the order in which they access that resource immaterial to the final result. Although such a strategy can technically lead to multiple computations, as in the center of the figure, that is due more to ScalPL's specific rules (i.e. our drive to simplify our rules by treating observations like any other access) than to any deeper difficulty. The issue is resolved if we consider the functionalized computations (as described in the previous chapter) corresponding to those computations. In that case, all of the computations are indeed the same, because resource states with unchanged content are merged. See the bottom of Figure 9.5.

To show that a given plan is result deterministic, we need to show that all of the computations producable from that plan will produce the same result. If the plan is computation deterministic, this is obvious (in that all the computations are the same, and a computation is a function), so the challenge is for computation nondeterministic (and therefore semideterministic) plans. The common technique is to show that certain portions (subgraphs) of different computations, although different, will produce identical results, and then to show that all of the differences in the different computations can be accounted for that way (by either converting the subgraphs of one into the other, or converting the subgraphs of both to a common representation).

Quite often, the demonstration that different subgraphs will produce the same result is based on properties commonly encountered in mathematics, most notably commutativity –i.e. that the order in which the operands are presented to some operations (like addition and multiplication, for example) is immaterial to the outcome, so "A operation B" (e.g. $a + b$) gives the same result as "B operation A" (e.g. $b + a$). Occasionally, other properties like associativity (e.g. $a + (b + c) = (a + b) + c$) and distributivity (e.g. $a(b + c) = ab + ac$) can also be used. It should be noted, however, that although certain properties (like these) may always be true in ideal math, they are often not always true when operations are only carried out to limited precision, as they are in most computers, calculators, and people's heads: The field of numerical analysis is indeed involved with (among other things) determining the best order to perform operations to preserve the most meaning with limited precision. That is beyond the scope of this text, and further examples will assume that commutative operations are indeed mathematically commutative in every way.

Consider the example plan at the top of Figure 9.6. (The plan is actually shown there twice, once in junction dot form, the other without, but they are the same plan.) In it, the subplan Comm activates three times, observing each of resources A, B, and C, and each time updating resource X, but the order in which these three activate is not determined, so (assuming that Comm is a tactic) there are six possible different computations. Two of the functionalized computations are shown at the bottom of the figure, where the final content of X is $Comm(B, Comm(C, Comm(A, X)))$ and $Comm(C, Comm(A, Comm(B, X)))$ respectively (expressing the roles in and to as the first and second arguments of Comm(), and the new value of to as its only result). If Comm was represented by the infix operator $\otimes$, those could be written $B \otimes C \otimes A \otimes X$ and $C \otimes A \otimes B \otimes X$, respectively. And if Comm (i.e. $\otimes$) is known to be a commutative operator (like

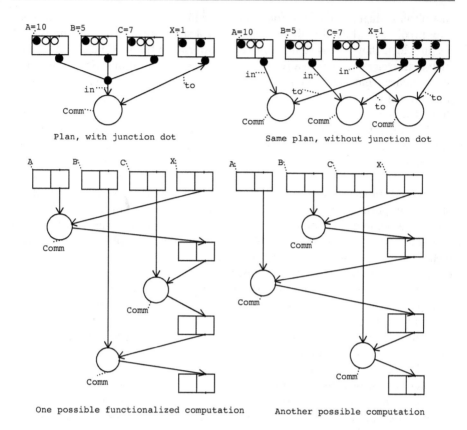

Figure 9.6: Plan Comm activates 3 times, each observing its **in** role and updating its **to** role.

× or +), these two expressions are easily shown to be equal.

Rather than first converting the results of the execution graph to some more common mathematical notation and demonstrating those equal, equivalence classes can be defined on computations through graph rewriting. For example, consider the graph rewrite rule in Figure 9.7, where #I and #J are intended to be replaced (consistently) by any resource state. Using this rule, the two computation graphs in Figure 9.6 can be shown to be equivalent in two steps.

Instead of considering whether computations can be mapped directly to each other, another approach is to simplify (or reduce) some or all of each computation graph to a simpler form. Since examples of such forms would require yet another set of notations and rules, we will not delve more deeply into this approach here, as it is largely beyond the scope of, and potentially confusing to, the points made in the rest of this book. Assuming that some representation is found for representing an entire class of computations (such as those differing only in order of application of commutative operations), it is reasonable to ask why any of these simplified computation graphs shouldn't be

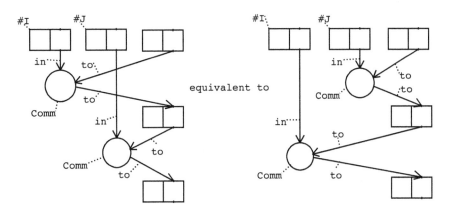

Figure 9.7: Computation subgraph equivalence rule for Comm (#I & #J generic).

considered as another form of plan: After all, we suggested that a plan could be considered as a folded up (or wound up) computation, and that's what such a simplified graph would seem to be. The point won't be argued here, just clarified that such abbreviated computations will generally be far less expressive than our plans (strategies) – technically because the rewrite rules don't rely on the content or control state of the resource states.

Commutativity here has been described in terms of mathematics, but defining when results (of differing order of application) are identical may be subjective. For example, if the operation Comm in Figure 9.6 is multiplication or addition (e.g. $to = to + in$ or $to = to \times in$), few people would question that Comm is commutative (at least over well-defined ranges). However, if the to role (bound to resource X in the example) is considered as a list, and Comm simply appends the number from in to the end of the list found on to (i.e. $to = to, in$), the two computation graphs in Figure 9.6 would yield results (on X) of 1, 10, 7, 5 and 1, 5, 10, 7, respectively. Whether these should be considered equivalent (and therefore Comm considered commutative) depends on the needs of the planner: Although obviously not equal *ver batim*, if the objective is to just represent a set of the four numbers (in the form of a list in this case), those two sets are effectively equivalent.

9.1.5 Re-creating Computations

By definition, deterministic strategies are capable of producing only a single computation for a given input. This has the convenient property that even if the computation is not kept around in the common case when only a result is required, the same computation (and result) can still be recreated later as long as we know the inputs. This is especially important for debugging, where we want to understand how a particular unexpected result came from a particular input fed to a particular strategy – i.e. when we want to more closely examine an computation which we didn't expect to occur. Strategies which are not deterministic, however, do not have this nice property. For these strategies, if we do not record the computation, then just having the input and the strategy is not enough to recreate it. If we wish to determine how the plan created a particular result, it may never recreate the same computation or result, or may especially "refuse" to do so when under our scrutiny (e.g. being debugged). This is one of the properties that has given nondeterminism a bad name, and which has led to the term "Heisenbugs" to refer to unexpected results which cannot be recreated.[1]

The question to be answered is: How much information about a computation, in addition to the plan and the input, must be recorded in order to rebuild the computation? If enough information is recorded to uniquely determine the activation (if any) which follows each resource instance in the computation, then that alone will be enough information (along with the input and plan) to recreate the computation, using exactly the same logic as was used above to show that non-shared control states lead to deterministic plans. For any resources with no shared control states, no information needs to be recorded, since the next acton is already uniquely determined by the control state. In other cases, where there are shared control states and there is no other way to statically determine the next tactic to activate, simply recording the order in which the control state-sharing activities access that resource is sufficient. In this way, there is no ambiguity in the computation: The activation (if any) which follows each resource instance in the computation will be known from either the structure of the plan or from the recording.

For a Director, recording that amount of information is relatively easy and non-intrusive. Since the information is associated with a resource already bound to the actons in question, that info can be recorded to the resource (e.g. with its control or content state) and passed around with the resource. (This may mean changing non-updateable resources to be updateable, and instrumenting the actons to record this information to the resource, but these modifications can be performed "under the covers".) Since only enough information needs to be recorded to denote which of the likely few contexts having one control state is activating next, it will likely be jst a couple of bits of information per activation – lightweight enough to be recorded whether or not it is known in advance that it will be needed.

9.1.6 Other Kinds of Nondeterminism

The way we've been using the term, nondeterminism implies that we don't know what an activity will do, within some range. Another common use of the term relates to similar initial conditions, but instead of considering it as not knowing what the result will be (which is sometimes called **erratic** or **uncontrolled nondeterminism**), it is considered as a specification of a set of all of the results which could occur. In many such cases, the use of the nondeterministic plan is not so much to activate it and see what happens as it is to understand

---

[1]This term is a pun on the name Heisenberg, who stated that the very act of observing a quantum system alters its state.

whether a particular postulated result or goal is actually produceable by the plan, thereby proving or disproving that the goal is a member of the set specified by the plan. In general, such cases are called **angelic nondeterminism**, in the sense that it can be considered as some unseen force pushing the computation in the right direction to lead to the goal. In practice, that unseen force is typically the use of backtracking (i.e. trial and error) to attempt certain nondeterministic options and keep track of which choices have been tried and which have not.

Angelic nondeterminism has little to do with concurrency, except that it may sometimes be possible to concurrently attempt many different potential computations, and then dispense of all but those which lead to the goal. In fact, we previously mentioned backtracking way back in Chapter 3, in relation to deadlock and serialization, when we discussed backing out of activities which were not serializable. This was, indeed, an example of trying different computations to find one which met a goal (serializability), and dispensing of those which did not qualify: The activities which were backed out were treated as though they had never happened, and thus were not part of the final computation.

Two particularly common uses of angelic nondeterminism are in language parsing and in logic languages, like Prolog.

1. In parsing, a nondeterministic finite automata (NFA) is devised to define (or alternately, generate or recognize) all legal constructs within a language. Then as the language is scanned, possible choices (computations) are considered which will lead to the scanned text. In finite cases, NFAs can be converted to DFAs (deterministic finite automata) which perform the same work, technically making backtracking unnecessary, but NFAs are often still a useful and more intuitive form.

2. In logic languages, the plan consists of a set of rules called clauses, each of which may allow progress towards the goal. Shortcuts are often employed to forbid backtracking at certain points for efficiency, often to avoid attempting searches which the planner (logic programmer, in this case) determines will be non-productive.

In the next chapter (Chapter 10), axioms will remove the necessity that computation graphs be constructed from beginning to end, thus leading to the potential of plan being interpreted angelically, but we will not develop that further here.

9.2 Atomicity

9.2.1 Definition

Atomic: Indivisible; having no discernible inner structure.

The goal behind atomicity is to hide the outward effects of inner structure in a plan's behavior (i.e. activity). It was a prime motivator in our design of actons and their plans (tactics) in Chapter 3, but sometimes we would also like to ignore the inner structure of non-acton activities as well. For example, even when it may be advantageous to use a more complex plan for performance

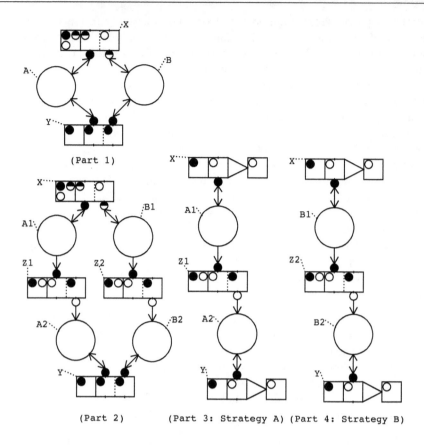

(Part 1)

(Part 2) (Part 3: Strategy A) (Part 4: Strategy B)

Figure 9.8: Top strategy (1) deterministic if A and B atomic, but not if decomposed (2) or strategies (3 & 4).

reasons (to facilitate concurrency) or to permit some flexibility ruled out by actons (like nondeterminism or persistent state), when it comes to using the strategy within another strategy, we might prefer to make its inner workings as inconsequential as possible. Most specifically, we may not want to consider the effects of the order in which the activity accesses its (external) resources, preferring instead to consider it as executing to completion or not completing at all, and of being live (not held up by deadlock).

Atomicity is often intertwined with nondeterminism. For example, consider Figure 9.8. The strategy at the top left is easily shown to be deterministic, if A and B are atomic and deterministic (such as being tactics), because the control state of X tells which will activate next. For the sake of concreteness, we'll consider that the internal implementation of A is to add 2 to X, and multiply Y by the result, and the implementation of B is to multiply X by three, and add the result to Y – i.e.

168

```
A: plan {<-> int X (done)
         <-> int Y (done)}
tactic {
        X = X + 2;
        Y = Y * X;
}
B: plan {<-> int X (done)
         <-> int Y (done)}
tactic {
        X = X * 3;
        Y = Y + X;
}
```

If X and Y both start at 1, then the result is for Y to be multiplied by 3, then incremented by 9, to end up at 12.

Now consider breaking A into A1 and A2 (and B into B1 and B2) as shown in part 2 of the figure, by having the first part perform the addition, storing the new value of X onto Z1 (or Z2) as well as back to X, and the second part to multiply this into Y. It is now possible for Y to be incremented (by B2) before it is multiplied (by A2), ending up as 30. This nondeterministic result (12 or 30) is possible whether A and B are split up where they are (in part 2 of the diagram), or are separate strategies (as in part 3 and 4 of the diagram).

So the question we address in this section is: Even if A and B are taken to be those separate strategies (from parts 3 and 4), what techniques can we use to make them act as if they are atomic (like tactics) when used in the part 1 strategy?

9.2.2 Atomicity Using an Atomic "Start" Acton

Perhaps the easiest way to ensure that a strategy is atomic is to use the activation of a single tactic within the strategy to represent the logical atomic activation of the strategy as a whole. The approach consists of binding a context, within the strategy and holding a tactic, to the initial control state of all of the strategy's formal resources, and to not allow any other role bindings to those initial control states within the strategy. When (and only when) all of the formal resources have their initial control state (meaning all of the actual resources in the parent have a control state corresponding to an associated access dot), this tactic can activate into an acton (called the **start acton** in this usage) at which point it will atomically steal the control state from all of the actual resources in the parent.

In part to help with this situation, but also many others, ScalPL supports a special tactic called $null, which has no roles, and therefore does nothing. In other words, it is used with only anonymous role bindings, which are (of course) predictable, so $null works especially well for use as a start acton. (Since $null is intrinsic, the Director generally directly performs all of its functions without even actually activating any tactic.)

See the left strategy of Figure 9.9 to see the strategy A (from part 3 of the previous figure) after inserting a start acton. For most intents and purposes, the

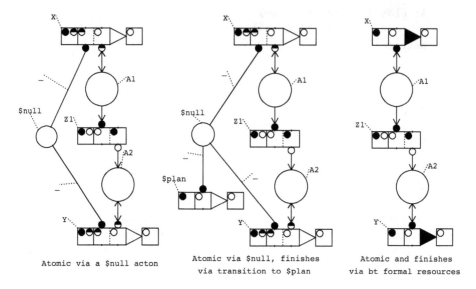

| Atomic via a $null acton | Atomic via $null, finishes via transition to $plan | Atomic and finishes via bt formal resources |

Figure 9.9: Strategy A from previous example modified to be atomic.

second control state for each formal resource effectively becomes its initial control state, since the real initial control state is now used only by the start acton. The strategy continues as usual, and when it transitions the formal resources to match a final dot, the control state is passed back to the corresponding actual resource in the parent as usual.

Note that the newly augmented strategy is not only atomic, it is effectively bottom-belted, because it atomically claims all of its actual resources from the parent at the same time the start acton does, and relinquishes them one by one via transitions, just as A would have acted had it been a tactic instead of a strategy. Among other things, this prevents deadlock.

In this particular example, the activity also does not preserve any internal state from one activation of the start acton to the next, since Z1 always ends up back with the initial control state, and from there, its content state is always replaced by the next activation of A1. In general, however, the strategy may hold some internal state from one iteration to the next, so care must be taken to explicitly reset content and control states of resources each time if this is not desired. Another way to do this is to finish the activity just as soon as the start acton activates, as in the center strategy in Figure 9.9. That is, by also binding the start acton to the $plan formal resource, and having it transition that resource to the done transition dot at the same time it transitions the other formal resources as already described, the strategy finishes as soon as it begins (i.e. after stealing the control state from all of the actual resources in the parent), and therefore the entire strategy will be garbage collected as soon as it finally transitions the last control state of the last formal resource back to the parent. When it is activated anew, it will have fresh resource states, so if it is otherwise deterministic (as discussed earlier in this chapter), it will appear

170

externally very much like an acton when it activates.

9.2.3 Atomicity Using Activation Formal Resources

These still leave an important issue. Although a strategy built as described above (with the start acton bound to the $plan formal resource) will activate (and bind its roles) anew before each activation of its start acton, it may in fact activate (and bind) *long* before that child activates. That is, the activation (and therefore binding) of the strategy and the activation of its child start acton are still independent to some extent, even if we would like to consider them as linked. The potential problems with this will become more apparent in future chapters, but since the solution to these problems can also offer another convenient means to achieve atomicity for a strategy, we'll address it here.

In addition to the "regular" formal resources described so far, ScalPL has another kind of formal resources called **activation formal resources** (or @ **formals** for short). These resemble regular formal resources except that the triangle connecting the transition box (on the right, containing the final dots) to the main rectangle is filled in: The rightmost diagram in Figure 9.9 shows Strategy A implemented with @ formal resources.

The difference between @ formal resources and others is that a strategy with any @ formals will not even activate (and therefore not bind) until the bindings to all of their corresponding actuals in the parent are ready. In this sense, it is as though the role bindings for these formal resources are activation role bindings (i.e. preceded by @ signs), as described in 7.3.2. But in addition, when the strategy *does* activate, it will atomically steal the control state from all of the actuals in the parent corresponding to the @ formals – even while the @ formals themselves maintain their initial control state. (For this reason, unlike for other formal resources, bindings to an @ formal *can* have transitions back to the initial control state.) In fact, unlike regular formal resources, if the strategy holding the resources finishes, @ formals do not lose their initial control state. Finally, once the strategy containing the @ formal(s) has activated, and an @ formal has (eventually) issued a transition to the parent (by virtue of a transition to one of its final dots), that @ formal is done, as though the strategy it is within has finished: It will never reattain its initial (or any other) control state, even if the corrsponding binding to the actual in the parent becomes ready again. The @ formal may be collected as garbage by the Director. So, the normal finishing rules don't apply to @ formals: They are effectively finished as soon as the strategy activates.

One result of these behaviors is that, if all of the formal resources within a strategy are @ formal resources, the strategy will be atomic and stateless. That is, the strategy will not activate until all of the bindings in its parent are ready, and then when they are ready, it will atomically steal the control state for all of them, and then go about its business until eventually perhaps issuing at most one transition to some or all of them. If it eventually issues transitions to all of them, the entire strategy can be garbage collected by the Director (since the activity will have no further contacts to its parent/environment), and if/when it activates again, it will be as a new strategy, with fresh control and content states.

The rightmost diagram in Figure 9.9 is therefore indeed atomic. As can be seen, this is a relatively easy, clutterless way to make a strategy atomic without significantly changing its implementation in major ways (or often, at all).

9.2.4 The Downside of Atomicity

Although atomicity can simplify reasoning about a plan, it can also negatively impact the amount of concurrency which can be exploited. For example, reconsider the example in Figure 9.8. We could have solved the problem of nondeterminism just as easily by adding an extra control state to Y, to mimic X, and leaving strategies A and B as non-atomic. This would have had the benefit of allowing the possibility of A2 acting concurrent with B1, which is not possible when A and B are atomic, since no part of B is then allowed to activate until A has issued transitions to both of its roles. The drawback of atomicity would be even more pronounced if there had been more branches, and/or if each branch consisted of more steps before issuing the transition to Y and allowing the next one to activate.

With the techniques introduced here, we can now indeed develop strategies which result in activities having varying combinations of properties up to those of an action. That is, we now know how to make strategies deterministic or non-, with persistent state or not, and atomic or not.

9.3 Summary

Nondeterminism and atomicity were covered as aspects which one may (or may not) wish various strategies to have, though they are always present within tactics. Nondeterminism was defined as some aspect of an activity not being determined completely by its initial state. (That initial state can be, and is here, considered to also encompass inputs). Atomicity is the property that some activity will be considered to have taken place or not to have taken place, but never to have just partially taken place.

Nondeterminism was first categorized by which result of the plan was not determined by its inputs. If the plan's computation is completely determined by the inputs, then so too are the outputs, so we call such a plan fully deterministic. If the plan's outputs are not completely determined by its inputs, then so too must its computations not be completely determined by its inputs, so we call such a plan fully nondeterministic. However, some plans will have outputs completely determined by its inputs, even though its computations are not, and we call such plans semideterministic. Generally speaking, semideterministic plans will depend on some (mathematical) equivalences to ensure that even different computations (withn some equivalence classes) will produce the same outputs. For example, commutative mathematical operations (like addition and multiplication) should provide the same result regardless of the order in which they are evaluated to contribute to a resource's content.

Techniques were then shown to determine whether a strategy is deterministic. The simplest is to ensure that no more than one context (holding a tactic) is bound to any single resource with the same (color/shade of) access dot. If this is true, then the control state of every resource fully defines the next context which can access it, so the computation is fully determined, and so are the outputs. More generally, if any set of control states fully determines the next context (holding a tactic) that can access each resource next, then the computation and outputs are fully determined. We called such cases, where the plan can be determined to be deterministic simply by observation of its form, syntactic (or strategy) computation determinism. However, there are also plans which are computation deterministic only because some of the tactics within the plan behave in specific ways which prevent multiple activities from being ready to access any one resource at one time. We called such cases semantic (or tactic) computation determinism.

Even for nondeterministic plans, if we can capture a trace showing the nondeterministic decisions made by the Director – i.e. which of (a generally small number of) activities accessed a resource whenever the control state of that resource allowed multiple to be ready at once – then even a nondeterministic computation can be reconstructed later, from the inputs plus the trace.

Regarding atomicity, the most primitive way to ensure it for strategies is to use a start tactic – i.e. a tactic which is bound to the initial control state of each of the fomal resources for the plan, and which transitions each to some other control state. By ensuring that the start tactic is the only context bound to those initial control states, the strategy effectively atomically reserves all of its resources (by stealing the control states from its actual resources) all at one time, thereby forming a belt for the activity. A particular intrinsic tactic, called $null, is especially useful for this purpose, because it does absolutely nothing else but activate and terminate, and the Director can often optimize these actions.

The use of a start tactic does not solve another problem, that the roles of the strategy may be bound (in its parent) long before the start tactic activates. The problems with this will become clearer in later chapters, but regardless, another form of formal resource, called an activation (or @) formal resource, is also available which solves both the atomicity and early binding problems. An activation formal graphically resembles a normal formal resource in almost every respect except that (1) the triangle connecting the transition box to the rectangle is filled in, and (2) transition bindings (new control state dots on role bindings) are allowed to go back to the initial control state. An @ formal acts different than a normal formal resource in that the plan containing the @ formal will not even activate until the role corresponding to the @ formal is ready (in the parent), and once it does activate, the control state will immediately be stolen from the actual (in the parent) corresponding to the @ formal. Once a transition is made to a @ formal corresponding to one of its final dots (in the transition box), and a transition is thereby issued back to the actual in the parent (returning the control state to it), the @ formal is finished. It will no longer regain a control state, even if the control state of the actual in the parent returns to match the access dot of the associated role binding, making the role ready again. If all of the formals for a strategy are @ formals, then any activity will effectively be finished after a transition has been issued to all of those roles.

With the constructs and observations presented here, a planner should now be able to construct strategies with or without any combinations of the three traits of determinism, atomicity, and persistent internal state.

Chapter *10*

Axiomatic Semantics

This chapter presents an alternate, more mathematically formal approach to specifying what a plan is and how it acts, in terms of axioms expressed in the form of set and function notation. First, we use the axioms (within theorems) to demonstrate that the resulting computations have the same sorts of familiar properties as those already discussed. These theorems will also provide an excuse to introduce other formal notation which may prove useful later. As a culmination, we discuss the instrumentation of plans, the collection of traces (as a result), and prove a theorem that the traces thus created, along with the original plan and initial marking, are sufficient to recreate the computations of even nondeterministic plans.

10.1 Intro

In Chapter 8, we presented an operational way of building a concurrent computation from a concurrent plan by watching (or pretending to watch) the plan as it executes according to aforementioned rules, and recording the results. We call this an **operational semantics**, because it emanates from simply recording the plan's operation. By its very nature, an operational semantics defines the computation in one direction (earlier to later), and relies on an explanation (which may be in common vernacular) for how a plan operates.

Another approach, which lends itself more to a formal, mathematical approach, is to simply consider the plan syntactically (according to its static form), and to then define some constraints on the form of the computations which may be produced from a plan, based on that form. If this set of constraints is clear and complete enough to always allow all, and only, the same computations from every plan that the operational semantics would allow, then it can be considered to define a semantics that is equivalent to the operational semantics, and we can consider these constraints as semantic **axioms** – i.e. the most basic "truisms" describing the nature of computations, from which other (perhaps less obvious) properties can be derived. Since the axioms just relate the structure of one construct (the computation) to another (the plan), the directional, time-based nature of computation becomes less onerous, allowing one to even

175

consider building the computation in a non-obvious order. This is one reason that the approach lends itself to a formal, mathematical description: Time is not explicitly represented except in the acyclic nature of the computation, so as long as we can formally represent the properties of both the plan and the computation, then it's simply a matter of associating those properties with one another.

It's no secret that mathematical approaches can be scary, both in their reliance on a small number of symbols to convey a lot of information, and in the fact that the symbols used may be unfamiliar to non-mathematicians. This chapter is intended only for those who wish to attempt to surmount these obstacles, and other readers can survive quite well by skipping this chapter, but nevertheless, effort will be made here both to back up the math with prose, and to introduce (and/or reintroduce) unfamiliar terminology or symbology before it is used. To that end:

- Sets. A lower case letter (like a, b, c or Greek like α, β, γ), with or without decorations (e.g. $\hat{\sigma}, \bar{\sigma}, \ddot{\sigma}, \sigma, \sigma_0$), represents a single value or function or tuple (see below). An upper case letter (like A, B, C, or Greek like Σ, Ω) represents a set of elements. The notation $b \in B$ means that b is a member of set B, and $A \subseteq B$ means that set A is a subset of set B, containing only some or all of its elements. The notation $|A|$ will represent the number of elements in set A. The specific notation $\mathbb{N}^+$ denotes the positive natural numbers (i.e. the infinite set $1, 2, 3, ...$). The notation $[x, y]$, where x and y are integers and $x \leq y$, represents the set of integers between (and including) x and y. The set difference between sets A and B, represented $A \setminus B$, signifies the elements that are in A but not in B. The notation $\wp(Z)$ (called the power set) for any set Z is the set of all subsets of Z, so each element of $\wp(Z)$ is a subset of Z. The special notation $A_\perp$, where A is any set, is shorthand for $A \cup \{\perp\}$ (i.e. A together with the special value $\perp$ defined elsewhere).

- Tuples. An n-tuple (where n is a positive integer) is an ordered set of n elements, often of heterogeneous (different) types or kinds, which we will represent by enclosing representative elements in order, in angle brackets (e.g. $< a, b, c >$). The notation $x \bullet b$ will be used to represent the element named b in tuple x. The notation $A \times B$ (i.e. cross product) represents the set of all 2-tuples where the first element is from set A and the second is from set B, and it can be generalized to more sets (e.g. $A \times B \times \cdots \times X$). The notation A^n, where A is a set and n evaluates to an integer, represents the cross product of A n times (i.e. $A \times A \times A... \times A$), so the elements are n-tuples with all the elements from A (or, similarly, sequences of length n).

- Functions. The notation $b : C \to D$ will denote that b is a function from set C to set D, meaning that when b is applied to an element of set C (denoted as $b(c)$, where $c \in C$), it will evaluate to exactly one element of D. $Im(b)$, the image set of b, will be the subset of D consisting of all elements which can actually result from b's evaluation – i.e. $\{y | x \in C, b(x) = y\}$. If

$D = Im(b)$, we say that b is onto D (or a surjection), represented symbolically as $b : C \twoheadrightarrow D$. Similarly, the notation $b : C \hookrightarrow D$ will denote that b is an injection (or one-to-one), meaning that it is not only a function from C to D, but also that different elements from C will always yield different results (from D). If a function is both an injection and surjection, it is called a bijection, represented $b : C \leftrightarrow D$, in which case there will always exist one inverse function (also a bijection), $b^{-1} : D \to C$, such that $b^{-1}(b(x)) = x$.

- Logical implication.

10.2 F-Net Syntax

The first step to making the association between the syntax of a plan and the semantics of its computation is to formally and mathematically define the syntax. To demonstrate the gist of the approach while not getting lost in needless details, we'll make a few simplifications, and to make clear when we are discussing this simplified formal model, we'll give it a name, F-Nets, different from the one we've been using for the full complete planning language (ScalPL).

The first simplification of F-Nets over ScalPL is that all resources will share the same content domain and control domain, which we'll call Σ and Ω respectively, and we'll call the initial control state ω_0. We'll also declare a single set Δ from which all of the transitions for all the roles will be drawn. (It is very tempting to just number the transitions – i.e. to draw them from $\mathbb{N}^+$ instead of defining a whole new set – but drawing them from a nondescript set reduces assumptions about ordering and other properties of $\mathbb{N}^+$ that are not required for transitions.) It should be clear that these are not restrictions, since no matter which domains were planned for each individual resource, it is possible to make one large (or general) enough to contain the individual domans anyway.

Then, we'll only deal with contexts that can only activate tactics (not strategies), and in fact, only one tactic per context – i.e. no $plan roles on contexts. Such restrictions may be troublesome in some cases, but the goal here is to introduce the reader to formalisms and ways of working with them, not to include the entire approach in the formalism. This chapter can be used as a sample of how a more complete formalism could be constructed, for those so motivated.

We will also only allow a single access dot on each role binding. As long as we are dealing only with tactics within each context, this also does not restrict the expressiveness in any substantive way, since any context with multiple constraint dots on its bindings can just be replaced with multiple contexts each with one constraint dot on each of its bindings, each context representing one of the combinations of constraint dots which would have allowed the original (multiple constraint dot) context to activate.

We will also not deal with permissions, just usages – in other words, will assume that permissions are always the same as the permissions, or if one prefers, that all permissions are update. Also, we'll not model anonymous role bindings. These also do not affect the expressiveness of the model. We also slightly simplify the notion of predictability to apply only to roles that have exactly one transition binding, not to roles having multiple transitions bound to the same control state.

With these simplificatons, we can now formally and completely describe the syntax of an F-Net plan (also known as just an F-Net), as set of resources, a set of tactics, and a set of contexts, as well as the content domain and control domain for all of its resources. Mathematically, we assign each of those a symbol (e.g. usually a roman or greek letter, capitals for sets) and represent the collection as a tuple, in angle brackets, so:

An **F-Net** (plan) p is a 7-tuple, $< \Sigma, \Omega, \Delta, \omega_0, R, T, C >$ where

- Σ is the content domain (for all resources)

- Ω is the control domain (for all resources)

- Δ is the transition domain (for all roles)

- $\omega_0 \in \Omega$ is the initial control state (for all resources)

- R is the set of Resources

- T is the set of Tactics

- C is the set of Contexts

Of these, Σ, Ω, Δ, and R need no further description: They are arbitrary sets, and the form of their elements is not important to the definition. The initial control state ω_0 can be any member of Ω. However, the elements of T and C (the Tactics and Contexts) have a very special form syntactically, so those must be defined further.

Each tactic in T has a number of roles, which we will number sequentially starting at 1. Each role has a usage, which is either observe, replace, both of those, or neither of those, so these can be specified by just specifying all the roles which have observe usage, and then all those with replace usage. For each role, we also specify the number of transitions. And, since a tactic is atomic and deterministic, the content results produced to the replace roles, and the transition produced to all of the roles, can each be specified as a function of the content state on the observe roles. For roles which have multiple transitions and/or replace usage, it is possible that no transition result (or, more specifically, a bottom ($\bot$) transition) will be specified for that role. So:

For each tactic $t \in T$, t is a 6-tuple $< u, I, O, \tau, \phi, \psi >$ where

- $u \in \mathbb{N}^+$ is the arity (or number of Roles)

- $I \subseteq [1, u]$ are the observe (or input) roles

- $O \subseteq [1, u]$ are the replace (or output) roles

- $\tau : [1, u] \to \wp(\Delta)$ is the transition signature for each role

- $\phi : \Sigma^{|I|} \to \Sigma^{|O|}$ are the content results

- $\psi : \Sigma^{|I|} \to \tau(1)_\perp \times \tau(2)_\perp \times \cdots \tau(u)_\perp$ are the transition results. (Technically, due to predictability, if $n \notin O \wedge |\tau(n)| = 1$, that domain set corresponding to n can be unaugmented, i.e. just $\tau(n)$ rather than $\tau(n)_\perp$.)

Each context in C is labeled with a tactic. For each of the roles in that tactic, the context specifies a role binding (i.e. the resource to which that role is bound), a firing constraint (i.e. the control state of the access dot), and a transition binding for each of that role's transitions. So:

For each context $c \in C$, c is a 4-tuple $< t, \beta, \gamma, \delta >$ where

- $t \in T$ is the tactic in the context

- $\beta : [1, t \bullet u] \hookrightarrow R$ is the role binding (and is one-to-one)

- $\gamma : [1, t \bullet u] \to \Omega$ is the firing constraint

- $\delta : [1, t \bullet u] \to (\Delta \to \Omega)$ is the Transition Binding,
  where, more specifically, any of the functions $\delta(k)$ needs only to be defined over the domain $t \bullet \tau(k)$ – which could be expressed something like $\forall k \in [1, t \bullet u].\delta(k) : t \bullet \tau(k) \to \Omega$

For convenience, for any particular context, we will define $G \equiv Im(\beta)$, the resources to which that context is bound, so $\beta : [1, t \bullet u] \leftrightarrow G$, and G has $t \bullet u$ elements.

10.3   F-Net Semantics

Now that we have a formal and mathematical representation by what we mean by a plan (in an F-Net), we can review the operational semantics to define the a computation. Before doing that, we will first need to define the form of the computation, and just like the plan, assign names to its parts, which are: the circles representing activations, rectangles representing resource states, "beginning" arrows from resource states to actons (called "pre" arrows in other chapters), "ending" arrows from actons to resulting resource states (called "post" arrows in other chapters), and labels associating each resource state with a resource in the F-Net and each acton with a context in the F-Net. The way that those pieces of the computation are assembled is obviously dependent upon the F-Net which it models and the initial content states of its resources, so those could also be considered part of the computation, but we will instead consider those as inputs constraining the form of the computation. Since each of the resource states has an associated control state and content state, those could also be regarded as part of the computation, but since they can be derived from the other information, there's no reason to do so formally. So:

An **F-Net computation** $\chi_{p,\iota} =< A, S, B, E, \hat{\sigma}, \bar{\sigma} >$ where p is the F-Net (plan) being modeled, $\iota : p \bullet R \to p \bullet \Sigma$ is the initial content marking, and

- A is the set of actons

- S is the set of resource states

- $B \subseteq S \times A$ is the set of pre (or beginning) arcs

- $E \subseteq A \times S$ is the set of post (or ending) arcs

- $\hat{\sigma} : A \rightarrow p \bullet C$ is the context labeling

- $\bar{\sigma} : S \rightarrow p \bullet R$ is the resource labeling

such that functions

- $\dot{\sigma} : S \rightarrow p \bullet \Omega_\perp$ is a control state labeling

- $\ddot{\sigma} : S \rightarrow p \bullet \Sigma$ is a content state labeling

exist, and Semantic Axioms 1 through 6 (below) hold.

Notation (aside): Now that we can refer to the parts of the computation, we can move on to formulate the axioms defining how that computation must relate to the F-net from which it springs, but before doing so, we'll introduce a little more notation to keep things short and sweet. For example, instead of writing $\hat{\sigma}(x), \bar{\sigma}(x), \dot{\sigma}(x)$, or $\ddot{\sigma}(x)$, for any node x, we'll usually just write $\hat{x}, \bar{x}, \dot{x}$ or $\ddot{x}$ respectively. We'll also use the elements (arcs) from B and E to define some shorthand. For example, $x*$ (called x's successors) will represent the set of all nodes which one can reach from node x by following one arc–i.e.

$$x* \equiv \{y | (x, y) \in B \cup E\}$$

and $*y$ (called y's predecessors) will represent the set of all nodes that can reach y by following one arc–i.e.

$$*y \equiv \{x | (x, y) \in B \cup E\}$$

Based on these, node x will be said to precede node y, represented by $x \preceq y$, if you can get from node x to node y by following some number of arcs, including 0. This can be defined recursively by saying that x precedes y whenever either x and y are the same node, or one of x's successors precedes y–i.e.

$$x \preceq y \equiv x = y \vee (z \in x * \wedge z \preceq y)$$

Since the concept of a context being "ready" will come up repeatedly, we will define what it means here first. A set of state nodes S' will be said to enable a context c (thereby making c ready), written $S' \triangleright c$, if and only if the elements of S' are named exactly for the resources to which c is bound, and the control state of each matches the firing constraint–i.e.

$$S' \triangleright c \equiv (\bar{\sigma} : S' \leftrightarrow c \bullet G) \wedge \forall s \in S'.\dot{s} = \gamma(c \bullet \beta^{-1}(\bar{s}))$$

10.3.1 Initialization Axiom

Each resource begins with the initial (green) control state and some initial content state.

First define the initial resource states S sub 0 as all of the resource states without predecessors:

$$S_0 \equiv \{s_0 \in S \wedge | * s| = 0\}$$

Based on that definition, there is exactly one initial resource state named for each resource, and it has the initial control state and the initial content state for that resource:

$$(\bar{\sigma} : S_0 \leftrightarrow R) \wedge (s \in S_0 \implies \dot{s} = \omega_0 \wedge \ddot{s} = \iota(\bar{s}))$$

10.3.2 Time Axiom

The only way that time is really embodied in the computation is that the computation is acyclic – i.e. that you can't get from a node back to itself by following the pre and post arrows.

$$x \preceq y \wedge x \neq y \implies \neg(y \preceq x)$$

10.3.3 Atomicity Axiom

Only one activity is permitted to access a resource at any one time. When that activity is finished accessing that resource, the resource is considered to be in a new state. So, each resource state node in the computation has at most one predecessor and at most one successor.

$$\forall s \in S. |s * | \leq 1 \wedge | * s| \leq 1$$

10.3.4 Safety Axiom

A tactic will only activate when all of the resources to which it is bound (by roles) have a control state equal to one of the access dots of the corresponding roles. So, the control state for each of the resource state nodes bound by pre arrows to an activation node correspond to the access dot of the corresponding role binding of the context.

$$a \in A \implies *a \triangleright \bar{a}$$

10.3.5 Liveness Axiom

If a tactic can activate, then a tactic will (eventually) activate. (It may not be the tactic you expected, but it will use at least one of the same resources.) So, if there are resource state nodes in the computation which make some particular context in the F-Net ready, then at least one of those resource states will have a pre arrow coming from it (to an activation node).

$$S' \subseteq S \wedge S' \triangleright c \implies \exists s \in S'. |s * | > 0$$

10.3.6 Firing Axiom

Now for the meaty axiom, which defines how an acton dictates the resulting control and content states of its resources based on their initial content states. In fact, it is so meaty that we will express it in terms of smaller sub-axioms.

To shorten some of these sub-axioms, we first introduce a new notation, $P \overset{c}{\ltimes} Q$, which can be pronounced "state nodes from P named for resources to which roles Q are bound by context c". That is, it returns a subset of P (which is, in turn, a subset of S, the states) as a sequence, selected and sequenced according to roles of context c which are named (i.e. enumerated) in Q, which are bound to those state nodes (or more properly, to the resources to which those state nodes correspond). So, the notation is defined as

$$P \overset{c}{\ltimes} Q \equiv (x_j) \text{ such that } x_j \in P \wedge (\bar{x}_j) = c \bullet \beta(Q^<)$$

This is well defined when Q is in the domain of $c \bullet \beta$ and $\bar{\sigma} : P \to R$ is one-to-one.

Structure

Each activation node will result from a set of state nodes, and will result in a set of state nodes, and the members of each of those sets will have names corresponding exactly to the resources bound to the acton's context.

$$\bar{\sigma} : *a \leftrightarrow \hat{a} \bullet \beta\left([1, \hat{a} \bullet t \bullet u]\right) \wedge \bar{\sigma} : a* \leftrightarrow \hat{a} \bullet \beta\left([1, \hat{a} \bullet t \bullet u]\right)$$

New Content States

For any activation, if you take the content states of the predecessor state nodes corresponding to (resources bound to) its input roles, and apply the ϕ (content results) function from the activated tactic, you will get the content states of the successor state nodes corresponding to (resources bound to) its output roles.

$$\hat{a} \bullet t \bullet \phi(\ddot{i_1}, \ddot{i_2}, \cdots) = (\ddot{o_1}, \ddot{o_2}, \cdots)$$

where $(i_j) = *a \overset{\hat{a}}{\ltimes} (\hat{a} \bullet t \bullet I)$ and $(o_j) = a* \overset{\hat{a}}{\ltimes} (\hat{a} \bullet t \bullet O)$.

Unchanged Content States ("Non-interference")

For any activation, for the acton's roles which are not output roles, the predecessor nodes and successor nodes representing resources bound to those roles will have equal content states. That's another way of saying that the acton won't change the content state of resources bound to roles that are not output roles.

$$(\ddot{i_1}, \ddot{i_2}, \cdots) = (\ddot{o_1}, \ddot{o_2}, \cdots)$$

where $Y = [1, \hat{a} \bullet t \bullet u] \setminus \hat{a} \bullet t \bullet O$ and $(i_j) = *a \overset{\hat{a}}{\ltimes} Y$ and $(o_j) = a* \overset{\hat{a}}{\ltimes} Y$.

New Control States

For any acton, if (similar to the "New content states", above) you take the content states of the predecessor state nodes corresponding to (resources bound to) its input roles, but now apply the ψ (transition results) function, you will get transitions for (resources bound to) all of the acton's tactic's roles. We'll use x_j to represent the transition it gives for role j. In most cases, the control state for the resource bound to any role j will be found by mapping that transition (i.e. x_j) through the transition binding δ for that role (i.e. by evaluating $\delta(j)(x_j)$). That means, in turn, that if $x_j = \bot$ (representing the case where the tactic never produces a transition for role j), the new control state for the resource bound to that role would be $\delta(j)(x_j) = \bot$, representing no control state. That is the wrong answer in one specific case; if the role is not a write role, and all the transitions for that role are bound (by $\delta(j)$) to a single control state. In that case, we'll ignore x_j, so even if $x_j = \bot$, the new control state will be the one to which all of the transitions for that role are bound.

$$\dot{o}_j = \begin{cases} \hat{a} \bullet \delta(j)(x) \text{ if } j \notin \hat{a} \bullet t \bullet O \wedge \hat{a} \bullet \delta(j)(\hat{a} \bullet t \bullet \tau(j)) = \{x\} \\ \hat{a} \bullet \delta(j)(x_j) \text{ otherwise} \end{cases}$$

where $(o_j) = a * \overset{\hat{a}}{\ltimes}([1, \hat{a} \bullet t \bullet u])$, $\hat{a} \bullet t \bullet \psi(\overset{..}{i_1}, \overset{..}{i_2}, \cdots) = (x_1, x_2, \cdots)$, and $(i_j) = *a \overset{\hat{a}}{\ltimes}(\hat{a} \bullet t \bullet I)$

10.4 Theorems

For now, the axioms are just a bunch of separate mathematical statements. We have no assurance that they will work together to produce the same kinds of computations as our earlier operational model. In this section, we'll prove that they do indeed imply that the computations described by these axioms have at least some similar properties. We hope that these, together with the common-sense understanding of the formation of each of the axioms, will provide the reader some confidence that the computations expressed here are in fact identical to those earlier ones.

10.4.1 Nodes in Computation Are Partially Ordered

Theorem 1 The operation $\preceq$ partially orders $A \cup S$
 (A partial order is a binary relation over a set which is reflexive, antisymmetric, and transitive.)

Proof of Theorem 1 $\preceq$ is reflexive by definition (i.e. $a \preceq a$ is true). Axiom 2 (Time) gives asymmetry. ∎

10.4.2 States for a Resource in Computation Are Totally Ordered

Define S_r as the set of state nodes named r – i.e.

$$S_r \equiv \{s \in S.\bar{s} = r\}$$

For $s, s' \in S, \bar{s} = \bar{s}'$, define relation "next becomes", represented $\rightsquigarrow$, as:

$$s \rightsquigarrow s' \equiv \exists e \in E.s* = \{e\} \wedge *s' = \{e\}$$

Based on $\rightsquigarrow$, define the relation "eventually becomes", represented $\precsim$, as its transitive closure:

$$s \precsim s' \equiv (s = s') \vee \exists s''. (s \rightsquigarrow s'' \wedge s'' \precsim s')$$

Note that, since $\precsim$ over S_r is embedded on $\preceq$ over $S \cup E$,

$$s \precsim s' \implies s \preceq s'$$

Theorem 2 All state nodes representing a given resource are totally ordered in a computation (i.e. form a chain in the partial ordering).

$$s, s' \in S_r \implies s \preceq s' \vee s' \preceq s$$

Lemma 2.1

$$s* \neq \emptyset \implies \exists s'.s \rightsquigarrow s$$
$$s \neq \emptyset \implies \exists s'.s' \rightsquigarrow s$$
$$s \rightsquigarrow s' \wedge s \rightsquigarrow s'' \implies s' = s''$$
$$s' \rightsquigarrow s \wedge s'' \rightsquigarrow s \implies s' = s''$$

Proof of Lemma 2.1 For the first statement, if $s* \neq \emptyset$ then by the Atomicity Axiom (3), $|s*| = 1$, so $\exists e \in E.s* = \{e\}$. Since $s \in *e$, by the Structure Axiom, there will be exactly one $s' \in e*$ such that $\bar{s'} = \bar{s}$. By the definition of $\rightsquigarrow$, it follows that $s \rightsquigarrow s'$. The same reasoning works in reverse, for the second statement, and the "exactly one" in the previous sentence proves the third and fourth statements.

Lemma 2.2 Every element of S has an element of S_0 that eventually becomes it.

$$\forall s \in S \exists s_0 \in S_0.s_0 \precsim s$$

Proof of Lemma 2.2 Assume false, and let s' be least element such that $s' \precsim s$.

$$s' \notin S_0 \implies *s' \neq \emptyset \implies \exists s''.s'' \rightsquigarrow s'$$

Then $s'' \precsim s'$ and therefore $s'' \precsim s$, so s' is not the least element such that $s' \precsim s \implies \Leftarrow$. Assumption incorrect.

Lemma 2.3 If one element of S eventually becomes two elements, then one of those eventually becomes the other.

$$s \precsim s' \wedge s \precsim s'' \implies s' \precsim s'' \vee s'' \precsim s'$$

Proof of Lemma 2.3 Let $s''' \in S_r$ be the greatest element such that $s''' \precsim s' \wedge s''' \precsim s''$. ($s'''$ exists and is well defined, since all the elements from s to s' and from s to s'' are ordered by $\rightsquigarrow$ and therefore by $\precsim$, and s''' is one of them.) If $s''' = s' \vee s''' = s''$ then substituting both into the antecedent,

$$(s' \precsim s' \wedge s' \precsim s'') \vee (s'' \precsim s' \wedge s'' \precsim s'') \implies s' \precsim s'' \vee s'' \precsim s'$$

and the Lemma is true. Otherwise, $s''' \neq s' \wedge s''' \neq s'' \implies s'''* \neq \emptyset \implies \exists s''''.s''' \rightsquigarrow s''''$ and since s'''' is unique, $s'''' \precsim s' \wedge s'''' \precsim s''$, but that means that s''' was not the greatest element eventually leading to both s' and s'', and there is no "otherwise" case. So the Lemma is true.

Proof of Theorem 2 From Lemma 2.2, $\exists s_0, s_0' \in S_0.s_0 \precsim s \wedge s_0' \precsim s'$. To be related by $\precsim$, $s_0, s_0' \in S_r$, but since S_0 has exactly one element named for each resource, $s_0 = s_0'$, so $\exists s_0 \in S_0.s_0 \precsim s \wedge s_0 \precsim s'$. From Lemma 2.3, $s' \precsim s'' \vee s'' \precsim s'$, and therefore, $s' \preceq s'' \vee s'' \preceq s'$. ∎

10.4.3 Computations as Functions

Theorem 3 The control state and content state labelings (functions $\dot{\sigma}(x)$, and $\ddot{\sigma}(x)$) for an execution graph are unique – i.e.

$$\vdash \dot{\sigma}, \ddot{\sigma}$$

In other words, the content and control state of any state node in the computation is determined completely by the initial content marking ι – roughly, inputs – so the computation (in some sense) represents a function from those inputs to the content and control state of all of its state nodes.

Proof of Theorem 3 Earlier, in Chapter 8, we argued that the control and content states of all the nodes in a computation were completely determined by the initial content states, but there, we were able to reason about each state and activation node as it was added to the computation. Here, there is no real concept of nodes being added to the computation over time: Time itself consists only of an axiom that the computation is acyclic. So, we need to be a bit more careful.

First, for a base case, pick any $s \in S_0$. From the Initialization axiom, we know that $\dot{\sigma}(s) = \omega_0$ and $\ddot{\sigma}(s) = \iota(\bar{s})$. So, the theorem holds for members of S_0.

Then, for the general case, we choose some other $s \in S \setminus S_0$. From the Atomicity axiom, $|*s| \leq 1$, and the assumption that $s \notin S_0$ means that $|*s| \neq 0$, so $|*s| = 1$. We'll call s's predecessor a – that is, $a = *s$. Consider $*a$ (or, identically, $**s$). From the Structure axiom (1), we know that those are elements of S named for the resources bound to context $\hat{a}$. Either $\dot{\sigma}$ and $\ddot{\sigma}$ are uniquely defined for all those nodes, or they're not.

First, we'll suppose that those functions are uniquely defined for all those nodes. In that case, the Firing axiom (6.2, 6.3, and 6.4 specifically) specify the values for $\dot{\sigma}$ and $\ddot{\sigma}$ for all of $a*$, which includes s.

185

So that leaves the case where either $\dot{\sigma}$ or $\ddot{\sigma}$ are not uniquely defined for at least one member of $*a$. Pick one. If we were to call it our new s, and repeat the previous logic, then either $\dot{\sigma}$ or $\ddot{\sigma}$ must not be defined for one of the predecessors of s's predecessor (i.e. $**s$). If we keep going "backward" in the computation, from predecessor to predecessor, we must eventually end up with an s with no predecessors – i.e. $s \in S_0$ – because the Time axiom (2) ensures that the computation has no cycles. But we've already shown that the functions are uniquely defined if $s \in S_0$, violating the assumption. Thus, the case described by this paragraph, where either $\dot{\sigma}$ or $\ddot{\sigma}$ are not uniquely defined for at least one member of $*a$, does not exist.

Hence, $\dot{\sigma}$ and $\ddot{\sigma}$ are uniquely defined for all members of S.■

10.4.4 Tracing a Computation

How much (or little) information is required, in addition to the F-Net itself, to completely determine a computation graph for that F-Net (up to an isomorphism)? This question is important for debugging non-deterministic plans, for it determines the amount of data that must be logged during a computation in order to reconstruct "what happened". In this subsection, we'll start by defining what we mean by instrumenting an F-Net, and then (as a result), defining what we mean by collecting a trace on the resulting computations. The next subsection will then use these definitions to prove that such instrumentation and resulting traces, together with the same initial marking, are sufficient to rebuild a non-deterministic computation.

First, we define what we mean by the resources **shared** by two contexts – i.e. simply the ones (if any) to which both are bound:

$$shared(c, c') \equiv Im\,(c \bullet \beta) \cap Im\,(c' \bullet \beta)$$

Then, we define the **contends relation** between two contexts $c, c' \in C$, represented $c \Diamond c'$, as

$$c \Diamond c' \equiv shared(c, c') \neq \emptyset \wedge$$
$$\left(\forall r \in shared(c, c').c \bullet \gamma \left(c \bullet \beta^{-1}(r)\right) = c' \bullet \gamma \left(c' \bullet \beta^{-1}(r)\right)\right)$$

That is, two contexts contend whenever they share at least one resource, and for all resources which they share, the firing constraint for the role bound to that resource is the same for each. Or put another way, they contend if the firing constraints of the resources which they share do not dictate which should execute next. Since they do share resources, the A nodes representing their activations will be related by $\preceq$, so the order in which they activate will affect the topology of the computation. This suggests (as argued earlier in Chapter 9) that contending contexts are the only source of non-determinism in an F-Net. We now add instrumentation to an F-Net to capture the order in which contending contexts activate, and thus capture the non-deterministic choices made during an F-Net execution. This is accomplished by (figuratively) coloring the contexts of the F-Net such that contending contexts always have

186

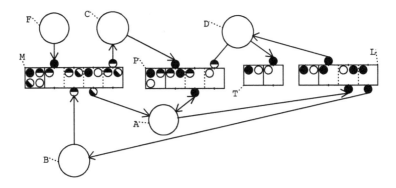

Figure 10.1: Sample F-Net with contention.

differing colors, then recording the color of each contending context every time it activates. This log of colors does not need to be shared by all contexts — it is only necessary that any two contexts which contend use a common log. Since contending contexts already have some shared resources, by definition, these resources can provide a handy (and local) site to store the logs. It is not necessary to assign a log to each shared resource, but to at least one resource shared by any contending contexts.

With this aim, we will define an **Instrumented F-Net** $\breve{p}$ as a 10-tuple, $< \Sigma, \Omega, \Delta, \omega_0, R, T, C, K, \rho, \lambda >$ where

- K is the set of Colors,

- $\rho : C \to K$ is a Context Coloring, and

- $\lambda : C \to \wp(S)$ is a Log Selector

such that

- $< \Sigma, \Omega, \Delta, \omega_0, R, T, C >$ is an F-Net

- $c \Diamond c' \wedge c \neq c' \Rightarrow \rho(c) \neq \rho(c') \wedge (\lambda(c) \cap \lambda(c') \cap shared(c, c') \neq \emptyset)$

- $\neg (\exists c' \in C.c \Diamond c' \wedge c \neq c') \Rightarrow \lambda(c) = \emptyset$

That is, for any two contexts which contend, the colors assigned to the contexts are different, and at least one of their shared resources belongs to the log selector of each context. If a context does not contend with any others, its log selector is null (and its color is immaterial). To illustrate, consider the F-Net in Figure 10.1. The only contexts which contend are B$\Diamond$C and B$\Diamond$D, so one possible instrumentation for this F-Net would be to color context B green and contexts C and D red, and to select resources L and M for context B's log, resource M for context C's log, and resource L for context D's log. In the more formal set/function notation,

- $K = \{red, green\}$

- $\rho(\mathtt{B}) = green, \rho(\mathtt{C}) = red, \rho(\mathtt{D}) = red$ (and the rest are immaterial)

- $\lambda(\mathtt{A}) = \emptyset, \lambda(\mathtt{B}) = \{\mathtt{L}, \mathtt{M}\}, \lambda(\mathtt{C}) = \{\mathtt{M}\}, \lambda(\mathtt{D}) = \{\mathtt{L}\}, \lambda(\mathtt{F}) = \emptyset$

Define a **Traced Computation** of Instrumented F-Net

$$\check{p} = <\Sigma, \Omega, \Delta, \omega_0, R, T, C, K, \rho, \lambda>$$

with initial marking ι, as a 7-tuple $\check{\chi}_{\check{p}, \iota} = <A, S, B, E, \hat{\sigma}, \bar{\sigma}, \theta>$ where

- $\chi_{p, \iota} = <A, S, B, E, \hat{\sigma}, \bar{\sigma}>$ is a computation for F-Net

$$p = <\Sigma, \Omega, \Delta, \omega_0, R, T, C>$$

  with initial marking ι

- $\theta : S \to K$ is the Trace Coloring

such that

- $\forall a \in A \forall s \in *a.\bar{s} \in \lambda(\hat{a}) \Rightarrow \lambda(s) = \rho(\hat{a})$

That is, for any activation, any of the activation's predecessors (i.e. state nodes) named for a resource in the context's log selector will be colored to match the context's color. To illustrate, consider the computation in Figure 10.2, in which the three colored state nodes have been annotated at their upper right. θ would therefore evaluate to those colors for those state nodes, and could evaluate to anything (or nothing) for any other state node.

A **resource trace** of a traced computation $\check{\chi}_{\check{p}, \iota} = <A, S, B, E, \hat{\sigma}, \bar{\sigma}, \theta>$ for resource $r \in R$, denoted $trace(\check{\chi}_{\check{p}, \iota}, r)$, is defined as

$$trace(\check{\chi}_{\check{p}, \iota}, r) \equiv \theta\left(\{s \in S_r.s* = \{a\} \wedge r \in \lambda(\hat{a})\}^{\preceq}\right)$$

where

- $\check{p} = <\Sigma, \Omega, \Delta, \omega_0, R, T, C, K, \rho, \lambda>$

- $\check{\chi}_{\check{p}, \iota} = <A, S, B, E, \hat{\sigma}, \bar{\sigma}, \theta>$

That is, the resource trace for a resource is the sequence of colorings of the state nodes named for that resource (totally ordered from "beginning" to "end" by $\preceq$), omitting those that do not immediately precede contending contexts. If the traced computation in Figure 10.2 is called $\check{\chi}$, $trace(\check{\chi}, \mathtt{L}) = green, red$ and $trace(\check{\chi}, \mathtt{M}) = green$ with the rest of the resources having empty (null) traces.

10.4.5   Computations with Identical Resource Traces are Isomorphic

In this subsection, we prove that instrumentation and tracing, as defined in the previous subsection, is sufficient to rebuild a non-deterministic computation – with very little overhead. But first, if we are going to claim that one computation is somehow identical to another, we must define what that means: After

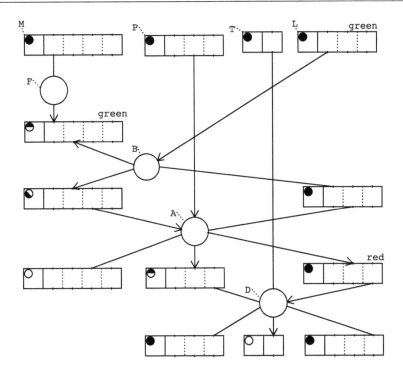

Figure 10.2: Possible traced computation for F-Net in previous figure.

all, they are different graphs, with different nodes, etc. We take the standard approach of using the concept of isomorphism. We define computations $\chi_{p,\iota}$ and $\chi'_{p,\iota}$ (both from F-Net p with initial marking ι, so we will subsequently omit those subscripts) as being **isomorphic** (denoted $\chi \cong \chi'$) iff there exist bijections $\tilde{s} : \chi \bullet S \leftrightarrow \chi' \bullet S$ and $\tilde{a} : \chi \bullet A \leftrightarrow \chi' \bullet A$ such that

$$(s,a) \in \chi \bullet B \Leftrightarrow (\tilde{s}(s), \tilde{a}(a)) \in \chi' \bullet B$$
$$(a,s) \in \chi \bullet E \Leftrightarrow (\tilde{a}(a), \tilde{s}(s)) \in \chi' \bullet E$$
$$\bar{\sigma}(s) = \bar{\sigma}(\tilde{s}(s))$$
$$\hat{\sigma}(a) = \hat{\sigma}(\tilde{a}(a))$$

That is, there is a one-to-one correspondence between the state and activation nodes, such that corresponding state nodes are named for the same resource, corresponding activation nodes are named for the same context, and all arcs (and only arcs) between corresponding nodes in one computation are present in the other. From Theorem 3 (or at least, its proof) that $\dot{\sigma}$ and $\ddot{\sigma}$ are uniquely defined for computations, it also follows that they correspond in the isomorphic computations:

189

$$\dot{\sigma}(s) = \dot{\sigma}\left(\tilde{s}(s)\right)$$
$$\ddot{\sigma}(s) = \ddot{\sigma}\left(\tilde{s}(s)\right)$$

Now we can formally state the big theorem of this chapter.

Theorem 4 If
$$\check{\chi}_{\check{p},\iota} =< A, S, B, E, \hat{\sigma}, \bar{\sigma}, \theta >$$
and
$$\check{\chi}'_{\check{p},\iota} =< A', S', B', E', \hat{\sigma}', \bar{\sigma}', \theta' >$$
are traced computations of instrumented F-Net
$$\check{p} =< \Sigma, \Omega, \Delta, \omega_0, R, T, C, K, \rho, \lambda >$$
with initial marking ι such that
$$\forall r \in R.trace(\check{\chi}_{\check{p},\iota}, r) = trace(\check{\chi}_{\check{p},\iota}, r)$$
then computations
$$\chi_{p,\iota} =< A, S, B, E, \hat{\sigma}, \bar{\sigma} >$$
and
$$\chi'_{p,\iota} =< A', S', B', E', \hat{\sigma}', \bar{\sigma}' >$$
for F-Net
$$p =< \Sigma, \Omega, \Delta, \omega_0, R, T, C >$$
are isomorphic.

That is, in addition to the initial marking (input) and instrumented F-Net, only the trace associated with each resource is required to uniquely determine the execution graph (to within isomorphism).

Proof outline for Theorem 4 (induction over partial order) For the proof, we will need to use the concept that the beginning of one computation is the same (i.e. isomorphic) to the beginning of another, and this idea of "beginning" needs to be defined formally first. We will say that Υ is a **prefix computation** of computation χ if Υ has the same form as a computation and the following conditions hold (instead of the earlier axioms):

$$\Upsilon \bullet S \subseteq \chi \bullet S$$
$$\Upsilon \bullet A \subseteq \chi \bullet A$$
$$\Upsilon \bullet B \subseteq \chi \bullet B$$
$$\Upsilon \bullet E \subseteq \chi \bullet E$$
$$s \in \chi \bullet S \wedge *s = \emptyset \Rightarrow s \in \Upsilon \bullet S$$
$$(s \in \Upsilon \bullet S \wedge (a,s) \in \chi \bullet E) \Rightarrow (a \in \Upsilon \bullet A \wedge (a,s) \in \Upsilon \bullet E)$$
$$(a \in \Upsilon \bullet A \wedge (a,s) \in \chi \bullet E) \Rightarrow (s \in \Upsilon \bullet S \wedge (a,s) \in \Upsilon \bullet E)$$
$$(a \in \Upsilon \bullet A \wedge (s,a) \in \chi \bullet B) \Rightarrow (s \in \Upsilon \bullet S \wedge (s,a) \in \Upsilon \bullet B)$$

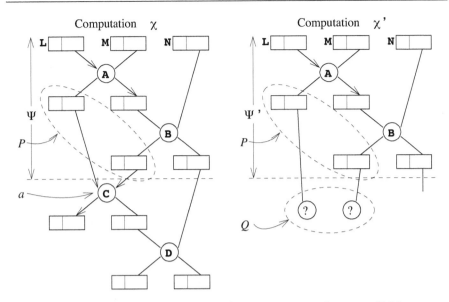

Figure 10.3: Two isomorphic prefix computations for same F-Net.

That is, the nodes and arcs of Υ are a subgraph (subsets) of those in χ, Υ includes all the initial stat nodes of χ,any node in Υ with a predecessor in χ also has that predecessor in Υ, and any activation node in Υ with a successor in χ also has that successor in Υ. Note that a prefix computation is often not a legal computation specifically (and only) because it doesn't adhere to the Liveness axiom. We will also use the same definition of isomorphism for prefix computations as we used for computations. Now we are ready to outline the proof of Theorem 4, as vaguely illustrated in Figure 10.3.

Base case: Show that the prefix computation of χ consisting only of its initial states (S_0), with all other sets (A, B, and E) empty, is isomorphic to the prefix computation of χ' consisting only of its initial states.

Inductive step: Suppose that there is a prefix computation Υ of computation χ which is isomorphic to a prefix computation Υ' of computation χ'. If either computation (say χ, without loss of generality) has any elements not in its prefix computation (Υ), then pick a least such element by partial ordering $\leq$ and call it a_χ. (It must be a member of $\chi \bullet A$ from the definition of prefix computation.) We will show that the other computation (χ') has an element $a_{\chi'}$ not in its prefix computation (Υ') such that adding a_χ, its pre arcs, post arcs, and successors to Υ is a prefix computation which is isomorphic to that obtained by adding $a_{\chi'}$, its pre arcs, post arcs, and successors to Υ'.

The result of this induction is that given any two traced computations with identical traces for all resources, all of both graphs can be pulled into Υ and Υ', so the computations themselves must be isomorphic.

191

Proof of Theorem 4   The base case follows immediately from the definition of S_0, the Initialization axiom, and the definition of a prefix computation. The rest of the proof will focus on the inductive step.

Construct Υ, Υ', and a_χ as indicated in the inductive step, and consider the set $*a_\chi$, which we'll refer to as P_χ. All members of this set must be in Υ (specifically, $P_\chi \subseteq \Upsilon \bullet S$), so by the inductive assumption, there exists a set $P_{\chi'}$ in Υ' such that $P_{\chi'} \cong P_\chi$. Now consider the successors of $P_{\chi'}$, which we'll call $Q_{\chi'}$. That is, $Q_{\chi'} \equiv \bigcup_{s \in P_{\chi'}} s*$, so $Q_{\chi'} \subseteq \chi' \bullet A$. We know from computation χ that $Q_{\chi'}$ cannot be empty, since there exists a context $(\hat{a}_\chi)$ which can activate based on the control states of the elements of P_χ, so from the definition of isomorphism (i.e. the elements of P_χ and $P_{\chi'}$ have the same names and control states) and the Liveness axiom, one of the elements of $P_{\chi'}$ must have a successor.

Pick a least element of $Q_{\chi'}$ and call it $a_{\chi'}$. Then $a_{\chi'}$ has at least one predecessor in $P_{\chi'}$ by construction (call it $s_{\chi'}$), which also has a counterpart (call it s_χ) in P_χ representing the same resource (i.e. $\bar{s}_\chi = \bar{s}_{\chi'}$). Since $P_\chi = *a_\chi$, and from the Structure axiom, both contexts $\hat{a}_\chi$ and $\hat{a}_{\chi'}$ must be bound to at least one resource (that one) in common, so $shared(\hat{a}_\chi, \hat{a}_{\chi'}) \neq \emptyset$. Let $R^{shared} = shared(\hat{a}_\chi, \hat{a}_{\chi'})$.

Moreover, because $a_{\chi'}$ was chosen as a least element of $Q_{\chi'}$, all of the predecessors of $a_{\chi'}$ which represent resources in R^{shared} must be in $P_{\chi'}$. Let $P_{\chi'}^{shared}$ be the elements of $P_{\chi'}$ representing those resources, and P_χ^{shared} be the elements of P_χ representing those resources. Since $P_\chi^{shared} \cong P_{\chi'}^{shared}$, they represent state nodes having the same control states, which (from the Structure axiom) means that the firing constraint for contexts $\hat{a}_\chi$ and $\hat{a}_{\chi'}$ for those shared resources is identical. In other words, $\hat{a}_\chi \lozenge \hat{a}_{\chi'}$.

Assume that $\hat{a}_\chi \neq \hat{a}_{\chi'}$. Then from the definition of an instrumented F-Net, at least one of the resources in R^{shared} will be in both of their log selectors (λ). Pick one such resource, call it r^{shared}. By the definition of a traced computation, the state node of P_χ^{shared} representing r^{shared} must be colored for $\hat{a}_\chi$, and the state node of $P_{\chi'}^{shared}$ representing r^{shared} must be colored for $\hat{a}_{\chi'}$, and from the definition of an instrumented F-Net, those contexts must have different colors (ρ), so the state nodes must also have different colors. But since $P_\chi^{shared} \cong P_{\chi'}^{shared}$, and moreover, $\Upsilon_\chi \cong \Upsilon_{\chi'}$, and by the theorem assumption, $trace(\check{\chi}, r^{shared}) = trace(\check{\chi}', r^{shared})$, the state nodes must have identical colors. $\Rightarrow \Leftarrow$. Therefore, the assumption that $\hat{a}_\chi \neq \hat{a}_{\chi'}$ was incorrect, so $\hat{a}_\chi = \hat{a}_{\chi'}$ and $P_{\chi'} = *a_{\chi'}$, so $a_\chi \cong a_{\chi'}$. As a result, pulling a_χ, $a_\chi*$, and all of a_χ's pre and post arcs into Υ, and $a_{\chi'}$, $a_{\chi'}*$, and all of $a_{\chi'}$'s pre and post arcs into Υ' will again yield isomorphic prefix computations.∎

10.5   Summary

An F-Net (a simplified form of plan/strategy) was defined completely in terms of a tuple of sets and functions, with the elements of some of those sets (specifically, the tactics and the contexts) themselves defined as tuples of sets and functions. At that point, no meaning at all had been formally assigned to any of the components. Then, a computation was also defined, again completely in terms of tuples of sets and functions. Then, some axioms were stated relating the sets/elements of the computation to the sets/elements of the F-Net. Specifically, those axioms were Initialization, Time, Atomicity, Safety, Liveness, and Firing (Activation). The Activation axiom was actually broken down into four others, specifying Structure, New content states, Non-interference (unchanging content states), and New control states.

With all/any "meaning" of these definitions and axioms to emerge only as a result of applying the axioms, some theorems were stated and proven to demonstrate that the F-Nets and computations defined here have properties which are at least similar (and arguably identical) to simple versions of the strategies described earlier. Specifically, Theorem 1 stated/proved that the computations specified are indeed partial orders (i.e. can be represented as Directed Acyclic Graphs, or DAGs), Theorem 2 stated/proved that all of the state nodes named in the computation named for any particular resource appeared in a sequence, and Theorem 3 stated/proved that a computation does indeed specify a function, in the sense that all of the activation nodes represent a function (tactic), and each of the state nodes has a unique control and content state which is a result of only the initial marking (input) and the computation itself.

We proceeded with a more substantive theorem dealing with the amount of information, in addition to the plan itself and initial marking (input), which is required to completely specify a computation. For deterministic plans, the answer is clearly "none", so the question pertains specifically to nondeterministic plans. To set this up, an extended form of F-Net, called an Instrumented F-Net, was defined to be one with three additional components: A set of colors, a coloring (i.e. the assignment of one of those colors to any context which could contend with any other context), and a log selector specifying a shared resource for each context to log its color to (also just for contending contexts). To capture the results of such instrumentation, an extended form of computation, called a Traced Computation, was specified to be a computation with some of its state nodes potentially colored, as specified by the coloring and log selector of the Instrumented F-Net. Finally, a resource trace was defined as the colors assigned to the sequence of state nodes associated with any particular resource.

The theorem being proved, then, was Theorem 4, that just having the resource traces, in addition to the initial marking (input) for an instrumented computation was sufficient to rebuild it, even if the F-Net from which it emanated was nondeterministic. The proof relied on the construction of a so-called prefix computation, which (conceptually) corresponds to a partially-completed computation, being built starting with the inital states toward the "end".

The proof of Theorem 4 has very practical applications. Even for rather large F-Nets, the corresponding Instrumented F-Net is likely to require just a small number (if any) colors, and just a small number (if any) resources listed within the log selectors. This means that each color can be represented by just a few bits in a computer, and those few bits only need to be recorded occasionally, so the overhead (in time, space, or communication overhead) is very low, and even in a high-performance real-world environment, might be so low as to make it practical to convert every F-Net (or strategy) to an instrumented form, and to trace every computation, just in case a planner might later wish to inquire

193

into "what happened".

Chapter 11

Sets

It is quite common to logically (if not physically) associate different resources into collections, based on such things as all having a common format or characteristic, or perhaps all forming parts of one conceptual whole. In the computer world, it is common, for example, to organize variables into so-called records or structures, and to organize files into folders or directories. In each case, these entities are hierarchical (i.e. can contain entities like themselves as members, to any level of nesting), and can be treated either as a unit, or as individual components depending upon the circumstances. In ScalPL, a primary goal of such collections (called resource sets) is to effectively allow an activity's visibility of a collection of resources (i.e. scope) to be controlled as easily as one, via a binding to a context. After all, such visibility/scope is itself information, and understanding where this information must be and when can facilitate scalability. This will play an especially important role in the subsequent chapter on object-oriented constructs.

11.1 Motivation

In descriptions so far, each context has been required to explicitly bind each role of the plan that is activated within it to resources in its immediate environment – even if those are in fact formal resources which may again represent roles it *its* parent, etc. However, there are cases where we would like to use a plan while only knowing or caring about a few of its roles, but would still like to allow the rest of the roles to be bound by somewhere else (e.g. in the parent) in contexts which *are* aware of those other roles. In other words, we'd like some "intermediate" plans to be able to carry role bindings in their parents to their children (i.e. plans within contexts of the intermediate plans) without the intermediate plan knowing much about those roles or bindings, or similarly, carrying the scope of the outside environment through to the internal child contexts, for them to bind to some or all of it.

For example, consider that we have a plan called `circle_points` which takes a center, radius, and arc degrees, and then repeatedly returns an x and y coordinate of the next location on the circle. With it, we wish to build a new plan,

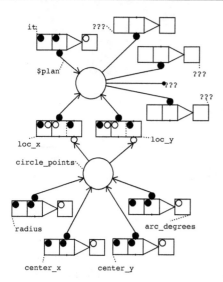 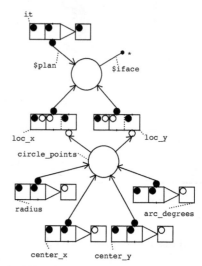

(a) circle_points pumps out coordinates on circle, and "it" does its thing at each, but can't bind it's roles without knowing what they are.

(b) $iface is set of all roles of activity not already bound on context, and * is set of formals for roles bound in parent but not otherwise represented here.

Figure 11.1: "Do it in a circle" plan takes "it" and applies it in a circle.

called `do_it_in_a_circle`, which takes those same circle point specifications, but also takes any plan (which we'll call it) that does something (we don't care what) at a specified point (say, `loc_x` and `loc_y`). This `do_it_in_a_circle` plan then repeatedly and progressively does it at each point around the specified circle. See Figure 11.1(a) – which is not an entire legal representation, due to the unknowns on the top right represented by question marks.

As suggested by the question marks in the figure, the problem in creating our new `do_it_in_a_circle` plan is that we don't know in advance what other roles it must have filled/bound (except for `loc_x` and `loc_y`) to do whatever it does. Even so, we want any context that binds `do_it_in_a_circle` to also be able to bind its roles as well, whatever they are. In other words, its roles somehow need to be fed from its context within `do_it_in_a_circle` out to the context in which `do_it_in_a_circle` is activated (where they can be bound), all without `do_it_in_a_circle` knowing what those roles are.

A solution, in Figure 11.1(b), makes use of **role sets**. That is, although each of the roles (and likewise, each of the formal resources) associated with an activity can be bound independently, they can also be bound collectively as a set. All of the roles belonging to any activity are always considered as belonging to a special role set named `$iface`, so the example shows all of the roles of it being bound to an asterisk. Since roles `loc_x` and `loc_y` of that context are already explicitly bound to resources, they are excluded from `$iface` in this case by a special rule, so `$iface` is all of the *other* roles. The asterisk is called a **wildcard**, and represents any formal resources not already

196

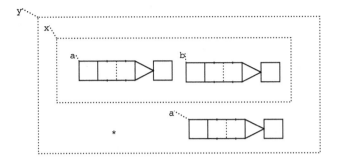

Figure 11.2: Formal sets (x within y).

explicitly represented that would be needed to satisfy any extra bindings when the plan is activated. In other words, when `do_it_in_a_circle` is activated, the asterisk in its implementation represents formal resources for all of the role bindings on that context, except for `it`, `center_x`, `center_y`, `radius`, and `arc_degrees`. The result: All of the other role bindings to the context binding `do_it_in_a_circle` (i.e. the asterisk) are passed along to `it` (on its `$iface` bound to that asterisk).

This is a very simple case of the use of role sets, skipping over several details, and even once those details are filled in, this solution may be suboptimal. For example, if `it` uses roles named `center_x`, `center_y`, `radius`, and/or `arc_degrees`, they will effectively be intercepted by `do_it_in_a_circle` before they ever get to `it`, and will not be represented by the wildcard. And if we wanted to make a slightly more flexible plan called `do_it_in_a_shape` which took any plan that produced shape points (in place of `circle_points`) as well as an `it`, the potential conflicts (between the shape points plan and the `it` plan) could become even more troublesome.

Four constructs will help us to iron out all the details: Formal sets, wildcards, bundlings, and paths.

11.2   Paths and Formal Resource Sets

A **formal set** is a set of formal resources and/or other formal sets, represented by enclosing those elements within a labeled, dashed box, as in Figure 11.2. Though a formal set may be nested within another formal set (i.e. shown by nested dashed boxes, as x and y in the example), formal sets cannot otherwise intersect: If one formal set contains any elements of the other, one must totally contain the other. The names of all of the elements of any one formal set must be unique within that set (alone), though they need not have unique names overall. For example a formal set named x could contain both a formal resource named y and another formal set named x which contains another formal set or resource named y. Put another way, with the advent of formal sets, each formal resource and formal set within a strategy is fully specified by a **set path**, rather than just a name. A set path, similar to the constant path described in 7.2.2, is a sequence of names separated by slashes (/) specifying how to find the specified formal set or formal resource starting from the top, so each name in the sequence (except for possibly the last) is a formal set, and each is an element of the previously-named formal set in the sequence. The "unique names" requirement above can therefore be reworded that each formal set and formal resource must have a unique path.

All of the formal resources and formal sets that are not otherwise shown as being contained in another formal set are considered to belong to a formal set called $iface. In other words, $iface is the top level formal set, within which all the other formal resources and formal sets are contained. It is up to the planner whether they want to explicitly represent the $iface formal set as a dashed box in the plan, or just to have its presence be implied, but if it is represented, all of the other formal resources and formal sets in the plan must be shown within it. Technically, the first name in every set path is therefore $iface (the formal set containing all other formals), but this can be (and usually is) omitted (implied) unless the set path is simply $iface alone.

11.3   Role Sets and Splice Bindings

Just as formal resources correspond to roles to be bound, formal sets correspond to **role sets** to be bound. A role set binding is represented on a context just like a role – i.e. as a line labeled with the name of the role set – but unlike a role which is bound to a resource, a role set can be bound only to a formal set (or resource set, described later), and/or can have some or all of its component roles broken out and bound individually.

Binding a role set to a resource set, using a **splice binding**, is shown as in Figure 11.3 by simply connecting the line representing the role set to any part of the dashed box representing the formal set. Just as in a role binding, if the role set (line) is not labeled, it will be considered to borrow its name from the formal set to which it is bound. In any case, the role set and formal set must correspond exactly in terms of the name and types of their elements – formal sets corresponding to role sets of the same name, formal resources corresponding to roles of the same name. And the elements of each are bound one-to-one, recursively if necessary (i.e. elements of role sets to elements of formal sets, etc.). For role bindings, the content type of the role must conform to that of the formal resource, and the transitions of each (i.e. transition domain of role and final dots of formal resource) must match exactly by name.

A splice binding pertains only to elements of the role set which are not bound explicitly. That is, if there is an explicit binding of some of the elements of the role set, such as by specifying the full path on a role binding, those take precedence over the splice binding. In Figure 11.3, then, the role set x has two of its elements (a and b) bound using the splice binding, and the third element (c) bound explicitly to resource u. This is the same rule which was used in the earlier example in Figure 11.1, where $iface/loc_x and $iface/loc_y were bound explicitly, but the rest of $iface was bound in a splice binding to the wildcard *.

198

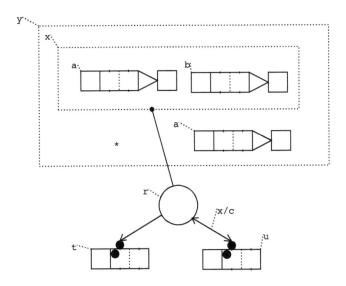

Figure 11.3: Splice binding to formal set x, one element of role set to u.

11.4 Bundlings

Some or all of the components of a role set can be broken out at once and bound independently through the use of a **bundling**, shown as a triangle (in any orientation) with the named role set line attached to the apex (or any corner) and the lines representing the component roles and role sets "emerging" from the base (or side opposite the role set line) each to be bound independently. See Figure 11.4 to see two bundlings, one bundling role bindings a and b into role set z, and another bundling that role set z with another role set x (containing roles j and k from a splice binding) and role binding y into role set m.

11.5 Wildcards

Some or all of the elements of a formal set may be represented by a **wildcard** (asterisk), in which case it represents any additional formal resources and/or formal sets necessary to match the bindings when this plan is inserted into a context, as described previously. Therefore, the way to represent a formal set with all unknown elements is as a dashed box containing a wildcard. As a special rule, a dashed box containing nothing (not even a wildcard) is taken to represent either a formal set (with any elements, as though it contained a wildcard) or a formal resource an appropriate content type and transition domain, depending on the binding of that name when this plan is activated within a context. Although a wildcard does not represent a formal set per se, it is possible to make a splice binding to it (as in the "do it in a circle" example), in which case it is effectively interpreted as a formal set. And as with other formals and formal sets, a wildcard outside of any depicted formal set is assumed to be

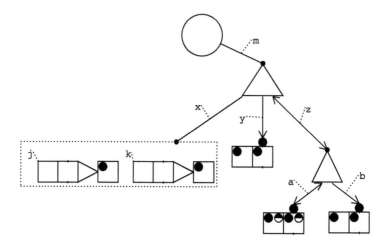

Figure 11.4: Using bundlings to bind role set m {x{j, k}, y, z{a,b}}.

in the $iface formal set (as those in previous examples here),

11.6 Resource Sets

Generally speaking, it is most convenient to allow a ScalPL syntax where any construct included within a set box other than a formal resource, formal set, or wildcard is ignored as a potential member of that set. This allows, for example, entire regions of a plan to be encompassed with a set box, while only intending it to contain any interface constructs that happen to fall within. There is another (and fairly recently adopted) exception, however: Such a set box is considered to be a **resource set** if it contains *only* non-formal resources (which may themselves be represented by the standard shorthand for constants) or other resource sets, and no other constructs at all.[1]

As shown in Figure 11.5, resource sets mostly offer a notational convenience which could be accomplished in other ways (e.g. via bundlings). Part (a) shows that a splice binding to a resource set effectively binds each component of the roleset being bound to the resource (or resource set) with the same name, and if a resource, always to the initial control state and always with a done transition bound back to the initial control state. In other words, these splice bindings offer no use of control state to arbitrate access, except (as usual) to prevent multiple concurrent accesses. Permissions to the bindings are borrowed from the permissions arrows shown on the roleset.

The right side of the Figure shows how resource sets can also be used to make struct constants more flexible, by preceding them with the keyword **set** to turn them into **set constants** – i.e. structure constants where each element is

---

[1] At some point, a different kind of box may be used to more clearly differentiate resource sets from formal sets.

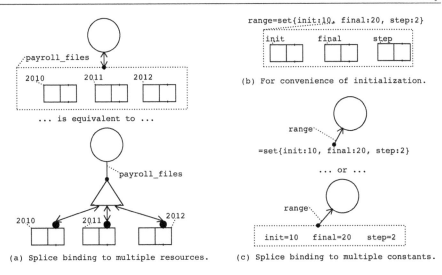

(b) For convenience of initialization.

... is equivalent to ...

... or ...

(a) Splice binding to multiple resources.

(c) Splice binding to multiple constants.

Figure 11.5: Resource sets and set constants.

considered a separate set element, designated by prefixing the structure constant with the keyword **set**. Specifically, as in part (b), set constants can be used to initialize some or all of the elements, and as in part (c), splice bindings can be used for multiple constants at once.

One reason for introducing resource sets is as a means of binding computer directories (or "folders") to the root context. In such a case, a high level directory can be bound to the root context as a resource set, making all files and subdirectories available, and thereafter, child plans can systematically "whittle down" the resulting role set by specifying only the directories and or files they need within their own formal sets to pass to their children, leaving the rest as wildcards. This approach is not especially useful if the context to which the set/directory is bound expects to alter the directory itself (i.e. to add or delete files).

11.7 Summary

Sets are a rather simple method for moving collections of role bindings, called role sets, from the context activating a particular strategy to one of the contexts within that strategy, without the strategy necessarily being aware of the properties of those bindings, such as their names, transitions, or permissions. In other words, they effectively a means of transfering **scope** from the parent to a child. As demonstrated here, this can be used for such diverse purposes as to provide a specific list of roles known by the child and parent, but not the intermediate strategy, or to provide visibility to the child of a relatively large set of resources from which the child can access only those it wishes.

The main constructs related to sets are the formal set, the role set, the bundling, and the wildcard. A formal set is represented by a dashed box containing formal resources, other formal sets, and/or wildcards, and therefore represents a hierarchical structure. A role set corresponds to formal set in the same way that a role corresponds to a formal resource, and like a standard set, is bound by the parent context to an actual (as depicted by a line to that formal), which may be a formal set, bundling, wildcard, or resource set. A wildcard, represented by an asterisk, represents any number of elements of a formal set (including zero) bound in the parent, but not otherwise represented within the formal set box. And a bundling, represented by a triangle, represents the collection of resource or set bindings into a new role set.

A binding of a role set to a formal set (represented by simply attaching the role set line to the formal set box or wildcard representing a role set) is called a splice binding, and can be considered either as simply importing visibility of the role set to the inner scope, or alternately, as binding every role and role set within the role set being bound to the corresponding element of the formal set (i.e. with the same name), to the initial control state and all transition bindings to final transitions of the same name.

A resource set is not a formal set, but has some similar syntax and properties. It is a collection of resources, and allows a splice binding of a role set, but the bindings are different in nature than to a formal set. That is, each resource in the resource set results in a role of the same content type bound to the initial control state (i.e. with that access dot), and a single **done** transition back to the initial control state. The permissions attributed to each role binding are signified by arrows on the role set itself. The resources can also be constants, either individually or as a set constant, the latter represented as a struct constant preceded by the keyword **set**. In this case, all permissions are observe only.

Chapter 12

Objects

Much earlier, we explicitly limited actons to not have persistent state, and now, even strategies have been defined to get fresh content and control state for their resources each time they are activated, excluding persistent state there (between activations), too. But there are times when we would like a strategy to not only possess persistent state, but to carry it around with the plan wherever it might be activated. This is a a hallmark of a kind of programming (and planning) called object-oriented (or OO). This chapter will introduce mechanisms to allow different activations of a single plan to communicate with one another through time and/or space, using persistent state, and with that ability, develop the means to exploit an object-oriented approach to planning, including the creation of classes and class hierarchies, subtype polymorphism, abstract superclasses, and other constructs and techniques which are long familiar to the OO community.

12.1 Intro to Object-Oriented Planning

So far, we have discussed planning from the perspective of activities. We have considered each activity in terms of what happens internally during its lifetime, and how it interacts with its environment (in the form of resources) through the role bindings of the context in which it lives (during its entire lifetime). If multiple activities are to act on a common resource (or set of resources), the standard approach is to make those resources accessible in the environment shared by all of the contexts, and then to bind all of the contexts to them. The resources themselves are static, simply storing information/state to be interpreted and manipulated any way that the accessing activities wish to do so.

This is rather different from the way we deal with entities in real life. Instead of considering an entity (such as a chair, a bag of marbles, a building, an animal, a helicopter, or a triangle) as a collection of information, or even a collection of "stuff", we consider it largely in terms of the actions that we can sensibly perform on it (or that we can prompt it to perform), or on the questions we can sensibly ask about it. In other words, we tend to think of these entities in

203

terms of how they interact with their environment, much like an activity.

But unlike the activities we've discussed so far, real-life entities have relatively long lives, and can work in a number of different contexts without losing their identity or properties between those contexts. That is, we'd like to be able to perform one operation to the entity in one context, and another to it in another context, where an "operation" is considered as any request, action, query, etc., that makes sense to perform on that sort of entity. Although the performing of each operation could be considered as a separate activity, we want to consider all of these activities as pertaining to one entity, as all revolving around (and perhaps accessing and/or modifying) the state of the entity: The entity embodies both the state and the operations which can be performed to that state.

This is the idea behind so-called **object-oriented** (or **OO**) planning. OO planning is based heavily on the more traditional principles of object-oriented programming and/or design, and even though the latter principles were developed in the world of sequential programming, we find that they can be applied straightforwardly in the context of concurrent planning. It is mostly a matter of making some slight extensions to the constructs we've already discussed, and then providing a translation between the terminology we've been using so far and that used in the OO world. (As you may already have guessed, the "entities" discussed in the preceding paragraphs would be considered **objects**, or class instances, in OO planning.)

We will not argue here that ScalPL in its current form is an especially natural way to express OO plans. Our objective here is to introduce a few constructs and concepts, and to demonstrate that important aspects of OO plans can be represented with them, in a way that fits naturally within the framework presented throughout the remainder of this book. If these are not found especially intuitive or easy-to-use in their current form, they can at least suggest an orderly way to (for example) extend ScalPL in the future with similar functionality.

12.1.1 Outline of (Some) OO Principles

Since the definition of the term "object oriented" can vary from one place to another, we start by reviewing those aspects as they will be discussed here. Though readers unfamiliar with OO principles may see this section as a general primer, it is surely not the best introduction available to such material, and some who are familiar with the principles may even quibble with some of the concepts presented here. This will, however, present the principles in terminology that fits naturally within the rest of the book.

The OO planning world is considered as consisting of objects of different **classes** (or **types**). An object of a given class is called an **instance** of that class, so a class can be considered (in part) as a set of objects/instances. The class to which an object belongs also defines the internal state which each object of that class maintains, as well as the **operations** (i.e. the transformations or queries) that can be performed to that object, and how those operations affect and are affected by) its internal state. In traditional OO, these operations are typically named for the so-called **methods** (plans) used by the class to carry them out, but we will use a different approach here in which users of the objects don't explicitly specify the operations being used (or the methods which implement them).

In a nutshell, OO planning (as described here) revolves primarily around

1. Defining classes, often in terms of other classes,

2. Creating instances of classes (i.e. objects), and

3. Invoking operations on those instances.

Since class instances are explicitly created (in the second step), it might also be assumed that they would be (or could be) also explicitly destroyed. However, this belies the fact that once an instance is created, it is stored somewhere – as the content state of a resource, in our case. Just as with anything else stored on a resource, if something else replaces it on the resource, or the resource becomes dead (i.e. reaches a control state ensuring that no other activity will access it), the (previous) content state of the resource is just as good as gone anyway, so it is (or can be) implicitly destroyed – i.e. garbage collected – by a Director. Garbage collection, rather than explicit destruction/reclamation, is used in most any OO environment to avoid unpredictable and/or unintended consequences from accidentally explicitly destroying still active objects (as can happen in computer languages like c), but it is even more important in concurrent planning: Just as in the case of terminating an activity, explicitly coordinating the destruction of an entity in one place with its potential asynchronous use in another place would generally be difficult, needless, and dangerous.

Another important aspect of OO methodologies is the "in terms of other classes" phrase in step 1 above. Although it is always possible to define a class from scratch by explicitly defining each operation that may be performed to members of that class, it is quite often more useful to rely on help from classes that have already been defined and/or implemented which are similar to the class being defined. One obvious advantage of reusing these other classes is that it saves work, not only from the aspect of coming up with the plans to do what is needed, but also in reducing the number of places that must be changed when upgrading and/or debugging plans over time. Another (perhaps less obvious) advantage of reuse is that, if the new class being created is a more specialized version of the one being reused, the instances of the new class (called a **subclass**) can be often be made to be usable anywhere (in any plan) that instances of the original class (called its **superclass**) could be used. The relationship between such a subclass and superclass is sometimes called an **"is-a" relationship** because the subclass is a – i.e. is an example of the – superclass. For example, since a circle, triangle, or line segment are all examples of geometrical shapes (e.g. a circle is a geometrical shape), this means that if the latter are implemented as subclasses of the former, they will all support operations which are valid for geometrical shape, and therefore any plan capable of dealing with instances of a "geometrical shape" class will also be capable of dealing with instances of "circle", "triangle", or "line segment" classes. Note that it does *not* usually work the other way around: A plan which expects to deal with instances of a line segment class (and therefore might perform operations like querying its length) would not tend to work with instances of the geometrical shape class in general, or of other subclasses of geometrical shape, like circle or triangle (which don't have a length *per se*). With the right tools, it is possible to keep track of these subclass-superclass relationships automatically.

Creating a subclass from a superclass is simplified by techniques usually called **inheritance** or **delegation**. In traditional OO, these two are rather different from one another, but they are both ways for a subclass to use of some or all of the superclass' plans, except for those which the subclass **overrides** by providing a replacement (or augmentation). The subclass can also override operations provided by the subclass, or add new operations which were not present at all in the superclass, meaning that the subclass may be able to do more than the superclass, but that's OK, as described earlier.

Many OO toolsets have the concept of **class variables** – i.e. state which is part of the class (set) itself, and shared among (and accessible by) all of the instances (members) of that class. In other words, the class contains some identity and state of its own, in addition to just being a collection of instances and a definition of how they act. Some toolsets, such as ScalPL, take that further, allowing **metaclasses**. Just as an object is created as an instance of a class, in ScalPL a class can be created as an instance of a metaclass, and the classes created as part of the same metaclass not only share state from the metaclass, but the instances of those classes can also share that metaclass state (as well as the class state).

In ScalPL, this instance-class-metaclass relationship can be carried to any level desired – e.g. a metaclass can be created as an instance of a meta-metaclass, etc. This facilitates the creation of "comprises" hierarchy (whole comprises parts). For example, consider a (metametaclass) school, considered as a building hosting a collection of (metaclass) grades, each of which can be considered as a collection of (class) homerooms, each of which can be considered a collection of (object) students. Thus, an instance of the school (metametaclass) is a grade (metaclass), and an instance of the grade (metaclass) is a homeroom (class), and an instance of the homeroom (class) is a student (object). All (and only) the student objects within a particular school or homeroom or grade would share resources pertaining to that school or homeroom or grade.

12.1.2   Strategies as Classes and Instances (Objects)

As it turns out, features already discussed in ScalPL provide much of the functionality required of OO planning. That is, we have already discussed how a single strategy (or plan of any kind) can be activated in different contexts, by feeding it to those contents (from a resource) on a `$plan` role binding. If, in addition, a strategy could be made to carry information (state, resources) along with it among/between activations, then the strategy could serve as an object, and activating it in different contexts would be rather like invoking operations within that obect (the strategy) in different contexts. Four primary issues need to be overcome to fully provide the functionality described in the preceding section associated with objects, classes, and metaclasses:

1. To act as an object, a strategy must be able to carry state (i.e. the control and/or content state of some or all of its resources) along with it as it moves from one context to the next, instead of being given new state for all of its resources each time the strategy is activated in a context. Resources that are maintained between activations will be called **instantiated resources**. A class, then, needs to define which resources are to be instantiated to create an object.

2. To act as an object, it should be possible to activate a strategy in a context which does not bind all of its roles. That is, since we may only need to invoke one method (or a few methods) in one context and another (or others) in another context, there should be a way to only bind roles which will be used by the operations that are desired in that context, while providing some protection against simply forgetting to bind some roles. This will be called **binding constraints** (or **partial binding**).

3. It should be possible to allow one strategy representing a superclass to "intercept" some or all of the roles from another, representing a subclass, thereby effectively delegating that functionality to the superclass. This will be handled primarily through set constructs introduced in the previous chapter.

4. Finally, since classes play the role of types in OO, and strategies are being proposed to fill the role of classes in ScalPL, it should be possible to declare the content domain (i.e. content type) of resources in ScalPL in terms of their ability to hold certain strategies. Moreover, if a particular resource is declared with a content domain capable of holding instances of a certain class (or metaclass, etc), then it should be automatically capable of holding instances of subclasses (submetaclasses, etc.) having an "is-a" relationship with that class (metaclass, etc.).

This will serve as the outline for the next four sections of this chapter (one section for each of the points above). Many of the constructs which support this functionality can be used in different ways, promoting a building-block approach which leaves the planner free to assemble these constructs in novel ways that do not correspond exactly to traditional OO usage, perhaps providing some unforeseen new patterns of use.

12.2 Encapsulated State

As has been described, each time a strategy is activated in a context, each of its standard resources is initialized with a new initial (green/solid) control state, and an initial content state declared for the resource, or a default content state if nothing is declared. We will call this act of giving a new initial control and content state to a resource the **instantiation** of the resource. As described so far, the control and content state for instantiated resources have been accessible only from within the same activity in which the resources themselves reside (i.e.

Figure 12.1: Resources with Instantiation Level 0, 1, 2, and 3.

Figure 12.2: Contexts with IL 0, 1, 2, and 3.

via contexts bound to those resources), so when that activity is finished and there is no further chance that the resource state will help to further progress within that activity, the resources can be collected as garbage.

There is, however, a way to alter when resources are instantiated, and how many activities may access them. Any resource can be drawn with any number of shadows, the number being called the **instantiation level** (or **IL**) of the resource, as in Figure 12.1. Contexts can also be drawn with shadows, the number also being called *their* instantiation level, as in Figure 12.2. The basic rule is that if a context is used to activate a strategy, it will instantiate all (and only) the resources, and bind all (and only) the formal resources, having the same instantiation level as the context itself. This allows us to pick and choose which resources to intantiate in a particular context. Since all resources and contexts up to now have had IL zero (i.e. no shadows), the IL of each context has matched the IL of all of the resources in the plan it is instantiating, so each context has instantiated all of the resources. Uninstantiated resources are not just considered "unready" (i.e. having no control state): Uninstantiated resources effectively don't exist at all, and as such, any contexts bound to them are also considered not to exist, so cannot activate any plans – even if those plans would not need that resource in order to proceed.

In SPLAT (the textual version of ScalPL), instantiation levels are shown as an integer with a percent-sign (%) prefix, after the description of the resource or context.

Instantiation levels only really help us to achieve OO because of another feature of contexts: Those with an IL higher than zero have an extra role, called $oplan, with replace usage. Sometime after the plan (observed on $plan) is activated in the context (and the appropriate resources have been instantiated), the context itself produces a new strategy to $oplan. In more detail, when a context instantiates each resource, it creates the new control and content state (in some unspecified location) and records a secret **instantiation name** for them. (If you like, you can think of this name as instructions for how to find this just-created state.) The resource in the strategy (i.e. the rectangle) is then

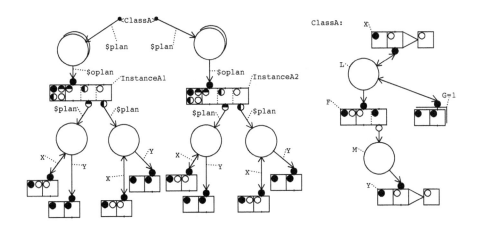

Figure 12.3: Left plan instantiates ClassA twice at IL 1, each twice at IL 0.

labeled with that instantiation name, both to show that the resource has been instantiated, and to associate the newly-created control and content state with this particular resource. When the strategy is produced to the $oplan role, all of these instantiation names are included, so the information on the content and control state of these instantiated resources is available to other contexts which might access this strategy.

The trick, then, is that when the strategy, with some instantiated resources, is then activated in other contexts (e.g. with a lower instantiation level) by virtue of being "fed" to them on their $plan role, the previously instantiated resources will remain instantiated, so all of the activities in those different contexts will effectively share those instantiated resources. That is the goal we were after. For example, see Figure 12.3 for a plan on the right (ClassA) which has one resource (G) with IL 1, and the rest with IL 0, and another plan on the left which instantiates it in various ways. Specifically, the left plan instantiates the ClassA plan twice at IL 1, into two different resources, InstanceA1 and InstanceA2, and each of those plans is then instantiated again (at IL 0) two more times, each time binding roles X and Y. Since the top two contexts separately instantiate resource G (since it is the only resource with IL1 in ClassA), and each of the lower contexts separately instantiate F and bind X and Y (those having IL 0), the two bottom left activities will share one instantiation of G, and the two bottom right activities will share a different one.

As the labeling in the example suggests, ClassA (on the right) can be considered a class, and in the plan on the left, the two IL1 contexts at the top can be considered the creation of instances (objects) of that class, the contents of InstanceA1 and InstanceA2 can be considered as holding those two instances of class ClassA, and the four IL 0 contexts can be considered invocations of (all of the) methods of those instances. This follows a general pattern regarding instantiation levels:

- Level 0 contexts are used to invoke instances, and level 0 resources within the invoked instance are those belonging to (i.e. local to) each invocation;

- Level 1 contexts are used to invoke classes (and thereby create instances), and level 1 resources within the invoked class are those belonging to (i.e. local to) each instance (all of its invocations);

- Level 2 contexts are used to invoke metaclasses (and thereby create classes), and level 2 resources within the invoked metaclass are those belonging to (i.e. local to) each class (and all of its instances, and all of their invocations); etc.

This means that any specific strategy should be instantiated from high IL to lower IL, decrementing the IL by one each time. There are cases, however, including one later in this chapter, where it is convenient to reinstantiate a strategy – i.e. to instantiate it at a level at which it has already been instantiated – to effectively create another class or instance of the same type. The result is as you might expect: The resources with that IL level are instantiated again, and so assigned new instantiation names. As always, the newly reinstantiated resources will start with their initial content and control state. If resources at lower ILs were also previously instantiated, they are uninstantiated – i.e. the instantiation names are removed from those resources.

The plan on the left of Figure 12.3 may appear to be computation deterministic, because there do not appear to be any shared control states (except for the observe-only constant at the top)–*but it's not!* Even if access to the ClassA constant was more regulated with control state (by specifying it as the initial content for a bona fide resource), it still would not be computation deterministic, due to the combination of two factors. First, even though the control state of InstanceA1 (or InstanceA2) controls the order in which the two IL 0 contexts below it are activated, the activities in both can be concurrent because the $plan role binding (for both) is predictable: The order in which the activities where initially activated is immaterial to the ordering of what goes on within them. Second, whenever a context is bound to resources of different ILs (as L in ClassA is), it effectively represents several contexts, because the lower IL resources will be instantiated more frequently than those with the higher IL, and the context will exist for each case of the lower IL resource instantiated. So L represents (potentially) many different contexts, one for each IL 0 instantiation of the class (i.e. invocations of methods on the class), but the single resource G (and its control state) is shared between all of them – a nondeterministic pattern, as per Chapter 9. Assessments of nondeterminism must now also be aware of this "non-matching IL" rule. (A description of why this does not apply if bound only to resources with the same IL, even a high IL, is given below.)

Note that ClassA does not have any formal resources of IL 1, so when it is invoked in an IL 1 context, it has no role bindings, only the bindings of the context's own $plan and $oplan roles. It is not unusual at all for a class/metaclass/etc. to have no formal resources with an IL greater than 0. The result of having no roles bound is the same as it has been previously when an activity has no remaining bound roles, such as sfter a strategy finishes (by transitioning its $plan formal resource to done) or uses only activation formal

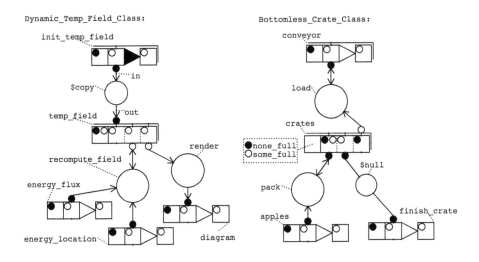

Figure 12.4: Examples with IL 1 formal resources.

resources–i.e. the activity is considered to be finished, and can be garbage collected, and the context can be reused to activate another (or the same) plan. But resources within a strategy are only garbage collected if they will (provably) not be accessed again, and instantiated resources such as G might be accessed again as long as any strategies which might access it (i.e. resources with its instantiation name) are active or might subsequently be activated. In this case, InstanceA1 holds just such a strategy. (In this particular example, if L can be determined to be atomic (e.g. a tactic), and it issues a transition to X, then it is indeed possible to eventually verify that L cannot activate any more, so G will not be accessed any longer, and can be collected.)

Now consider some possible outcomes when a strategy *does* have formal resources with IL greater than zero. Figure 12.4 shows two examples. The left one, Dynamic_Temp_Field_Class, uses an @ formal to bind the IL 1 formal resource init_temp_field exactly once, during which time the content state is simply copied into the instance state, temp_field. This is a convenient approach to initialize the state of an instance at the time that the instance is created, after which time the IL 1 activation of the class finishes, and each invocation of the instance simply continues to use the internal instance state, temp_field in this case. The example strategy on the right, Bottomless_Crate_Class, is perhaps less intuitive and more surprising, in that the IL 1 activation/invocation does virtually nothing other than instantiate crates and bind the formal resource, conveyor, to an actual resource in the parent, and does *not* finish. (load cannot activate because crates has the wrong control state.) Only later, when the instance is (therefore concurrently) activated in one or more contexts, is it possible that (say) pack will put enough apples into the crates to determine that a crate is (or some crates are) full (some_full), thereby enabling load to put the crate(s) onto the conveyor–which remains bound in the IL 1 activation, by

211

a context completely separate (and effectively hidden) from the "users" of (i.e. contexts activating) the instance in the IL 0 activations. On a computer, one can imagine that `crates` might represent an I/O buffer, and `conveyor` might represent an I/O device.

These two examples also highlight two minor complexities. First, consider, in `Dynamic_Temp_Field_Class`, that instead of using an @ formal, one might prefer to use the technique of a `$null` start acton (as described in Chapter 9) which finishes the activity by transitioning the `$plan` resource to `done` at the same time it transitions the formal to its non-initial control state. This implies that the `$plan` resource must have IL 1, since it is bound by an IL 1 context. But it may also be desirable to have an IL 0 `$plan` resource, for the instance activations to use. This is indeed possible, to have multiple formal resources (`$plan` or any other) with different ILs but the same name: They are different resources.

Second, notice, in the `Bottomless_Crate_Class` example, that the `load` context is bound only to resources with IL 1, but (as mentioned earlier) it is not even possibly activated until instances are activated in IL 0 contexts. Does this context potentially exist in every IL 0 activation of the strategy? If so, since all will share access to the same resources and control states, they could introduce nondeterminism. Nothing would be helped or solved by this. So, the answer is, a context is considered to exist only once for every instantiation of highest resource to which it is bound. In other words, the context containing `load` will exist just once, effectively created when the class is invoked (in an IL 1 context), at the same time the `conveyor` and `crates` resources are instantiated. That context will *not* exist multiple times for the multiple IL 0 instantiations.

12.3   Partial Binding

The IL 0 context examples above are unsatisfying. We described activations within IL 0 contexts as instance (object) invocations, but in a typical OO language, one doesn't invoke an instance (object), one invokes a method on an instance. In our case, that would correspond to just binding some of the plan's roles (and therefore formals) in any given context, just enough to activate the desired subplans to carry out the method or operation. However, the plan-context conformance rules developed in Chapter 2 require all of a plan's roles to be bound by each context in which that plan is activated. There were good reasons for that rule, primarily to prevent the user of a plan from just forgetting to bind some of the roles. In some plans (like tactics, or any atomic plan), leaving any of the roles unbound would necessarily make it impossible for the plan to ever activate at all – clearly an undesireable result, so unreasonable to consider perfectly legal.

Now, however, we have good reason to wish to bind some of the roles of a class instance (i.e. a plan) in one context, and other roles in another context, in effect invoking just a particular method (or methods) in each. It is OK for some parts of the plan to be useless (due to unbound roles) in the one context, because the useful (bound) parts can still have an effect on the instantiated resources, and the different activations of the same plan elsewhere can still interact with this context through those instantiated (higher IL) resources. However, we don't want to just throw out the binding rules completely, to allow binding any old combination of roles at any time: We would still like to allow only "sensible" combinations of bindings, to ensure that the user of an instance doesn't just forget to bind certain roles, or misunderstand how the planner intended them to be used in combination. In other words, we would like the planner to have a firm hand in stating the kinds of bindings intended (required) for a particular strategy.

12.3.1   Binding Constraints

ScalPL addresses this challenge with **binding constraints**, which are declarations of the combinations of bindings for that strategy which are legal from the perspective of the planner. A binding constraint is considered part of the interface of a strategy, and is expressed right after the role declarations, preceded (separated) by the keyword "binds". Each instantiation level of a strategy can have a separate binding constraint, since only one level is bound at any one time, and each has its own set of formal resources. To specify the binding constraint for a particular IL, it should be preceded by %n, where n is the IL being specified by that constraint, otherwise it will be assumed that it is for IL 0. A binding constraint for a particular IL consists of a logical expression which must evaluate to "true" in order for a binding to be considered legal. The expression consists of terms connected with "and", "or", "exclusive or", and "not" operations, which are typically represented by &, |, !, and ~, respectively, and optionally grouped with parentheses to control precedence. Each term in the binding constraint may be the name of a role (i.e. a formal resource) of the strategy having that instantiation level, in which case that term will evaluate to "true" if and only if that role is bound by the context containing the strategy. For example, IL 0 binding constraints for the two classes in Figure 12.4 might (respectively) be

- (energy_flux & energy_location) | diagram

- apples | finish_crate

(Strictly speaking, the parentheses would not be required in the first example, since & is typically considered to have a higher precedence than | or !.) In general, different methods (i.e. parts of a strategy/instance) can be invoked concurrently, whether those methods are invoked from a single context, or from different contexts. The decision of which methods to invoke (i.e. roles to bind) from a particular context are governed more by the convenience of the resources being bound to those roles than by a desire to constrain the bindings to ensure that only one method at a time is invoked.

Two special forms of binding constraint consist of just a solitary & or a solitary |, which represent all of the role names of the strategy linked with either & or |, respectively, the first thereby allowing only bindings where all the roles are bound (as is the default) and the second allowing bindings where any of the roles are bound (as long as at least one is).

Partial binding and binding constraints can also be used to some advantage outside of OO techniques. For example, even if a strategy has no resources with IL higher than 0, it may still be considered as a collection, or library, of operations, any of which may be selected and bound at each activation using binding constraints.

12.3.2 Methods

Although binding constraint expressions solve the "partial binding" problem, they can still leave the user hoping that (and wondering whether) they have bound the proper toles to accomplish what they really want to accomplish, which in most OO approaches would be accomplished by naming the method they want to invoke. To solve this, any number of the terms of the binding constraint can also consist of an **method name**, differentiated from a role name by being followed by matched parentheses. A method name evaluates to "true" if and only if the context in which the strategy is bound has a label with a suffix containing that operation name. That is, the label on a strategy is now considered to be of the form *plan*::*methods*, where *plan* is as before (looked up in the repository), and *methods* is any list of method names separated by commas. If the context has an explicit $plan role (as it will almost always have when invoking an instance!), it would not normally be labeled at all, in which case the label (if any) must just be of the form ::*methods*. Unlike many other OO techniques, method names in ScalPL don't (necessarily) correspond to any named entity within a class or object (such as plan): They are just used to establish a correspondence between the intentions of the user of a plan (as specified in the context label) and the intentions of the planner (as specified by the binding constraints) regarding the role bindings that are required to perform different operations. The only place the method names are used is to evaluate the truth of the binding constraint.

With that in mind, any number of terms of the binding constraint can also be of the form *method*(*role*1,*role*2,...,*role*n), where *method* is a method name and all of the *role*i are role names. A term of that form evaluates exactly the same as an expression of the form (*method*() & *role*1 & *role*2 & ... & *role*n). That is, it suggests that if the user wants to perform *method*, then they must bind roles *role*1, *role*2, ..., and *role*n. For the previous two examples, then, more fitting binding constraints for IL 0 might be (respectively):

- `new_source(energy_flux, energy_location) | render(diagram)`

- `pack(apples) | finish_crate`

and the first (`Dynamic_Temp_Field_Class`) might be invoked as shown in Figure 12.5. The fact that the method name `render` is the same as the name of the plan invoked via the `diagram` role (in the implementation of the class) is coincidental: They could have had different names with no difference in behavior. Also, in the example, the `$copy` activity is included primarily to drive home the idea that even if the instance (object) is copied from place to place, both copies represent the same instance, and invoking (activating) either copy will access the same instantiated (IL 1) resources: The only thing being copied by

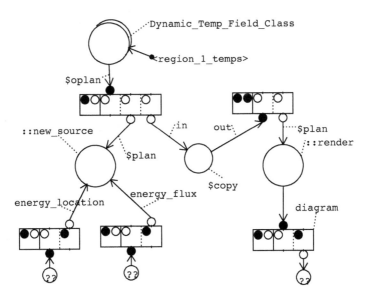

Figure 12.5: Method invocation example.

$copy is the plan, and the two activities (invocations) can be concurrent. The small circles at the bottom are intended to suggest other parts of the plan not explicitly included here.

12.4 Delegation

The third piece of the OO puzzle is the ability to delegate some of the operations (in our case, roles) from one class (or, specifically, an instance of that class) to another class (or, specifically in our case, an instance of that class). Among other things, this will allow us to refine existing classes by adding and/or over-riding some operations while allowing the original (base) class to handle others as-is. The primary tool for accomplishing this was described in the previous chapter (11) on sets.

To illustrate, suppose that a CellPhone class exists which represents a (limited) cell phone device with a user interface (UI) consisting of screen, buttons, etc., and also an application program interface (API) accessible from apps or the cloud, such as to play sounds (PlayWave), or to retrieve the text currently hilighted on the phone's screen (HilitText). We now wish to define a new class, SpeakingCellPhone, which does everything a CellPhone does plus some speech synthesis. Rather than reinvent the wheel, we would like to base SpeakingCellPhone on CellPhone, to which we will just add the novel functionality. To the User Interface, we'll add the following:

SpeakHilitButton Speak the text which is currently hilighted on the screen.

And to the API, we'll add the following:

215

LangNo   Set the language which will be spoken, so that the phone can install the proper default text-to-phoneme dictionary, etc. For illustration purposes, this step will be required when an instance of the class is first created (which can be considered to be when it is configured at the factory or provider).

Jargon   An external speaking dictionary that may be provided, offering extra text-to-phoneme (and grammar, stress, etc.) rules for words or terms not in the default language dictionary.

SpeakPace Set the pace at which speaking occurs (if the default speed is not desired).

SpeakVoiceNo Set the voice used for speaking (if the default voice is not desired).

SpeakTextIn Speak a text block at the defined pace in the defined voice.

SpeakRaw Speak a phoneme stream at the defined pace and in the defined voice (allowing more control than SpeakText).

(We don't pretend that this is a realistic example, or that all bases have been covered. For example, there would likely be ways to change the voice or language from the user interface as well. Also, we are here modeling the cell phone as a stand-alone device, with no attempt to model interaction between cell phones, though that could be added.)

Each instance of SpeakingCellPhone will use an instance of CellPhone internally which will handle all of the non-novel methods. This will require two "tricks":

1. SpeakingCellPhone must pass any roles which were bound in its parent, but which are not any of the new roles which it is handling, through to the CellPhone instance.

2. That instance of CellPhone within SpeakingCellPhone must be instantiated at the same rate/instantiation level as the instance of SpeakingCellPhone in which it resides, if it is to have the proper internal state and act/react properly to invocations of its methods at that instantiation level.

The first part is pretty easy, based on what we learned in the previous chapter. That is, the role bindings can be effectively passed from the parent of an instance of SpeakingCellPhone to one of its children, and specifically, an instance of CellPhone, by using set bindings and wildcards. The second part is also not so hard once you see how it's done. See Figure 12.6 for an example of the SpeakingCellPhone class.

All of the constructs used here should be familiar except for maybe three. First, the resources called Dict and Voice are arrays, indicated by "things going on" on the left end, which will be covered in Chapter 13. All you need to know for now is that the arrow coming in on the left end selects one of the elements in that array for further access, so the integer in Langno selects an element of Dict,

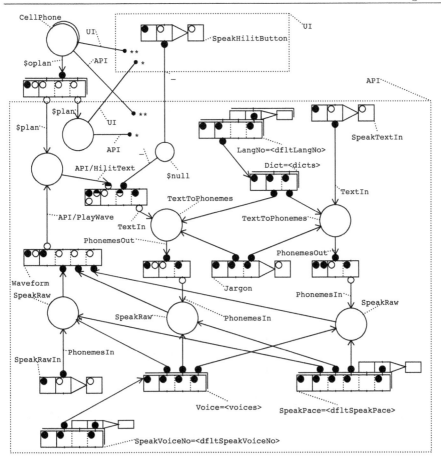

Figure 12.6: SpeakingCellPhone class, based on CellPhone.

and henceforth, `Dict` acts like a regular resource. Likewise with `SpeakVoiceNo` selecting an element of `Voice`.

Second, the double asterisks in the upper left are simply IL 1 wildcards, representing all of the role bindings in the given sets when this strategy is activated at IL 1. In a perfect world, an IL 1 wildcard would have been represented by one asterisk with one shadow, to be consistent with IL 1 iconography for formals, but for simplicity, one asterisk is IL 0, two are IL 1, etc.

The other new construct used here is the funny-looking "tail" on the `LangNo`, `SpeakPace`, and `SpeakVoiceNo` resources. Looking carefully, that tail is actually just a (resized) formal resource stacked on top of another resource, and it is just a shorthand for a very common construction, as shown in Figure 12.7. This construct, called a **ported resource**, signifies the ability for the parent plan (i.e. the one invoking this instance) to cause content to be copied to (if the formal resource is on top) or from (if the formal resource is on the bottom) a resource, usually a resource one with a non-zero IL (i.e. an attribute of the instance). In other words, the "port" (in some sense) makes the resource/attribute

217

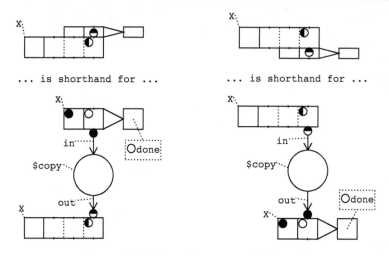

... is shorthand for ...   ... is shorthand for ...

Figure 12.7: Ported resource shorthand.

visible to the invoker. By default, both the formal and regular resources are named the same, but it is possible to label each independently. Note that the access, transition, and final dots (and names and control states) on the formal resource after expanding are all fixed by the shorthand, and the two dots shown in the shorthand are used for the access and transition dots on the other resource. However, other aspects of the formal resource in the shorthand, such as whether it is an activation formal (indicated by a filled-in triangle) and its instantiation level (indicated by shadows), are carried over to the expansion. It is also possible to exend this shorthand, for example by having formals both above and below the regular resource (as long as they are given different names), or even multiple formal resources above or below with different instantiation levels (and perhaps names).

So, with these new constructs in mind, we can look at the example. The most important parts, for this illustration, are the two contexts and one resource at the top left corner. There, a `CellPhone` strategy, which represents the superclass, is activated at IL 1, but because the `$oplan` role is bound to a resource at IL 1, this will only happen if this `SpeakingCellPhone` strategy (subclass) that it is within is *also* being activated at IL 1, and the resulting instantiated `CellPhone` (i.e. the new instance of the superclass) will be recorded to that resource (in this instance of the subclass). As a result, any activations of this subclass (`SpeakingCellPhone`) instance will use that instance of the superclass. And the bindings of superclass instances, to wildcards in the appropriate UI and API sets, will ensure that any invocations of this subclass with bindings for those roles will be passed along (delegated) to the superclass (instances) at the same IL.

Aside from this, the rest of the example should be fairly straightforward. There are two plans used within, `TextToPhonemes`, which converts a list of words in the selected language to some internal form we call phonemes, using the selected language dictionary and (if supplied) jargon dictionary, and then

SpeakRaw converts this internal phoneme form into a sound waveform which is played using the an invocation of the CellPhone instance using the current voice and pace. Likewise, when the SpeakHilitButton becomes ready (i.e. the button is depressed), the $null tactic transitions the control state of the resource so that it will accept the highlighted text from the CellPhone instance and run that through the same steps to speak it.

12.5 Class Structure (Subtyping)

The constructs described provide the basic tools required to implement OO principles, but the planner's intentions are not reflected in the interface. That is, ScalPL can do more than just provide enough tools to let one build things that act like instances, subclasses, and superclasses. In some cases, it makes sense to tell ScalPL of those intentions, so that it can help to insure that the constructs are being used correctly relative to one another.

Consider the earlier example of CellPhone and SpeakingCellPhone. Although our intention was to make the second a subclass of the first, the planner was required to explicitly form the interfaces to be compatible to make that work. Without any additional support, the planner would also be required to ensure that instances of the subclass could be used anywhere instances of the superclasses might be. By allowing the planner to more clearly declare the intended relationships between different classes (strategies), it becomes easier to build such relationships and to check that they are being obeyed, sometimes automatically.

The following three subsections will visit three elements of ScalPL intended to help in the construction of class structure. First, we introduce the ability to use a particular strategy (not just its interface) as a content domain (i.e. type) for resources, so that if that strategy is considered a class, we can treat that class as an abstract data type. Second, we introduce a way to declare a superclass-subclass relationship between different strategies, thereby allowing further checking and assumptions to follow. Finally, we discuss the concept of abstract (super)classes, a class meant only to be a superclass to other classes, and thereby to combine them under one heading (class, type).

12.5.1 Strategies as Content Domains

The introduction of instantiated resources introduces new intricacies related to content domains. That is, until now, it didn't make much sense to say that the content domain of a particular resource consisted of just one particular strategy. Since a strategy is a constant, it would be akin to specifying a content domain of 4 for a resource, which (aside from control state) would have little merit over just using the constant 4 in place of the resource altogether. With instantiated resources, however, it becomes sensible to specify a particular strategy as the content domain for a resource, since:

- different instantiation names are created each time resources are instantiated, so a strategy name plus an instantiation level now potentially describes an entire set of constants (having different instantiation names) instead of just one, and

- even a single instance of an instantiated strategy can effectively have different values (and exhibit different effects) depending upon the content domain of its instantiated resources.

One can, of course, specify a content domain for a resource so that it can accommodate any plan (or more specifically, strategy) having a particular interface. But the interface embodies only part of the description of a class or instance: The planner often wishes for a resource to hold only plans with particular *behavior*, and that is embodied by the class itself, which represents its behavior (and interface), as well as behavior (and interface) owned by all of its subclasses.

So, when specifying the content domain of a resource, one valid content domain is the word `class` followed by a path to where a strategy (representing a class) resides on the repository. To ensure that the path remains valid regardless of where the root is, the path should be relative to the home repository (i.e. the repository holding the plan referencing the strategy/class), rather than to the root repository.

12.5.2   Superclass Designation

We have described how to implement a strategy such that it can delegate certain roles to another strategy, and have likened this relationship to that of a subclass and superclass. However, a subclass-superclass relationship is based on more than just its internal behavior. It is based on the ability to use an instance of the subclass anywhere one can use a superclass, so both the implementation (behavior) and the interface must be asserted to be compatible: Simply allowing any class that conforms to a particular interface is not sufficient.

ScalPL allows the planner to declare one class (i.e. plan) as a subclass of another in the interface, by following the role declarations and any binding constraints with the keyword `extends` followed by a path to the superclass. Usually, then, this will be the same path used in the implementation to instantiate the superclass (to which roles are delegated via wildcard when not otherwise handled), though not necessarily. For example, one might override all of the roles of an abstract superclass, to the point where actually including the superclass in the implementation of the subclass would be more troublesome than helpful.

The inclusion of `extends` has three outward effects.

1. It allows the subclass to be used as the content in any resource having a content domain specified as the superclass (or its superclass, etc.), using the `class` keyword.

2. It declares that any roles of the superclass which have not been overridden (i.e. explicitly declared) in the interface declaration in this class (the subclass) will be as they are in the superclass. In other words, it suggests that any roles not explicitly declared in the interface were delegated to the superclass with a wildcard-`$iface` binding in the implementation,

as described earlier. This specific effect of the `extends` keyword can be accomplished in another way, by adding another construct, `roles(path)`, to role declarations in the interface, but if the other effects of `extends` are desired anyway, this makes it unnecessary to express the path twice in the interface. (The `roles()` option in the interface declaration also allows one to exclude roles of using minus, i.e. `roles(path - role - role...)`, to signify those roles which were explicitly bound and not overridden in the implementation.)

3. In large part to support the above, `extend` ensures that the interface of this plan (as augmented with #2 above, if necessary) conforms to the interface of the superclass plan. Specifically:

- All of the roles of the superclass must be represented in the subclass with the same transition domains and same atomicity requirements.

- The usages for each role in the subclass must be a subset of the usages for that same role in the superclass, except for the usual exception that `nodata` is not allowed to be used as a subclass of `replace`.

- Subclass roles with usage of `observe` (and/or `update`, by virtue of being defined as `observe` + `replace`) must have a content domain that is a superset of (or equal to) that of the corresponding superclass role.

- Subclass roles with usage of `replace` (and/or `update`, by virtue of being defined as `observe` + `replace`) must have a content domain that is a subset of (or equal to) that of the corresponding superclass role.

- Any binding constraints in the superclass must be matched by binding constraints that are at least as general in the subclass. That is, any expression which would be true for the superclass must also be true for the subclass. Logically, this means that if the binding constraint is in disjunctive normal form (i.e. $X_1 \mid X_2 \mid ... \mid X_n$ where each X_n is a conjunctive expression of the form $r_1 \& r_2 \& ... \& r_m$ where each r_i is a role or method name), the conjunctive expressions can be shorter in the subclass, and there can be more such expressions added in the subclass (as disjuncts).

Abstract methods must be defined or redeclared as abstract, as explained in the next subsection. Moreover, if the superclass is abstract, then any abstract operations in the superclass must either be defined in the subclass or declared again as abstract in the subclass. "Defined in the subclass" in this context means that the formal resources for the operation are explicitly represented in the subclass and are each bound to at least one context containing a "real" plan (i.e. not labeled as abstract).

12.5.3 Abstract Classes

The purpose of a class definition may have little to do with actually providing plans for operations which work for any instance of that class. Instead, the class may be meant only (a) to specify the general sorts of functionality required by all of the subclasses of that class, and similarly (b) as a means of referring collectively to all of the subclasses of the class (and their instances) by defining a node in the class hierarchy. In these cases, the class is meant only to serve as a superclass, and might not contain many (or any) plans or operations at all, and is instead only (or primarily) a specification of the minimum interface (the roles and their domains and usages) required of the subclasses, and the binding constraints relating to that interface. Such classes are sometimes referred to as **abstract (super)classes**.

The most obvious way to implement abstract classes in ScalPL is to simply create a class that has no implementation except for formal resources with the appropriate content and transition domains (with no contexts or role bindings), and an interface consisting of those with appropriate usages and binding constraints (e.g. to introduce appropriate method names). That is, if a formal resource has no contexts bound to it, it is considered abstract. The result is that any role bindings for the associated role (in the parent context) is considered an error. In other words, such a formal resource exists only to be overridden in a subclass, and if overridden by another formal that does have bindings to it, of course the associated role can be bound in the parent (of the subclass).

12.6   Example

Here is a more indepth example of delegation which demonstrates some of the complexities – some of which may be addressed more naturally in future versions of ScalPL.

Consider that we have an existing class, `Inf_Int_Class`, which implements infinite-length integer registers (e.g. on a computer), such that the result of any operation (within limits) will be accurately represented internally, regardless of magnitude. Part of the interface is here:

```
plan {
    --> init %1 (done) int        // Initial value
    <-- clone (done) class .      // Returns clone
    --> plus (done) class .       // Plus ...
    --> minus (done) class .      // Minus ...
    --> mult_by (done) class .    // Multiply by ...
    --> div_by (done) class .     // Divide by ...
    <-- remainder (done) class .  // Remainder of div_by
    --> exponent (done) class .   // Raise to the ... power
    <-- to_native (done) int      // Current value in native
    ...
}
```

(This assumes that the interface is defined with its associated class within a BASE constant in a repository, so the single-dot path after the **class** keywords refers back to the same repository as home, and therefore back to the same constant. This is not recursion, in that the constant at that location is not expanded here.)

When an instance of the class is first created, it is supplied an initial integer (often just a zero) on `init` in the default computer representation and length, and it converts and stores it in some internal representation which is hidden (a common principle of OO planning). Subsequently, math operations such as addition, multiplication, division (with or without remainder), and exponentiation, can be performed to the register, supplying another register with the first operand. There is also a means of converting an infinitely-long integer back to the computer's native integer format, assuming the latter is capable of representing (holding) it.

We would now like to create a new subclass of `Inf_Int_Class` called `Digital_Inf_Int_Class`. This new class does everything that `Inf_Int_Class` does, but also contains the notion of the base that the number is in, allowing the user to (say) extract a particular digit of the representation. Upon creating a new digital register (i.e. instance of this class), we can now also supply a `number_base` (in native computer integer format). If supplied with that, the class supports one more operation than `Inf_Int_Class`, in which you can ask it for a digit particular digit (where zero is the rightmost digit), `digit_to_get`, in native integer format, and it will return that digit in `digit_out`, also in native integer format. In other words, it has the same interface as above, with those two additions:

```
plan {
    --> init          %1 (done) int
    --> number_base   %1 (done) int
    --> digit_to_get (done) int
    <-- digit_out (done) int
    --> new_super_obj (done) class Inf_Int_Class
    --> new_inf_number_base (done) class Inf_Int_Class
    <-- clone (done) class .
    ...
}
```

Figure 12.8 shows a possible class definition for `Digital_Inf_Int_Class` in terms of `Inf_Int_Class`, with the new functionality encompassed within the plans `clone`, `deep_init`, and `get_digit`, which will be described shortly. Note first that its IL 1 attributes (resources) consist of `super_instance`, an instance of the `Inf_Int_Class` which will be used for almost everything, and `inf_no_base`, the number base for the register, stored itself as an infinite integer register to facilitate further computation. The formal resources `number_base`, `digit_to_get`, and `digit_out` are as just described. The rest of the formal resources will be described shortly. First, we'll turn our focus to the three contexts at the top left.

When this class is instantiated at IL 1, resources `super_instance` and `inf_no_base` are instantiated, and the formal resource `number_base` is bound. This permits the IL 1 context at the upper left to activate `Inf_Int_Class` at instantiation level 1, effectively creating an instance of that class in `super_instance`. The other top context also allows `Inf_Int_Class` to activate at IL 1, creating another instance of that class in `inf_no_base`. That one

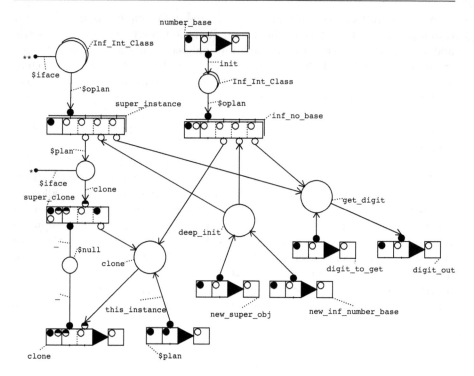

Figure 12.8: Digital Infinite Integer Class extends Infinite Integer Class.

is initialized with the value in number_base. But what of the other? Shouldn't it have an init role, too? The answer lies in the binding at the left, labeled $iface, bound to the double asterisk (**). $iface represents all of the roles (in this case, at least init) of the plan within that context (i.e. Inf_Int_Class at IL 1) that are not explicitly bound by role bindings on that context (which in this case is none). The double asterisk is an IL 1 wildcard, representing formal resources for all of the IL 1 role bindings of the context activating this plan in the parent (presumably at least init) except for those represented explicitly in this plan by IL 1 formal resources (i.e. number_base). The wildcard (*) is a special case of a formal set (set of formal resources), and $iface is a special case of a binding set (set of role bindings), both covered in more detail later in this chapter.

So, this construct effectively carries all of the bindings (except number_base) from this activity's context in its parent, right through this plan to the activation of Inf_Int_Class – delegating the handling of those roles to the instance of the superclass. In this particular case, if we knew that Inf_Int_Class only every had one role at IL 1, named init, and we knew all of its transitions, etc, then we could have replaced the ** and $iface binding with a formal resource init and a normal role binding (for init), but doing so would not only be more complicated, it would introduce potential needless difficulties if the definition of Inf_Int_Class was to change.

224

Now consider what happens when our plan is instantiated at IL 0. The rest of the resources (IL 0) are instantiated, or if formal, potentially bound. This will (usually) allow the instance of `Inf_Int_Class` in resource `super_instance` to activate in the context below it. Here, we see the real power of the wild-card/`$iface` construct for delegation. It again binds (via `$iface`) all the IL 0 roles of that `super_instance` activation except for `clone` (which is bound explicitly on that context) to (via the asterisk) formals representing all of the role bindings for this this plan (instance of `Digital_Inf_Int_Class`) in the parent, except for those represented explicitly here by IL 0 formals (i.e. `digit_to_get`, `digit_out`, `new_super_obj`, `new_inf_number_base`, and `clone`). In effect, these IL 0 formals here override these roles by intercepting these bindings from the parent before they get to `super_instance`. The binding constraints of `super_instance` will determine whether the bindings that "get through" form a legal combination. In the case of `clone`, which produces a "deep" copy of an instance, `Digital_Inf_Int_Class` overrides the method so that it will produce a clone of the subclass instance instead of a superclass instance, but must also create a superclass instance clone to be part of the subclass instance clone.

The constructs at the upper left of this class are a common ScalPL pattern when constructing classes which inherit from other classes. That is, there is a context activating the superclass at IL 1, to which class level operations can be delegated, with `$oplan` bound to a resource of IL 1 to hold an instance of that superclass, which is in turn fed to an IL 0 context with `$plan`, to which instance level operations can be delegated. This way, the superclass (and its instances) are instantiated at the same level as the subclass (and its instances). For each of the contexts, some roles may be bound explicitly to prevent default delegation, and the use of wildcards and $iface constructs allows other bindings of the subclass (or instances thereof) to be passed directly onto the superclass (or instances thereof), effecting the delegation. The same pattern can be extended further, to higher ILs, for metaclasses, metametaclasses, etc.

Note that the `$null` context in the lower left activates when and only when the `clone` formal is bound by the parent (optional in the binding constraints for the class), thereby causing the superclass instance to create a clone into `super_clone` which is then passed to the `clone` plan to create a clone of the subclass.

Figures 12.9 and 12.10 show implementations for the remaining plans (methods) used in `Digital_Inf_Int_Class`. Plan `get_digit` works by creating a clone of the register to have the digit extracted, then dividing it by `number_base` to the `digit_to_get` power (shifting the desired digit to the right), then dividing it again by `number_base` to get the desired digit as the remainder. Note that it creates two additional infinite registers (clones) during the calculations, which are collected as garbage when the plan finishes, which (thanks to the use of all bt formals) can occur as soon as it returns its result (or sooner). Also note that, in `clone`, `this_instance`, an (IL 0) instance of `Digital_Inf_Int_Class`, is instantiated at IL 1 again, effectively treating it like a class instead of an instance. The `deep_init` plan is not intended for public usage, but `clone` requires it. (In fact, `deep_init` is a rather clumsy approach here, but it helps to illustrate such control.)

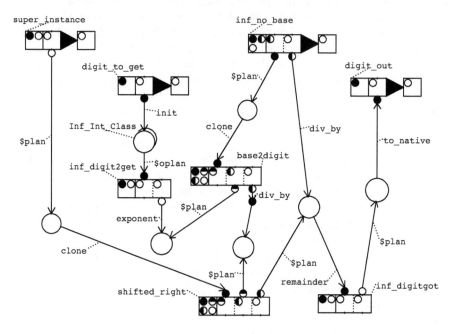

Figure 12.9: get_digit, implementing method in Digital_Inf_Int_Class.

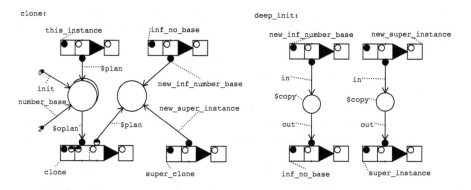

Figure 12.10: clone and deep_init, methods in Digital_Inf_Int_Class.

12.7 Summary

Object Oriented Programming was originally developed in a sequential setting, roughly build upon concepts and constructs like methods and messages. Here, we have delved further into the precise base-level concepts which give OO its power, including persistent encapsulated state, the sharing of certain state among class instances, and the ability to relate classes to one another. Our strategies have served as the basic framework required for a class, as long as we could add persistent state (via instantiated resources) and the ability to bind roles selectively (via partial binding), as well as to provide constructs to allow classes to extend others in a subclass-superclass relationship.

The result here is a style of OO planning which does not suffer from some of the drawbacks of traditional OO. For example, while some criticism is leveled against OO as leading to design being too centered around nouns ("objects") instead of verbs, ScalPL started by giving nouns (resources) and verbs (activities) equal footing, and our formation of classes just provide ways of integrating and combining them in novel ways.

In addition, the constructs presented here are not limited to some specific template of OO. Instantiation levels, for example, can be extended far higher than required for class/instance/invocation (IL 2, 1, and 0). Higher instantiation levels can be used to create hierarchical systems of classes, such as might be found in a school district: IL 5 could be the level for instantiating district level info, IL 4 for school level, IL 3 for grade level, IL 2 for homeroom level, and IL 1 for student level. In such a construction, all invocations of methods (plans) on a student would not only act upon the student's own state (instantiated resources), but would also allow access to the state (higher level instantiated resources) associated with his homeroom, grade, school, and district, all in a form efficiently implemented in a distributed concurrent setting.

Other constructs presented here, such as role sets, resource sets, bundlings, and wildcards, allow scope to be efficiently provided to inner invocations, essentially forming a well-managed porthole through which those inner invocations can view the world outside of their parent. In the computing world, that outside world can be as diverse as libraries, file systems, or devices, bound to the root context and then accessed from deep within complex strategies.

In all, then, even though this chapter has only introduced a few new concepts, they are very powerful ones, and the majority of the effort here has been lent to describing how they might be used to facilitate concepts like OO planning.

Chapter 13

Arrays

While deriving the allowable behaviors of actons, we considered the possibility of allowing inter-resource dependences – i.e. allowing an acton to determine some of the resources it would access by first consulting the contents of some other resources. We ruled against allowing such dependences within actons in order to simplify their specification and deadlock-free scheduling, and this, in turn, implied that the set of resources to be accessed by each acton could be determined (and specified) before the acton commenced. That is, since the decision of which resources an acton will access can't depend on other resources, and actons don't retain state, then the decision of which resources to access must depend on nothing, and therefore must be constant. But what about those cases where we do need to institute such dependences, where an activity must compute the identities of some of the resources it needs (**secondary resources**) based on the content of other resources (**primary resources**)? As was illustrated in Figure 3.6, these cases can already be at least theoretically addressed, though not by a single acton, by breaking the activity down into multiple actons in conjunction with some additional control state.

That approach becomes rapidly cumbersome when there are more than a few secondary resources (or combinations of secondary resources) which the primary resources may designate for the activity. Such a situation is not at all uncommon, like when those potential secondaries come from a large collection of resources which are similar (of the same "type"), each indexed by some unique ID or key or address calculated from the content of the primaries. In mathematics and traditional computer languages, collections of similar resources like this are often arranged within tables, arrays (or vectors), or as records in a file. In most computer languages (and in some real-life situations), it is also possible to simply create or allocate new resources on-the-fly, as they are needed, while keeping track of where they are (i.e. their "addresses" or "handles") for later reference. When dealing with any such collection, then, the primaries contain enough information to calculate the indices or keys or locations of the secondary resources that are to be accessed.

To simplify such cases, this chapter will introduce mechanisms for accomplishing such indexing within ScalPL. That is, we will here re-introduce the possibility of inter-resource dependences. We had good reasons for avoiding them in the first place: Their absence facilitated bottom-belted activities, thereby preventing the potential of deadlock and simplifying the specificaion and independence of actons. So the reader could be justified in wondering why we would reverse that decision now, to seemingly re-introduce complications we earlier avoided.

The main answer to that is that we are introducing a very limited and tightly controlled version of such dependences. Specifically, the dependences will occur within the context itself, even before the plan within the context is activated. That is, it will not be the activity within the context, but the context (and, more specifically, the Director) itself, which finds and binds the context's secondaries on the basis of the contents of its primaries, and does so in such a way that the activity within the context can not even sense whether any inter-resource dependences exist: The dependences are all resolved by the time the plan in the context is activated.

This approach does not make the difficulties of inter-resource dependences disappear, but it does make them less costly, and easier to handle by the Director. For example, although this could theoretically reintroduce the possibility of deadlock, it would be between two contexts trying to bind their roles, so (a) the Director, involved in facilitating that binding, can detect and react to it, and (b) if the Director must indeed back out of one or more such bindings, it is before the plan in the associated context has even been activated, so no great amount of work is lost if it is necessary to back out. In a sense, the bottom of these activities (visualized as pebbles) is still very flat, just not quite as flat, as the Director resolves the dependences in order to create the bottom belt. The bottom line is that the planner can still treat an acton as atomic, bottom-belted, and non-deadlocking, even with inter-resource dependences when they are expressed the way to be presented.

Just as in most computer languages, arrays are convenient and powerful for reasons other than just facilitating non-deadlocking inter-resource dependences, so regardless of the initial motivation for their introduction here, they can be used for a variety of activities that may or may not be actons.

13.1   Resource Arrays

13.1.1   Form and Terminology

To begin to address these issues, we define a **resource array** (or **array**, for short) as a set of similarly-shaped (i.e. identically-typed) **elements**, each a full-fledged resource in itself, possessing both content and control state. Each element is uniquely identified/addressed within the array by an **index** consisting of a tuple (i.e. fixed-length sequence) of integers. The number of integers in each index for a particular array is fixed, and is called the **dimensionality** of that array. So, each element of a one-dimensional array would be addressed with a single integer, those of a two-dimensional array with a pair of integers, etc.

In the graphic representation of a plan, a resource array is represented as

Figure 13.1: Resource arrays of dimensionality 0 (usually called "scalar"), 1, 2, and 3.

a rectangle just like a **scalar** (conventional non-array) resource, but with hash marks in its left (or, if vertical, top) end, equal in number to the array's dimensionality, as shown in Figure 13.1. There is no difference between a scalar and a zero-dimensional array: They are different names for the same thing.

In computer languages (and often in mathematics), it is quite common to envision an array as a dense rectangular region of elements, with the indices representing the location of an element within that region by designating the row, column, level, etc. where that element resides. In fact, computer languages often go so far as to dictate how elements of an array are to be packed in a computer's memory relative to one another. In general, resource arrays are *not* constrained in these ways, though the planner is always free to regard them as being dense and rectangular if it simplifies planning. In fact, unless further constraints are placed upon the indices (descibed later), each index of a resource array is free to range over the entire set of integers (including negative and zero), so these arrays are effectively infinite. In their default form, they do not so much provide a fixed memory region to be selectively filled up as they do provide a coordinate system into which new elements can be selectively embedded as needed. In other words, resource arrays do not have a size *per se*, and can be considered more like n-dimensional space than n-dimensional arrays in the traditional sense, with the dimensions of the resource array playing the role of axes in space and the indices in the array playing the role of coordinates along those axes – a dimensionality 1 resource array being akin to an infinite line, a dimensionality 2 resource array to an infinite plane, dimensionality 3 to normal 3-dimensional space, etc. It is the Director's job to keep track of which elements have a control and/or data state different from their initial, and to maintain and make these available to activities as needed. If a previously unaccessed element is accessed, it is expected to provide a fresh one to the activity, with initial content and control state.

This view of resource arrays as a bunch of independent but labeled elements makes them applicable to situations that may not be well suited to arrays in normal computer languages. For example, so-called "sparse arrays", where the majority of elements are unused, may be difficult to model with traditional computer arrays, but are naturally modeled using resource arrays by simply accessing only those elements/indices that should have content, and making those elements easy to differentiate from the empty elements, such as by assigning them unique control states or keeping track of their indices elsewhere. Likewise, in any situation where an unknown number of elements of some type of resource will be needed (e.g. sheets of paper, or personnel records in a file), the planner can consider them elements of a one-dimensional array, accessing new ones whenever needed. Some techniques for helping with this will be described

231

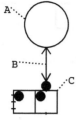
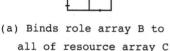
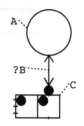

(a) Binds role array B to   (b) Bindany binds scalar role
    all of resource array C   B to arbitrary element of C

Figure 13.2: Bindall (default) and Bindany (with ? label prefix).

later.

13.1.2   Default Binding, Bindall

By default, binding a context to a resource array (as in Figure 13.2(a)) binds it
to all of the elements in that array – i.e. infinitely many, by default! Within the
strategy, the associated formal resource must also be an (infinite) array of the
same dimensionality (designated by the hash marks on the left), and the role
being bound is also considered as an infinite array of that same dimensionality,
binding (by default) each element of the formal to the corresponding element
of the actual.

Because of this, the activity within the context in this (default, infinite)
case cannot be an acton, because that would require infinitely many elements
to become ready before the acton could activate, and the activation would need
to result in issuing a transition to all infinity of them, taking infinite time (in
the general case). However, when the plan activated within the context is not
a tactic, but a strategy, a binding like this can be useful, essentially carrying
all infinity elements of the actual into the formal in the child where they can
be accessed by contexts there. The remainder of this chapter will discuss ways
for activities to selectively bind to certain elements or collections of elements
from a resource array, thereby allowing any kind of activity to access elements
of resources arrays.

13.1.3   Bindany

Figure 13.2(b) shows a **bindany**, where a scalar role is bound to only one
arbitrary element of the resource array. Generally, the planner would like to
have some control over the element to which that binding occurs, such as one
with the specified control state, and that will indeed happen *if* the plan (A in
this case) atomically binds that role, such as if the plan is a tactic and/or uses
either an activation role binding or an activation formal for that role, because in
those cases, binding can only occur if the plan can be simultaneously activated.
If, on the other hand, A is a strategy, and does not use one of those constructs,

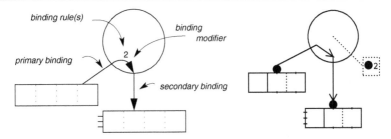

Figure 13.3: Binding modifer: The pieces, and as represented in tools.

then a bindany construct can easily bind to any arbitrary element of C, including one which will never attain the desired control state (i.e. that of the access dot associated with the binding). Such a usage has such limited utility that it should likely be considered indication of an error (unintended usage).

13.2 Binding Modifiers

To modify a binding to a resource array, so as to restrict the binding to something less than the entire array (such as to one or more specific elements of the array), or to change the correspondence of the indices between the elements of the role array (formal resource) and the elements of the actual resource array, the binding is specified in conjunction with one or more **binding modifiers**. All binding modifiers consist (at least) of a **secondary binding**, which is the binding to a resource array which is being restricted or modified, and (2) **binding rules**, which describe the sort of restriction or modification being made to the secondary binding. In addition, most binding modifiers reference another **primary binding**, to another resource (often scalar), which supplies parameters used by the modifier to determine precisely how the secondary binding is to be modified. The remainder of this chapter describes the possible formats and meanings of binding rules (and therefore, the different kinds of binding modifiers).

When a binding modifier has both a primary and secondary binding (as is usual), it is illustrated as an arrow within the context, from the primary binding to the secondary binding and labeled with the binding rules, as in Figure 13.3. A binding modifier without a primary (and there is only one that doesn't use a primary, called a permutation) is specified by labeling the secondary in a special way. Since it may be difficult for drawing tools to manage the placement of binding modifier arrows and the associated binding rules, especially when there are many within a single context circle, it is common to just draw the binding modifier arrows with different colors, shades, or line styles/dashes, and then to provide an associated legend which associates each of those colors/shades/styles with a binding rule. (The figure shows a black dot in the legend next to binding rule "2", meaning that the rule is associated with the black binding modifier arrow, which is the only one shown in this case. Multiple arrows would be in differing shades, indicated by multiple dots of those same shades.)

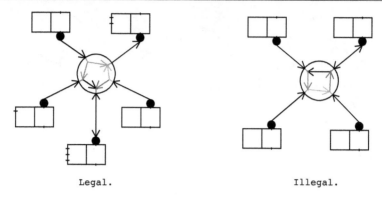

Legal. Illegal.

Figure 13.4: Primary bindings can also be secondaries, but cycles not allowed.

A single binding can serve as both a primary and a secondary binding, as in the lower left binding in the left of Figure 13.4, and any binding can be shared among any number of different binding modifiers. A binding modifier evaluates only after all of its primary receptacles (if any) are bound and ready, at which time the secondary binding occurs. Therefore, if a secondary binding is also a primary binding (for some other modifier), then it must be bound as a secondary before it can be used as a primary. This implies that these modifier chains must be evaluated in the order suggested by their arrows (primaries at the tail of the arrows bound before the secondaries at their heads can be bound), and implies that binding modifiers cannot form cycles (i.e. may not be specified such that binding modifier arrows can be followed from a given binding back to itself).

Binding rules take five basic forms, which will be described much further in the remainder of this chapter: **Reductions, mappings, selections, translations,** and **permutations**:

- A reduction[1] fixes one dimension's index for the secondary role to a particular value, as read from the primary, thereby effectively deleting that dimension of the secondary from subsequent consideration (i.e. reducing the dimensionality of the secondary formal with respect to the actual). If all the dimensions of the secondary role are thus reduced, the secondary role becomes zero-dimensional – i.e. just one scalar element – because fixed indices have been specified for every dimension. So, reduction (as we use the term) is effectively the same thing as piecemeal "subscripting" or "indexing" in other computer or mathematical notations.

- A selection restricts the accessible indices in a particular dimension of the secondary role (and the associated formal resource array) to a particular range, read from the primary. It effectively specifies a temporary size for the array in that dimension.

---

[1]This use of the term "reduction" here is different from, and not to be confused with, the use of the same term when used to signify the creation of a single scalar result over the contributions of several sources like vector or array elements, such as in a dot product.

- A translation shifts the indices of the secondary role (and the associated formal resource array) in a particular dimension relative to the secondary resource array, in a direction and distance read from the primary. If the array is considered as a graph, a translation is like moving the axes of the graph.

- A permutation changes the correspondence between the dimensions (i.e. the order in which the indices are expressed) of the secondary role (and the associated formal resource array) and the dimensions of the secondary actual array. If the array is considered as a graph, this is effectively the same as transposing the axes of the graph. For example, as a result of a permutation, the first three indices specified for the role index may be used to index the third, first, and second dimensions of the resource array, respectively, instead of the usual case of indexing the same first, second, and third dimensions. Permutation is the only modifier that doesn't use a primary binding.

- Unlike the other binding modifiers, a mapping uses an array instead of a scalar for its primary role, but after specifying (on each access) an element of that primary array, the mapping acts like a reduction (into the secondary) using that primary element. Computer programmers might refer to this as indirection – specifying elements of the secondary array indirectly via the contents of the primary array. To specify the index into the primary, additional "ghost" dimensions are added to the primary, so the activity in the context is generally not even aware of which secondary indices are being used to directly specify elements of the secondary actual resource array, and which are being used to specify elements of the primary array (the contents of which is then used for the secondary). The result is a powerful way of making many non-sequential elements of the secondary accessible by a single activity, and of controlling the indices associated with those elements, all based on the contents of the primary.

Figure 13.5 depicts the way that each of these (except for selection) affects indices presented by the activity within the context, though these will become clearer with further explanation. Generally speaking, (a) indices presented by the activity are used for dimensions of the secondary in the same order, skipping over those dimensions in the secondary fixed by reductions or mappings (c). Mappings (e) will intercept some indices from the activity to index the primary, which will then be used to index the secondary. The order in which indices from the activity will satisfy dimensions of the secondary can be explicitly altered using permutation (b), and the indices (from the activity, reductions, or mappings) can be adjusted before indexing the secondary by incrementing or decrementing them from the primary using translations (d).

Many selections and translations can be specified for the same secondary, even in the same dimension, but the dimensions can only be flipped around with a permutation once, and only one reduction or mapping can be specified for a particular dimension of the secondary, since after that the dimension is effectively gone, out of contention for any other modifiers.

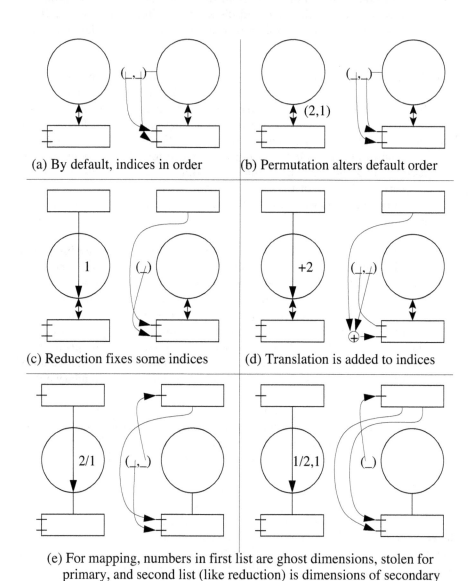

(a) By default, indices in order

(b) Permutation alters default order

(c) Reduction fixes some indices

(d) Translation is added to indices

(e) For mapping, numbers in first list are ghost dimensions, stolen for primary, and second list (like reduction) is dimensions of secondary

Figure 13.5: In each pair, left diagram is legal syntax, and right diagram shows what it represents in terms of flow of data during indexing. Parens enclose a hypothetical index issued by activity, and hash marks on array resource act as "address lines" for each dimension, from top to bottom.

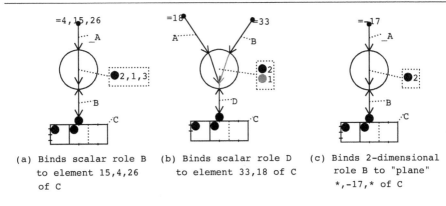

(a) Binds scalar role B   (b) Binds scalar role D   (c) Binds 2-dimensional
     to element 15,4,26   to element 33,18 of C   role B to "plane"
     of C   *,-17,* of C

Figure 13.6: Sample reductions.

Each of these will now be described in detail. These modifiers have the form
they do to provide maximum functionality while simultaneously preserving the
property that the context can determine all of the resources which are being
bound to. Specifically, the set of resources which must be ready for the plan in
the context to activate is well-defined.

13.2.1 Reduction

The simplest and most important form of a binding rule is called a **reduction**,
which corresponds closely to the concept of subscripting, or indexing – and has
nothing to do with a very different use of the term "reduction" in some computer
languages (where it often denotes applying a single operation to an entire array
or set of numbers to yield a smaller number of results – often one). A reduction
in ScalPL is denoted by listing some dimensions (as integers) in the binding rule,
and is evaluated by reading one integer from the primary binding for each of
those dimensions, and using those integers as indices in those dimensions in the
secondary resource. So, for example, if the binding rule is "2,1,3", it means
that three integers will be read from the primary binding and used to index
dimensions 2, 1, and 3 (respectively) of the secondary resource (which must be
an array of dimensionality at least three in this case). If the secondary resource
is an array resource of dimensionality exactly three for this example, then this
would specify a single element of that resource, to which the secondary role
will be bound. The activity in the context would see the secondary as simply
a scalar role, with no indication that it was bound to anything other than a
scalar resource. See first part of Figure 13.6.

The binding rule is not required to list all of the dimensions of the secondary
as it does here, it may list only a subset of those dimensions. In either case,
the dimensionality of the secondary binding (and therefore of the role being
bound and its associated formal resource) is equal to the dimensionality of the
secondary actual resource minus (i.e. "reduced by") the number of dimensions
specified by the binding rule. Dimensions not reduced will remain to be indexed by the activity within the context, or perhaps by other reduction binding

modifiers which use the same secondary, as shown in the center and right of
Figure 13.6. The right diagram shows a binding rule for a reduction listing
only one dimension, and the secondary resource is a three-dimensional array, so
the resulting secondary will bind a two-dimensional role (i.e. the three dimensions of the array minus the one of the reduction) to a single plane or square
(two-dimensional slice), extracted from the secondary array resource by fixing
the one index mentioned in the binding rule to the value read from the primary binding. For all that activity can tell, the binding is to a two-dimensional
resource array, without any binding modifiers at all.

Only integer fields from the primary binding will be used to supply indices
for the dimensions mentioned in the binding rule, so non-integer fields will be
ignored. If the primary binding is to a resource holding more than just the
appropriate number of integers (as designated by the binding rule), then it may
be necessary to more carefully specify exactly which fields from the primary
are to be used to supply the indices. This is accomplished by following each
dimension in the binding rule with an equal sign ("=") and the name of the field
to supply the index in that dimension.

13.2.2 Selection

A **selection** restricts bindings of the secondary to elements with indices within a
particular range in some dimension(s). The binding rule specifies the dimensions
over which the selection is being made (i.e. the dimensions being restricted)
listed within square brackets. Each list dimension results in two integers being
read from the primary, and interpreted as a low-end and high-end of a range in
that dimension. As a result, subsequent bindings for that dimension will only
occur within that range. That is, if the selection is the only modifier specified for
a particular dimension, then the secondary will effectively be bound to all of the
elements in the range specified by that selection (read from the primary), but
if multiple selections are specified for that dimension, then the secondary will
be bound only to indices in that dimension falling within their union (i.e. only
indices which fall within the range of all of the selections), and if a reduction is
specified for the same dimension as one or more selections, then the secondary
role will only be bound if the index for the reduction is within the range defined
by the selection(s). If, for any dimension, the ranges in multiple selections do
not overlap, or a reduction specifies an index outside of the range of specified
selections, the result is a **null binding** of the secondary, which has the same
behavior as if the binding succeeded but was to an element (or elements) which
never becomes ready (so can never be accessed). Any attempt by an acton to
access an unbound role (i.e. to an element outside of the selected range) will
have no external effect, and the effect on the activity itself will be defined by the
semantics of the activity, such as the language in which its tactic is expressed:
It might terminate, or generate some sort of local exception, but in any case, if
it is an acton, it must behave consistently (i.e. deterministically).

Multiple selections, or selections and reductions, can be specified within
the same binding rule, and even within the same square brackets if they are
consecutive. See Figure 13.7 for three examples.

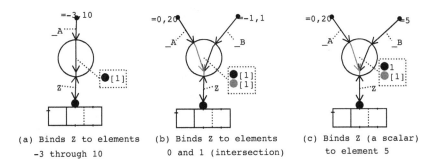

(a) Binds Z to elements   (b) Binds Z to elements   (c) Binds Z (a scalar)
    -3 through 10   0 and 1 (intersection)   to element 5

Figure 13.7: Selections restrict other bindings, including other selections.

Under no circumstance do selections alone reduce the number of dimensions of the secondary, as reductions do. That is, even if the range in some dimension specified by selections contains one element, that dimension of the secondary will still remain to be indexed: It will just have only one usable index in that dimension.

13.2.3 Translation

A **translation** moves (or "translates") one dimension of the secondary role array a particular distance in a positive or negative direction relative to the indices of the secondary resource array. That is, the translation specifies an integer (obtained from the primary) to be added to (or subtracted from) each index in a particular dimension before actually indexing the resource bound to the secondary. The same operation can be regarded as moving the indices for that array in that dimension the same distance in the other direction relative to the array elements. All subsequent bindings and accesses to the array are evaluated according to the translated indices.

The binding rule for a translation binding is an integer representing the dimension (just as in a reduction) preceded or followed by a plus (+) or a minus (-) sign. An integer is read from the primary binding to determine the offset to be added (if a plus sign) or subtracted (if a minus sign) from each index in the specified dimension of the secondary role array to determine the element of the secondary resource array to which it is bound. Multiple translations can be specified for the same dimension (e.g. from different binding modifiers), in which case they work together (add up).

Translations always take place before reductions, because there would be no index to translate if reductions took place first. The order in which translations take place relative to selections in the same dimension is more flexible. It is most common for translations in any dimension to take place before any selections ("early translation"), so that the range determined by the selection is imposed after translating the indices, and this is what happens if the plus or minus sign precedes the dimension number in the binding rule. However, there

239

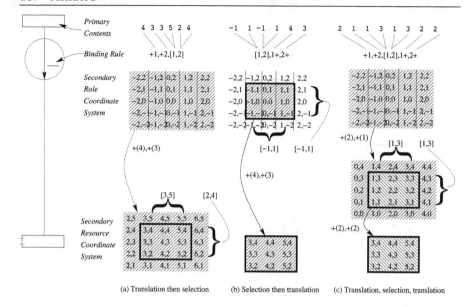

Figure 13.8: Examples of early and late translation.

are also cases where the translation should take place after the selection ("late translation"), so that the range specified in the selection is based on the "raw" indices, and the indices are shifted (perhaps again) after the selection only for the benefit of the activity to execute within the context. This can be made to happen occur by placing the plus or minus sign in the binding rule after the dimension number. Late translations can come in handy if some activities in a plan expect zero-based indexing, such as is used in the C programming language, and others expect 1-based indexing, as is used in the Fortran programming language. If no selections are specified in some dimension, there is no difference in effect between early and late translation.

See Figure 13.8 for some examples of using translation and selection together, all of which associate element 0,0 of the role array (as seen by the activity) with element 4,3 of the resource array, and restrict the activity's access to just that element and its immediate neighbors. The contents of the primary resource, and the binding rule, are shown at the top of each example, and the rest illustrates the transformations of the array coordinate systems. In the first (a), 4 and 3 (respectively) are added to the two indices of the role array to obtain indices to the resource array, and the resulting indices are then restricted (respectively) to be between 3 and 5, and between 2 and 4. In the second example (b), the indices of the role array are first restricted to be from -1 to 1 in each dimension, and then 4 and 3 are added to the indices (respectively). Finally, in (c), 2 is first added to both indices of the role array to obtain a temporary form of array, the indices of that array are then restricted to the 1 and 3 in each dimension, and then the array is translated again by adding 2 to the first index. The one of these most convenient for any particular circumstance would probably depend on the convenient availability of resource contents for

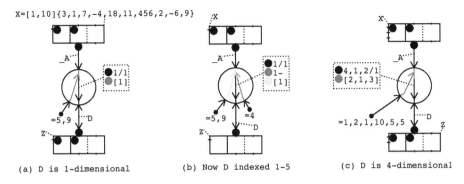

Figure 13.9: Mappings, simple and not-so-simple.

the appropriate selections and translations.

13.2.4 Mapping

A **mapping** is similar to a reduction, except that the primary is an array rather than a scalar. This creates a form of indirection, where an element of the primary array is first denoted (by the activity), and the contents of that element are then used to help specify an element of the secondary. So, in order to access the secondary, the activity within the context must somehow first specify an element of the primary from which those integers will be read. This is done by adding "ghost" dimensions to the secondary (i.e. dimensions in the secondary role which do not correspond to the secondary resource), and whenever an element of the secondary is accessed, any indices provided for those ghost dimensions are used to index the primary instead of the secondary. Once an element of the primary is so identified, the mapping acts like a reduction, reading indices from that element of the primary and using them in some dimensions for the secondary.

The binding rule for a mapping consists of two comma-separated lists of integers, separated by a slash. If the binding rule contains other binding modifiers in addition to the mapping, the mapping rule is generally completely enclosed in parentheses (to delimit the two integer lists from other integer lists for, say, reductions). The first list specifies ghost dimensions in the secondary, in the order which the indices for those dimensions will be used to index the primary, after all other binding modifiers (including translations) have been applied to it. The first list must therefore have a length equaling the dimensionality of the primary (after applying any reductions to the primary). The second list is just like a reduction – i.e. the list of dimensions of the secondary resource to be fulfilled by the integers read from the primary. Note that the same integer (like 2) might appear in both the first and second lists with very different meanings: as an ordinal ("the second index specified") for the first list, and as a dimension in the secondary array ("dimension 2") in the second. See Figure 13.9 for some examples (the dark arrows).

It is natural to consider a mapping as an extended form of a reduction, but there are important differences. A reduction binds to only one index of the secondary in the stated dimension, and that index (i.e. the one sitting on the primary) can be determined during "binding time", when the secondary role for the context is bound. For a mapping, there is insufficient advance knowledge about which indices the activity will specify for the "ghost" dimensions, and therefore about which elements of the primary would be indexed by those indices, and therefore about which elements of the secondary could ultimately be indexed. This would seem to be a problem, because the whole goal of using binding modifiers is to allow the context to be bound before the activity within the context begins.

This difficulty is ameliorated by requiring that the primary role have a restricted size, by way of a selection (as stated here or abbreviated as described later). Every accessible (i.e. selected) element of the primary is then considered as containing indices into the secondary which could potentially be used by the activity, so (1) a binding is made to all selected elements of the primary, (2) all of those elements of the primary must be ready for the binding of the secondary to occur, and (3) a binding is made to any element of the secondary which is indexed (through the mapping's second list) by any selected element of the primary. This may include elements of the primary and secondary which are never actually referenced.

For example, in the first part (a) of Figure 13.9, the values for 10 elements (1-10) of array resource X are initialized, but _A binds to only 5 (5-9), due to the specified selection. Since those contain the values 18, 11, 456, 2, and -6, those (and only those) are the elements of array resource Z which will be bound to D – so if the activity in the context is atomic, (only) those elements of Z must be ready before the activity can begin. In any case, since the index to D from the activity will be stolen to index _A, D will act as though it has indices 5-9. Example (b) of the figure is the same, but the additional translation for _A alters the indexing on D to now have indices 1-5. In example (c), even though array resource Z is only 2-dimensional, the activity in the context sees D as 4-dimensional: Indices 4, 1, and 2 to D, in that order, are used to index dimensions 1, 2, and 3 of role _A, with the contents of that element (from _A, i.e. X) to index dimension 1 of array Z. Index 3 of D (the only one unaccounted for) is used to index the remaining dimension (2) of array Z.

Mappings permit the chance for **aliasing** to occur on the secondary role. That is, whenever multiple elements of the primary role contain the same index, then multiple elements of the secondary role array will refer to the very same element of the secondary resource array, without the activity even being aware. "Aliasing" here means that such an element in the secondary resource is referred to by multiple names (i.e. elements of the secondary role bound to it). This is often a troublesome condition in most languages, causing hard-to-find errors, especially when the aliasing is accidental, because the activity (or other program form) may not even know that the resource accessed under one name is changing when the same resource, accessed by another name, is changed.

In ScalPL, however, an activity cannot access aliased resources. Specifically, any tactic with multiple roles (or role elements) bound to the same resource (or resource elements) will (by definition) never activate into an acton, so instead of a potentially incorrect answer, an alias condition will manifest itself as some part of the plan potentially not progressing. This behavior is consistent with the notion that a strategy knows when to activate by counting the number of its resources that are ready until that number equals the number of roles bound to those resources: If the total number of resources (and therefore control states) is smaller than the total number of roles, these two counts will never be equal.

13.2.5 Permutation

A **permutation** potentially changes the order in which indices for the secondary array role are used to index the secondary array resource. That is, while any element (a, b, c) of a role array would normally be bound to element (a, b, c) of its associated resource array (lacking any other binding modifiers), a permutation might instead make it bound to element (b, a, c), or (c, b, a), of the resource array. In other words, the dimensions (and therefore indices) of the role array are permuted relative to the dimensions (and indices) of the resource array to which it is bound.

Unlike arrays in many common computer languages, the layout of ScalPL arrays in space (e.g. in computer memory) is not dictated. This means that there is no fixed interpretation or convention (as there might be in computer languages) of the meaning of any particular index, such as one index (e.g. the first) representing the row, another (e.g. the second) representing the column, etc. The meaning of the order of the dimensions (and thus indices) is left to the planner. This means that different plans (perhaps implemented by different planners) may have different conventions of the order in which they specify their indices even when they agree on all other matters such as the sorts of data which will reside in an array and the dimensionality of the array. Permutation helps to address these matters by allowing one activity to specify the indices to an array in a different order than another activity, even though the contexts for both are bound to the same array. It can also serve to effectively perform matrix transpositions, but instead of moving data, only the meanings of the indices are altered (which may, indeed, result in data movement for efficiency in some cases).

Unlike the other binding modifiers, permutations do not utilize a primary binding and therefore are not represented by an arrow within the context. They are associated directly with the secondary binding, as part of the label on the role binding, shown as a comma-separated list of dimensions and potentially asterisks, enclosed in a set of parentheses, as in Figure 13.10.

The n elements of the permutation represent the n indices of the n-dimensional role array (not the resource array to which that role array is bound), as seen by any activity within the context. The ith position of that permutation (i.e. corresponding to the ith dimension of the role array) is an asterisk, if i is a ghost dimension (i.e. i is listed before the slash in a mapping for this secondary), or is an integer representing a dimension of the resource array to which this role is bound, if not. If this role is the secondary for reductions and/or mappings, some of the dimensions of the resource array (i.e. those mentioned in the reductions and/or in the after-slash list of the mappings) will

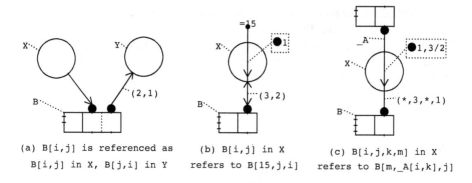

(a) B[i,j] is referenced as
B[i,j] in X, B[j,i] in Y

(b) B[i,j] in X
refers to B[15,j,i]

(c) B[i,j,k,m] in X
refers to B[m,_A[i,k],j]

Figure 13.10: Examples of permutation binding modifiers.

have already been specified there, so integers representing those dimensions must not appear in a permutation, but all other dimensions of the resource array must be listed. (In other words, when using a permutation, each integer 1 through n must be mentioned exactly once, in either the permutation itself, in a reduction, or in the after-slash list of a mapping.) So, as a special case, if there are no reductions or mappings using this role as a secondary, the permutation must consist of just the integers 1 through n, in some order, specifying the order in which indices will be used to index the resource array, hence the name "permutation".

Figure 13.10 shows three examples of permutations. The first, (a), has no other binding modifiers, so both contexts see a 2-dimensional role array named B, but any element of that array accessed by indices i,j by context X will be accessed by indices j,i in context Y, since the permutation (2,1) on Y's role binding flips the indices. In (b), the 1st index of resource array B is filled by the reduction, so the role array is only two dimensional, and the two indices supplied by the activity will be used to fill the 3rd and 2nd indices of the resource array, respectively – i.e. the reverse order in which they are specified. In (c), the 1st and 3rd indices of the role array B are ghost dimensions stolen by the mapping, which returns an index to the 2nd dimension of the resource array, thereby leaving only the 1st and 3rd indices into that resource to be specified directly by the activity. The permutation indicates that those will be supplied by the 2nd and 4th indices (respectively) for the 4-dimensional role array.

Even if a permutation is technically not required, it may still be wise to include it in complicated cases, just make clear which index will be used for what. For example, in Figure 13.10, it might have been wise to include the permutation even if it was (2,3) for B, or (*,1,*,3) for C, even though they would not have changed any behavior, but they would have clarified the use of each index supplied by the activity for the role.

A permutation only affects the activity within the context, and has absolutely no effect on the use of the role as a primary or secondary for other binding modifiers, since they already have complete flexibility when specifying index order. That is, the index ordinals listed before the slash for a mapping or in a translation refer to those of the primary or secondary roles, before any permutation is applied, even if a permutation is specified for those roles.

13.2.6 Combining Binding Modifiers

In summary, when accessing an element of a resource array bound to a secondary array, each of the indices for that element is supplied either from the activity itself, or from the primary (via a reduction or mapping). In either case, these indices may be modified by adding and/or subtracting values from one or more primaries (via translations) as they make their way to the secondary, and they may be restricted to be within ranges specified on one or more primaries (via selections). From the other direction, each of the indices supplied by the activity will index either the primary (via a mapping, if the index is for a ghost dimension of the secondary), or the secondary after being potentially translated or restricted (if it is not for a ghost dimension). Those indices that go to the secondary will (by default) be used in the same order they are specified by the activity, but that order can be changed (via a permutation).

From this, we can see that the dimensionality of any role can be calculated by starting with the dimensionality of the resource to which it is bound, and then for all binding modifiers using that role as a secondary:

- Subtract the number of reductions – i.e. the number of dimensions listed in any reductions

- Subtract the number of mapped dimensions – i.e. integers listed in any mapping's second list (after the slash)

- Add the number of "ghost" dimensions – i.e. unique integers listed in any mapping's first list (before the slash)

To see the effect of combining all of the binding modifiers for a particular (secondary) role, start with the resource array bound to a role, give each dimension an axis labeled with the dimension number while leaving a spot on each for a new label/number, and then apply all of the binding modifiers in roughly reverse alphabetical order (as described below) to come up with how the activity eventually perceives that resource array via that role.

1. For each pre-translation of the form "+x" or "-x", add (or subtract, respectively) the offset (read from the primary) to (from) all the indices in the given dimension (x) to shift the axis in that dimension.

2. For each selection of the form "[...x...]", restrict the indices on the axis in the given dimension (x) to the range (read from the primary), effectively deleting all the elements outside of the range. If there are no elements left in that dimension (because multiple selections in that dimension don't intersect, or because the beginning of a range is greater than its end), quit this procedure and leave the secondary role unbound.

3. For each post-translation of the form "x+" or "x-", add or subtract (respectively) the offset (read from the primary) to (from) all the indices in the given dimension (x) to shift the axis in that dimension.

4. For each reduction of the form "x", effectively flatten the array in that dimension (x) by keeping only the elements in that dimension having the given index (read from the primary), and then remove the axis for that dimension from the array. If the given index doesn't exist on the axis (because it was excluded by a previous selection), quit this procedure and leave the secondary role unbound.

5. For each mapping of the form "x1, x2, ..., xn / y1, y2, ... ym", consider the array as a "meta-array" (array of arrays) by preserving only the dimension(s) listed after the slash (y1, y2, ..., ym), in the order they are listed, by (if necessary) making each meta-array element represent an array in itself containing the other dimensions. (For example, if the original array is 3-dimensional, and only one dimension, 2, is listed after the slash, then the meta-array will be a one-dimensional array of two-dimensional arrays each containing the original dimensions 1 and 3.) Then rearrange some or all of the meta-array elements into a new meta-array having the same size and shape as the binding modifier's primary role array (n-dimensional, where n is the number of integers before the slash): To determine which element X of the original meta-array belongs in any specific element Y of the new meta-array, read X's indices from the element of the primary role array element corresponding to Y. When done rearranging in this way, assign the dimensions before the slash in the binding rule (x1, x2, ..., xn), in the order they are listed, as new labels for the axes in the new meta-array, and then re-expand the elements of the new meta-array to again form a regular single array. (New axis labels aren't considered to conflict with an old axis label with A single number may be used as a new label by one axis and an old label by another, which is why old and new should be kept separate.)

Finally, consider all of the remaining axes (not removed by a reduction or mapping) that haven't yet had a new dimension label assigned (by a mapping). Assign new labels (starting with one) to those axes sequentially, either progressing in the order of the original axis labels, or if a permutation is present on the secondary role, in the order that the original axis labels are listed in the permutation. In either case, refrain from using any new labels which would conflict with those already assigned by a mapping.

The order, above, in which the modifiers are applied to the secondary is mostly dictated by common sense. Permutation comes last, because the other modifiers can already clearly specify which indices (i.e. in which dimensions) they deal with, so nothing is to be gained by permuting those indices before applying these modifiers. Of the remaining modifiers, it doesn't make sense to evaluate a reduction or mapping for a dimension before a selection or translation for that dimension, since the reduction or mapping elides the dimension, leaving nothing for the selection or translation to act upon. Therefore, reductions and mappings are always evaluated next to last, just before permutations. The order of selection and translation is left flexible so that the selection range can be relative to the "raw" pre-translated indices of the resource array, or the post-translated indices of the role which will be seen by the activity, or something between the two.

The primary role for a mapping must have a fixed size in each dimension (e.g. as the result of a selection binding modifier). Since the primary role may also be a secondary role of another binding modifier (which is evaluated first), the primary role doesn't necessary correspond exactly to its actual resource array. Specifically, if the primary of a mapping is also the secondary of a (previous) mapping, then the ghost dimensions of this mapping which are used to index the primary may in turn it be considered as ghost dimensions again to index *its* primary. Though this may sound confusing, the planner should only need to remember that the coordinate mapping of a secondary binding is established by the binding modifiers from its primary bindings, and once that mapping is established, it will be used by both the activity within the context and by any subsequent mapping which may use it.

13.2.7 Alternate Representations for Binding Modifiers

Instead of using directed arcs and binding rules to represent the correspondence between role elements and resource elements, the same information can sometimes be conveyed more naturally in a textual format by simply following each role label (for roles bound to resource arrays) with a tuple of the form [i1, i2, ..., im] which, when evaluated, represents the index to a single element of the m-dimensional resource array to which the role is bound. Each expression i sub j in the tuple consists of terms connected with plus or minus signs, where each term can be an integer constant, a role index of the form #j which represents the jth index supplied by the activity to index the role, or the name of another role bound to the same context, subject to the following restrictions:

a. If a role with dimensionality greater than zero is named within any i sub j expression, then it must itself be bollowed by a subscript in braces consisting only of other role indices separated by commas, and those subscripts must be the same everywhere that role is mentioned within any of that role's i sub j expressions. (This is because the subscript in this case represents a mapping.)

b. No expression can contain multiple role indices at the same level (such that they are to be added or subtracted from each other, or themselves), though a role index can be present both within an expression and within a subscript associated with a role name within that expression.

13.3 Delimited and Undelimited Resource Arrays

The constructs described in this chapter provide the ability to declare and work with arrays, without the necessity to declare the sizes of the arrays upon which these operations work. One reason for this marked difference with more traditional treatment of arrays in sequential computer languages, where the size of an array is a central trait, lies in the costs and benefits of requiring a specific layout versus not. Unsized resource arrays can simplify formal semantic descriptions and kill two birds with one stone. That is, most languages use one construct for arrays, where elements are regularly arranged into rows and columns of predictable sizes, and another for situations where elements must be invented as they are needed with no logical spatial relationship between element locations, commonly known as dynamically-allocated memory. Here, though, we capitalize on the similarities of these cases – i.e. the ability to store and manipulate element names – to use a single set of constructs for both. The trade-off is that, if the size of an array is not known, it may not be as convenient or efficient to store it all together, such as organized by rows and columns packed together. Also, common matrix operations (like multiplication, dot product, etc.) are not well-defined.

In most sequential computer languages, an array is a data structure with many small elements which are local to a program running on a processor. Even if some elements are not to be accessed immediately, it is expected that most of them will eventually be accessed by that processor, so there is at least some benefit to having them reside in memory to reduce access time. (In cases where only a few elements of a large array are likely to be accessed and/or to contain unique information, a different data structure, sometimes called a sparse array, is often used to store the elements.) Given that the elements will be in memory, and that they may very well be accessed repeatedly and/or in differing orders (which is often the reason for indexing the elements in the first place), it is important in those languages to reduce the overhead for access to each element, which includes the overhead of mapping the element's index to the element's location/address. This mapping can easily be optimized by arranging the elements of the array into fixed-length rows, columns, planes, etc., and juxtaposing them in memory so that a simple computation can be performed to an index to find an element. Such arrangement and computation can be optimized if the arrays are rectangular and fixed in size (in at least all but one dimension). Specifying the array size also permits memory to be efficiently managed: Since all of the array elements have similar lifetimes, memory for the entire array can be allocated and/or deallocated all at once.

While a resource array is superficially similar to these other traditional arrays in that it consists of many elements addressed by indices, the role of these elements is not related to having a single "process" (acton) access all of them repeatedly or sequentially. For cases where that *is* the goal, it is suitable (and in many ways preferable) for the planner to place the entire array on a single scalar resource. The goal of resource arrays is to enable dependent resource bindings, where the resources (in this case, resource array elements) to be accessed by an acton are decided dynamically, and to allow different actons to access different elements concurrently. Since the actons accessing different elements (even sequential elements) may very well reside on different processors, there is often no reason for some of the elements to exist on some of the processors, so it would surely be wasteful to allocate space for all elements on all processors.

Still, there are plenty of cases where it is convenient to convey the size of an array if the size is intrinsic to the plan, whether it is for storage efficiency or understanding the intent of the planner.

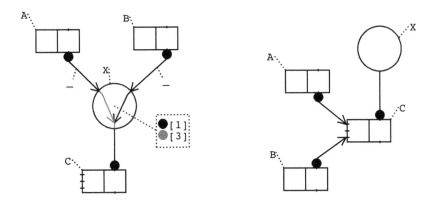

Restricting index ranges with selections...   or delimiter.

Figure 13.11: Array delimiter for dimensions 1 and 3 of C.

13.3.1 Establishing Array Size: Delimiters

If the intended index range of an array, in one or more dimensions, is known by the planner, there are advantages to expressing that knowledge explicitly: It can serve as a double check to ensure that array accesses are indeed within the intended range, it can convey information from the planner to someone else reading the plan, and when all or most of the array elements end up in the same part of the platform, it can facilitate the same sort of storage and mapping optimizations that are used for arrays in sequential languages (described earlier).

An array size declaration is effectively an alternate form for expressing a selection binding modifier, but instead of being associated with any particular context, it is associated with the array itself. That is, instead of a separate selection applied to every context bound to the array resource, the resource containing the index range (and perhaps step) for those selections is associated (via something resembling a binding) directly with a dimension dot of the array resource itself, as shown in Figure 13.11. The effect is exactly as if that resource was used as the primary for a selection modifier in the same dimension on every context bound to that array. (The selection in this case is applied before any translations on those contexts.) The specification of such an index range for an array dimension is called an **array delimiter**.

13.3.2 Sensing Array Size

If a context possesses a role binding to a resource array with restricted indices in one or more dimensions (as the result of array delimiters or just selections), it is often useful for the activity within the context to determine the indices in those dimensions which have actually been bound – i.e. which are within the delimited limits in the parent. For this purpose, a formal resource array representing the role can have so-called **size sensors**, as shown in Figure 13.12. That is, arrows

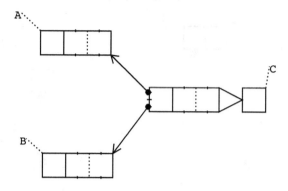

Figure 13.12: Formal resource size sensor (dimensions 1 and 3).

(resembling bindings) are drawn *from* the dimension dots on the end of the formal resource array to scalar resources (usually just their corner), and this results in the content state of each those scalar resources being initialized (when they are instantiated, usually at activation time) with two integers representing the lowest and highest indices bound in the parent in that dimension. (No other initial content state can be specified for those resources.)

If size sensors are specified for certain dimensions of a formal array, then it is considered an error if the plan is bound to a non-delimited array (in those dimensions), and the binding will not occur.

13.4 Example: Bounded Buffer Object (Queue, FIFO)

This section offers very simple example of an object which collects, and regurgitates, items of a given type. There is a given limit to the number it can store at any one time, and it regurgitates them in the same order in which they were submitted for collection – a so-called First-In, First-Out (or FIFO) object. It is also the way a queue (line) works, such as in a supermarket, where the first to get there is the first to be served. Many programming or planning methodologies, especially those based upon a dataflow or message passing model, have constructs such as this built in, though the number and type of elements may be unspecified.

This particular object is instantiated at IL 1 with one role, n_records, specifying the number of elements it is to accommodate, as an integer. Subsequent IL 0 activations can then bind either rec_in (to feed entries in) or rec_out (to retrieve records) or both. It is not atomic at either IL 1 or IL 0, and remains bound. (Although it does not rebind each time, it can easily be modified to do so, to make it act more like a traditional object with atomic operations, at the cost of some efficiency required to rebind it each time which may not be constructive.)

250

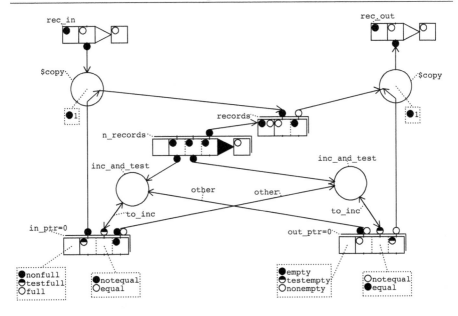

Figure 13.13: Bounded Buffer strategy.

```
inc_and_test: plan tactic {
    to_inc += 1;
    if (to_inc >= n_records) to_inc = 0;
    if (to_inc == other)
        issue equal to to_inc;
    else
        issue notequal to to_inc;
}
```

Figure 13.14: Tactic inc_and_test, used in Bounded Buffer Strategy.

13.4.1 The Plan

The Bound Buffer strategy is shown in Figure 13.13, with the lone tactic used therein, `inc_and_test`, shown in Figure 13.14.

The workings are simple and efficient. `records`, a one-dimensional array, holds the records that have been gathered so far between (and including) indices 0 and `n_records` - 1, stored sequentially in increasing order if those end elements are considered as wrapped around to touch each other, as if in a circle. `out_ptr` is the index of the next record to regurgitate, so therefore the beginning of the sequence of stored records, and `in_ptr` is the index of the next record to store, so therefore the one after the end of the stored sequence. If `out_ptr` and `in_ptr` are equal, then there are either no records stored, or `n_records` stored. Clearly, if they become equal as the result of a new record coming in, that means the buffer is full, and if they become equal as the result of a record going out, that

251

means the buffer is empty. These full or empty conditions are recorded to the control states of `in_ptr` and `out_ptr`, respectively.

So, the story is primarily told by the control states, and just as the strategy is very symmetric, the empty and full conditions are also. As the top two contexts suggest, a new record can come in (or respectively, go out) only if the buffer is `nonfull` (or respectively, `nonempty`). After a record comes in (or respectively, goes out), `inc_and_test` ensures that the buffer is no longer considered `empty` (or respectively, `full`). It also increments `in_ptr` (or respectively, `out_ptr`) modulo `n_records`, and if it now equals the other pointer, the control state is changed to `full` (or respectively, `empty`).

13.4.2   Analysis

This plan expresses significant concurrency for being so simple. For example, elements can be copied into and out of the buffer concurrently. In fact, due to the large number of predictable bindings throughout, very few activities potentially interfere with each other.

The formal resources `rec_in` and `rec_out` could easily be replaced with activation formals, with only a subtle change in behavior. That is, the plan would re-bind for each element or removed. This would, for example, be useful if used in a context where `rec_in` and `rec_out` were secondaries of binding modifiers, which should be reevaluated for each element added or fetched. Usually, though, bounded buffers are used as a relatively static channel between two other plans, and repeatedly rebinding is mostly wasted time.

This plan would theoretically work just as well if the control domain of `records` was restricted to only one element – i.e. the initial control state – since the indices supplied by `in_ptr` and `out_ptr` already assume that the same element won't be accessed by both `copys` at the same time. The advantage of using two control states comes in providing ready information to the Director (or others who might observe the plan). For example, consider the role binding from `$copy` on the upper right to `records`. Because it transitions the element back to its initial control state, it becomes obvious that the content state of that element will never be observed again, because nothing observes an element with the initial control state. It is also obvious that the old content state associated with `rec_out` will subsequently be completely ignored, due to the replace permission. So, since the Director knows that `$copy` copies content unchanged, it may very well be able to effect the overall result of that copy by simply internally relabeling the content state of the element from `records` to now be the content state of `rec_out`, with no actual copying at all. (The same sort of trick may be possible with `rec_in`, depending upon other bindings to its actual resource in the parent.)

Similarly, this plan would work the same without delimiting the `records` array to `n_records`. However, this makes it obvious to the Director that there will be no accesses to any elements in `records` except those at 0 through `n_records` - 1. On some platforms, this can allow the Director to store and access those elements much more efficiently, by simply allocating appropriate memory for all of them at once.

13.5 Summary

An array resource consists of an infinite number of elements, each a resource in its own right with its own control and content state. Each element is identified/addressed within the array by a (short) sequence of integer indices, all sequences of equal length. The length of those sequences for any particular array is called the dimensionality of the array, and it is represented graphically by adding that number of dots or hash marks along the left side of the resource rectangle. A scalar (non-array) resource, as has been presented so far, can also be considered a 0-dimensional array, with no hash marks, and zero-length sequences for indices (i.e. none).

By default, a binding to an array binds to all infinity elements. The array is represented within the child plan by an array formal resource of the same dimensionality, and the role binding (by default) associates each element of the formal array with the same element of the actual array, so the role itself can be considered an array. A bindany, indicated by prefixing the label on the role binding with a question mark, instead binds a scalar role to just one element of the array, but the element is not specified.

Binding modifiers can be added to array role bindings to either limit the binding to certain elements of the actual array, or to alter the correspondence between the indices of the role array (i.e. formal array) and the actual array, or both. In the presence of a binding modifier, the role array being bound to the actual is called the secondary binding. Another binding on the same context, called the primary binding, is required for most binding modifiers (all except permutation). The binding modifier is (usually) specified as an arrow within the context circle, from the primary binding to the secondary binding, labeled by a binding rule.

There are five kinds of binding modifier, designated by the form of the binding rule. Multiple binding modifiers can be integrated into the same binding rule, to use the same primary and secondary. The five are:

- Reduction: Essentially equivalent to subscripting in mathematics or computer languages, reduction reads indices (integers) for certain dimensions (specified in the binding rule) from the primary, using them for to index the secondary.

- Selection: Selection reads index ranges (i.e. two integers) for certain dimensions (specified in the binding rule) from the primary, using them to limit the index range being bound to in the secondary. Binding rule is enclosed in square brackets ([])

- Translation: Transition reads an offset (integer) for certain dimensions (specified in the binding rule) from the primary, and adds or subtracts them to indices in those dimensions for the secondary, before or after selections, as specified by the binding rule. Binding rule uses + or - to specify whether to add or subtract the offset, and prefix or postfix notation to specify whether to perform before or after selections.

253

- Mapping: Mapping adds ghost dimensions to secondary (specified in the binding rule), and uses any indices specified for those dimensions by the activity to index the primary instead, which (unlike other binding modifiers) is an array. Otherwise, it behaves like a reduction: It reads indices (integers) for dimensions (also specified in the binding rule) from that element of the primary, using them to index the secondary. The binding rule consists of the list of ghost dimensions, followed by a slash(/), and the reduction dimensions.

- Permutation: A permutation allows the activity within the context to specify indices to the secondary role in a different order than the dimensions actually exist on the actual array bound to that role. A permutation has no primary binding, and is denoted by an annotation on the secondary role consisting of sequence of unique integers and asterisks enclosed in parentheses, representing an index sequence as provided by the activity in the context. The integer (if any) in the nth element of the permutation represents the dimension of the actual array (on the secondary) for which the nth index (provided by the activity in the context) is to be used. Dimension numbers specified by reductions (or by the second list in a mapping) for the same secondary are not shown within the permutation, since the activity in the context doesn't provide these. Ghost dimensions, specified in the first list of a mapping for the same secondary, are shown as asterisks in the permutation: They aren't used to index the secondary at all.

Instead of providing a selection for each context bound to a particular array, the selection can be applied to the array itself using a delimiter construct. This consists of drawing an arrow from a scalar resource to a hash mark on an array resource. The result is effectively to constrain access in the dimension represented by that hash mark to the range specified in the scalar, and is as though a selection using the same scalar (on the primary) was applied to that array (on the secondary) for every context bound to that array.

For formal arrays, it is possible to determine the indices accessible in the actual array, if they have been constrained using selections (or delimiters), by using a size sensor construct. This is shown by an arrow from a hash mark of an formal array resource to the corner of a scalar resource. The result is to initialize the content state of the scalar resource with the range of indices accessible in the formal in that dimension, when the scalar resource is instantiated. (No other initial content state can be specified for the scalar resource.)

Chapter 14

Data Parallelism

The preceding chapter described how to bind a particular context to a particular element or portion of an array, and to customize the mapping of the coordinates between the role binding (used by the activity within the context) and the actual resource array by using binding modifiers. By themselves, these modifiers facilitate concurrency only by minimizing potential conflict between activities in different contexts bound to the same array (with write permission) by allowing them to bind to different parts of it at once. However, the amount of concurrency is still essentially restricted to the number of contexts bound to that array, which is basically fixed within the plan. This is unfortunate, because if each each element (or each few elements) of an array can be operated upon by a separate activity, then the number of activities which could be acting on that array concurrently would be proportional to the number of elements in the array, if only there were enough contexts to hold them all.

Plans where the amount of potential concurrency increases (scales) directly with the amount of data (such as the size of arrays) are said to exhibit **data parallelism**. Data parallelism is central to the ability to take maximum advantage of highly concurrent platforms (a term being constantly redefined, but which suggests having far more processors than the number of plans in a typical activity). It is also central to overcoming Amdahl's Law, as suggested in the intro with Gustafson's Law, by allowing concurrency to grow at an almost unbounded rate while leaving any "inherently serial" setup time constant.

14.1 Creating Contexts Dynamically

To enable data parallelism, we need a way to create a desired number of contexts dynamically, for varying numbers of activities to have a place to live. The construct to do this in ScalPL is called a **dup** (pronounced "doop", short for duplication). It simply replicates a single context a given number of times to effectively become many contexts. In itself, a dup has nothing to do with resource arrays, but (as will be described in an upcoming section) it works very well with the binding modifiers described in the previous chapter to support data parallelism by effectively creating many contexts in which plans can acti-

255

vate, and providing each context with one or more unique integers on bindings which can in turn be used in binding modifiers (e.g. reductions) so that each can access unique array elements.

14.1.1 Basic Function of Dup

A dup is specified by identifying one or more bindings on a context as a **dup binding**, by prefixing its name (if any) with an asterisk (*), in which case it is called a **dupall** or plus (+), in which case it is called a **dupany**. The binding must be scalar, the content must include 1, 2, or 3 integers, the transition domain must consist only of the transition **done**, and the role binding must not have replace (or update) permission. It may be (and often is) an anonymous binding (with a name, therefore, like *_). If the number or location of the integers in the resource are not obvious, the names of the fields containing those integers may be shown in parens between the asterisk or plus prefix and the role name (e.g. *(first_slot,last_slot)slot)

When any/all dup bindings are ready (i.e. bound to an actual resource with the same control state as its access dot), and before any plan is activated within the context being bound, and even before binding modifiers are evaluated, the context is effectively replaced by some number of replicants of itself, the number being specified by the integer(s) on those dup bindings. The dup binding for each replicant is replaced by a **post-dup binding**, which is a normal scalar binding with the same name (minus the asterisk or plus prefix) bound to a unique integer constant, that constant also being specified by the integer(s) on the original dup binding. At the time of this replication, the **done** binding is issued on the original dup binding. The other (non-dup) bindings on the replicants are (by default) identical to the bindings on the original context. See Figure 14.1 (the top bindings on all of the "In plan..." snippets).

Each replicant context will never activate more than one plan, but after a dup completes, it may then replicate again, in which case each of the new replicants can also activate a plan, etc. The conditions under which a dup is considered to be complete depend on whether it is a dupall or dupany; If the dup is a dupall, the replicants effectively exist until a plan has activated once in each of the replicant contexts; If the dup is a dupany, the replicants exist until a plan has activated in exactly one of the replicant contexts. As will be seen, it is quite common for a dupany to replicate over and over again, though in actuality, the Director can usually avoid creating any of the replicants except the one that results in an activation.

14.1.2 Number of Replicants

The number of replicants created, and the integer constant bound to each, is determined as follows, as illustrated in the first three examples of Figure 14.1. If the original binding was to a resource with one integer, then that number of replicants will result, and the integers associated with each post-dup binding will range from 0 to one less than the integer on the original dup binding. (If the integer is negative, no replicants result.) If the original binding was to two integers, i and j in that order, the number of replicants is $j - i + 1$, and the

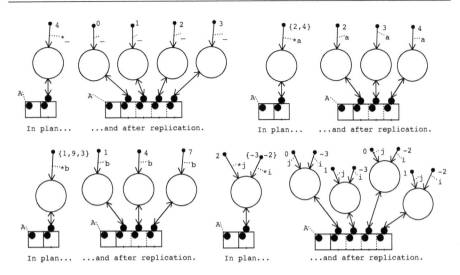

Figure 14.1: One-, two-, and three-parameter form, plus 2 dups on 1 context.

integers range from i to j. (If i is greater than j, no replicants result.) And if the original binding was to three integers, i, j, and k, the number of replicants is $(j - i + 1)/k$, rounded down to the next integer, and the integers are i, $i + k$, $i + 2k$, etc., not to exceed j. In other words, one integer i represents the range 0 to $i - 1$, two integers i and j represent the range i to j, and three integers i, j, and k represent the range i to j in steps of k.

14.1.3 Behavior of Role Bindings

As mentioned, aside from the transformation of the dup bindings to post-dup bindings, the default case is for each replicant to have the same role bindings as the original context, meaning that, lacking appropriate use of binding modifiers (as described in the next section), each original role binding will result in many identical bindings to the same resource, one for each replicant. For dupanys, or dupalls where the transition bindings always transition back to the same control state, and especially when the bindings are predictable, these shared resources don't bring much contention. However, for other cases – specifically, where a dupall has one or more role bindings with transition bindings to a new control state – this implies that there can be significant contention among the replicants, and that another activity (on the new control state) will need to at least transition the control state back repeatedly to allow all of the replicants to eventually access the resource. Care must be taken to ensure that this default is indeed the desired behavior. Role A of Y in Figure 14.2 shows this, where plan X may need to "pass" the control state of A back to Y repeatedly to allow all of the replicants of Y to access A. (Role C transitions the control state back to initial, predictively, and more on the anonymous role bound to B shortly.)

It is not uncommon to desire that some action take place (i.e. some transition be issued) only after a plan has activated within all of the replicants of a

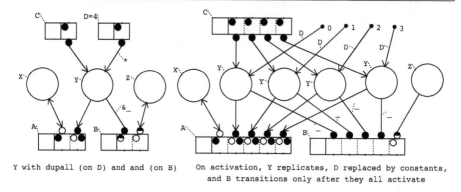

Y with dupall (on D) and and (on B)   On activation, Y replicates, D replaced by constants, and B transitions only after they all activate

Figure 14.2: Assorted bindings in conjunction with dup.

dupall. One way to accomplish this would be for each replicant to increment a count within one of the shared resources, and to perform that transition only when the count reaches the total number of replicants. Or, the replicants could always transition the control state so that another context (like X in the example) could count the activations and only pass the control state back to the replicants if the count has not been reached. However, these are circuitous, and since the Director needs to keep track of when all the replicants have activated anyway (to know when the dupall has run its course), ScalPL has a more direct approach, called an **and binding**, designated by prefixing the name of any predictable role binding on the context with an ampersand (&), as in the binding from Y to B in Figure 14.2. For such a binding, instead of the specified transition occurring as the result of each activation in each replicant, it will occur just once after all of the replicants have issued the transition (if ever). Specifically, when used on an anonymous role binding, this will therefore issue a transition if and only if a plan has activated in each of the replicants. (The transition bindings for B in the diagram on the right are incapable of representing this accurately.) As a special case, the dup binding itself can be made an and binding (i.e. *&name), so that instead of issuing its done transition as soon as the replication occurs, it, too, will only be issued after a plan has activated in all of the replicants.

A dup obviously cannot produce replicants until the dup binding(s) is/are ready. As a matter of course, it also will not produce replicants until all/any anonymous bindings, and all/any activation bindings and formals (including $plan), are ready. To replicate before this could easily leave lots of replicant contexts that might never be prepared to activate a plan. (Whether a dup binding is actually *defined* not to replicate until these conditions are met is left as an open issue for now.)

14.1.4 Combining Dups

Multiple dup bindings may be specified for a single context, in which case the results are generally multiplicative, as in the bottom right example in Figure

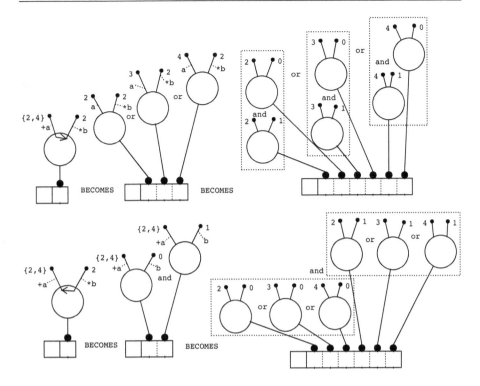

Figure 14.3: Dup order may matter, such as when dupall and dupany are mixed.

14.1. That is, first dup binding replicates the context, and then the other dup binding replicates each one of those contexts, etc. The overall result is similar to a rectagular array of replicants, with a unique combination of integers from the dup ranges being bound to its post-dup bindings of each.

In many common cases, the above rules make the order in which the multiple dups are evaluated immaterial, specifically, in cases where all of the dups are of the same sort (i.e. all dupall or all dupany), and none of the transitions (done) for the dup bindings change the control state of the associated resource. In this case where the dups are all dupalls, the standard rules dictate that a plan is activated in each of the resulting replicants, and where the dups are all dupanys, standard rules dictate that a plan is activated in exactly one of the resulting replicants, before the dup is considered to have run its course and is ready to be re-evaluated.

In other cases, though, the order in which multiple dups replicate can affect the outcome. For example, if one dup is a dupall, and the other is a dupany, it will still result in (effectively) a rectangular array of contexts, each with a unique combination of integers from the dup ranges, but the conditions under which it will finish depend upon the order in which the dups are expanded. (Fortunately, these cases are rare, so the rest of this subsection will concern only relatively few readers.) Figure 14.3 shows two small plans at the far left, identical except for the small **dup precedence arrow** within the context circle. That precedence arrow, which resembles a binding modifier but is used instead with dups, can be used to dictate the order in which the replication of dups takes place. In each case here, role binding a is a dupany, from 2 to 4, and role binding b is a dupall with a 2 – i.e. from 0 to 1. In the top case, the dupany replicates first, to create three contexts, each with a dupall, one of which must activate a plan to finish. The dupall on each of those then replicates, resulting in the arrangement on the top right. In the bottom case, the dupall replicates first, to create two contexts, each with a dupany, all of which must activate a plan to finish. The dupany on each of those then replicates, resulting in the context arrangement in the lower right.

The top case may require further clarification. According to the dupany rules, only one of the contexts from the first (dupany) round of replication is allowed to activate a plan, and yet each of those contexts becomes two (dupall) replicants, which must *each* activate a plan for the entire compound dup to complete. So what if other bindings on the contexts (not shown) were to allow a plan to activate in one of a particular vertical pair (in the top right example), but not the other in that pair, keeping that pair from completing, even if another pair might be able to? This is considered just a special case of a situation that can arise for any dupany, when an activity begins but does not complete in one of the contexts. It is not the Director's job to "back out" that activity, and try to find another in another dupany replicant which would allow the dupany to complete. Likewise, it is not the Director's job to keep trying different pairs in the dupany above until it finds a pair in which both contexts will activate a plan. Once a plan has been initiated in one context (or set of contexts) of a dupany, the other contexts (or sets of contexts) are effectively locked out of further consideration. For this reason, if no dup precedence arrows are specified in a compound dup, all dupalls replicate before any dupanys (like the bottom example in the figure) by default, since it is more likely to provide a produce a meaningful and productive result.

Even when all dups are of the same sort, the order of replication may matter, such as when at least one of the dup bindings binds the "done" transition to a new control state. The precedence arrow may be used any time the order of evaluation of dups needs to be clarified.

14.2   Using dups with binding modifiers for data parallelism

Replicating contexts as in the last section actually isn't very useful on its own. There are actually fairly few cases when activating a single plan concurrently, all accessing the same resources other than a unique integer, is really needed. The true value in using dups is when using the dup binding as the primary binding for binding modifiers (specifically reduction or translation) for other bindings on the same context. In that way, each replicant can access different elements of an array resource, allowing each to work concurrently on very different resource content.

For example, every element of a one- or two-dimensional resource array

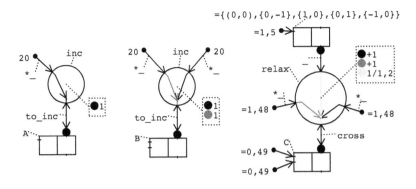

Figure 14.4: Using dups in binding modifiers.

might be processed with a plan like the first two in Figure 14.4. In each case, these dup binding is (bindings are) anonymous, but they replicate the context containing the inc plan so that each replicant can access one element of a 20 element (or 20-by-20 element) array via reductions. Note that the inc plan itself is given no indication that its context is being replicated, each replicant just sees one scalar role (to_inc) which it updates.

The rightmost plan in Figure 14.4 is a more in-depth example, which stamps out a cross template across an array. Again, the context has two anonymous dup bindings, replicating the context with every combination of integers from the range 1 to 48 on the post-dup bindings. But in this case, the dups are used as primaries for translations (instead of reductions) on the cross role binding. cross is also the secondary of a mapping, from the top anonymous binding, such that an access to element 1 of cross (by the relax plan) is mapped through the top resource to actually access element (0,0) of the C resource array, which is then translated by the post-dup receptacles. Likewise, element 2 of cross accesses element (0,1) of C before translation, etc.

So, consider any particular replicant context corresponding to values i and j on the post-dup anonymous receptacles. The relax plan within that replicant sees cross as a 5-element 1-dimensional array, containing some of the elements of C, specifically (in order) C(i,j), C(i,j-1), C(i+i,j), C(i,j+1), and C(i-1,j) – i.e. the element at i,j plus each element immediately adjacent to it (horizontally or vertically, in "clockwise order", in some sense). This is a common cross template that can be used in physics relaxation codes, to update each element of an array based on the value within it and its immediate neighbors. Note that with this particular approach, each replicant i,j has update permission to the entire cross of elements centered at i,j in C, so no two crosses will access the same element concurrently. Also, unlike many relaxation algorithms, there is no particular order in which the different replicants access C: The replicants activate nondeterministically relative to each other.

Dupalls are generally used in cases where every element of the array (or section of the array) is to be processed in lockstep, in phases, or at the same general rate, while dupanys are used when the elements are processed in a

261

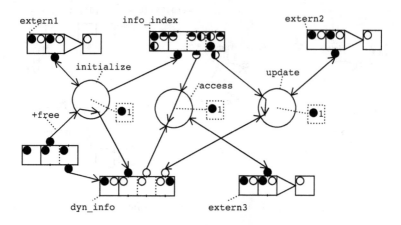

Figure 14.5: Allocating and accessing free element of `dyn_info`.

less regular manner, such as when the next element to process is determined dynamically based on its control state. That is, a dupany is often evaluated repeatedly, each time accomodating one activity to operate on one element or collection of related elements, while a dupall is usually evaluated once for an entire phase of activities, each operating on a single element or collection.

A dupany is most often used to find and access any element of an array (perhaps within some range) having a given control state, perhaps repeatedly. That is, it can be used with a reduction so that each replicant attempts to access one element of an array, and if the plan withindoesn't bind until activation (i.e. is a tactic, or uses an activation binding or formal), then only an array element with the appropriate control state will allow the plan within the associated replicant to activate. Figure 14.5 shows plan `initialize` binding to any free element of `dyn_info` (designated by its initial control state) using a dupany, replacing the content within, recording the index of that element to `info_index`, and transitioning the element's control state to non-initial to record that it is in use. Other plans `access` and `update` can then access it at will by using `info_index` as the primary of a reduction modifier, until there is no further need for that element, in which case the element is returned to a free state by transitioning its control state back to initial, allowing it to be found again by `initialize` at some later time. (Note that since `initialize` has replace permission to `dyn_info`, there is no need for `update` to "clean up" the content of the `dyn_info` element before effectively returning it to the available pool.) Resources `extern1`, `extern2`, and `extern3` are meant to suggest pathways to other activities outside of this snippet. Perhaps a more satisfying (though also more complex) example of dynamically allocating elements is provided in the Linked List example in the next section, as it allows concurrent access to different elements.

14.3 Examples

One would expect to find many plans like the examples we will present here in a standard plan library, obviating the need for the planner to ever deal with them (especially down to the level of single operations as they will be handled here), but we have chosen them here because they are familiar to many readers and illustrate a number of approaches. The three primary examples chosen here are a linked list object, a matrix multiply plan, and a (recursive) quicksort plan.

14.3.1 Linked List Object

Intro

This is a slightly more realistic use of dynamic allocation than provided earlier, using dupany with arrays. It implements (internally) a single-linked list in a rather simplistic fashion, for illustration of basic use of constructs rather than of more advanced concurrency techniques (like skip lists). The goal is to construct (internally) a list of "records", each containing a so-called key and other data (sometimes called a payload) in such a way that the keys of the records are in order, and new records (with new keys) can be added, and old records can be deleted, without repositioning all the existing records, as would be necessary if they were all simply packed into sequential elements of an array. This is accomplished here by including some sort of indicator (called a link) internally on each record indicating where (in the array of records) the record having the next sequential key is. To find, add, or delete a record, this usually requires that the record closest to the one with that key is found internally starting at the beginning and linking one record at a time.

A linked list object is created by instantiating the given plan at IL 1, which requires two role bindings:

```
--> index_range (done): {integer beg, integer end}
--> init_data (done): P
```

The index range designates the range of integers that will be used to identify the elements of the list, as well as (by its size) the number of records. (The record at `beg` will actually be used internally.) `init_data` specifies the default payload for a new record, when it is added. We have just specified its type as P, for now.

The methods available on the object (at IL 0) are:

- `find(FIND, key, index)`: Find entry with key `key` and return `index`

- `insert(INSERT, key, index)`: Insert new entry with key `key` and return `index`

- `delete(DELETE, key, index)`: Delete entry with key `key`

- `update(index_in, content_in)`: Update content of element at index `index_in` with the new payload `content_in`

263

- retrieve(index_in, content_out): Retrieve payload of element at index index_in, as content_out

(So, this will form of the binding constraint expression, linking all of these with "&".) All of these methods are atomic. The success or failure of find, insert, and delete is reflected in the transition performed to the index role. The success of update and retrieve is indicated by the done transition to its roles, but they simply fail to complete if the specified record is not part of the list (or equivalently, until it is). The roles themselves (at IL 0) are as follows:

```
--- @FIND (done): nodata
--- @INSERT (done): nodata
--- @DELETE (done): nodata
<-- @key (done): K
<-- @index (success, fail): integer
--> @index_in (done): integer
--> @content_in (done): P
<-- @content_out (done): P
```

Here, K is the type of the key. The at signs (@) indicate that these are activation formals.

The Linked List plan

The Linked List plan is shown in Figure 14.6 with the tactics used therein shown in Figure 14.7. (Here, all transition names are assumed to be the same as the control states to which they are bound, and all unstated binding modifier expressions are "1" – i.e. reductions in the first dimension.) Generally speaking, the three contexts at the upper left, init_base, init_search, and next, are for finding the record closest to key for the methods that need it. The plans in the remaining "large circle" contexts, insert, delete, retrieve, and update, implement the unique aspects of the methods with those same names. The three small contexts at the bottom, activating $null plans, ensure that proper transitions are issued to index in leftover cases for the find, delete, and insert methods, and (via resource cleanup) they enable the other $null plan on the right to reset the control state of an element in records, to be discussed. Resource array records holds the records in the linked list, each with a data type (content domain) of approximately: {key:K, payload:P, link:integer}. And resource prev_index holds the index to the record visited previously (generally, linking to the one at index) while searching.

   The concept here is that plan init_base is activated exactly once, after the linked list is instantiated (at IL 1), at which time it allocates one element of records (at beg, from the index_range resource) and initializes the link field to contain beg – i.e. to point back to itself. This record is designed to act as though it immediately precedes the first, and follows the last, "real" record in the list. So, it will always be fetched first, and whenever the link of any record points to this record, it will mean that there are really no more records in the list.

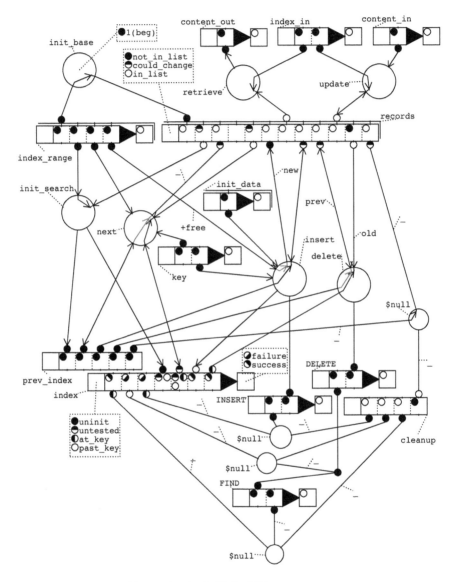

Figure 14.6: A Linked List strategy.

```
init_base: plan tactic {
  records.link = index_range.beg;
}
init_search: plan tactic {
  prev_index = index_range.beg;
  index = records.link;
  if (index == index_range.beg)
    issue past_key to index;
  else
    issue untested to index;
}
next: plan tactic {
  if (records.key > key)
    issue past_key to index;
  else if (records.key == key)
    issue at_key to index;
  else {
    prev_index = index;
    index = records.link;
    if (index == index_range.beg)
      issue past_key to index;
    else
      issue untested to index;
  }
}
insert: plan tactic {
  new.payload = init_data;
  new.key = key;
  new.link = records.link;
  records.link = free;
  index = free;
}
delete: plan tactic {
  prev.link = old.link;
}
retrieve: plan tactic {
  content_out = records.payload;
}
update: plan tactic {
  records.payload = content_in;
}
```

Figure 14.7:   Tactics used in Linked List strategy.

After that, whenever a `find`, `insert`, or `delete` method is invoked (i.e. any one with an `index` role binding), `init_search` activates. It sets the content of `index` to point to the first real record, if any, and its control state will record whether or not we already know we won't find a record with the desired key (because there are no records).

Then, `next` can activate, repeatedly, as long as the control state of `index` remains at `untested`. Each time, it tests if the record indicated by `index` is at or past the key, and if so, it sets the control state of `index` to reflect that, but if it hasn't reached the key yet, it records the value of `index` (the record it just checked) into `prev_index`, sets `index` to the next record following the one at `index` (from its `link` field), and if it hasn't bumped into the end, it sets the control state back to `untested` (allowing it to be activated again). When the `next` plan finally stops activating, `index` will have advanced to (or past) the key, perhaps to the end of the list, and the control state set of `index` will accurately reflect whether it is `at_key` or `past_key`, and `prev_index` will be left pointing to the record previous to the one where it stopped.

If this was all set into motion by a find method invocation, then that's all the info we need, and the `$null` activities at the bottom will convert the control state of `index` (i.e. `at_key` or `past_key`) to a transition on that role (`success` or `failure`, respectively). If this was all at the behest of an insert method invocation and the key was already found, or a delete method invocation and the key was not found, those `$null` activities will issue a `failure` transition to `index`.

If this was an insert method invocation and the record with the key was *not* found (as desired), the `insert` plan is invoked, with its `new` role bound to any `free` record, as per the dupany binding from `index_range` used in the reduction. It initializes the `payload`, `key`, and `link` fields of the new record (`link` pointing to the record formerly after the previous record), and then it updates both `index` and the link of the previous record to point to the new record. The control state of the new record is altered to now be `in_use`, and `success` is issued to `index`.

If this was a delete method invocation, and the record with the key was found (as desired), the `delete` plan is invoked, which just sets the `link` field of the previous record to the `link` field of the record being deleted (so that it points past it), and then effectively deallocates the deleted record by changing its control state back to `free`. And, finally, if this is a retrieve or update method, the `retrieve` or `update` tactics just copy the appropriate values between the formal resources and the appropriate record.

After any activation of `init_search` or `next`, the entry of `records` pointed to by `prev_index` is set to `could_change`. This is because, as a result of finding or not finding the key, the link in that record could change (either in `delete`, by linking past, instead of to, the record at `index`, or in `insert`, by linking to, instead of past, the new entry). This control state is set back to `in_list` as soon as `next`, `insert`, or `delete` has finished processing it, or in all other cases (such as from a successful find method, or a failure condition on one of the other methods), by the `$null` operation on the right. The primary purpose of the `could_change` control state is to prevent concurrent invocations from interfering with each other's proper operation. For example, if a `delete` method was invoked concurrently with a `find` or another `delete` method, this would prevent them both from operating on the same record at the same time: One would be forced to follow the other through the list.

Analysis

Clearly, to make this plan "industrial strength", the plan would (at the very least) be provided additional methods to step sequentially through the list, as well as more robust behavior (e.g. error transitions) if a `retrieve` or `update` attempted to access a record not in the list, and perhaps ways to keep a record locked after it is found to ensure that it can be accessed or updated without concurrent access. Even so, this plan helps to illustrate how dynamic linked structures can be negotiated in ScalPL.

One question prompted by this example is: Where is the concurrency? It is indeed true that there is very little concurrency in any one method invocation, largely because the data structure dictates it: The only way to get to any particular record is to proceed through every preceding record, sequentially. Even so, this plan facilitates more concurrency than some other implementations of linked list. For example, multiple methods may concurrently operate on the list, with the `could_change` control state of the `records` entries ensuring that the different searches through the list follow one another. Also, the method of linking through the list demonstrates latency hiding. That is, because the next entry to be accessed cannot be known until the previous entry is accessed, there may be a significant delay between the two accesses, because the items may be physically far apart. Since each access here is by a separate acton (i.e. `next`), no transient resources are in use while waiting: Other work can continue unobstructed. Even so, there are better plans for implementing concurrent linked list: This is primarily for illustration of how reduction on resource arrays can be used for linked list structures.

14.3.2 Matrix Multiply

Matrix multiply is constructed from three related plans (strategies):

`fmatmult`, which multiplies two two-dimensional arrays and produces a two-dimensional array as a result, such that element i, j in the result is defined to be the dot product of the ith row of the first with the jth column of the second (under the constraint that the number of columns in the first must equal the number of rows in the second).

`fdotprod`, which performs a dot product. A dot product is defined on two equal-length vectors as the sum of the products of corresponding elements. For example, if one vector is (1, 6, 2, 4) and the other is (3, 5, 8, 7), the dot product would be 1*3+6*5+2*8+4*7=3+30+16+28=77.

`ac_red`, which performs a generic scalar reduction of a vector using any associative and commutative scalar operation. Examples of associative and commutative scalar operations are addition, multiplication, min, max, and, and or. A scalar reduction of the vector (3,6,9,2) with the multiplication operator would be 3 * 6 * 9 * 2 = 324.

268

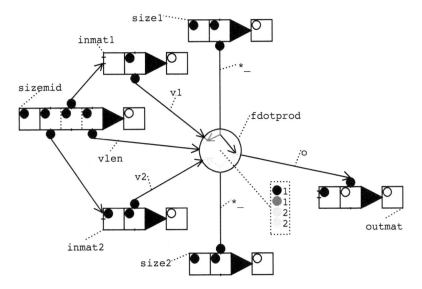

Figure 14.8: fmatmult: Matrix multiply.

fmatmult

One simple implementation of fmatmult (the matrix multiplication plan) in terms of fdotprod (the dot product plan) is shown in figure 14.8. Simply put, this plan declares that each element i, j of the output matrix is defined as the dot product of row i of the first input matrix and column j of the second input matrix.

This plan has six formal resources (and therefore roles): inmat1 and inmat2 are the input matrices, outmat is the result matrix, size1 is the number of rows in inmat1 and outmat, size2 is the number of columns in inmat2 and outmat, and sizemid is the other dimension of both input arrays. (ScalPL arrays don't really have rows and columns: The terms are used here only by convention to mean the first and second dimensions of the arrays, respectively.) The size of inmat1 in its second dimension, and of inmat2 in its first dimension, is given by the range in sizemid, as indicated by the delimiting arrow from sizemid to the corresponding dimension hash marks on the others. The plan works by replicating the middle context once for every element in the output array-i.e. once for every combination of values from the range on the size1 resource and the range on the size2 resource. This "dupall" replication is represented by the asterisk prefixing the label on the roles (lines) leading from those resources to the context. Each resultant context replicant sees a unique combination of numbers on those roles from within those two ranges, but because those roles are anonymous (labels starting with underscore, after the asterisk), the plan within the replicants won't see them at all – they are used here only as primaries for the binding modifiers, shown by the arrows within the context circle. The context's binding modifiers (shown by the the legend to its lower right) show that the value from the size1 range for each replicant will be used

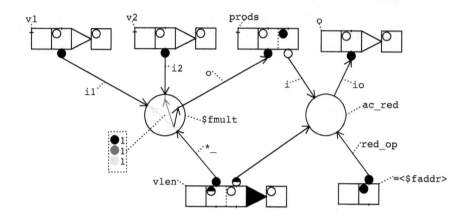

Figure 14.9: fdotprod: Dot product.

to index the first dimension of both the `inmat1` array and the outmat array, while the value from the `size2` range for each replicant will be used to index the second dimension of both the `inmat2` array and the outmat array.

The result, then, is that each replicant will contain the `fdotprod` plan (as per the label), and for each, a single row of inmat1 will play its `v1` role, a single column of `inmat2` will play its `v2` role, and the one element of outmat in the same row and column will play its o role. The `sizemid` resource will play the `vlen` role for each replicant. The `fdotprod` plan, described below, will have no awareness of rows and columns: It knows only that it is getting two one-dimensional arrays (also called vectors) on its `v1` and `v2` roles and a length on its vlen role, and that it is producing a scalar on its o role.

As per the role control states, each context replicant containing `fdotprod` can only access the resources when they are in their initial control state. The transition bindings show that the `inmat1` and `inmat2` elements will remain in that control state, as will `vlen`, but the `outmat` elements will turn final (empty) as each is produced. `size1` and `size2` will turn final after plans have been activated in all of the context replicants.

Every formal here is marked as an activation (or @) formal, meaning that the `fmatmult` strategy won't activate until all of the roles on its parent context are ready, and they will not be under contention with contexts in the parent when they are in their initial control state. Although this plan never explicitly issues transitions to `inmat1`, `inmat2`, and `sizemid` formals, the parent strategy can assume that these transitions will occur because these roles are predictable (i.e. not written to, and with only one transition dot).

fdotprod

Figure 14.9 represents the strategy named `fdotprod`, which is used in the previous plan to perform a floating point dot product. The strategy has four formals: `v1` and `v2` are the input vectors, `vlen` is the range of indices to be processed on those vectors, and o is the resulting scalar. v1, v2, and prods, are all one-dimensional arrays (vectors).

The context on the left is replicated once for every number in the range found on vlen, as represented by the asterisk (dupall) prefix on the corresponding role's label. Each replicant performs the pairwise floating point multiplication (using the predefined constant plan $fmult) of corresponding elements from v1 and v2 into the corresponding element of prods, as shown by the three binding modifier arrows within the context using the single integer from the dupall as an index into all three, but since it is again anonymous (starting with an underscore), it will not be seen by the $fmult plan in the replicated context. As a result, each $fmult activity operates in a very simple context where it gets one floating point number on its scalar i1 receptacle, another on its scalar i2 receptacle, and produces a result on its scalar o receptacle.

The context on the right adds the resulting floating point products from prods together, in no particular order, producing the output resource, o. The plan in that context, ac_red, is defined in the next subsection, and can perform any associative and commutative scalar reduction which it finds on its red_op receptacle. In this case that operation is a floating point add ($faddr). ac_red finds the input elements for the reduction in the array playing its i role (in this case the prods vector), in the range found in the resource playing its vlen role (in this case the vlen resource), producing a result on the resource playing its io role (here the o resource).

ac_red

One possible implementation of the ac_red (associative commutative reduction) plan is shown in Figure 14.10. The context on the left will activate first, producing an identity element for the reduction operation to o, after which that resource will transition to the half-dot control state as per the associated transition dot. The reduction operator is assumed here to produce its identity (i.e. the value which can be applied to any other number by the operator to produce the number itself) to the resource (o) playing its identity role. As a result, the context on the top right can replicate (as per the dupall role) and the replicants can activate, in no particular order, performing the reduction operator for every input element (on i) to o. (Note that the context on the right binds different roles of the operation red_op than the left context did.) When the replicants finish, the and binding transitions vlen to the half-dot control state, which allows the $null plan at the bottom to transition both vlen and identity to their final dots.

14.3.3 Matrix Multiply Variations

The three examples given work well in general, and are easy to understand, but there are some potential tradeoffs. This section will explore alternate implementations for ac_red and fmatmult which have some different properties.

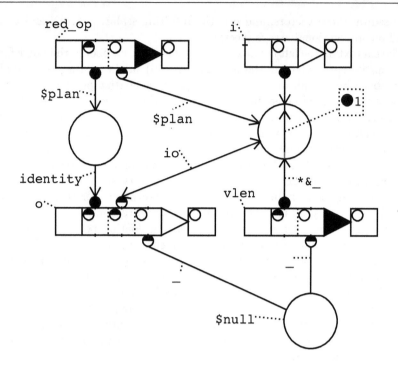

Figure 14.10: ac_red: Associative Commutative reduction.

ac_red revisited

The implementation for `ac_red` given above is unsatisfying in that it contains no concurrency! That is, even though the replicated contexts containing the reduction operator can execute in any order, only one can execute at one time, due to the fact that they all update the same resource, o. The implementation also relies on an identity initialization and an initial reduction with that identity that are not strictly necessary. At the expense of some additional complexity, the implementation shown in Figure 14.11 addresses both of these issues:

Since this plan uses bindanys (designated by the question marks) which activate repeatedly instead of a single dupall (as previously) to access all of the inputs, completion cannot be easily gauged using an *and* binding, so instead, an extra array called `todo` is employed, with no content state, just to keep track of when all of the inputs have been processed, at which time (as described shortly) one of the `$copy` plans at the bottom can activate to move the result to o. Unlike the previous example, instead of reducing all of the input into a single scalar resource (o), a vector of partial results is kept (`partials`). The additional contexts provide as few restrictions for the order in which these operations occur as possible. If there are two roles from the same context to the same resource, they will not both be bound to the same element.

The three contexts along the top each perform a single scalar reduction, but each in different ways. The first reduces any two elements of i (the input),

272

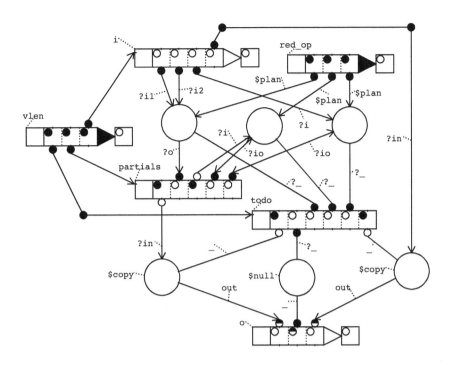

Figure 14.11: ac_red, another implementation.

playing its i1 and i2 roles, to produce a partial result into any element of the **partials** vector, playing its o role. The second reduces any one **partial** result playing its i role into any other playing its io role. The third reduces any one input element playing its i role into any partial result playing its io role. Control states of the **partials** elements are initial when unused (or emptied), and otherwise (empty circle) when they hold a valid partial value. These three contexts can be performed in any order or in parallel. (In fact, since the reduction op is assumed to be atomic, any one of these may execute concurrently with another instance of itself.) The strategy's **red_op** formal plays the **$plan** role for each of these contexts, and each binds only the roles it needs.

This implementation performs one fewer reduction operation than the original strategy, so one element of the **todo** vector must be transitioned to the red control state without a reduction. This is performed by the middle context on the bottom holding the **$null** plan. The other two contexts at the bottom (both containing a **$copy** task) can only activate when **todo** is all transitioned to the half-dot control state, and one or the other is used to copy the answer to the output resource, **o**. There are two of them because the answer could be in two different resources: It will usually be in **partials**, as the only element there with the proper control state, but in the special case where there is only one input element to the strategy, no reductions need to occur, so the answer

273

will still be in the only (still initial) element in i.

fmatmult revisited

The original matrix multiply strategy was completely atomic-i.e. all of its formals were activation formals. This has both potential advantages and disadvantages. For advantages, all of the input roles (size1, sizemid, size2, inmat1, and inmat2) are predictable, so the parent can immediately and accurately know the outcome for these roles the moment the strategy activates, and can predictively perform other actions based on that knowledge. A disadvantage (shared by solutions in many other parallel programming paradigms) is that the plan will not activate until all of the input elements are ready and all of the output elements are ready to accept the results. In some cases, this could result in the plan sitting idle waiting for one or two input or output elements to become ready even when there is plenty of work to do and perhaps plenty of compute resources available to support it.

For applications where those sorts of cases are likely, we can consider an alternate matrix multiply in a more streaming form, which is capable of performing any dot product as soon as its own unique input and output elements are ready, instead of waiting for all of them first. The dot product plan already works in a streaming fashion, allowing any single multiplication or addition to be performed as soon as possible, so that property can now extend to the entire matrix multiply, as in Figure 14.12.

The only differences between this and the original implementation is that the input and output matrices are no longer initial, and two resource arrays (t1 and t2) and four contexts containing $null tasks have been added. These changes are necessary to record when the strategy is finished with each input element, and to bid goodbye to each at that time. Specifically, a row of inmat1 can be transitioned to a final dot (issuing a transition to the actual) when the associated row of o has been computed, and a column of inmat2 can be transitioned to final when the associated column of o has been computed. However, since the elements of o are transitioned to final just as soon as they are calculated, and since some of those may even become available for the next iteration/matrix before this iteration/matrix has finished, the control states of o cannot be used to keep track of what has been done in this iteration. To make up for that, the control states of elements in local arrays t1 and t2 are used to record the completion of each element of o, and a $null task between t1 and inmat1, and between t2 and inmat2, activates when an entire output row or column have been calculated, issuing a transition to the appropriate input row or column and resetting the control state of that row or column in t1 or t2 for the next iteration/matrix.

The other two $null contexts (at the top and bottom) are solely for to steal the control state from the actuals in the parent by transitioning the control state of the input elements from initial to non-initial: The input formals are no longer activation formals, so they no longer automatically steal this state, and v1 and v2 can't be used to effect this transition because each will need to access each element multiple times and this transition can only be performed once for each element.

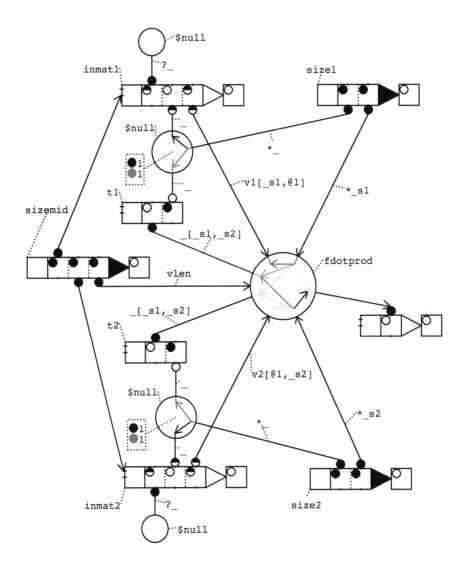

Figure 14.12: Matrix multiply revisited.

Note that the three size formals in this plan are still initial, so they will be supplied just once and used throughout the lifetime of the plan, regardless of how many input matrices are supplied and output matrices are produced.

Matrix Multiply Optimization

The program, as specified, will run correctly on many different platforms, and there is a tremendous amount of concurrency to be exploited. For example, when the fmatmult fragment is executed, all of the size1 * size2 dot products can execute concurrently, and for each of those, all of the multiplies (within fdotprod) can execute concurrently, and many of the additions (within the revised ac_red) can also occur concurrently. The problem is that the concurrency can only be exploited when potentially concurrent operations are on different processors at the same time, and it may not be obvious to a Director how to make that happen, especially since transferring data to a processor (so that an operation can execute) takes time in itself. The overhead of these operations can often be reduced by pre-scheduling operations on the processors (i.e. to determine which processors which will be free to perform each operation in advance, rather than sensing and deciding it at runtime), and also by transferring several data items at one time when the source and destination are the same for all. In some cases, the amount of data to be transferred (and therefore overhead) can be reduced by clever scheduling.

For example, in the program under consideration, if each subplatform adds up all of the local products into a partial sum before summing those partial sums across the entire platform into an overall sum, then at most only one item per subplatform needs to be transferred to accomplish the overall sum. The availability of special hardware (for computer platforms), such as pipelined processors and combining networks, can also affect scheduling decisions. Picking among all of the scheduling and embedding options available in plans like this may be too much for a Director to handle efficiently and effectively. More likely, hints offered by a planner to the scheduler (such as by annotations to the plan) can help the scheduler to determine (for a given platform) which non-deterministic choices to avoid altogether, and how to schedule and embed the remaining operations.

14.3.4 Quicksort

Traditional Definition and Approach

A very common example of the use of recursion in computing is the so-called "quicksort", a means of sorting entries by picking some item in the list (called the pivot), putting it at the correct position in the output (so that all of the items before it should come before it and all those after should come after), and then doing the same thing (recursively) to the lists before it and after it, until each element is at the correct position. If a list ever gets down to one (or zero) elements, then that list is considered already sorted.

The characteristics of the sort can change significantly depending upon how the pivot is chosen. If the original list is fairly randomly ordered, then choice of the pivot is not so important, since any element is just as likely as any other to fall about in the middle of the pack, so subsequent invocations of the sort (on those elements less than and greater than the pivot) will deal with about half of the remaining elements. However, for example, if the list is already completely sorted and the pivot is always chosen as the first element in the list, then all of the subsequent elements will always be compared with it (and found to come after it), and then all of those subsequent elements (all but the first) will be compared to that new first (overall second) item (and found to come after *it*), etc., leading to among the least efficient sorting processes possible. To prevent this, many forms of quicksort determine the overall character of the input (at the beginning or at each step) to determine how sorted it is before deciding on a pivot (or whether to use a different kind of sort, or whether a sort is needed at all).

Quicksort usually occurs in place, in a linear list, to easily keep track of which items are less than and/or greater than the pivot. That is, one pass through the data usually consists of picking the pivot, then comparing it sequentially with each other element in the current (sub)list, swapping places with those in the wrong order, then recursively invoking quicksort on the two new (sub)lists. Concurrency is therefore primarily exploited when the two quicksorts are invoked, as they share no data. Since each of these can eventually invoke two more, etc., it can eventually lead to substantial concurrency, but not until enough levels of sorting have been initiated.

High Level Approach

We will take a very different approach here, adapted to ScalPL's strengths, to get plenty of concurrency "right out of the gate". For example, since each element of the list (i.e. resource array) can have its own control state, we will simply compare (concurrently) the pivot against every other element in the list and use the control state of each element to record whether it's less than, equal to, or greater than the pivot, while counting the number of elements in each category. The count of these control states will leave us with enough information to determine the position (in the answer) where the three sublists (less than, equal to, and greater than the pivot) should go while identifying the elements to be passed to each next level of invocation. Because of this, the classic advantages of sorting in place evaporate: It would not help us to keep track, and would in fact hurt concurrency by adding artificial dependences between different elements in the list. And, if we use a $copy activity to move the records from the input array to output array, we may not even impose much copying overhead (since it can often just put a new name/label on resource contents to say that they now belong to a different resource).

This also means that, except for any issues in choosing a pivot, we can actually start work on a list (i.e. comparing and counting) even before the entire list is present. Specifically, this would allow us to initiate subsequent invocations of the sort (for the lists smaller and larger than the pivot) even before the current invocation is done. To achieve this, we will indeed allow a pivot to be chosen even before the entire list is present – specifically, as any element of the list, nondeterministically. If there is very little of the list available (such as from a previous invocation) from which to choose it, then it might be advantageous to choose one of those elements which does become available early, but we will leave that aspect completely unstated, at least at this level of specification. (It is not necessarily true, in a distributed, concurrent platform, that the elements will become available in the same order in which they are stored, so this approach might even still work well for lists which are, in some sense, already highly ordered.)

Adding all of this potential concurrency does come with some complications. One is that, although we like the idea of invoking subsequent recursive sorts on the sublists soon, we can't invoke them *too* soon (such as even if there's no work to do), or each sort will instantly launch two more, and those will each launch two more, etc., and we'll get infinite recursion. To prevent this, we'll formulate the sort (at least the one we call recursively) so that it requires at least one element – a pivot – before it can activate, by making the pivot an explicit activation formal to the sort. (If it was easy to do, we might have waited until there were at least two elements before recursing, but just the pivot will do.)

Another complication is determining when any particular invocation is complete. We have said that we'd like an invocation to *begin* work even before the list to be sorted is fully determined – i.e. before we know how many items there will be, or before we have seen that many items – but we can't let it *finish* before we're sure we have all the input. We also can't let it finish before any recursive sorts have been invoked, since those activities will need to access $plan, which will go away when the invocation finishes. And, since any elements of the output array which still have their initial control state will be made unavailable when the invocation finishes, those will first need to be transitioned to some other control state, too, even if they have not yet been filled with their eventual output.

ScalPL Plan for Quicksort

Figure 14.13 shows a strategy for Quicksort following the high-level approach just outlined. Along with the $plan role itself, the plan has six roles, described textually in Figure 14.2. The in_data and result roles are one-dimensional arrays, as shown by the "^1" qualifiers. None of the input data to this plan, including the input records in in_data, is modified by this plan, as shown by the observe usages (indicated by -->). Instead, the sorted list (including the pivot) is written to elements result_base through result_base+n of result. As indicated by the at signs (@), the plan itself will not activate until pivot and compare_key are ready, since they are activation roles (formals). All of the roles have just one transition, done, shown in parens, though the plan that plays the compare_key role has three transitions (lt, eq, and gt) on one of its roles (rec1). Although in_data, pivot, result, and the roles of compare_key all have contents of some type described here as R, there is no need to actually specify R.

The input records need not be within any particular index range within in_data, and need not be contiguous. Processing of input records may begin before n is ready, and regardless, it is important to not allow more than n elements of in_data to become ready, such as for subsequent sort iterations,

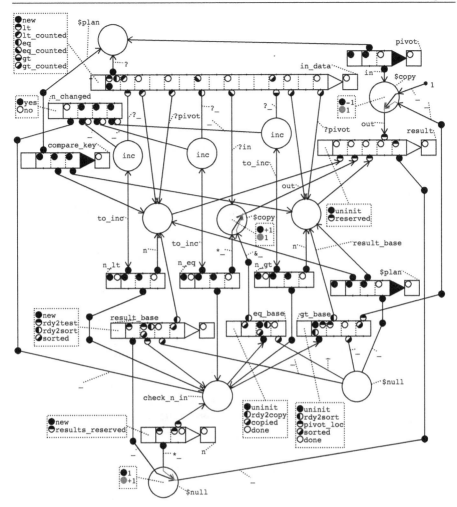

Figure 14.13: Recursive Quicksort in ScalPL.

until the current plan finishes, as indicated by a **done** transition to its **n** role.

High-Level Implementation Description

The activity at the top compares **pivot** against any **new** element of **in_data** and transitions that element's control state based on the outcome: to **lt** if less than the pivot; to **eq** if equal to the pivot; or to **gt** if greater than the pivot. (Since all roles are either predictable or unique, many elements of **in_data** can be compared concurrently.) The three **inc** (i.e. increment) activities shown below **in_data** tally the number of elements with each of those control states into resources **n_lt**, **n_eq**, and **n_gt**, respectively, while again transitioning the input element control states, to **lt_counted**, **eq_counted**, and **gt_counted**, respectively. When there is at least one element with control state **lt_counted**

279

Role	Description
`--> in_data^1 (done): R`	Input records (of type R)
`--> n (done): int`	# of input records to process (including pivot)
`--> @pivot (done): R`	Input record to treat as initial pivot (may be a member of in_data)
`--> @compare_key (done): plan {--> in_data (lt, eq, gt): R; --> pivot (done): R}`	Input plan for comparing keys and deciding if the one in rec1 is less than (lt), equal to (eq), or greater than (gt) that in rec2
`<-- result^1 (done): R`	Ordered output records (of type R)
`--> result_base (done): int`	Index into result preceding first output record

Table 14.2: Roles for qsort (quicksort) strategy

(and/or `gt_counted`), the `pivot` role can bind for the recursive quicksort(s) indicated by the contexts below the left (and/or right) `inc`, allowing them to activate and begin processing any other input items which have been given an `lt_counted` (and/or `gt_counted`) control state.

Once resources `n` and `result_base` become ready (i.e. control state `new`), two main things occur. First, `n` locations in `result`, starting at `result_base`, are transitioned to a new control state (`reserved`) by the `$null` activity at the bottom, effectively reserving them for the eventual sorted (sub)list output. Then, the `check_n_in` plan is invoked, perhaps repeatedly, to determine whether `n` elements have actually been tallied yet from `in_data` by comparing `n` with the sum of `n_lt`, `n_eq`, `n_gt`, and 1 (for the pivot). To keep `check_n_in` from activating needlessly, we have added another resource called `n_changed`, near the upper left, which has no salient content state, but which has a control state of `yes` if and only if the sum of `n_lt`, `n_eq`, and `n_gt` has changed since `check_n_in` previously activated – i.e. when at least one of them have been incremented by an `inc` activitiy since then. Note that there is no harm done, and in fact work saved, if multiple `inc` activations occur before a subsequent activation of `check_n_in`. Also note that the check could have been integrated directly into each of the `inc` plans instead of having a separate plan for that, but that would have meant checking after every tally, and disallowing them from working concurrently since they would be updating shared resources.

Once `check_n_in` finds that all `n` items from `in_data` have indeed been accounted for, it prepares the contents of resources `eq_base` and `gt_base` to specify the places in the result array where the output items equal to the pivot and greater than the pivot (respectively) will begin, as `result_base+n_lt` and `result_base+n_lt+n_eq+1` (respectively) – the "+1" to make room for the pivot itself. `check_n_in` then transitions the control states of those bases to `rdy2sort` (ready to sort) or `rdy2copy`, to make them visible to the recursive sorts or `$copy` – unless some of the counts are zero, in which case those control states are transitioned directly to `sorted` (or `copied`). If the bases are transitioned to `rdy2sort`, the recursive sorts will find their own `result_base` roles ready, and so they too will be able to finish up, and when they do, they will transition the bases to `sorted` (or `copied`). When all sorts and copies are finished, the `$null` activity on the lower right will finish the activity by transitioning the `$plan` formal resource to `done`.

Concurrency Analysis

Consider how each input element progresses through the different comparisons at the different recursive iterations to produce the output. Each iteration first selects one incoming element as a pivot, and then compares each other incoming element against its pivot, gathering those equal to it, or immediately sending those less/greater than it to the next iteration which either selects it as a pivot or compares it to its pivot which is respectively less/greater than the previous level's pivot. As many recursive iterations become active all at once, and pivots are chosen for each, the recursion tree exactly becomes a binary comparison tree, with each incoming element either sticking at that level of recursion if it compares equal to that pivot, or going down the "left" or "right" levels of recursion (i.e. branches of the comparison tree) if it is less or greater than the pivot. When considered in this time/space form, this is perhaps as generic as a sort can get, simply comparing each input element with as many (and only as many) previous elements as necessary to determine where it belongs relative to those elements. Its efficiency depends primarily on how balanced the tree ends up, and recursion overhead.

Finer Points

A usable implementation of `inc` consists of a simple interface declaration plus one line of C:

```
plan {<-> to_inc (done): int}
tactic {| (*to_inc)++; |}
```

That is, it increments the integer present on its one role whenever it activates. The done signal is issued by default when it finishes.

An implementation of `check_n_in`, in C, is:

```
plan
{ --> n            (done) int;
  --> n_lt         (done) int;
  --> n_eq         (done) int;
  --> n_gt         (done) int;
  --> result_base (n_not_in some none) int;
  <-- eq_base      (n_not_in some none) int;
  <-- gt_base      (n_not_in some none) int;
}
tactic
{|
```

```
     int total = *n_lt + *n_eq + *n_gt + 1;
     if (total != *n) {
        issue n_not_in to result_base;
        issue n_not_in to eq_base;
        issue n_not_in to gt_base;
     } else {
        if (n_lt) {
           issue some to result_base;
        } else {
           issue none to result_base;
        }
        if (n_eq) {
           *eq_base = *result_base + *n_lt;
           issue some to eq_base;
        } else {
           issue none to eq_base;
        }
        // gt_base must be valid even if n_gt zero
        // since it will still be used to copy
        // pivot to result.
        *gt_base = *result_base + *n_lt + *n_eq + 1;
        if (n_gt) {
           issue some to gt_base;
        } else {
           issue none to gt_base;
        }
     }
  }
|}
```

14.4   Embedding/Scheduling Data Parallel Plans

A general problem with expressing parallel plans (such as these) is that the optimal way to execute them depends highly on the target platform and/or on the size and shape of the inputs.

Rather than asking the programmer to recode the plan (program) for every target platform (architecture) or data characteristic, some languages offer higher level data structures with operators that do not micromanage the lower-level operations, and may provide a mechanism for the user to hint or suggest how to optimize them. For example, Fortran90 provides array operations, so the above programs could be expressed directly in those languages, and HPF additionally provides "structured comments" that allow the programmer to say how the rows and columns of those arrays should be distributed among processors, which in turn implies which processor will be used to perform operations. Even so, for any particular language, that approach only solves the issue for those particular abstractions which the language designers have chosen to include as primitives, and even then, only in those cases and for those platforms which the compiler (and runtime) implementers have spent the time and effort to optimize. Hinting and mapping mechanisms, like those used in HPF, are also restricted in their expressiveness (i.e. using the "owner computes" rule).

ScalPL provides a much more general approach to solving such problems which does not depend on language designers and implementers to be steps ahead of any particular programmer's wishes. The general approach is for the programmer to first state the algorithm in the most general and least restrictive terms possible, by specifying the operations that must be performed to each input to produce outputs while excluding mention of the order in which operations must execute relative to one another except for cases where one operation directly depends upon the other. The result of this step is an executable algorithm, or program, which can run on a number of platforms, but it may not be obvious to a runtime system how to execute it optimally on some or all. After the initial programming task, ScalPL then allows the programmer to offer much more help in suggesting how it might be executed on a particular platform using mapping and specialization.

These suggestions take place in three stages. First, a conceptual abstract platform tree is imagined, which has (as its name states) a tree topology. Each node in the tree at a particular level is conceptually named by sequential integers, and any specific node in the tree is named by a sequence of integers, representing the path to the node from the root.

A strategy is then annotated to give contexts and/or resource control states expressions that evaluate to sequences of integers, stating the node within the abstract platform tree to which that context or control state is to be assigned. These expressions can depend on parameters passed down through the invocation tree – i.e. from parent to child of each context. The basic concept is to assign activities which are likely to communicate often to close (connected) nodes in the tree, and to assign activities which are likely to be able to work concurrently to different nodes. (This approach has an obvious weakness, in that communication topologies are not always tree-based, but (a) a tree can often be stretched into other topologies, such as by having long parallel branches representing parallel rows or columns in a grid, and (b) communication does not have to follow the tree topology, the final assignment to the platform is all that really matters, the tree just forms a convenient and flexible coordinate system.)

Finally, when the strategy is assigned to an actual platform, the planner has the option of assigning nodes and/or complete branches of the abstract platform tree to specific parts of the platform, such as by specifying a function from tree node name (i.e. integer sequence) to platform node. The planner can also leave that tree to be assigned to the platform automatically by the Director, letting it rely on the assumption that nearby nodes in the tree are more likely to communicate often than far apart nodes.

14.5 Summary

Data parallelism is a property by which the amount of concurrency in an activity increases with the amount of data being processed by that activity. Since the concurrency is variable, so must the number of contexts be, and while one way of achieving varying numbers of active contexts might be through recursion,

ScalPL provides a mechanism called a dup (pronounced "doop") to replicate a given context. The number of replicants is obtained from one of the role bindings of the context, called the dup role binding, designated by prefixing the name on the binding with an asterisk (*) or plus (+) to indicate that it is a dupall or dupany, respectively. A dup binding must have oberve permission, and just one transition binding, for transition **done**. When the dup binding is ready, the context itself replicates some number of times, and the dup receptacle (with prefix removed) becomes a post-dup scalar receptacle bound to one integer. The number of replicants, and the integer appearing on the post-dup receptacle for each, is dictated by the contents of the resource bound to the dup receptacle, being one, two, or three integers. If one integer, it represents the number of replicants to create, and the post-dup constants are integers from 0 to the integer minus one. If two integers, they represent a range, so the number of receptacles are their difference plus one, and the integer on each post-dup receptacle is one of the integers in the range. If there are three integers, they represent a range and step.

The usual use of a dup receptacle is as a primary receptacle for either a reduction or translation for access into an array. This allows each replicant to access a different element, or subset of elements, of arrays, thereby allowing each to work concurrently on different parts of a large dataset.

The difference between a dupall and a dupany is that an activity must activate in each replicant of a dupall, and in exactly one replicant of a dupany, before the dup is considered finished, at which time it may replicate again when conditions are reached (e.g. the dup receptacle is ready). By default, the transition will take place to the dup role binding as soon as it replicates, and any binding other than the dup role binding will be carried unchanged to each replicant. For a dupalls, the issuing of a transition to the dup role binding, or to any other predictable role on the context, can be delayed until a plan has been activated in all of the replicants, by prefixing the receptacle name with an ampersand (&). (These role bindings are technically no longer predictable in this case.)

When uses of dupany and dupall are mixed for a single context, they are (by default) interpreted as a dupall of dupanys – i.e. one of each of the dupanys must activate. This can be overridden with a dup precedence arrow within the context circle from the earlier dups to evaluate to the later ones. This arrow represents the arrow for a binding modifier, but without a binding rule.

Chapter 15

Engineering Correct Plans

With these tools under our belts, how can we best use them in practice? We briefly describe how one might go about establishing correspondences between specifications and plans (which are in themselves specifications), such as separation of liveness and safety issues. Similarly, we briefly describe methods of converting/refactoring one plan (especially strategy) into another with perhaps more concurrency. Finally, we briefly discuss some other formal models which have been developed, from which techniques and proof methods might very well be ultimately borrowed to help with analysis of ScalPL/F-Net plans.

15.1   Introduction

Planning (of which programming is one example) can be considered as the creation or verification of a correspondence between a specification and a plan. Usually, that correspondence is established by being given a specification (however vague or formal) and creating a plan which meets that specification. It can also work the other way, as is familiar to so-called maintenance programmers who are given a program and must figure out what it's doing and why – i.e. the specification to which that plan might have been written. And then, there's the act of debugging, which is determining why a particular plan does not meet its specification, or verification, where one proves (in some sense or other) that the plan does meet its specification. Generally speaking, we'll call a plan and a specification correct, with respect to one another, when the plan meets the specification. Precisely what it means for a plan to "meet" a specification is difficult to further define without restricting the form of one or both, but since they are both descriptions of activity at a level of detail required for the task at hand, they must (at some level of detail) describe the same activities.

15.1.1   Correctness of Tactics

The plan for an acton is (by definition) a tactic. As described in Chapters 3 and 10, one possible specification for a tactic is a function from the initial content states of the observable roles to the new content states of the replaceable roles and control state transitions for all the roles. For the purposes of showing the correctness of any plan, this is the only specification required for each tactic. However, showing that a tactic satisfies such a specification is beyond the scope of this book. Depending on the form which a tactic takes, there are a number of techniques which have been developed over the years to show just such correspondences. For example:

- If a tactic takes the form of a function (being expressed in mathematical functional composition or using a functional computer language), then the specification and the tactic may be one and the same, in which case there is no correspondence to demonstrate. The functional programming community sometimes uses the term "executable specifications" to describe this property.

- The field of Denotational Semantics is concerned with defining computer programs (expressed in certain languages) in terms of mathematical functions. If a denotational semantics exists for the language in which the tactic is expressed, then it may be possible to show mathematically that the function to which that tactic corresponds is equivalent to (or at least an example of) the specification.

- Other proof techniques, such as loop invariants, etc., have been developed to demonstrate certain properties of sequential programs.

Although it may take some effort to show that a particular tactic satisfies a particular specification expressed as a function from contents of observable roles to contents of replaceable roles and transitions for all roles, it can be much easier to ensure that the tactic satisfies *some* specification of that form, as we have already discussed at several points (e.g. in Chapter 5).

15.1.2 Correctness of Strategies

A strategy is a plan constructed from other plans. Showing correctness of a strategy (i.e. conformance to its specification) is much more complex than showing it for a tactic, because both the plan and the specification are typically much more complex. For example, formal specifications for concurrent plans have traditionally been expressed in languages such as temporal logic or LOTOS (Language of Temporal Order Specification). Forming such a specification from user requirements, and showing that it is consistent with those requirements, can be difficult in itself, even before showing the correctness of the plan with respect to that specification. So, one question we will approach here is whether there are better ways to express a specification for a concurrent plan.

The correctness of any plan with respect to a specification can be largely decomposed into two basic issues called **liveness** and **safety**. Liveness is the property that the plan will eventually get around to doing some particular thing that it is supposed to do. Safety is property that the plan won't do anything that it's not supposed to do. In the case of strategies, the axioms help to show these properties for each step (e.g. acton) making up a larger activity. For example, the axiom which states that a tactic will only activate when all of its roles are ready is an important way of showing safety of a particular step, by showing that the logical AND of the corresponding control states represents the conditions under which that acton should execute. The liveness axiom shows that a desired acton will eventually result when the proper conditions exist, and the remaining axioms ensure that that acton will do what it is specified to do (and only that).

The remaining step is to show that the specification for each acton carries the states of its resources from consistent states to consistent states. That is, resources will often have some aspect of internal consistency, such as when the control state must accurately reflect some property of the content state. Then there are cases where the control states of several resources must collectively be consistent with one another to reflect a larger property or constraint, particularly when all of those resources are bound to a single context. The way to maintain such collective consistency is for an activity to operate on them collectively and ensure that they are not "released" (i.e. control state returned to them) in an inconsistent state.

Roughly, then, the things to show are:

1. That each tactic can activate when it is supposed to, and only when it is supposed to, according to the control states of the resources playing its roles.

2. That each resource's internal consistency will be preserved by each acton that accesses it.

3. That each acton preserves the collective consistency of each set of resources which it accesses.

4. That the content state of the resources, as determined by the computation performed by the strategy, is the desired functional mapping of the input states (i.e. that the function specified by each computation is correct, as a composition of the tactic functions).

The last step is almost always the most difficult. Even if one can show that activities will continue to occur, and that after every activity, the state of the resources are somehow consistent, these are tangential to the purpose of developing the plan in the first place, which is to perform the desired computation.

This brings up a philosophical question: Must every activity within a plan perform some sort of "useful" purpose, pushing the computation closer to the desired solution, in order for the plan to be deemed "correct"? Clearly, if some activities do (or might) act contrary to the goal of the plan, and keep it from meeting its specification, then the plan is wrong. In fact, even if a particular tactic does not in itself need to act contrary to the computation to interfere with liveness, since simply offering alternatives to productive work can do that (with the absence of fairness constraints). For example, in Figure 3.7(b), if acton Z was necessary to move the computation forward, then even if acton Y does nothing to change the content or control state of any resource, its very presence can keep Z from necessarily activating. But if some activities (or parts thereof) neither advance the plan towarfd the specified result nor prevent other activities (or parts thereof) from meeting the specification, then the plan must be deemed correct (in some sense), as it continues to meet the specification.

15.1.3 Specifications for strategies

What is a natural form for someone to use to specify the desired behavior of a strategy? Mentioned above, LOTOS and temporal logic can be used, but constructing and assuring the correspondence between the actual customer requirement and LOTOS, and then doing the same for the correspondence between LOTOS and a strategy, may be both difficult and unneeded. After all, a strategy is itself as formal as one wishes to make it: It is completely formal in specifying how component plans activate and interact, so the question of formality of a plan is reduced to the formality of the specifications of the component plans. If some of those component plans can be described in terms of functional mappings (from start contents of observable roles to end contents of replaceable roles and transitions for all roles) then those mappings serve as complete formal specification of those plans (and facilitates their later implementation as tactics). If some component plans cannot be so described, they can themselves be described as formal strategies of sub-components, repeating the process. There are few convincing reasons to believe that there are any better ways of describing/specifying plans that are more understandable and verifiable to both the customer demanding the plan and the people and tools implementing the plan than either a functional mapping or a strategy. This divide-and-conquer approach in the specification process becomes one and the same as the planning process, allowing a plan to double as a executable specification, at least down to the implementation of tactics, and blurring the line between high-level programming and specification.

This equating of specification and high-level implementation raises seemingly philosophical conundrums. For example, the long-taught software engineering goal of separating the interface specification from the implementation becomes impossible when the implementation *is part of* the interface specification. This raises immediate questions as to whether we have taken a wrong turn, and prompts re-examining both why the separation of interface and implementation is a goal and why that goal should be forsaken (in some cases). After all, "tell me what to do, not how to do it "is a general philosophy adopted by many employees, teams, or entire companies, and is the basis for legal contracts as well as the freedom and flexibility which lead to job satisfaction and future optimization. It is not something to be dispensed with lightly, and in fact, we have already alluded to the fact that even we advocate preserving it in some cases – i.e. where the interface can be summarized as a function. This encompasses cases where the implementation consists of some stateless sequential plan

Most specification languages, like LOTOS, help in extending functional specifications with transformations to persistent internal state, thereby transforming these functions into abstract data types (classes). The general approach is to specify how groups of functions/operations behave when they are invoked (or composed) in certain sequences, rather than describing what state they should or should not hold inside and how they should transform it. Since there may be many such functions or operations, the rules must be sufficient to simplify any sequence of such operations.

There are two problems with this approach. One is that great effort is expended to avoid obvious implementations, even if those implementations are what the customer has in mind and therefore can most easily verify as expressing their intention, and in fact are almost required in order to make proper behavior. The other problem with the LOTOS approach is the very use of sequences (temporal ordering) of operations to specify functionality. In a concurrent systems, the temporal ordering of different operations may not be defined. Since the very goal of concurrent planning is to reduce the need to sequence operations, it is sometimes awkward and artificial to require the specification of such plans to use sequences as a primary building block. ScalPL already offers a formal semantics. (A primary difference between CCS, a foundation of LOTOS, and ScalPL, is that CCS uses non-atomic actions and atomic state changes, while ScalPL uses atomic actions (actons) and (potentially) non-atomic state changes to resources.)

So, is it sufficient to simply conflate the implementation and the specification of a plan? To say that if a user of a plan wants to understand a particular plan, they should simply dive inside to see how it's implemented? There is a difference between *an* implementation and *the* implementation. For example, a queue specified by (or to) a customer as in Figure 4.2(b) might be implemented in any number of ways, such as that in Figure 13.13, which might not be as obvious to a customer or user. In the best of cases, someone (e.g. the planner) will have verified that the equivalence of the behaviors of the specification and the actual implementation.

15.2 Refactoring

A sequential plan can be considered as a special form of concurrent plan. For example, in a sequential programming model, each instruction or statement can be considered as a tactic in ScalPL, the program counter (which tells which instruction/statement to perform next) can be considered as a resource with no content but lots and lots of control states (one for every instruction/statement), and each register or variable in the program can be regarded as a resource with just one (i.e. the initial) control state. Advancement and/or branching in the control flow is represented by transitions to the control state of the program counter. For example, see Figure 15.1 for a straightforward translation of the sequential binary search (TDSP) from Chapter 8 into a ScalPL strategy. All role bindings to the bottom resource, representing the program counter, should likely be empty, except for the while and if tactics, which explicitly alter the control state of that resource based on the result of their comparisons.

Note that, in such a representation, most control state transitions (to the program counter) are predictable, so although the program counter forces all instructions to be serialized, it does not necessarily keep "downstream" instructions from starting before upstream ones have finished. (Except for conditional branching instructions, all bindings to the program counter resource can there-

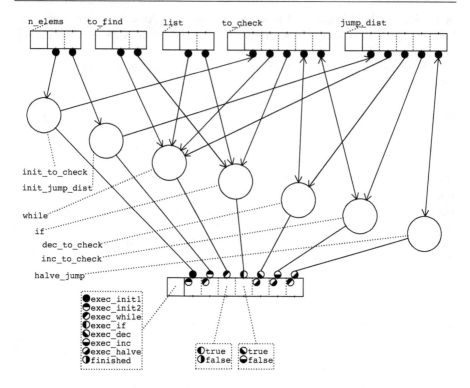

Figure 15.1: Simple translation of binary search from Chapter 8.

fore be anonymous.) This closely matches how modern language processors and computers work, allowing concurrent and/or out-of-order execution of seemingly "sequential" instructions, as long as the result is consistent with sequential execution.

15.2.1   Refactoring Control State

Given that a sequential plan can be represented in this way, the so-called parallelization (or concurrentization) of such a plan can be considered, in part, as migrating as much control control state as possible away from the program counter and towards the resources representing registers/variables. Moving the control state to the resources in this way enforces the proper ordering over accesses to each register/variable resource without enforcing a total ordering of the accessing activities with respect to every other activity. In terms of a computation graph, the goal of such control state migration from the program counter to the resources can be seen as producing a plan which produces identical computation graphs as the sequential plan except that some of the activation nodes are not bound to the program counter state nodes. (In the extreme, it would be possible to completely factor out the program counter resource.) Since the program counter resource carries no content state, the function evaluated for the computation is identical.

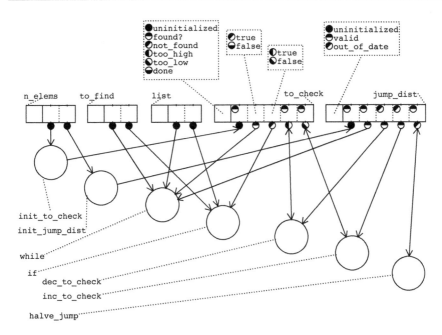

Figure 15.2: Removing program counter resource from binary search.

See Figure 15.2 for one example of how the program counter resource in the binary search example (in figure 15.1). Note that resources n_elems, to_find, and list have not been altered in any way, and still have only a single (initial) control state. The bindings to the other resources have only been changed by adding control states and transitions from the program counter, most of them to the to_check resource, which now has six control states, representing:

- uninitialized: The content state is meaningless so far.

- found?: The content may or may not point to the correct list entry.

- not_found: The content does not point to the correct list entry.

- too_high: The content points above the correct list entry.

- too_low: The content points below the correct list entry.

- done: The content points to the correct list entry, or the entry doesn't exist.

Likewise, resource jump_dist has been given three control states:

- uninitialized: The content state is meaningless so far.

- valid: The content state is valid and can be used.

- out_of_date: The content state should be updated before being used again.

It can be statically determined that this strategy is still deterministic. This is easy to see for all contexts except `init_jump_dist` and `halve_jump`, because the control state of `to_check` uniquely determines which of those can activate next. Although `init_jump_dist` and `init_to_check` can activate in any order or concurrently, they can only activate once (due to control state transitions and access dots), and those activations do not affect one another and must both occur before any other context (i.e. `while`, in this case) bound to their other resources activates the first time. `halve_jump` is also well-ordered relative to other contexts accessing `jump_dist`. The only concurrency that has been added to this plan over the initial sequential version is the initialization, limited in part due to the character of the algorithm itself.

15.2.2   Refactoring Tactics

Migration of control state is just one factor involved in concurrentization. First of all, this approach posits a one-to-one correspondence between variables and resources, and between statements/instructions and tactics. While this can produce a working plan, multiple statements are more naturally grouped into a single tactic if they will naturally execute as a unit and be applied to (or produce) a cohesive collection of contents or information. Correspondingly, contents are more naturally grouped into a single resource if those contents are naturally perceived and dealt with as a unit (e.g. by common tactics) so that they can share control state. In this sense, tactics correspond more naturally to so-called basic blocks than to statements, and resources correspond more naturally to object state than to variables or registers. And second, refactoring is far more complex if one is to model subroutine or function calls in the sequential language just using ScalPL constructs, and the benefits of doing so are less than obvious. It is often better to rethink such constructs completely, especially since sequential ("synchronous") subroutine calls effectively return all of their results at once to one place: Issuing a transition in ScalPL effectively returns a single result (or, similarly, part of the whole result) at a time, and to perhaps a different consumer than for another result (or part of the whole result).

Perhaps most importantly, sequential plans are always deterministic. They simply cannot take advantage of the power of non-determinism, because there is no way to express non-determinism in them, so introducing non-determinism will mean altering the very character of the plan: It's not something that can be done by rote in a refactoring, because there's no way to know, in the general case, whether the programmer would find it acceptable or desirable to introduce non-determinism.Formal Models

15.3   Related Formal Models

There have been many formal models of computation proposed, some of which lend themselves to concurrent computation better than others. We discuss here some which have enough resemblance to ScalPL (and/or its formal computational model, F-Nets) to merit some further comparisons, and further investigation by the reader interested in advancing some of the formal aspects of ScalPL. (This is not to suggest that there are no other models from which analogies and similarities can also be discovered and learned from.)

15.3.1 UNITY/Guarded Commands

In their book "Parellel Program Design: A Foundation", K. M. Chani and J. Misra introduced a formal model called UNITY, in which a plan (using the terminology in this book) was expressed as a set of atomic expressions, unrelated except for the variables (resources, in our terminology) which they shared. There was virtually no control over which expression would evaluate/activate next, except for a rather strong fairness constraint which required them to each execute (roughly) the same number of times in any fixed amount of time – or, as they put it, each an infinite number of times. However, each expression could (and usually would) also include a predicate, or guard, that would be evaluated as part of the overall expression, and if the predicate/guard evaluated to false, the entire evaluation would be guaranteed to have no overall effect – i.e. to be so-called idempotent. So, the predicate/guard would effectively serve as a condition under which the rest of the expression would be evaluated, and the predicates (at least) would be checked regularly. UNITY has since been argued to be equivalent to a subset of Dijkstra's Guarded Commands.

Clearly, there are large similarities and large differences between these models and ScalPL/F-Nets. They are similar in that they all consist of atomic actions reading/observing and/or writing/updating some subset of a global state, and the circumstances under which any particular action will take place are controlled by some logically separate part of the expression. However, ScalPL/F-Nets uses a special construct, control state, which is used *only* for controlling the ability of these actions to access parts of the state/environment. We argue that this separation of control and content state in ScalPL/F-Nets allows more information that can be used in proofs, in optimization, and in simply human understanding and communication, by reducing the size of the domain of values related to deciding which parts of the computation can follow from previous parts.

15.3.2 Petri Nets

A well-studied form of formality for concurrency is called a Petri Net, or place/transition network. Although these come in many styles, they virtually always consist of a set of place nodes (represented graphically as circles) and a set of transition nodes (represented graphically as vertical lines or rectangle) connected by directed arcs (i.e. arrows), one kind of node to the other – that is, in a bipartite directed graph. (The graphs are not generally acyclic.) An arc from a place to a transition symbolizes an input place for the transition, and an arc from a transition to a place represents an output place for that transition. After being assigned some initial marking, which is just a specification how many tokens (represented by dots) are to be assigned to each of the places, the network operates by "playing the token game", meaning that transitions fire, effectively moving tokens from place to place. Generally, the rule is that a transition may fire when there is at least one token in each of its input places for each arc from that place to the transition, and as a result of the firing, those tokens are consumed, and one token is produced to each output place for each arrow from the transition to that place. Rather than have multiple arcs to (from) a single place from (to) a single transition, a single arc is often shown with an integer (called a multiplicity) indicating the number of tokens which will be produced (or consumed) there. Variations include whether places are restricted in the number of tokens which each place can hold (so that a transition cannot fire if its result would be to place more than that number), and/or whether inhibitory arcs are allowed which can prevent firing if there is a token on a given place. Nets with different syntax restrictions (e.g. no place being an input to more than one transition, transitions always having the same number/multiplicity of input and output arcs) are studied for their unique properties. Extensions, such as adding color to tokens/arrows, also exist.

There are many similarities, in spirit if not in precise semantics, between Petri Nets and F-Nets/ScalPL. Most specifically, consider a ScalPL plan (or F-Net) with only nodata roles, and therefore no content state of any consequence on any of the resources, and therefore with only predictable role bindings. Such a plan can be easily modeled as a Petri Net, by modeling each control state of each ScalPL/F-Net resource as a Petri Net place, an initial marking with a single token on the places representing initial control states, and each ScalPL/F-Net context represented by a Petri Net transition, with arcs from each place representing the ScalPL/F-Net access dots of its role bindings, and arcs to each place representing the ScalPL/F-Net new control state (transition binding) dots of the role bindings.

Endowing such a Petri Net with color – i.e. the ability to carry data on its tokens – and requiring all of the places representing any single resource to be of the same color (type) can bring an even closer analogy to full F-Nets (with content state). The idea of tokens carrying data is actually more similar to many dataflow models than to F-Nets, but if the Petri Net is taken to only model the behavior (rather than the implementation) of the F-Net, the fact that there will only be a token at a time on any one place representing a given resource means that moving content/tokens from one such place to another (within the resource) could be considered (and implemented) as just updating the content in place.

Perhaps even more important than correlations between specific F-Nets and Petri Nets, Petri Nets are (like F-Nets) considered to unfold into partial orders (DAGs) (called occurrence nets) similar to our computations (computation graphs), resulting in Petri Nets being "structured" according to our earlier definition. The formalization for F-Nets in Chapter 10 was modeled (at least initially) after that commonly used for Petri Nets.

15.3.3   Turing Machines

This book started with a mention of Alan Turing and the model of computation he developed, often called the Turing Machine, or TM. It was further mentioned that a TM was, in some sense at least, capable of representing any computation that could be

A TM has many acceptable forms which are all effectively equivalent in their computational power. We'll first consider a "classic" version which consists of:

- A one-ended tape, consisting of an infinite number of squares in a single line, each capable of holding one symbol from its finite alphabet. One element of the alphabet is differentiated as a "blank" symbol, which originally fills all of the tape squares outside of a finite distance from the tape beginning (i.e. an infinite number of them).

- A head that sits over one square of the tape at a time, so it can just be considered as an integer signifying a square of the tape (counting from the end).

- A finite set of possible machine states, with one singled out as the initial machine state.

- A transition table consisting of a set of transitions, each uniquely indexed by a (machine state, alphabet element) pair, and each consisting of a new machine state, a new alphabet symbol, and a direction (Left, Right, or None).

The machine starts with the head over the first tape square, and a machine state equal to the initial state, and then repeatedly finds the transition associated with the (current machine state, tape symbol under the head) pair, replaces the machine state with the new machine state from the transition, replaces the symbol under the head with the new symbol from the transition, and moves the head left one, right one, or leaves it where it is, as per the direction from the transition. The machine continues until either (a) some combination of machine state and tape symbol found doesn't match a transition, or the tape falls out of the machine (head moves too far left), or some predetermined "halt" machine state is reached. The "input" to the function computed by the machine can be considered as the initial tape contents, the "plan" as the transition table, and the "output" as the content of the tape when it halts (and, in some cases, the position of the head at that time).

Such a machine is capable of virtually any complexity of computation, technically, of evaluating partial recursive functions. The power of the machine is mostly attributable to the infinite length of the tape, which is used to leverage the finite number of machine states and finite number of symbols in the alphabet.

Now consider an Multi-Tape TM (MTTM), like the TM above except that:

- It possesses n heads (numbered 1 through n) and n tapes under them (for some fixed n).

- The transition table entries are now indexed by a machine state and a sequence of n alphabet symbols, and each entry contains a new machine state and a sequence of n (new tape symbol, tape direction) pairs. In addition, one tape symbol is differentiated as a "no tape" symbol (which the head sees when there is no tape below it).

The machine works similar to the one-tape TM described before it, but instead of just looking at the one tape symbol, it looks at all n of them, and gives each tape a new symbol and movement, as dictated by the corresponding entry from the transition table. If a tape head moves off of the left end of a tape, or is assigned "no tape" as a new symbol, that tape "falls out" of the machine, and any further new symbols or movements for that tape from the transition table will be ignored, but the machine keeps going until/unless either (a) all of the tapes fall out, or (b) there is no transition matching the current state plus the combination of current tape symbols (some of which may be "no tape"), or (c) some special "halt" machine state is reached.

An MTTM like this can be shown to have no more or less power than a more traditional one-tape TM like that described above it. The interesting aspect, in our case, is in considering a collection of such MTTMs passing tapes back and forth. To keep track, consider a map showing a number of MTTMs, each as a circle, and a number of tapes (to go into them), each as a rectangle. Lines labeled 1 through n from each circle represent the n heads, and connect the circle (MTTM) to the rectangle representing the tape to be associated with that head. In general, each tape in the map may be associated with heads of multiple different MTTMs (one MTTM at a time), so there will be multiple lines from the same tape rectangle.

Perhaps it's clear where this is going: The map is analogous to our strategy, the MTTMs to our tactics, the heads to our roles, and the lines to our role bindings. An MTTM (tactic) can be made to start (activate) when there is a tape available for each head, according to the map. When a tape falls out of a machine, the symbol in the first square can be interpreted as a transition, and translated to a control state (using the transition bindings on the map) to determine which MTTMs the tape can be used for next. (The first square of the tape will be erased before transferring it to a new machine, to prevent the previous transition from being used/interpreted as content state.)

Yes, there are some tricks that would need to be played here to honor the precise semantics of ScalPL/F-Nets, such as The usages now apply to heads, and can be handled in various ways. Even heads without replace (or modify) usage need to be able to write new transitions to the tape. One way to address that is to make a copy of any observe-only or nodata tape before the MTTM begins to feed to the machine, and then using just the first square of the result on that tape for the transition from the head. Likewise, for heads without observe usage, always put a new (blank) tape into the machine for that head.

This makes it pretty clear that an F-Net (i.e the computational model for ScalPL) or ScalPL plan is neither more nor less powerful than an MTTM, and therefore than a one-tape TM, in its ability to compute any particular thing. It is, however, a clear, concise, and formal way to specify how multiple TMs can interact. It (or other concurrent/parallel models) can also be considered more powerful than TMs, in a sense, because it embodies nondeterminism as one of the things which can be expressed, which a single TM alone cannot express.

Other completely different analogies between F-Nets and TMs can be imagined. For example, each resource in an F-Net can be considered as one square on the TM tape, and each context in the F-Net can be considered to correspond to a transition in the TM. The analogy quickly becomes cumbersome, however: Each transition would need its own heads (role bindings), permanently bound to certain squares of the tape (resources), so the tape wouldn't move. The state of the machine would become, roughly, the control states for each square on the tape, to control which transitions could be performed at any one time. In the long run, such an analogy becomes so strained that it is hardly worth making.

15.3.4 Chemical Abstract Machine (CHAM)

An interesting and attractive analogy for computation as a set of chemical reactions has been proposed by G. Berry and G. Boudol in the Chemical Abstract Machine. Without going into detail, the idea is that molecules can react to become new molecules, without any specification about precisely where or when such reactions might take place. Some such reactions are only allowed to occur within a barrier called a membrane, with only certain interactions allowed between the solutions within and outside of the membrane.

It is indeed tempting to use a similar analogy for F-Nets. Here, the actons would essentially specify the potential reactions, and the resources and their control states would specify the molecules. Whenever the proper molecules were present in solution (what we have called the environment) in the proper number, the reaction (activation) can take place, consuming some molecules and producing others. In our case, strategies would conform to membranes, as suggested in Figure 6.1.

Even in this case, the analogy is stretched for F-Nets. (For example, different control states suggest different molecules, even of the same resource, suggesting that the molecules in solution essentially oscillate in amount as the reactions evolve.) Even so, the insight of having the resources essentially floating free and the actons specifying how they might react in groups in unison (atomically) seems to have merit. No further attempts will be made here to associate these models, however.

15.3.5 Other Models

Any number of other models and constructs could be said to be at least distantly related to F-Nets, including (but not limited to) the Actor model (by C. Hewitt and G. Agha), Linda's Generative Communication/Tuple Spaces (D. Gelernter and N. Carriero), Kahn-McQueen Networks, dataflow models of various kinds, and others. However, the correspondences are tenuous enough to often be more obstructive than illustrative in this volume.

Chapter *16*

The Future: What If?

If this book is considered as a vector, it has so far specified a direction more than a magnitude. What are some possible results of pursuing this direction? What is left to be done if this approach is to reach its potential?

16.1 Publishing More Existing Research

Several chapters dropped off of this book as time and resource limitations became apparent. Two rather important resulting omissions are related to duties we ascribed to the Director: Honoring real-time constraints and embedding/scheduling issues – especially, in the latter case, for data parallel plans. In a sense, these omissions are more glaring for ScalPL than in other computational and/or planning approaches in which the programmer or planner is allowed/asked to tackle these in more direct brute-force (though less portable) ways. That is, ScalPL cleanly factors these aspects out of the planning process, so there should be a way to integrate them again after the initial planning is done, also cleanly. We have, indeed, made significant progress in these directions, but in the end, the scope of this book, and the time and resources to create it, were necessarily limited. We expect subsequent publications to explain these in more detail. (They do not require a re-thinking of what has already been described here.) Far more could also be written regarding the relationship between ScalPL and other concurrent/parallel programming and planning approaches (with more adequate citations), and metrics of concurrency based on ScalPL computations.

Relatively short shrift has also been given here to SPLAT, the textual form of ScalPL. A primary issue is in how to make the notation as unobtrusive and compact as possible in cases where the full power, flexibility, and expressiveness is not required. In the best of cases, simple collections of concurrent tasks should be at least as easy to express and obvious as they might be in an existing textual parallel language. The authors have indeed invested significant time into researching this goal, and in developing parsers and processors to convert between SPLAT and fully graphical ScalPL representations, including the format and processing of structured comments for including/encoding visual information relating to positioning, colors, sizes, etc. Again, further publication on these topics can be expected.

But even with such work remaining in describing even the basic approach, working on any project like this naturally sparks forward thinking into what could be accomplished down the line if this effort and direction was well accepted and driven forward by the planning and computing communities at large. How might ScalPL be integrated into a world a decade from now?

16.2 Making "Scalable Planning" Simply "Planning"

Scalable and/or concurrent planning (and programming) is, after all, still just planning (and programming). Making special categories for concurrency or scalability seems not only unnecessary, but doomed to failure, since it means starting each planning task with the question "Will this be concurrent (and/or scalable) or not?", which immediately diminishes both the expected return on investment of devising the plan, and the customer base of those offering tools, platforms, or Directors to facilitate plans. Instead, if scalability and concurrency can become viewed as a natural part of the planning process, everyone benefits. [1]

One way to help this happen is to ensure that plans developed for concurrent environments still perform well in sequential environments, where the platform is only a single person (or processor) to carry it out. We believe that ScalPL scores high in this regard. Another factor motivating scalability in the computer realm is the current (as this is being written) demand for more and more functionality to be made available on cell phones and tablets, and for the bulk of data (if not computation) to be held (or processed) remote from those phones or tablets, in the so-called "cloud" (which used to be called the "grid", and before that, the internet, etc.). Without knowing which parts of a computation or data store might be needed on the phone or in the cloud, and when, and without knowing how that decision may evolve over time or depending on load, it can be advantageous to "factor out" those details during planning by using a scalable approach like ScalPL. And even just for those parts that do end up in the cloud, being ready to exploit as much distributed, concurrent processing power as possible will itself bring advantages.

But even lacking a concurrent or distributed target platform, and even if there might be some slight additional overhead on a sequential platform, can an approach like ScalPL be justified? We argue that it provides benefits which have long been sought by the sequential programming community. These include:

1. ScalPL naturally integrates design and implementation and documentation (and perhaps even specification). That is, instead of creating the specification, then the design, then implementation, then documentation, each as a separate document or plan to be individually verified, stored and/or lost, with no tight coupling between them, ScalPL effectively integrates them all into one.

---

[1]This suggests that a successful ScalPL will eventually need a new name, like UPL, Universal Planning Language.

2. ScalPL strategies form a powerful pattern language, in both the sequential and concurrent domain.

3. ScalPL brings formality (back) to software. There has long been a tension between the relative formality (but seeming lack of flexibility) of hardware design methods, yielding advances in performance and miniaturization along an exponential curve known as Amdahl's Law, and the relative flexibility and complexity (but lack of correctness criteria) of software design methods, yielding an expectation of bugs in almost any new software. A ScalPL strategy is nearly as formal as any hardware design approach – and is often confused as one by those first encountering the notation – but is clearly a software design method, complete with all the inherent power and "softness" of software.

4. ScalPL is a complete and expressive visual langage for Object Oriented planning, integrating what might take many different diagrams in an approach like UML (Universal Modeling Language) into one.

16.3 Creating a ScalPL-Friendly World

Without doubt, easy-to-use visual editing tools will be of extreme importance if ScalPL is to meet its potential as a graphical planning paradigm. Much has already been done (and learned) in this area, but other advances such as integrating automatic layout algorithms (e.g. gleaned from hardware design approaches) will help a planner to stay focused on the planning task rather than with prettying up the design by manually arranging elements (contexts and resources) on a screen. Such an environment is also very natural for debugging and "code browsing".

While not expert on getting new planning approaches accepted into (say) the business community, we can comment some on issues in the computer realm. For example, there is no very good reason that CDS (Cooperative Data Sharing, explained in Chapter 5) could not be integrated, at a low level, into even existing operating systems such as Linux and Unix, as an alternative to shared memory and/or messages for inter-process communication (IPC). This would provide great portable functionality to a wide range of programs, without impacting existing ones, but would also establish a foundation for further advances of ScalPL.

Further, one can imagine the creation of a ScalPL Transport Protocol (SPTP), analogous to the HTTP (Hypertext Transport Protocol) currently used in web activities, so that servers would be prepared to accept descriptions of work in the form of strategies and/or tactics, and understand the form in which results should be returned, efficiently, whether to a different part of the platform or to be kept local for later use there. In fact, that SPTP could resemble (or use as part of its specification) SPLAT to specify an activity to a remote processor in a platform. At a high level, ScalPL's strategies and tactics can be considered to do the same job for computation that packet switching does for data within the net. That is, a tactic can be considered as an independent packet of activity, that can find its way through a cloud on its own, and strategies help

301

to reconstruct all of the results of those tactics (i.e. activities) into something more meaningful by having them interact correctly.

At a much lower level, if ScalPL's approach became widely used for programming even fine-grain concurrency, computer architectures could be optimized to facilitate the model. This could range anywhere from new instructions to efficiently manage the decrementing, incrementing, and comparisons of multiple reasons counts (outlined in Chapter 5), to compiling ScalPL strategies to optimize routing between tactics using FPGAs, to optimizing on-chip access to the CDS whiteboard and/or managing chip-to-chip communication and allocation of whiteboard regions.

Common obstacles to accomplishing all of these advances lie simply in (a) establishing standards, and (b) finding people motivated to do the work. Creating a demand, perhaps by elucidating a vision of a potential brighter future such as the one you are reading, will hopefully help to motivate both of those. Now that the principle core of concepts and insights that motivated ScalPL's design have been explained (in this text), a logical next step would be to employ a standards body comprising sufficiently diverse backgrounds and skills to ensure that this approach has wide applicability and consistent/cohesive terminology for a sufficient domain of target disciplines.

16.4   Rethinking Apps

If ScalPL was ubiquitous, with receptive platforms as available as web servers are now, the "web" would become more like a collective consciousness or distributed intelligence than a data repository. That is, instead of writing an app to be utilized by a human, a contributor might create an "expertise agent" in the form of a plan (e.g. strategy) embodying some aspect of their knowledge or expertise in a manner intended primarily for integration into other plans. Planners could then work independently at different levels of hierarchy to either contribute/sell such knowledge or expertise agents, or to integrate existing ones from a wide range of sources in novel ways to produce ever more useful, professional, productive, or lucrative consolidations. In a sense, this is a vision of "mental mashups", with people integrating different areas of expertise in new and unexpected ways, without necessarily having access to the people providing the raw expertise (or assembled expertise at a lower level of hierarchy), just to the plans/agents into which they have encoded that expertise. In other words, when interfacing different applications, physical aspects like location become inconsequential, and the focus goes completely into understanding the cooperative aspects of the different parts.

Since, unlike the current web, most such expertise agents would interact with other plans/agents rather than with human users, such an infrastructure would also require an economic environment in which to work which was not driven by "eyeballs" (advertising) and product sales. The author has speculated elsewhere on approaches to providing such environments, under names like PICA (people, instruments, computers, and archives) and AO (abstract owner).

16.5 Conclusion

This book represents an attempt to take a fresh look at concurrency, scalability, planning, and programming, and to present cohesive and forward-looking methods and mechanisms that might carry us into the era of global interaction and cooperation that seems imminent. We hope that readers will find the possibilities as exciting as we have in writing about them, and look forward to seeing how the world might further employ and exploit these ideas.

12.5 Conclusion

Index

$ prefix, 119

A
abstract (super)classes, 222
access dots, 27
ACID transaction, 68
activating, 21
activation circle, 146
activation formal resources, 171
activation role binding, 131
active, 114
activities, 21
activity binding, 34
actons, 43
aliasing, 242
and binding, 258
angelic nondeterminism, 167
anonymous role bindings, 131
array constant, 128
array delimiter, 249
atomic, 46
atomicity, 46
axioms, 175

B
BASE, 126
basis, 44
belt, 49
belted, 50
binary search, 138
bindany, 232
binding constraints, 207, 213
Bipartite Graph, 147
bottom control state, 61

bottom transition, 61
bottom-belted, 51
broadcast, 72
buffering, 73
bundling, 199

C
CDS, 94
CDS queues, 95
CDS regions, 95
CDS ticket, 95
CDS virtual processors, 95
CDS whiteboard, 95
circular time dependence, 49
class keyword, 220
class variables, 206
classes, 204
collective constants, 128
commit, 46
conform, 35
consistent, 68
constant, 23
constant path, 125
contends relation, 186
content dead, 153
content domain, 23
content state, 23
contents, 22
context, 22
context switch, 93
control domain, 26
control state, 26
Cooperative Data Sharing, 94
$copy, 79

D
DAG, 147
data parallelism, 255
deadlock, 53
delegation, 206
deterministic, 44
Directed Acyclic Graph, 147
Director, 21, 84
dollar-sign prefix, 79
double buffering, 73, 79
dup, 255
dup bindng, 256
dup precedence arrow, 260
dupall, 256
dupany, 256

E
erratic nondeterminism, 166
executing, 21
extends keyword, 220

F
fairness, 58
FIFO, 73
final box, 112
final dots, 113
finish, 119
formal resource, 112
formal set, 197
frames, 72
fully deterministic, 157
fully nondeterministic, 158
functionalized computation, 143

G
garbage collection, 211
growing phase, 51

H
home repository, 126

I
$iface, 198
IL, 208
implementation, 34
independent, 43
inheritance, 206
initial contents, 23

initial control state, 27
instance, 204
instantiated resources, 207
instantiation, 207
instantiation level, 208
instantiation name, 208
Instrumented F-Net, 187
interface, 34
inter-resource dependences, 55
is-a relationship, 205
isomorphism, 189

J
junction dot, 30

L
latency, 9
latency hiding, 15
link time, 125
livelock, 54
liveness, 44, 58, 286
logically adjacent, 144

M
mapping, 234, 241
metaclasses, 206
method name, 214
methods, 205
mobility, 91
MTTM, 295
multi buffering, 73
Multicast, 72
mutual time dependence, 49

N
new control state dots, 28
nodata permission, 24
non-belted, 50
nondeterminism, 210
$null, 169

O
object-oriented, 204
objects, 204
observe permission, 24
OO, 204
operational semantics, 175
operations, 204

$oplan, 208
overrides, 206

P
partial binding, 207
partial order, 149
partial recursive function, 142
partially ordered, 147
pebble puzzle, 48
pebbles, 45
permissions, 23
permutation, 234
$plan, 21, 119
$plan role binding, 130
platform, 83
P.O., 149
ported resource, 217
post-dup binding, 256
predictable role, 63
prefix computation, 190

Q
queue, 73

R
race conditions, 161
RC, 85
reasons count, 85
reduction, 234, 237
replace permission, 24
repository, 124
resolution, 125
resource set, 200
resource state rectangle, 146
resource trace, 188
resources, 22
rivalry, 88
rivals, 88
rivals relation, 88
role binding, 23
role set, 198
role sets, 196
roles, 32
rollback, 46
root repository, 125

S
safety, 44, 286

scalar constants, 128
scope, 201
searchback, 127
selection, 234, 238
semideterministic, 158
sequence constant, 128
serializability, 44
serialized, 48
set constant, 200
set path, 197
shared resources, 186
shrinking phase, 51
side effects, 47
signature, 34
size sensors, 249
snapshot, 75
SPLAT, 38, 208
splice binding, 198
start acton, 169
strategy, 21
stream, 72
structure constant, 128
structured plan, 144
subclass, 205
superclass, 205
supplemental re-execution, 47

T
tactic, 43
tactic language, 128
TDSP, 138
throttling, 73
top-belted, 51
traditional deterministic sequential
        plans, 138
transaction, 68
transient resources, 83
transition, 32
transition binding, 32
transition domain, 32
translation, 234, 239
two-phase, 51
types, 204

U
uncontrolled nondeterminism, 166
update permission, 24
usage, 33

W
wildcard, 196, 199